PERGAMON INTERNATIONAL LIBRARY
of Science, Technology, Engineering and Social Studies
The 1000-volume original paperback library in aid of education,
industrial training and the enjoyment of leisure
Publisher: Robert Maxwell, M.C.

Planning for small enterprises in Third World cities

THE PERGAMON TEXTBOOK
INSPECTION COPY SERVICE

An inspection copy of any book published in the Pergamon International Library will gladly be
sent to academic staff without obligation for their consideration for course adoption or
recommendation. Copies may be retained for a period of 60 days from receipt and returned if
not suitable. When a particular title is adopted or recommended for adoption for class use and
the recommendation results in a sale of 12 or more copies, the inspection copy may be
retained with our compliments. The Publishers will be pleased to receive suggestions for
revised editions and new titles to be published in this important International Library.

Pergamon Urban and Regional Planning Advisory Committee

Planning for small enterprises in Third World cities

Edited by

RAY BROMLEY

Centre for Development Studies, University College of Swansea, UK.
and
Regional Planning Program, State University of New York at Albany, USA

PERGAMON PRESS

OXFORD · NEW YORK · TORONTO · SYDNEY · PARIS · FRANKFURT

U.K.	Pergamon Press Ltd., Headington Hill Hall, Oxford OX3 0BW, England
U.S.A.	Pergamon Press Inc., Maxwell House, Fairview Park, Elmsford, New York 10523, U.S.A.
CANADA	Pergamon Press Canada Ltd., Suite 104, 150 Consumers Road, Willowdale, Ontario M2J 1P9, Canada
AUSTRALIA	Pergamon Press (Aust.) Pty. Ltd., P.O. Box 544, Potts Point, NSW 2011, Australia
FRANCE	Pergamon Press SARL, 24 rue des Ecoles, 75240 Paris, Cedex 05, France
FEDERAL REPUBLIC OF GERMANY	Pergamon Press GmbH, Hammerweg 6, D-6242 Kronberg-Taunus, Federal Republic of Germany

First edition 1985

Library of Congress Cataloging in Publication Data

Main entry under title:

Planning for small enterprises in Third World cities.
(Urban and regional planning series; v. 34)
Includes indexes.
1. Small business—Developing countries—Addresses, essays, lectures. 2. City planning—Developing countries—Addresses, essays, lectures. I. Bromley, R. J. II. Series.
HD2346.5.P4   1984   338.6'42'091724   84-2988

British Library Cataloguing in Publication Data

Planning for small enterprises in Third World cities.—(Urban and regional planning series, ISSN 0305–5582; v. 34)
1. Small business—Government policy—Development countries
I. Bromley, Ray   II. Series
338.6'42'091724   HD2346.5

ISBN 0-08-025236-2 (Hardcover)
ISBN 0-08-031333-7 (Flexicover)

Printed in Great Britain by A. Wheaton & Co. Ltd., Exeter

Preface

Small enterprises have been founded, have prospered, have faltered and have terminated on innumerable occasions throughout human history, and for much of the duration of human prehistory. Initially they were the only form of enterprise, but increasingly they have come to coexist and compete with larger State, private and collective enterprises in both capitalist and socialist economic systems. They have shown, and continue to show, strong signs of adaptability, innovation and competitiveness, filling many of the economic niches left vacant by larger enterprises and providing an important source of income opportunities, on-the-job training and entrepreneurial skills.

Despite the enormous variety and significance of small enterprises, there is no universal agreement as to their definition or role, and there is not even the basis for a broad consensus as to the policies which should be adopted towards such enterprises. Many types of small enterprise, particularly in the service sector, have received remarkably little research attention, and policy statements tend to be full of vacuous generalities which neither tackle the basic problems faced by small enterprises nor show any capacity to distinguish between different types of enterprise with strikingly different needs and perspectives. A high proportion of current writings follow a naively simplistic and positivistic line, congratulating energy, initiative and enterprise, extolling Samuel Smiles and Horatio Alger cases of thrift, effort and good luck, and lauding the "self-made man" (usually forgetting both the "self-made woman" and the numerous men, women and children who helped the so-called "self-made" to get where they are). What has been sadly lacking in much of the small enterprise literature is a realization that such enterprises must now exist in a socioeconomic context which is dominated by larger enterprises, by the increasingly all-embracing powers of the State, and by international monopoly capitalism.

In the specifically urban context, and most notably in the case of the cities of the so-called Third World, there has been a particular lack of consideration of the relationships between small enterprise policies which are intended to encourage employment generation, economic growth and the satisfaction of basic needs, and physical planning strategies and urban government procedures intended to create a pleasant, healthy, homely and functional urban environment. All too often the actions of national and urban governments, combined with the behaviour of private sector investors and speculators, have led to the suppression of small enterprises, the removal of their principal sales outlets, the reduction of available employment opportunities, the spatial segregation of the urban population, and increases in the cost of living. Physical, social and economic objectives have become remarkably uncoordinated, and many hard-working individuals have been persecuted for trying to make a living in some way which, though not in any sense anti-social, fails to correspond to official standards, regulations and concerns.

However noble the virtues of entrepreneurship, those who run small enterprises often show grave tendencies towards the hyper-exploitation of those who work with, or for, them. To some extent this may result from the economic pressures of working in highly competitive situations without adequate capital, equipment or premises, and without appropriate training, credit or technical assistance. To some extent, also, it may result from the cut-throat competition of larger enterprises or foreign firms with access to higher levels of technology, scale economies and more cost-effective labour. In other cases it may result from the sub-contracting procedures of larger enterprises, delivering tasks which must be performed at rock-bottom prices if the small enterprise is to continue receiving such contracts. Finally, in almost all cases, the hyper-exploitation of labour results in part from the lack of adequate supervision and support from the State, from the protection, subsidies and costly infrastructure given to large enterprises, and from the widespread availability of tax- and customs-dodging opportunities to competing importers and large enterprises. Small enterprises may sometimes be congenial working environments and training grounds, but more often they are precarious ventures continually in danger of extinction because of their vulnerability to changing economic, political or physical environmental circumstances, or dangerous, insanitary sweat-shops which are only viable as long as they can exceed the norms for safe and reasonable labour utilization.

This book is intended to provide a general synthesis of the issues relating to urban small enterprises as they are likely to affect students, teachers and practitioners of urban and regional planning, urban researchers and specialists in employment policy. It attempts to provide a representative selection of authors and topics, including both those with a strongly positive and adulatory tone, and those with a much more critical and problem-oriented style. Case studies are drawn from a broad range of Asian, African and Latin American countries, and from both manufacturing and service sectors.

The approach taken to defining "planning", "cities", and "small enterprises" is deliberately broad and flexible. Planning is treated as governmental activity concerned with formulating and implementing economic, social and physical environmental policies, and with achieving an appropriate spatial organization for human activity. Cities are defined as continuous urban areas with over 50,000 inhabitants. Small enterprises are considered to be any economic activities or businesses with less than 20 persons contributing their labour power, and with no currently valid legal claim to be part of a larger enterprise. Within these limits, this book is particularly concerned with the problems and perspectives of the smallest enterprises, and with those possessing little capital and relatively low levels of technology. Nevertheless, cases of slightly larger, more capitalized and higher technology enterprises are considered in Chapters 8, 10, 17 and 18, so that the rationale and limits of "smallness" and the degree of commonality of problems with medium-scale enterprises can be adequately explored.

The definition of "Third World" is considerably more problematical than any of the previous definitions. The term has been used in different ways by different authors, and it is an awkward mix of euphemism, banner to rally disparate interests to a common cause, and crystallization of 1950s and 1960s radical analyses of the structure of the world economy. Here, it is used synonymously with the terms "peripheral capitalism" and "dependent capitalism" in the world system, as a means of designating those countries which are "subordinated to" or "dependent upon" the capitalist system, but which are not part of the central "cores" of that system in North America, Western Europe and Japan, or of the extensions of those cores in Australia, New Zealand, and (in a distorted form) in South Africa and Israel. This definition of the Third World excludes the socialist countries of the COMECON block (the so-called Second World), and also those formerly Third World countries which have deliberately, and apparently "permanently" largely opted out of the capitalist system: for example China, North Korea, Vietnam, Laos, Cambodia and Cuba.

The 19 Readings chosen for inclusion here vary considerably in length, style and vintage. Ten are reprints—sometimes in full, and sometimes abridged—of outstanding essays which have already been published in English elsewhere, but which, in most cases, are now difficult to obtain. Two are translations of outstanding essays previously published in Spanish or Portuguese. The remaining seven are original essays written specially for this book. These 19 Readings are organized into six sections. Each of the first five has an editor's introduction, briefly outlining the issues and arguments presented, and the sixth and final section is an editor's concluding chapter.

It goes almost without saying that this book could not have been prepared without the efforts and collaboration of its contributors. More than anything else, it is a collection and synthesis of their prolific ideas, and a considerable debt of gratitude is owed to them for their patience and inspiration. For their inputs to the translation and editing processes, a special vote of thanks is due to Nelly Acevedo, Rod Burgess and Chris Gerry, all of whom had a great influence on my thinking on petty production and small enterprise policies. Finally, thanks are also due to Beryl Appleyard, Janine Calderbank, Gwynneth Goodhead and Deirdre Slater for typing and re-typing various sections of the manuscript, and to all the publishers, journals and individuals who have authorized the translation and reprinting of papers originally published elsewhere.

Cali, Colombia   RAY BROMLEY
April 1983

Contents

List of contributors

ANTI-SLAVERY SOCIETY   180 Brixton Road, London SW9 6AT,
                                England.

ASHE, JEFFREY   ACCION International/AITEC, 10-C
                                Mount Auburn Street, Cambridge,
                                Massachusetts 02138, U.S.A.

BATLEY, RICHARD   Development Administration Group,
                                Institute of Local Government Studies,
                                Birmingham University, Birmingham,
                                England.

BEAVON, K. S. O.   Department of Geography, University of
                                the Witwatersrand, Johannesburg, South
                                Africa.

BREMAN, JAN   Comparative Asian Studies Programme,
                                Erasmus University, Rotterdam,
                                Netherlands; and Institute of Social
                                Studies, The Hague, Netherlands.

BROMLEY, RAY   Centre for Development Studies, University
                                College of Swansea, Swansea, Wales; and
                                Regional Planning Program,
                                State University of New York
                                at Albany, Albany, New York, USA.

COHEN, DENNIS J.   Management and Behavioral Science
                                Center, The Wharton School, University of
                                Pennsylvania, Philadelphia, Pennsylvania,
                                U.S.A.

EADES, J. S.   Faculty of Social Sciences, University of
                                Kent, Canterbury, Kent, England.

GERRY, CHRIS   Centre for Development Studies, University
                                College of Swansea, Swansea, Wales.

HARPER, MALCOLM	Enterprise Development Centre, Cranfield School of Management, Cranfield, Bedford, England.
HARRISS, JOHN	School of Development Studies, University of East Anglia, Norwich, England.
HUANG WEN-HSIEN	United Nations High Commission for Refugees, Geneva, Switzerland.
JIMÉNEZ, CARLOS	Current whereabouts unknown.
LEWIN, A. C.	Von-Einem-Strasse 17, 4300 Essen 1, Federal Republic of Germany.
MEIER, ALAN K.	Energy and Environment Division, Lawrence Berkeley Laboratory, University of California, Berkeley, California, U.S.A.
MIDDLETON, ALAN	Department of Town and Regional Planning, University of Glasgow, Glasgow, Scotland.
DE OLIVEIRA, FRANCISCO	CEBRAP (Centro Brasileiro de Análise e Planejamento), Rua Morgado de Mateus 615, 04015 São Paulo, SP, Brazil.
PRADILLA, EMILIO	Apartado Postal 70380, Ciudad Universitaria, México 20, D.F., México.
ROGERSON, C. M.	Department of Geography, University of the Witwatersrand, Johannesburg, South Africa.
SCHAFFER, BERNARD	Institute of Development Studies at the University of Sussex, Brighton, England.
SCHUMACHER, E. F.	Dr. E. F. Schumacher, who died in 1977, was Economic Adviser to the British National Coal Board from 1950 to 1970 and was also the originator of the concept of intermediate technology for developing countries and Founder and Chairman of the Intermediate Technology Development Group Ltd. He also served as President of the Soil Association and as Director of the Scott-Bader Company (pathfinders in common ownership).
VAN DEN BOGAERT, MICHAEL	Xavier Institute of Social Service, Purulia Road, P.O. Box 7, Ranchi 834 001, India.

SECTION I

The beauty of smallness

"Development has had the same effect in all societies: everyone has been enmeshed in a new web of dependence on commodities that flow out of the same kind of machines, factories, clinics, television studios, think tanks. To satisfy this dependence, more of the same must be produced: standardized, engineered goods, designed for the future consumers who will be trained by the engineer's agent to need what he or she is offered. . . . Different cultures become insipid residues of traditional styles of action, washed up in one world-wide wasteland: an arid terrain devastated by the machinery needed to produce and consume."

(Ivan Illich 1978, *The Right to Useful Unemployment*, 22)

"The things the craftsman produced in the days before modern capitalism were objects of joy and beauty, because the artisan loved his work. Can you expect the modern drudge in the modern factory to make beautiful things? He is part of the machine, a cog in the soulless industry, his labour mechanical, forced. . . . He hates his job or at best has no interest in it except that it secures his weekly wage."

(Alexander Berkman 1929, *What is Anarchist Communism?*, quoted in Woodcock (ed.) 1977, 336)

Introduction

This first section presents the case for small enterprises in its simplest and most eloquent fashion. Four relatively short essays have been included praising small enterprises on a wide range of counts. Such enterprises are seen as human in scale, congenial to work in, convenient for clients, cheap and strongly competitive, and favourable to the development of entrepreneurial skills and technological innovation. In addition, they are viewed as labour-intensive, employment-generating, energy-efficient, adaptable, able to operate with local skills and materials, and suitable for the use of appropriate (rather than excessively sophisticated, costly and transplanted) technologies. Of even broader significance, they are portrayed as being closely adjusted to local needs, the only realistic alternatives to domination by multinational corporations or gross dependence on imports, and the most obvious potential basis for relatively self-reliant regional and national economies. The alienating character of large-scale factory production is avoided, and small enterprises can contribute both to on-the-job learning and to convenient part-time combinations of income-earning work with domestic labour and formal education.

The first essay, by the late E. F. Schumacher, is a compilation of two extracts from his *Small is Beautiful*, probably the most influential book ever written on the advantages of small enterprises and the disadvantages of so-called "scale economies". It provides a remarkable synthesis, not only of Schumacher's own views and of the thinking underlying the Intermediate Technology Development Group which he founded, but also of a wide range of "conservationist", "ecological", "neo-anarchist", "libertarian" and (in Kitching's terms; 1982) "populist" thinking. Powerful arguments are elicited in favour of reversing the trend towards larger and larger enterprises, ever-increasing State control, the relentless advance of consumerism and the throw-away society, and the growing power of multinational corporations in the world economy. Equally powerful reasons are given for reducing the pace of utilization of non-renewable natural resources, for adopting more appropriate and energy-efficient technologies, and for reversing the trend toward ever-larger metropolitan agglomerations. What is sought, above all, is an economy and society on a more human scale, with patterns of resource

3

utilization which are more self-sustaining and ecologically viable in the long term.

The force of Schumacher's arguments is reproduced in a dramatized Third World context by Malcolm Harper in his debate between Mr. Pro small enterprise and Mr. Anti small enterprise in Chapter 2. Mr. Pro runs rings around Mr. Anti, and the arguments cited provide solid foundations for the assumption that substantial numbers of small enterprises will continue to exist in both urban and rural areas of Third World countries for many, many years to come.

A tremendous admiration for the efforts and initiative of "ordinary" people is reflected in Michael van den Bogaert's "Barefoot Management in India" (Chapter 3). This essay emphasizes the enormous conceptual gap which separates most government planners and administrators from the millions of poor people working in small enterprises, and it tries to explain in simple yet persuasive terms why a major change of attitude is required: replacing negative, restrictive government policies with positive, promotional ones. Above all, this paper challenges the assumed superiority of "modern" technology and sophisticated civil servants over the rudimentary techniques and on-the-job learning of those operating small enterprises. It shows that planners and administrators have much to learn before they can design appropriate promotional policies for small enterprises, and that most of that learning must be from existing petty entrepreneurs; they often know all too well the factors restraining the growth of their enterprises, the applicability of new technologies, and the possibilities of creating new market niches. It is only once existing status distinctions and hierarchies of authority have been called into question that there can be any effective unification of minds and efforts to design and implement more effective promotional and regulatory strategies for small enterprises.

Van den Bogaert's admiration for "barefoot entrepreneurs" is paralleled by Alan Meier's fascination for low-cost para-transit technology in Southeast Asian cities (Chapter 4). Meier gives numerous examples of extraordinary skill and ingenuity in designing, adapting and operating passenger and cargo vehicles, and his paper calls into question both conventional concepts of mass-transit and traffic management, and also the wholesale transfer of urban design concepts from so-called "developed countries" to the cities of the Third World. His work is part of a broader re-examination of para-transit systems (see e.g. Kilby *et al.* 1975; OECD 1977), and given a change of attitude by most Third World governments, para-transit could well be one of the principal growth areas for small enterprises over the next two decades.

All of the essays in this first section have a remarkable common-sense simplicity about them. Their arguments are well marshalled and initially convincing, but they raise serious questions as to *how* governments and big-businesses can be persuaded to change their attitudes, *how* existing status distinctions and prejudices can be reduced, and above all, *how* international monopoly capitalism can be persuaded or forced to assume a lower profile and to reduce its dominance and its total market share. If dozens of governments and hundreds of millions of consumers can be convinced of the merits of small enterprises and the disadvantages of large-scale and multinational enterprises, a major shift in favour of small enterprises may well be achieved. If such a broad conviction is not achieved, however, changes are likely to be smaller-scale, more localized, and relatively short-lived. There is no danger that small enterprises will disappear altogether or diminish in numbers to relative insignificance. There is little sign at present, however, of the sorts of radical and large-scale changes which will give small enterprises a higher status and a larger share in total employment and economic activity.

REFERENCES

ILLICH, Ivan (1978) *The Right to Useful Employment: And its Professional Enemies*, Marion Boyars, London.
KIRBY, Ronald F. *et al.* (1975) *Para-transit: Neglected Options for Urban Mobility*, Urban Institute, Washington D.C.
KITCHING, Gavin (1982) *Development and Underdevelopment in Historical Perspective*, Methuen, London.
OECD (Organization for Economic Cooperation and Development) (1977) *Para-transit in the Developing World*, OECD Development Centre, Paris, 2 vols.
WOODCOCK, George (ed.) (1977) *The Anarchist Reader*, Fontana/Collins, London.

CHAPTER 1

Issues of size and technology*

E. F. SCHUMACHER

A question of size

I was brought up on the theory of the "economics of scale"—that with industries and firms, just as with nations, there is an irresistible trend, dictated by modern technology, for units to become even bigger. Even today, we are generally told that gigantic organizations are inescapably necessary; but when we look closely we can notice that as soon as great size has been created there is often a strenuous attempt to attain smallness within bigness. The great achievement of Mr. Sloan of General Motors was to structure this gigantic firm in such a manner that it became, in fact, a federation of fairly reasonably sized firms. In the British National Coal Board, one of the biggest firms of Western Europe, something very similar was attempted under the Chairmanship of Lord Robens; strenuous efforts were made to evolve a structure which would maintain the unity of one big organization and at the same time create the "climate" or feeling of there being a federation of numerous "quasi-firms". The monolith was transformed into a well-coordinated assembly of lively, semi-autonomous units, each with its own drive and sense of achievement. While many theoreticians—who may not be too closely in touch with real life—are still engaging in the idolatry of large size, with practical people in the actual world there is a tremendous longing and striving to profit, if at all possible, from the convenience, humanity, and manageability of smallness. This, also, is a tendency which anyone can easily observe for himself.

Let us now approach our subject from another angle and ask what is actually *needed*. In the affairs of men, there always appears to be a need for at least two things simultaneously, which, on the face of it, seems to be incompatible and to exclude one another. We always need both freedom and order. We need the freedom of lots and lots of small, autonomous units, and,

*Extracts from pp. 53–62 and 122–33 of E. F. Schumacher, *Small is Beautiful: A Study of Economics as if People Mattered,* Abacus Edition published by Sphere Books Ltd., London, in 1974. Copyright © 1973 by E. F. Schumacher. First published in Great Britain by Blond & Briggs Ltd., London, and in the United States by Harper & Row Publishers, Inc., New York; reprinted here with the permission of Blond & Briggs, and of Harper & Row.

at the same time, the orderliness of large-scale, possibly global, unity and coordination. When it comes to action, we obviously need small units, because action is a highly personal affair, and one cannot be in touch with more than a very limited number of persons at any one time. But when it comes to the world of ideas, to principles or to ethics, to the indivisibility of peace and also of ecology we need to recognize the unit of mankind and base our actions upon this recognition. Or to put it differently, it is true that all men are brothers, but it is also true that in our active personal relationships we can, in fact, be brothers to only a few of them, and we are called upon to show more brotherliness to them than we could possibly show to the whole of mankind. We all know people who freely talk about the brotherhood of man while treating their neighbours as enemies, just as we also know people who have, in fact, excellent relations with all their neighbours while harbouring, at the same time, appalling prejudices about all human groups outside their particular circle.

What I wish to emphasize is the *duality* of the human requirement when it comes to the question of size: there is no *single* answer. For his different purposes man needs many different structures, both small ones and large ones, some exclusive and some comprehensive. Yet people find it most difficult to keep two seemingly opposite necessities of truth in their minds at the same time. They always tend to clamour for a final solution, as if in actual life there could ever be a final solution other than death. For constructive work, the principal task is always the restoration of some kind of balance. Today, we suffer from an almost universal idolatry of giantism. It is therefore necessary to insist on the virtues of smallness—where this applies. (If there were a prevailing idolatry of smallness, irrespective of subject or purpose, one would have to try and exercise influence in the opposite direction.)

The question of scale might be put in another way: what is needed in all these matters is to discriminate, to get things sorted out. For every activity there is a certain appropriate scale, and the more active and intimate the activity, the smaller the number of people that can take part, the greater is the number of such relationship arrangements that need to be established.

What scale is appropriate? It depends on what we are trying to do. The question of scale is extremely crucial today, in political, social and economic affairs just as in almost everything else. What, for instance, is the appropriate size of a city? And also, one might ask, what is the appropriate size of a country? Now these are serious and difficult questions. It is not possible to programme a computer and get the answer. The really serious matters of life cannot be calculated. We cannot directly calculate what is right; but we jolly well know what is wrong! We can recognize right and wrong at the extremes, although we cannot normally judge them finely enough to say: "This ought to be five per cent more; or that ought to be five per cent less".

A most important problem in the second half of the twentieth century is the geographical distribution of population, the question of "regionalism". But regionalism, not in the sense of combining a lot of states into free-trade systems, but in the opposite sense of developing all the regions within each country. This, in fact, is the most important subject on the agenda of all the larger countries today. And a lot of the nationalism of small nations today, and the desire for self-government and so-called independence, is simply a logical and rational response to the need for regional development. In the poor countries in particular there is no hope for the poor unless there is successful regional development, a development effort outside the capital city covering all the rural areas wherever people happen to be.

If this effort is not brought forth, their only choice is either to remain in their miserable condition where they are, or to migrate into the big city where their condition will be even more miserable. It is a strange phenomenon indeed that the conventional wisdom of present-day economics can do nothing to help the poor.

Invariably it proves that only such policies are viable as have in fact the result of making those already rich and powerful, richer and more powerful. It proves that industrial development only pays if it is as near as possible to the capital city or another very large town, and not in the rural areas. It proves that large projects are invariably more economic than small ones, and it proves that capital-intensive projects are invariably to be preferred as against labour-intensive ones. The economic calculus, as applied by present-day economics, forces the industrialist to eliminate the human factor because machines do not make the same mistakes as people. Hence the enormous effort at automation and the drive for ever-larger units. This means that those who have nothing to sell but their labour remain in the weakest possible bargaining position. The conventional wisdom of what is now taught as economics by-passes the poor, the very people for whom development is really needed. The economics of giantism and automation is a left-over of nineteenth-century conditions and nineteenth-century thinking and it is totally incapable of solving any of the real problems of today. An entirely new system of thought is needed, a system based on attention to people, and not primarily attention to goods (the goods will look after themselves!). It could be summed up in the phrase, "production by the masses, rather than mass production". What was impossible, however, in the nineteenth century, is possible now. And what was in fact—if not necessarily at least understandably—neglected in the nineteenth century is unbelievably urgent now. That is, the conscious utilization of our enormous technological and scientific potential for the fight against misery and human degradation—a fight in intimate contact with actual people, with individuals, families, small groups, rather than States and other anonymous abstractions. And this presupposes a political and organizational structure that can provide this intimacy.

What is the meaning of democracy, freedom, human dignity, standard of living, self-realization, fulfilment? Is it a matter of goods, or of people? Of course it is a matter of people. But people can be themselves only in small comprehensible groups. Therefore we must learn to think in terms of an articulated structure that can cope with a multiplicity of small-scale units. If economic thinking cannot grasp this it is useless. If it cannot get beyond its vast abstractions, the national income, the rate of growth, capital/output ratio, input–output analysis, labour mobility, capital accumulation; if it cannot get beyond all this and make contact with the human realities of poverty, frustration, alienation, despair, breakdown, crime, escapism, stress, congestion, ugliness, and spiritual death, then let us scrap economics and start afresh.

Are there not indeed enough "signs of the times" to indicate that a new start is needed?

Technology with a human face

The modern world has been shaped by its metaphysics, which has shaped its education, which in turn has brought forth its science and technology. So, without going back to metaphysics and education, we can say that the modern world has been shaped by technology. It tumbles from crisis to crisis; on all sides there are prophecies of disaster and, indeed, visible signs of breakdown.

If that which has been shaped by technology, and continues to be so shaped, looks sick, it might be wise to have a look at technology itself. If technology is felt to be becoming more and more inhuman, we might do well to consider whether it is possible to have something better—a technology with a human face.

Strange to say, technology, although of course the product of man, tends to develop by its own laws and principles, and these are very different from those of human nature or of living nature in general. Nature always, so to speak, knows where and when to stop. Greater even than the mystery of natural growth is the mystery of the natural cessation of growth. There is measure in all natural things—in their size, speed, or violence. As a result, the system of nature, of which man is a part, tends to be self-balancing, self-adjusting, self-cleansing. Not so with technology, or perhaps I should say: not so with man dominated by technology and specialization. Technology recognizes no self-limiting principle—in terms, for instance, of size, speed, or violence. It therefore does not possess the virtues of being self-balancing, self-adjusting, and self-cleansing. In the subtle system of nature, technology, and in particular the super-technology of the modern world, acts like a foreign body, and there are now numerous signs of rejection.

Suddenly, if not altogether surprisingly, the modern world, shaped by modern technology, finds itself involved in three crises simultaneously. First, human nature revolts against inhuman technological, organizational, and political patterns, which it experiences as suffocating and debilitating; second, the living environment which supports human life aches and groans and gives signs of partial breakdown; and third, it is clear to anyone fully knowledge-able in the subject matter that the inroads being made into the world's non-renewable resources, particularly those of fossil fuels, are such that serious bottlenecks and virtual exhaustion loom ahead in the quite foreseeable future.

Any one of these three crises or illnesses can turn out to be deadly. I do not know which of the three is the most likely to be the direct cause of collapse. What is quite clear is that a way of life that bases itself on materialism, i.e. on permanent, limitless expansionism in a finite environment, cannot last long, and that its life expectation is the shorter the more successfully it pursues its expansionist objectives.

If we ask where the tempestuous developments of world industry during the last quarter-century have taken us, the answer is somewhat discouraging. Everywhere the problems seem to be growing faster than the solutions. This seems to apply to the rich countries just as much as to the poor. There is nothing in the experience of the last 25 years to suggest that modern technology, as we know it, can really help us to alleviate world poverty, not to mention the problem of unemployment which already reaches levels like 30 per cent in many so-called developing countries, and now also threatens to become endemic in many of the rich countries. In any case, the apparent yet illusory successes of the last 25 years cannot be repeated: the threefold crisis of which I have spoken will see to that. So we had better face the question of technology—what does it do and what should it do? Can we develop a technology which really helps us to solve our problems—a technology with a human face?

It is almost like a providential blessing that we, the rich countries, have found it in our hearts at least to consider the Third World and to try to mitigate its poverty. In spite of the mixture of motives and the persistence of exploitative practices, I think that this fairly recent development in the outlook of the rich is an honourable one. And it could save us; for the poverty of the poor makes it in any case impossible for them successfully to adopt our technology. Of course, they often try to do so, and then have to bear the more dire consequences in terms of mass unemployment, mass migration into cities, rural decay, and intolerable social tensions. They need, in fact, the very thing I am talking about, which we also need: a *different* kind of technology, a technology with a human face, which instead of making human hands and brains redundant, helps them to become far more productive than they have ever been before.

As Gandhi said, the poor of the world cannot be helped by mass production, only by production by the masses. The system of *mass production*, based on sophisticated, highly capital-intensive, high energy-input dependent, and human labour-saving technology, presupposes that you are already rich, for a great deal of capital investment is needed to establish one single workplace. The system of *production by the masses* mobilizes the priceless resources which are possessed by all human beings, their clever brains and skilful hands, *and supports them with first-class tools*. The technology of *mass production* is inherently violent, ecologically damaging, self-defeating in terms of non-renewable resources, and stultifying for the human person. The technology of *production by the masses*, making use of the best of modern knowledge and experience, is conducive to decentralization, compatible with the laws of ecology, gentle in its use of scarce resources, and designed to serve the human person instead of making him the servant of machines. I have named it *intermediate technology* to signify that it is vastly superior to the primitive technology of bygone ages but at the same time much simpler, cheaper, and freer than the super-technology of the rich. One can also call it self-help technology, or democratic or people's technology—a technology to which everybody can gain admittance and which is not reserved for those already rich and powerful.

Although we are in possession of all requisite knowledge, it still requires a systematic, creative effort to bring this technology into active existence and make it generally visible and available. It is my experience that it is rather more difficult to recapture directness and simplicity than to advance in the direction of ever more sophistication and complexity. Any third-rate engineer or researcher can increase complexity; but it takes a certain flair of real insight to make things simple again. And this insight does not come easily to people who have allowed themselves to become alienated from real, productive work and from the self-balancing system of nature, which never fails to recognize measure and limitation. Any activity which fails to recognize a self-limiting principle is of the devil. In our work with the developing countries we are at least forced to recognize the limitations of poverty, and this work can therefore be a wholesome school for all of us in which, while genuinely trying to help others, we may also gain knowledge and experience how to help ourselves.

I think we can already see the conflict of attitudes which will decide our future. On the one side, I see the people who think they can cope with our threefold crisis by the methods current, only more so; I call them the people of the forward stampede. On the other side, there are people in search of a new life-style, who seek to return to certain basic truths about man and his world; I call them home-comers. Let us admit that the people of the forward stampede, like the devil, have all the best tunes or at least the most popular and familiar tunes. You cannot stand still, they say; standing still means going down; you must go forward; there is nothing wrong with modern technology except that it is as yet incomplete; let us complete it. Dr. Sicco Mansholt, one of the most prominent chiefs of the European Economic Community, may be quoted as a typical representative of this group. "More, further, quicker, richer", he says, "are the watchwords of present-day society". And he thinks we must help people to adapt "for there is no alternative". This is the authentic voice of the forward stampede, which talks in much the same tone as Dostoyevsky's Grand Inquisitor: "Why have you come to hinder us?" They point to the population explosion and to the possibilities of world hunger. Surely, we must take our flight forward and not be fainthearted. If people start protesting and revolting, we shall have to have more police and have them better equipped. If there is trouble with the environment, we shall need more stringent laws against pollution, and faster economic growth to pay for anti-pollution measures. If there are problems about natural resources, we shall turn to synthetics; if there are problems about fossil fuels, we shall move from slow reactors to fast breeders and from fission to fusion. There *are* no insoluble problems. The slogans of the people of the forward stampede burst into the newspaper headlines every day with the message, "a breakthrough a day keeps the crisis at bay".

And what about the other side? This is made up of people who are deeply convinced that technological development has taken a wrong turn and needs to be redirected. The term "home-comer" has, of course, a religious connotation. For it takes a good deal of courage to say "no" to the fashions and fascinations of the age and to question the presuppositions of a civilization which appears destined to conquer the whole world; the requisite strength can be derived only from deep convictions. If it were derived from nothing more than fear of the future, it would be likely to disappear at the decisive moment. The genuine "home-comer" does not have the best tunes, but he has the most exalted text, nothing less than the Gospels. For him, there could not be a more concise statement of his situation, of *our* situation, than the parable of the prodigal son. Strange to say, the Sermon on the Mount gives pretty precise instructions on how to construct an outlook that could lead to an Economics of Survival.

— How blessed are those who know that they are poor;
   the Kingdom of Heaven is theirs.
— How blessed are the sorrowful;
   they shall find consolation.
— How blessed are those of a gentle spirit;
   they shall have the earth for their possession.
— How blessed are those who hunger and thirst to see right prevail;
   they shall be satisfied.
— How blessed are the peacemakers;
   God shall call them his sons.

It may seem daring to connect these beatitudes with matters of technology and economics. But may it not be that we are in trouble precisely because we have failed for so long to make this connection? It is not difficult to discern what these beatitudes may mean for us today:

— We are poor, not demigods.
— We have plenty to be sorrowful about, and are not emerging into a golden age.

— We need a gentle approach, a non-violent spirit, and small is beautiful.
— We must concern ourselves with justice and see right prevail.
— And all this, only this, can enable us to become peacemakers.

The home-comers base themselves upon a different picture of man from that which motivates the people of the forward stampede. It would be very superficial to say that the latter believe in "growth" while the former do not. In a sense, everybody believes in growth, and rightly so, because growth is an essential feature of life. The whole point, however, is to give to the idea of growth a qualitative determination; for there are always many things that ought to be growing and many things that ought to be diminishing.

Equally, it would be very superficial to say that the home-comers do not believe in progress, which also can be said to be an essential feature of all life. The whole point is to determine what constitutes progress. And the home-comers believe that the direction which modern technology has taken and is continuing to pursue—towards ever-greater size, ever-higher speeds, and ever-increased violence, in defiance of all laws of natural harmony—is the opposite of progress. Hence the call for taking stock and finding a new orientation. The stocktaking indicates that we are destroying our very basis of existence, and the reorientation is based on remembering what human life is really about.

In one way or another everybody will have to take sides in this great conflict. To "leave it to the experts" means to side with the people of the forward stampede. It is widely accepted that politics is too important a matter to be left to experts. Today, the main content of politics is economics, and the main content of economics is technology. If politics cannot be left to the experts, neither can economics and technology.

I have no doubt that it is possible to give a new direction to technological development, a direction that shall lead it back to the real needs of man, and that also means: *to the actual size of man*. Man is small, and, therefore, small is beautiful. To go for giantism is to go for self-destruction. And what is the cost of a reorientation? We might remind ourselves that to calculate the cost of survival is perverse. No doubt, a price has to be paid for anything worthwhile: to redirect technology so that it serves man instead of destroying him requires primarily an effort of the imagination and an abandonment of fear.

CHAPTER 2

Why should we try to help small enterprises?*

MALCOLM HARPER

Before we can go into the details of how small enterprises can be helped to play their part in nation building, we must understand what it is that they do for a country and why they need assistance. There are a number of good arguments against small enterprises and it is important to understand these and their counter-arguments if we are to become involved in small enterprise development. We should remember that arguments in favour of small businesses are not necessarily arguments against big ones; society needs a range of different sized enterprises. With this caution in mind it may be useful to present the arguments for and against small enterprises in the form of a conversation between "Mr Pro" small enterprise and "Mr Anti" small enterprise.

Mr. Anti: You believe we should encourage and assist the small enterprises in our country, don't you?

Mr. Pro: Yes I do.

Mr. Anti: Well, I disagree. Our country's goal is to develop the economy so that we can be as wealthy as the industrialized countries. They are rich and successful because of big firms, many of which operate in different countries; these firms are big enough to afford the latest machines and techniques; how could a mechanic in one of our villages ever make a car to compete with Ford or Volkswagen?

Mr. Pro: Our market for cars is not big enough to support a large car factory. We need products which are appropriate for our stage of development.

Mr. Anti: You are condemning our people to second-rate and old-fashioned products and working conditions, which can never compete on world markets. Have you never heard of economies of scale?

---

*Pp. 2–4 in Malcolm Harper (1977) *Consultancy for Small Businesses*, published by Intermediate Technology Publications Ltd., London. This essay is reprinted here in slightly modified form with the permission of the author and publisher.

Mr. Pro: In industrialized countries, firms are big because they have to be. Only a big company can afford to buy and operate the machines that they must have because labour is so expensive. Look at all our unemployed people and look how short we are of the foreign exchange which is necessary to buy machinery. Small enterprises are the best way to make the most of our most plentiful resources, willing workers, without using much of our scarcest, foreign exchange.

Mr. Anti: Foreign companies will build big factories here if we encourage them to do so, and they will employ our surplus labour in safe factories.

Mr. Pro: Foreign companies come here to make a profit; in the end they will want to take their profit out, which is only reasonable since they put the original investment in. We need foreign firms for some activities, but if it is possible to use local management, local money and local labour we should do it. Small enterprises are the best way to do this. They employ five, ten or more times as many people for each unit of output. Perhaps their wages are lower and the roof may leak during the rainy season, but experience in industrial countries has shown that people are happier working in small units where they know everybody and are involved in the whole manufacturing process. Physical comfort may not make up for loneliness and lack of satisfaction. In any case is it better to employ one person in ideal conditions or ten in slightly less comfort?

Mr. Anti: Big businesses will build their factories in our cities and provide jobs for the thousands of unemployed who live in shanty towns on the edge of every large town. Small enterprises are scattered all over the country and are quite impossible to control.

Mr. Pro: We need jobs in the city but even more we need jobs in the country to encourage people to stay at home. Every time you create a job in the city, two or three people come to the city to try and get it, so that it creates more urban unemployment in the end. Small enterprises can be scattered across the country as our people are.

Mr. Anti: But what about the products and services of small enterprises? They are so often poorly designed and made of scrap material like old tins. Compare the sandals made by a village shoemaker out of an old car tyre with the ones made in the factory out of plastic. No wonder the rough village sandals are half the price.

Mr. Pro: Did you know that the shoe factory spends more money on imported raw materials than it does on wages, that most of its managers are foreigners and that they need three thousand dollars worth of imported machinery for every man they employ? A village shoemaker uses material that would otherwise be thrown away and his only machinery is a hammer, a pair of pliers and a piece of old iron he uses as an anvil; he probably employs at least one relation and possibly another assistant and people who could never afford the plastic sandals can pay for his. The finest product in the world is no good to the person who cannot afford it.

Mr. Anti: What about the risks? We all know how many small businessmen fail; they lose their money, their employees lose their jobs and if anyone has been foolish enough to sell materials to them on credit, they never get paid. Is this good for the country?

Mr. Pro: Haven't you heard of the survival of the fittest? We need our own entrepreneurs and managers who can run big businesses as well as small ones and the best way to learn is in the hard school of experience. Businesses fail because their competitors do better; this is good for the general public and the standards of products and services are improving all the time.

Mr. Anti: That may be, but a successful small businessman may become very rich; are we not committed to a policy of redistribution of wealth?

Mr. Pro: Rich men become rich because they create wealth, for themselves and the community. Heavy taxation can redistribute the wealth once they have made it but if we never let them make it, society will be all that much poorer. Small enterprises can also be owned by cooperatives or village groups too; they don't have to be private.

Mr. Anti: What about their designs though? How can a small business match the efforts of a large corporation with hundreds of scientists?

Mr. Pro: Large research laboratories develop products for large scale manufacture. Our country is made up of many different types of people growing different crops and having different needs; we may all be threatened by the diseases and it is reasonable to fight diseases with the standardized drugs developed in big laboratories. We may need large numbers of different shapes of hoe, or different types of cart, or different types of service from shops. Only small enterprises are flexible enough to change and adapt when our needs change. Really new things are invented by individuals not by committees. In the same way, small enterprises come up with good ideas far more quickly and far more often than large ones do. If they fail the individual cost is small, but big firms cannot risk failure; this means that they often fail to introduce new ideas at all.

Mr. Anti: What about capital and management? Big firms can go to the banks and try to influence government investments and they can train or hire the best managers from around the world. How can our small enterprises compete for management or for money?

Mr. Pro: As you know, our society is based on the family; progress is destroying many of the links and loyalties on which we have relied but small enterprises can actually strengthen the family. A typical small enterprise can be managed and staffed by a family and how else can all the capital or the human ability which is hidden away on our farms and villages be put to profitable use? Many people do not trust banks and they have no access to stocks and shares. They will, however, invest their savings in their own businesses and people will even sell surplus cattle or land to raise money for a business.

Mr. Anti: Yes but how can government possibly control all these small enterprises? We are trying to plan the development of our country and officials can personally speak to a few big business managers to make sure that they conform to the national plan. Nobody even knows how many small enterprises there are in our country so how can we control what they do?

Mr. Pro: Government represents the people and maybe thousands of small enterprises owned and managed by our own people are more likely to reflect national goals than a few large businesses which may be largely foreign owned and managed. When we set up our own businesses we still have serious problems; when the government tries to set up large national corporations they are, as you know, often inefficient or corrupt. If government directs and encourages the activities of small enterprises by assisting them to develop in certain areas or activities, it can have greater effect on the nation as a whole than can be achieved through a few large enterprises.

Mr. Anti: Most of the industrialized countries have moved towards small numbers of large enterprises. Why should we be trying to encourage large numbers of small enterprises?

Mr. Pro: All the industrialized countries reached their present prosperity because large numbers of small-scale business people started new enterprises and developed new techniques. There is no reason to suppose that our country can jump direct to large-scale enterprises; many industrialized countries are now regretting the large proportion of their economic activity which is in the hands of large companies and are trying to reverse this trend.

Mr. Anti: Small-scale business people are often dishonest and in our society we tend to despise them as thieves rather than looking up to them as leaders in economic development. Why should we try to help these people?

Mr. Pro: I do not think you will be able to give me many examples of dishonest business people who have succeeded for very long. Let me ask you a question; quite apart from the poverty of our country, what sort of personal failings have prevented our country from developing and prospering as it might?

Mr. Anti: Well I suppose people tend to be cautious, to lack initiative, to delay making decisions, to refuse to face up to problems, they are unwilling to take responsibility or to show imagination and self reliance and are unwilling to work together. Nowadays people always seem to expect someone else, usually the government, to solve their problems for them. It is often said that our public and private sector managers are not as effective as they might be because they are always looking for short-term returns.

Mr. Pro: Yes that is a reasonable list of human failings. You will find that a successful small-scale business person suffers from few or none of these weaknesses. He *has* to make decisions, to take calculated risks, to face up to and solve problems and to take responsibility for what he is doing because otherwise his enterprise will fail. Success in small business very often involves investing money in the business rather than withdrawing it for personal expenditure. Qualities of this sort, such as self-restraint, imagination, initiative and self-reliance are present in every successful small enterprise. Small enterprises can provide a school for this type of behaviour, a source of effective managers and an example to the rest of the community.

CHAPTER 3

Barefoot management in India: a humanitarian stand*

MICHAEL VAN DEN BOGAERT

Modern management in India today is the tip of an iceberg, one-eighth of which emerges above the water. It can only do so because it rests on the mass of the seven-eighths hidden below the surface. This hidden mass is the unorganized sector of the economy, manned by barefoot managers. Without the seven-eighths hidden below the surface we, in the remaining one-eighth, would not be able to catch the rays of the sun that the organized sector of the economy provides us. I am afraid that till now too little thought has been given to these seven-eighths. We ignore it, and at the same time make use of its services. I do not speak of the managers of small-scale industries, as currently understood in India, but of the self-employed people, of whom there are millions in India: the hawkers, *panwallas*, fruit sellers, laundry men, porters and coolies and *thela ghari* men, the wayside shop owners, cycle repair men, cane juice crushers, and a whole host of other crafts and avocations carried out in this city or in India's villages.

I shall cover the following subjects:

1. The dynamism of little people.
2. The human aspect of barefoot management.
3. What can be done to promote barefoot management.

The subsistence and even growth of the unorganized sector of our economy is the outcome of the determination of the common man to make a living with the very meagre resources that are at his disposal. It is an affirmation of hope in the future, an affirmation of life.

A great communication gap separates us from the common man as a result of which we go our own way without caring to understand the values of the other, or his needs.

---

*A reprint of Michael van den Bogaert (1977) *Barefoot Management: A Humanitarian Stand*, originally published by Action for Food Production (AFPRO), New Delhi, and republished here with the permission of both the author and AFPRO.

For us who commute to work by car or other means, the streets of the city are arteries of traffic, and we utter a sight of relief that the administration is finally removing from the streets, the vendors and their illegal encroachments.

The dynamism of little people

To the small man, a street, an alley, a park, or a railway station, have a different meaning. They are places to live on, to trade, to carry on one's craft, to sleep, and to put up a pandal when Saraswati or Durga Puja comes along. Having been given no other opportunity to earn his living, no berth in organized society, it is but natural that he considers it his right to encroach on public property, and from the point of view of social justice he may be right. In this seething mass of common people the barefoot managers, whose number has never been estimated, are the driving force, the earners of bread for families tucked away in the slums or in the hinterland of Bihar, Orissa or Uttar Pradesh. They ask for recognition of their human dignity, and an opportunity to earn and slowly grow more prosperous.

But is it not stretching the concept of management too far to call these people managers or entrepreneurs? Yes, perhaps, if one goes by the concepts of business management that we have learned from the West. No, if we look a bit closer to what these people do. They fulfil all the functions of management, though on a tiny scale. They manage their financial resources, a particular space on the footpath, their tools and machinery. They also engage in marketing and show often a degree of inventiveness that would leave us in admiration. They are surely great risk takers.

They make extremely productive use of the resources at their disposal. Witness how in contrast to the civilization of the West, which has become a civilization of waste and affluence, our barefoot managers recycle and use the waste products that come from the organized economy over and over again till these products finally fall to dust. Old cardboard, scraps of newspapers, tarpaulins, *dalda* tins, gunny bags all are put to productive use. Their input–output ratios would compare favourably with those of the organized sector of the economy.

True, the world of the barefoot managers is not a rosy one. Theirs is a hard struggle in which only the most inventive or ruthless survive. There is cut-throat competition and no hesitation to make an extra buck from an unsuspecting tourist or outsider. There is cheating, even petty crime, but that is the only way to survive. Being in the unorganized sector of the economy, the law of the jungle prevails.

Theirs is a culture of "Machismo", of showing one's manhood by doing dangerous acts and daunting the police and other authorities. Make as much money and as fast as you can seems to be the lesson they have learned and practise assiduously.

For us such behaviour works on the nerves. The little people who use their services put up with it uncomplainingly and side with the barefoot managers when it comes to a confrontation with the police or the *bhadralok*.

Theirs is an economy that we in the organized sector do not understand, but that is not without rationality when one realizes that these people operate from a short time perspective, and provide to the common man the services he needs, and at a cheap rate, never mind the inconveniences with which he has to put up.

The barefoot managers have also expenses that cannot be entered in the books, if books are kept at all. Hands have to be greased, of inspectors, policemen, *dadas* and others in order to be allowed to ply one's trade, to park one's vehicle, or to overload it.

I see this bustling world of barefoot managers, with the positive and negative points as a plea on the part of the common man to be allowed to exist, and to be respected for what he is and tries to become. Instead of seeing this world as an eyesore or a nuisance to be wiped off, why can't we see the little way-side restaurants, tailor's shops and repair sheds, as the primary schools in which the common people learn the art of management not from the books, as we have done, but through the hard struggle for survival?

We recognize in the poverty syndrome and the culture of marginality the traits that characterize or characterized till recently, the outlook of people at the bottom of the Indian iceberg, the *harijans*, tribals and backward communities.

Barefoot management is gaining ground amongst these people also and indicates that they are moving out of this culture of marginality and want a place and recognition in Indian society.

The human aspect

In terms of human progress, one barefoot manager amongst such people means a more significant step forward to their emancipation than any project for their uplift, whether launched by the government, non-governmental organizations or even enlightened managers. It means that those people are keen to take their own lot in hand and once this attitude is deeply entrenched half the battle of development is won.

This human factor is not merely a thing to be talked about at seminars, it plays a vital role in the performance of the Indian economy. We in the organized sector can continue to ignore it only at the expense of ourselves and the country.

A recent study by Xavier Labour Relations Institute, Jamshedpur, on the pattern of distribution of consumer goods in Singhbum district of Bihar should be an eye-opener to marketing managers in industry. The authors advise that it would be in our own interest to locate the many "marketing gaps" that still dot the rural map of India, and remark that we have by far not exploited to the full the weekly markets or *hats* that are held all over the country. We could learn a lesson from the barefoot entrepreneurs, hawkers and traders who carry their wares from market to market on their cycles. The consumer goods companies, so the authors say, could do the same by moving their products in the rural markets by mobile vans, they could also enlist the barefoot managers as allies.

I would say on the basis of my own experience that most of the decisions that our barefoot managers make in the unorganized sector are decisions with a rationale behind them, are indeed rational decisions, within the parameters of resources, values and culture in which the barefoot managers operate. Agricultural development in the more advanced states of India has shown that if proper incentives are given these barefoot managers know how to maximize their outputs and profits very well. It is not necessary to tell them what is best for them; they know this by themselves. It is rather a question for the administration and the organized part of the economy to create the right opportunities, to tone up the administration and to make the necessary inputs available at reasonable prices.

Finally, in the perspective of the human aspect of barefoot management, I would plead that we throw bridges of communication between ourselves and the barefoot managers. Today a huge gap separates us from them. For this we are primarily responsible. We move in an air-conditioned world, we speak a jargon that barefoot people do not understand, we have a set of values that makes us ignore them, as being of no importance or at best a nuisance or an encroachment on the growth of the organized sector. The more enlightened amongst business managers are awakening to the potentialities stored up in barefoot managers but find it difficult to shake off an attitude of paternalism.

Promotion of barefoot management

What can be done in the face of barefoot management? Two basic approaches seem possible; number one: do nothing and wait till the organized sector expands and occupies the vacuum so that eventually everybody is in the organized sector; number two: make a special effort to promote the upsurge of barefoot entrepreneurship and accommodate it as a valuable ally in the drive for economic and social growth.

ILO is in favour of the second alternative. At the present rate of growth of the organized sector it may take two or three generations till everybody can be given employment in the organized sector. By that time, the amount of capital required to create every additional job will be so staggering as to make the proposition impractical. ILO is of the opinion that the informal and unorganized sector offers the greatest opportunities for creating additional work opportunities with far smaller investments.

The thinking of the Government of India is also in favour of the second alternative. At the Fourth International Training and Development Conference in New Delhi, 16–20 November 1975, the Deputy Chairman of the Planning Commission made a strong plea that far more be done for the training of barefoot managers than has been the case till now. How to do this, is a challenging question to which some of our best minds will have to give attention.

The promotion of ancillary industries or small-scale industries and provision for self-employment training for unemployed youth are by now well established programmes of the Government of India. They are far from touching the real barefoot managers. They cater to a group of middle-level entrepreneurs who compared with the barefoot managers are an elite, to which some of the latter can aspire to make a break-through one day.

The efforts carried on by Xavier Institute of Social Service prove that it is not so difficult to promote barefoot management and entrepreneurship. Our staff members have organized games in cooperation, achievement motivation, creativity and self-understanding for groups of rural people, such as potters, basket weavers, blacksmiths, farmers, to whom commercial banks had issued small loans. They found that though these people may be illiterate, they are not dumb. As a matter of fact, untrammelled by the masks that business managers wear, these people seem to grasp often more quickly the meaning and lesson of such games than is the case with the former.

Nor is the conveying of basic ideas of management, accounting, finance, marketing, project planning, such an impossible task as appears at first sight. Even PERT, CPM, ABC analysis and other gadgetries can be taught to tribal entrepreneurs, provided one conveys them in local language shorn of all the jargonry.

The working out of concrete programmes is not that difficult. What is more vital is the change of attitudes that has to be brought about in the one-eighth of the iceberg that sticks out of the water. If the promotion of barefoot management is to become a reality in India, all of us have to go through what Paulo Freire has called a "conversion of heart". A process whereby we are willing to leave our certainties, our jargon, our ideosyncracies and the masks we wear, in order to put ourselves at the level of barefoot people, meet them as human beings, and go along with them through a common learning process.

For many this sounds just foolishness. To the few that dare to believe in the dignity and potentialities of the small man in India, it opens a road of discovery of one's own humanity. It throws open the windows of management and training circles where the air has become somewhat stuffy. It provides us an opportunity to again get "grounded", i.e. to go back to the grassroots from where we all take our origin. Finally, it may be the only way in which we as managers or academicians can survive, justify the privileges we enjoy, and maintain relevancy and acceptability in a society that is growing day by day more socialistic and popularist.

CHAPTER 4

Becaks, bemos, lambros and productive pandemonium*

ALAN K. MEIER

The streets of Southeast Asia are more than channels of transport. They are active centres of commerce and social interaction; the streets serve as residents' living rooms, kitchens, and sometimes bedrooms. Businesses use the streets as offices and warehouses. When water is scarce, the gutters may act as baths, laundries and sewers. Peddlers and tradesmen, offering an incredible variety of goods and services, fill the streets with their wares and calls for customers. Some are firmly established at profitable intersections; others move slowly along through the crowds.

Almost miraculously, traffic also flows through these streets. The most striking feature of this traffic is its variety—animals, pedestrians, and vehicles with two, three, or four wheels all jockey for passage through the choked thoroughfares. Closer examination reveals a method to the transportation madness, for each vehicle appears to serve a specific function in the transportation mix. Transportation engineers, or engineers in general, should not be surprised by this technological evolution to meet special requirements. However, the curious socially-induced differences in the traffic mixtures between cities, even within the same country, are particularly intriguing.

The differences are not so much found in cars, buses or trucks—which are all of Western design and scarcely change from country to country—but among the smaller, more primitive vehicles. It is upon the carts, bicycles, tricycles, motorcycles, motorized three-wheelers, and minibuses that the differing cultures exert their influence, constrained by economics and technology.

Transportation is perhaps even more vital in Southeast Asia than in the West. Telephones, postal services, and other communications facilities are notoriously unreliable, so the personal encounter is all-important to social and business interaction. Because personal trips are so frequent and

*Reprinted from *Technology Review*, vol. 79, no. 3, January 1977, pp. 56–63, with the permission of the author and of the editors of the journal. Copyright (1977) by the Alumni Association of the Massachusetts Institute of Technology.

necessary, the vehicles must be especially economic, using as few scarce resources as possible and depending primarily on the one resource plentiful in the area—human labour. It is especially surprising then, that the vehicles in Southeast Asian cities have such a great variation in efficiencies. Even the most fundamental form of transportation of goods—carrying them on foot—varies from place to place. For instance, in Korea, goods are carried on the back using a wooden frame, but in Indochina, the load is divided into two parts, hung from the ends of a split bamboo pole, then balanced across the shoulder.

The bicycle is the most basic intermediate technology vehicle. In my travels over Southeast Asia I was amazed at the differences among countries in the speed and effectiveness of their bicycles. For example, once the Saigon government banned importation of motorcycles in the 1960s because of the economic crisis, bicycles with sturdy, simple frames began to evolve. Extra seats over the rear wheels allowed transportation of both people and freight. Small-wheeled bicycles with low frames were especially suitable for new or elderly riders. The Saigon bicycles were designed in sophisticated Saigon shop industries, which had turned from motorcycle maintenance and reconditioning. In fact, after the fall of South Vietnam, it was reported that Saigon bicycles spread rapidly north to Hanoi, where they contrasted sharply with the staid, simpler North Vietnamese bicycle.

The rapid adaptation of the effective Vietnamese bicycle was successful because of the economic need for it in the collapsing economy, and its ease of use by all kinds of people. The open structure of the society also encouraged bicycle use, because there were no social taboos against women or the elderly riding bicycles. Also, a traffic law designed to protect motorcyclists from automobiles benefited bicyclists. By this law, large yields to small, so when bicycles came on the scene they inherited a legal advantage over all the other vehicles.

The effective, rapid evolution of the bicycle in Saigon contrasts sharply with the virtual stagnation of design in India. The Indian bicycle in use today is identical to that used generations ago, which, in turn, was an imitation of the standard English model of the earlier era.

This slavish imitation is remarkable when one considers the sharp difference in the bicycle's function between the two countries. The English bicycle was designed to carry one person and move quickly on a paved road. Moreover, careful maintenance was expected. In contrast, an Indian bicycle must carry one, two, or possibly more persons, and sometimes a substantial amount of goods as well. Indian roads are often poor, and bicycle maintenance is minimal. In the summer, the roads get so hot that tyre patches fail. The dust finds its way into every moving part, hastening deterioration. During the monsoon, bicycles are ridden on roads that resemble rivers. The greatest contrast between England and India, however, is in the attitudes of the riders toward their bicycling. In England the bicycle was a means of transportation much more rapid than walking; in India the object is to reach the destination quickly, but more importantly, to maintain a lower level of exertion. Thus, while Indian bicycle traffic seems to move more slowly, it is still a highly efficient mode of transportation for Indians, when considered in terms of conservation of energy, and the low value on time.

The Indian bicycle has not been redesigned to enhance its energy efficiency, ease of maintenance, or cargo-carrying ability, in large part because of India's strong social divisions. First of all, bicycle repairs are almost never done by the riders, but by repairmen of very low social status. These repairmen have established themselves along the major urban bicycle corridors, or simply under convenient shady trees. They own just enough tools to repair the most common malfunctions. Such a social taboo rules out any change in bicycle design which might enable the rider to repair his own vehicle. For instance, exchanging the currently used hex nut on the rear axle for a butterfly nut would enable the rider to tighten his own chain without tools (chain slackening is the most common malfunction on the Indian bicycle). However, such innovation is unlikely.

Similarly, bicycle designs with smaller wheels and a smaller frame will be slow to appear in India, for they would allow women in their saris to ride bicycles. Currently, most women are restricted to riding side-saddle as passengers on the luggage rack over the rear wheel. Innovations offered by organizations such as the Indian Institute of Design will almost certainly be stymied by conservatism and social prohibitions.

Of course, bicycles are by no means merely passenger carriers in the East. The luggage racks on Asian bicycles often carry up to 50 kilograms of goods strapped clumsily on the back. Jugs of milk, packages of food, and other perishables of high value are delivered rapidly by bicycles. Bakeries often use bicycles with large, wooden bread-boxes attached.

Three is better than two

The most widely-used human-powered freight-carriers in Southeast Asia are the tricycles, perhaps the most fascinating form of intermediate transport. The pedal tricycle, alternatively known as the becak, cycle-rickshaw or pedicab, is always manufactured locally, and rarely exported outside the city of its manufacture. Tricycle "factories" are small shops, employing only a few persons. Families often pass the trade from generation to generation. Locally available materials and parts are used as much as possible; hence, standard bicycle frames and wood usually constitute the tricycle base. Welding is an important technology, but machine tools are rarely used. Considering the similarity of basic materials and the cost restraints throughout Southeast Asia, the wide variation in both appearance and efficiency is surprising.

Tricyclists can carry up to 175 kilograms for level distances up to several kilometres. This capacity and distance depends greatly, of course, on the efficiency of design and the level of maintenance. The three fundamentally different tricycle designs place the driver either in front of the cargo or passengers, behind them, or the load on a side-car. In the driver-in-front tricycle, steering remains as on a regular bicycle, with power transmitted via a long chain to the two rear wheels. The driver-in-rear configuration features two front wheels, with power supplied to a single rear wheel. Steering is accomplished by turning the entire front compartment.

Each design has its own advantages and disadvantages. The driver-in-front design, used mostly in India, is lighter and easier to pedal and steer. However, side-car and driver-in-rear design, found in Indonesia, Malaysia, and Vietnam, can carry heavier loads, because power is transmitted more directly.

The importance of tricycles in the urban transport mix of Southeast Asian cities varies immensely. In the largest cities, they must compete with motor traffic and contend with an unsympathetic government administration which often discourages their use because they are "inhumane" or "a hazard to traffic". (Usually the government really means that the tricycles are a hazard to the autos belonging to the wealthy.) But government policies are not always effective in limiting the tricycles. In the city of Jakarta, Indonesia, about three times as many becaks run the streets as legal government licences for them have been issued. The owners duplicate their licences so as to run more than one vehicle. As a result of such large-city constraints, the tricycle is usually more important in the smaller cities.

Of all the tricycles, the Malaysian-type manufactured in Penang appears to be the most successful. These sturdy vehicles, some of which have lasted over 20 years, are used primarily to carry freight and serve as vehicles for food vendors. Stores own fleets of tricycles to make deliveries, and entire restaurants-on-wheels, complete with seating and kitchens, are operated from the front compartments of some vehicles. Freight-carrying will probably continue to be the forte of tricycles, for they can negotiate narrow city streets better than almost any motor vehicles, yet carry almost as much freight. The freight tricycle is still evolving, with gear ratios slowly dropping, and new, smaller wheels appearing (from motorcycles) to improve capacity and smooth the ride. Passenger tricycles, however, have all but disappeared due to competition from motor vehicles. One of the few remaining passenger functions of the tricycles is to transport small children to and from school.

Motors for muscle

As a city's economy improves its technology advances, and motor transport almost invariably comes into wide use. The smallest motor vehicle in Southeast Asia is the "mo-ped"—a reinforced bicycle with a small gasoline engine attached. The engine is usually less than 50 cc. and usually produces less than two horsepower. The driver of a mo-ped can pedal, motor, or do both. Although a passenger or freight can be carried on the back, the motor must really strain, and often sputters to a halt if it is even a bit out of tune. The real centre of current mo-ped activity is in India, where it is a vehicle of the upper classes. It is hoped that the mo-ped will soon be drafted to haul freight, pull two-wheeled carts, or be cannibalized to provide tricycle engines as they have been in Indochina.

With the addition of 20 cc or so to its engine displacement, the mo-ped becomes a motorcycle, and can function as an excellent passenger and freight carrier. For example, in Vietnam, entire families of up to six people ride on a single 50 cc motorcycle.

The technological evolution of a city to support motorcycles means not only a growth of repair facilities, etc., but also the improvement of roads. Potholes slow the motorcycles to bicycle speeds and shorten the life of the more expensive vehicle. In the Fiji Islands, the motorcycle's popularity skyrocketed when roads were paved. So quickly did the boom develop that some members of the motorcycle gang in Lautoka still rode motorcycles with a learner's "L" on their plates! Surprisingly, the wet weather of Southeast Asia plays a very minor role in motorcycle use, and the riders always seem to triumph over the weather. One unusual method motorcyclists use throughout Southeast Asia to protect themselves against rain is to wear their plastic raincoats backwards.

The Southeast Asians have developed the motorcycle into an effective intermediate-technology transport vehicle mainly by learning to "abuse" it to their advantage. They have discovered rather quickly that European and Japanese specifications for their motorcycles are very conservative, and in reality, the motorcycles can carry much greater loads than specified. Instead of two passengers, the motorcycles can carry three or four with additional seating in front of, or behind the driver. The motorcycle can also be adapted to carry an incredible variety of goods, including live pigs and chickens, bottled gas, sacks of rice, and bricks.

One of the most interesting adaptations of the motorcycles is not a change in technology, but of attitude—the idea that motorcycles can be used as taxis. In Saigon in the late 1960s motorcycle owners supplemented their income by transporting soldiers from barracks to night clubs. As the economy deteriorated in the 1970s, the incentive to profit from machines soared, and although illegal, the "honda-ôms", as they were called, flourished. A bargain at half the price of a taxi, they were also safer at night than riding a motorcycle alone; so, even motorcycle owners left their vehicles at home to use them.

Three wheels and a motor

Just as the tricycle evolved logically from the bicycle, so the three-wheeled motor vehicle has come from the motorcycle. These are called variously helicaks, minicars, bemos, mebeas, auto-rickshaws, four-seaters, tempos, cycle-motors, lambros, and samlors. Each of these vehicles is distinctly different, due to the many, small local manufacturers, who vary the simple main design. The three wheels make them stable so they can be constructed more heavily. Thus, they are unlike motorcycles, where balance and weight reduction is vital. And they require far less sophisticated brakes, suspension, transmission and steering systems than regular automobiles, so the technology does not far outstrip local resources.

The range of technological sophistication in these vehicles is enormous. The crudest three-wheelers are simply reinforced tricycles, with an engine replacing the driver's legs for locomotion. Because the tricycle frames cannot usually stand the strain of motor-power for long, the need for a stronger frame is immediately apparent, and the design proceeds to an even greater complexity. More sophisticated three-wheelers have been imported from Italy or Japan. These have engines of around 175 cc and can carry from three to nine passengers. However, in many Asian countries, local industries have begun to produce a third generation of three-wheelers. Some countries, such as India, are merely importing the manufacturing technology, while others, such as Indonesia, have designed their own vehicles for local conditions. But most importantly, the influence over design is returning to the area of use, and is no longer merely an adaptation of semi-obsolete European and Japanese vehicles.

Undoubtedly the oddest three-wheeler is the helicak—a driver-in-rear motor vehicle with an egg-shaped, enclosed compartment resembling a helicopter cockpit. The helicak, with its tinted windows, is a high-status vehicle for its passengers, but there was concern at their introduction that the zippy vehicles would present quite a hazard to passengers in a collision. Despite cartoons, such as one showing a helicak with a mattress strapped to the front, there appeared, however, to be few serious accidents with the vehicles.

The three-wheeler is not equally popular in all countries. While huge numbers of the three-wheelers roam streets in India, the vehicles have already come and gone in Saigon and Bangkok, replaced by four-wheeled taxis and buses.

While the three-wheeler is widely used as a taxi, its real vocation is as a minibus. As three-wheelers came into use as minibuses, they grew larger, with about 500 to 700 kilograms of capacity. Seating arrangements changed from one seat facing forward into two benches facing each other, and the driver's compartment was separated from the passenger compartment. As with most transportation in Southeast Asia, fares were bargained over before the trip began. The price depended on the time of day, the amount of luggage, and whether competitive transportation was available. For example, if the local bus service was on strike, fares might double.

Most of the three-wheeled minibuses originated during the period of 1958 to 1965, and manufacturing ceased after that time. So, the minibuses now used in such places as Vietnam, Indonesia, and Thailand are being driven until they collapse. However, new three-wheel minibuses are approaching the production stage in both Indonesia and Greece. The minibus has proven economically and even politically important to Southeast Asia. For instance, the "lambro" minibus was used as a political weapon in Vietnam. The South Vietnamese government, in an attempt to give rural peasants a stake in the government, encouraged the drivers of these buses in the countryside to also become their owners. Presumably the Viet Cong would not tolerate this form of free enterprise, thought government officials, and the driver-entrepreneur would, thus, have an economic interest in keeping the South Vietnamese government in power. Eventually this idea spread to Saigon, where fleets of lambros operated on fixed routes in the city. However, in 1967, as thousands of motorcycles were imported into Vietnam, the minibus lost an important source of customers—middle-class commuters. The lambros held on until late 1974 when buses were introduced that offered more comfortable seating and a lower fare.

As I indicated previously, when technology and economics allowed, three-wheeled vehicles were replaced by four-wheeled vehicles. However, some re-engineering was still performed on the basic four-wheelers to adapt foreign vehicles to Asian users. For instance, the Indonesian "opelets" were based on an Austin automobile chassis. The rear end of the body was removed and a station-wagon-type body made of wood was substituted. The opelet carried about nine passengers on two parallel bench seats in the rear. Besides the driver, there was invariably a boy manning the rear door, collecting fares, and calling out the opelet's destination to pedestrians.

Although such route-varying "jitneys" in Southeast Asia—as elsewhere—offered more flexibility and greater frequency than buses, the governments of Southeast Asia have discriminated against jitneys, because they are not as easily regulatable as buses. In Jakarta, for example, the opelets are limited to certain routes, thus depriving them of their flexibility. Fortunately, the jitneys are responding with improved, comfort-oriented technology to keep their market. For instance, small pickup trucks have been adapted as jitneys to give better rides. These have proven so successful that within three years of their introduction in Bandung, Indonesia, they had virtually displaced the opelets. Although such rapid transformations of transportation technology are quite common in Southeast Asia, a similar quick turnabout in the huge, capital-intensive transportation systems in U.S. cities is unimaginable.

Many of the transportation forms discussed here have arisen spontaneously in response to social needs, but the hand of the government has also been felt in Southeast Asian transport, both for good and bad. Motorcycles were deliberately introduced into Vietnam, on the advice of American economic advisors, to sop up excess dollars being earned by the Vietnamese workers. The Indian government sponsored the tricycle to replace hand-pulled rickshaws, because the former were more "humane". The officially approved driver-in-front design, however, was the only tricycle encouraged, using such policies as low-interest band loans. Similarly the Indian government has limited motorized three-wheeler design by allowing importation of only a few designs.

Sometimes government transportation policy has little to do with technology or "humaneness". There is a story, perhaps apocryphal, that the Japanese bemo three-wheeler was introduced into Indonesia because the Japanese were so delighted when Sukarno married his Japanese mistress that they gave him a special deal on them. Questionable bargains of some type often play a role in transportation and other government decisions in Southeast Asia, but they are obviously difficult to trace.

This incomplete description of intermediate transport in Southeast Asia illustrates the diversity of solutions available to answer the problem of moving people and freight around a city with a minimum of resources. The intermediate technology transport sector is ideally suited to these societies, because the marginal cost of additional transportation capacity is small for the entrepreneur and, for the government, often nothing. Usually the organization required to sustain the network arises spontaneously and is efficient, at least until it achieves a monopoly. Therefore, the one transportation policy really essential to Southeast Asia is that competitive modes of transport should be encouraged. These modes would provide slightly differentiated transport packages. For instance one mode might be like another, except the second can carry freight; one mode might be slightly more expensive than another, but faster. Thus, each mode would have a definite market, but would be able to assume a competitor's responsibility in the event of a strike or similar disturbance.

The key to effective urban transport in Southeast Asia is flexibility. Rapid change has been seen to occur in a transport system, even in peacetime. The last thing a rapidly growing city should do is make long-term commitments to urban transport, such as fixed rail systems. The city may be completely transformed before the plans leave the drawing board. Any government commitment should be to insure that the poor have a means of transport, as well as a livelihood in the transport industry (even if it means driving an "inhumane" tricycle).

Southeast Asian vehicle use will certainly grow, although the direction depends upon a myriad of social, political, and economic factors. In a situation where private entrepreneurs are encouraged, there will be a move toward small motorized vehicles and, later, buses. At almost every level of passenger transport, motor vehicles are more efficient. One motorized three-wheeler can substitute for (or displace) 15 to 40 passenger tricycles. The individual entrepreneur can realize a better return on the motorized three-wheeler than on a fleet of tricycles. On a national scale, however, the shift to motorized transport is a disaster. Unemployment in Indonesia is estimated by some experts to be over 25 per cent. Can the government tolerate a shift to motor vehicles when each new three-wheeler deprives 15 to 40 persons of jobs?

Thus, there is an inherent contradiction of national and private interests. On the other hand, motorized transport may transform the society into an even more productive entity, stimulating a need for labour greater than any displaced. This appears to be happening in many small villages in Greece. There, the introduction of a sturdy, motorized three-wheel farm vehicle has re-established the farm as a viable, economic unit. Still, there is no guarantee that the motorization of transportation will be successful enough to reconcile the conflict of private and national interests.

Such intermediate-technology vehicles may soon blossom in the developed countries as a variety of factors leads to the future de-emphasis of private automobiles. Besides environmental and economic restraints on autos, there have arisen auto-free areas, in the form of pedestrian malls and residence complexes, which may also encourage the friendly, neighbourhood minibus. As such areas increase in size, more sophisticated transport service, for both passengers and freight, will be required. Here, too, smaller vehicles—bicycles, motorcycles, and three-wheelers—could provide efficient unimposing service that does not disrupt pedestrian activity.

SECTION II

One system, not two

"The facts utterly refute the opinion that is widespread among us that 'factory' and '*kustar*' (village handicraft artisan) industry are isolated from each other. On the contrary, their division is purely artificial. The connection and continuity between these two forms of industry are most direct and intimate. The facts very clearly prove that the main trend of small commodity production is towards the development of capitalism, in particular towards the rise of manufacture, and before our very eyes, manufacture is very rapidly growing into large-scale machine industry. Perhaps one of the most striking manifestations of the close and immediate connection between the consecutive forms of industry is the fact that a number of big and very big manufacturers were, at one time, the smallest of small tradesmen and passed through all the stages from 'people's industry' to 'capitalism'. Savva Morozov was first a serf peasant (he purchased his freedom in 1820), then a shepherd, carter, weaver in a mill, then a 'kustar' weaver, walking to Moscow to sell his cloth to merchants; then he became the owner of a small establishment for giving out work to outdoor workers, and finally a factory owner. At the time of his death in 1862, he and his numerous sons owned two large cotton mills."

(V. I. Lenin 1936, *The Development of Capitalism in Russia*, 329–30)

Introduction

This second section presents two major essays, the first by Jan Breman and the second by Francisco de Oliveira, arguing that it is vital to consider the economy (urban, regional, national or world) as a whole, avoiding "dualist" divisions of enterprises and of the labour market into two contrasting sectors. These sectors have been given a wide range of names, but the most persistent labels are, on the one hand, the "modern" or "formal" sector, and on the other, the "traditional", "backward" or "informal" sector. In their simplest form, such divisions reflect a distinction between large, capitalist enterprises and government activities ("modern/formal"), and small-scale workshops, shops, stalls, household and peasant enterprises ("traditional/backward/ informal"). "Traditional" activities are viewed as those which existed before, and continue in the face of, Western capitalist penetration, while modern activities are those which result directly from foreign influence and investment, the application of advanced technologies, and the advent of sophisticated professional and governmental activities. The dualist approach has become the theoretical basis for an extensive literature and has become almost institutionalized in liberal and neo-classical analyses of Third World economies (see e.g. Fei and Ranis 1964; Lewis 1954; Paauw and Fei 1973).

The two essays presented here are "classics" which have never achieved the diffusion or fame that they deserve because they were originally published in the Third World (Breman in English in India, and Oliveira in Portuguese in Brazil) in journals which have relatively little circulation outside their countries of origin. It is a mark of the quality of these two essays, however, that their conclusions seem as convincing, coherent and original today as when they were first published (Oliveira in 1972 and Breman in 1976).

Breman's essay (Chapter 5) is based on long periods of anthropological fieldwork in rural and urban areas of Gujarat (see especially Breman 1974, 1977), and it combines a rich knowledge of local realities with an extensive review of the "informal sector" literature. It was one of the first major critical reviews of the "informal sector" concept (for others see e.g. Bromley 1978; Moser 1978), and it helped to establish a trend towards studies of small enterprises within the context of the "total" economy rather than as some sort of autonomous "small enterprise sector" (see e.g. Bromley and Gerry (eds.) 1979; Portes and Walton 1981).

Oliveira's essay (Chapter 6) is one of the principal works of the outstanding group of radical Brazilian social scientists associated with CEBRAP, the Brazilian Centre for Analysis and Planning located in São Paulo, and undoubtedly one of the principal centres of academic excellence in the Third World. It is based on two decades of close observation and analysis of Brazilian capitalist development, and on well-founded criticisms of the economic development strategies recommended by CEPAL (the UN Economic Commission for Latin America, ECLA) in the 1950s and 1960s. The essay presents a comprehensive attack on the sorts of "crude dependency theories" which imply that there is no possibility of sustained capitalist economic development in the Third World. It follows a line much closer to Cardoso and Faletto's (1980) concept of "associated dependent development", recognizing the possibilities for major industrialization in parts of the Third World and the gradual realignment of the world economy (see Warren 1973). Of greater specific relevance to this book, it explains how and why petty production not only survives in coexistence with capitalist industrialization, but may actually increase in significance by performing roles which are essentially complementary to, and supportive of, large-scale production. Furthermore, Oliveira shows how new small enterprises may be founded to perform functions which did not even exist before the advent of industrialization or the large-scale importation of high-technology consumer goods; for example the repair of liquidizers and hairdryers, the renting of video-cassettes, and the guarding and repair of—and sales of spares and accessories for— motor vehicles. Such activities cannot possibly be included in a "traditional" or "backward" sector, and their very existence is conditional upon the dynamism of the "modern" sector.

There is much to be said for a strict avoidance of dualist frameworks. Such avoidance reflects a greater enthusiasm for studying relationships and interactions than for defining and studying specific categories, sectors or segments of the population, and also a strong belief that dualistic (two-sector) models have outlived their utility for academic analysis and policy-making. All models and theories abstract from the complexity of the real world to present a simplified view, emphasizing divisions and relationships which are considered to be particularly important. The criticism of dualistic models, therefore, is not so much that they simplify, as that they emphasize the wrong divisions and relationships, consequently underplaying the significance of the relationships which are most important. An awkward division between "modern/formal" and "traditional/backward/informal" is being made precisely where the dominant focus of attention should be the vertical interlinkages between large and small. The study of these interlinkages could reveal the patterns of exploitation and accumulation maintaining and even accentuating socioeconomic inequalities, while the study of the individual sectors may do little more than confirm the characteristics which were assigned in their original definition.

In criticizing dualistic models, it is very important to distinguish between two strikingly different conceptions of dualism. Those two-sector models which assume either that there is no relationship between sectors, or that relationships are essentially benign, are shown by Breman, Oliveira and numerous other analysts (see e.g. Bromley and Gerry (eds.) (1979) to be entirely inappropriate, perpetuating misconceptions and leading inevitably to misguided policy formulations. In contrast, those two-sector models which assume that one sector dominates and subordinates the other, and that inter-relationships are both important and fundamentally exploitative, present credible and relatively useful images of Third World economies. Thus, the conclusions of Breman and Oliveira's analyses present no fundamental objections to Williams and Tumusiime-Mutebile's (1978) model of the inter-relations between capitalist production and petty commodity production, to Santos's (1979) model of the inter-relations between the upper and lower circuits of the economy in Third World cities, to Berger and Piore's (1981) model of segmented labour markets in industrial societies with a recurring tendency to generate a need for a secondary labour market, or even to Tokman's (1978, 1071–72) model of the "heterogeneous subordination" of the informal sector to the formal sector.

Despite the lack of fundamental objections to dualistic models emphasizing domination, subordination and exploitation, there are good reasons for avoiding their use. They have considerable didactic value for relatively simplistic explanations of how national and urban economies function in the Third World, but the substantial analytical problems of "structural overlap" between the two sectors (see Breman's essay, and Harriss 1978) make such models more an impediment than a help for advanced and detailed analyses. In both research and policy-making activities, it is much more useful to define specific categories for specific purposes (e.g. "small enterprises", "small shops", and "small-scale passenger transport firms") than it is to define broad, aggregate categories (e.g. "formal" and "informal" sectors) fitting into highly questionable "universal frameworks".

References

BERGER, Suzanne and PIORE, Michael J. (1981) *Dualism and Discontinuity in Industrial Societies*, Cambridge University Press, Cambridge.

BREMAN, Jan (1974) *Patronage and Exploitation: Changing Agrarian Relations in South Gujarat, India*, University of California Press, Berkeley.

BREMAN, Jan (1977) "Labour relations in the 'formal' and 'informal' sectors: report of a case study in South Gujarat, India", *Journal of Peasant Studies*, Vol. 4, pp. 171–205 and 337–59.

BROMLEY, Ray (1978) "The urban informal sector: why is it worth discussing?", *World Development*, Vol. 6, No. 9/10, pp. 1033–39. Reprinted in Ray Bromley (ed.) (1979) *The Urban Informal Sector: Critical Perspectives on Employment and Housing Policies*, Pergamon, Oxford.

BROMLEY, Ray and GERRY, Chris (eds.) (1979) *Casual Work and Poverty in Third World Cities*, Wiley, Chichester.

CARDOSO, Fernando Henrique and FALETTO, Enzo (1980) *Dependency and Development in Latin America*, University of California Press, Berkeley.

FEI, J. C. H. and RANIS, Gustav (1964) *Development of the Labor Surplus Economy*, Irwin, Homewood, Illinois.

HARRISS, Barbara (1978) "Quasi-formal employment structures and behaviour in the unorganized urban economy, and the reverse: some evidence from South India", *World Development*, Vol. 6, No. 9/10, pp. 1077–86. Reprinted in Ray Bromley (ed.) (1979), *op. cit.*

LENIN, V. I. (1936) "The development of capitalism in Russia", in V. I. Lenin, *Selected Works, Volume 1*, Lawrence and Wishart, London, pp. 219–385.

LEWIS, W. Arthur (1954) "Economic development with unlimited supplies of labour", *Manchester School of Economics and Social Studies*, Vol. 22, pp. 139–91.

MOSER, Caroline (1978) "Informal sector or petty commodity production: dualism or dependence in urban development?" *World Development*, Vol. 6, No. 9/10, pp. 1041–64. Reprinted in Ray Bromley (ed.) (1979), *op. cit.*

PAAUW, D. S. and FEI, J. C. H. (1973) *The Transition in Open Dualistic Economies*, Yale University Press, New Haven, Connecticut.

PORTES, Alejandro and WALTON, John (1981) *Labor, Class, and the International System*, Academic Press, New York.

SANTOS, Milton (1979) *The Shared Space: The Two Circuits of the Urban Economy in Underdeveloped Countries*, Methuen, London.

TOKMAN, Victor E. (1978) "An exploration into the nature of informal–formal sector relationships", *World Development*, Vol. 6, No. 9/10, pp. 1065–75. Reprinted in Ray Bromley (ed.) (1979), *op. cit.*

WARREN, Bill (1973) "Imperialism and capitalist industrialization", *New Left Review*, No. 81, pp. 3–44.

WILLIAMS, Gavin and TUMUSIIME-MUTEBILE, Emmanuel (1978) "Capitalist and petty commodity production in Nigeria: a note", *World Development*, Vol. 6, No. 9/10, pp. 1103–04. Reprinted in Ray Bromley (ed.) (1979), *op. cit.*

CHAPTER 5

A dualistic labour system? A critique of the "informal sector" concept*

JAN BREMAN

Most discussions of the "informal sector" take as their point of departure the dualistic character that is ascribed to the urban economy of the non-socialist countries of the Third World.[1]† This implies that the term "informal sector" refers to a dichotomy in which the characteristics of the two parts form each other's contrasts. The "formal sector" is taken to mean wage labour in permanent employment, such as that which is characteristic of industrial enterprises, government offices and other large-scale establishments. This implies (a) a set number of inter-related jobs which are part of a composite, internally well-organized labour structure; (b) work situations which are officially registered in economic statistics; and (c) working conditions which are protected by law. Some authors therefore speak of the organized, registered or protected sector. Economic activities which do not meet these criteria are then bundled under the term "informal sector", a catchword covering a considerable range of economic activities which are frequently marshalled under the all-inclusive term of "self-employment". This is employment of a sort that is very little organized if at all, which is difficult to enumerate and is therefore often ignored by official censuses and, finally, employment in which working conditions are rarely covered by legal statutes. As this description of the "informal sector" is rather inadequate, the lack of a proper definition is very often, although not satisfactorily, compensated by a somewhat arbitrary listing of those activities which meet the eye of anyone who strolls through the streets of a city in the Third World: street vendors, newspaper sellers, shoeshine boys, stall-keepers, prostitutes, porters, beggars, hawkers, rickshaw drivers, etc. In other words, the extensive collection of

---

*A slightly abridged version of Parts I and II of the article with the same title published in *Economic and Political Weekly* (Bombay), vol. 11, 1976, no. 48, pp. 1870–76, and no. 49, pp. 1905–08. This essay is published here with the permission of its author and of the editor of *Economic and Political Weekly*.
†Superscript numbers refer to Notes at end of chapter.

small tradesmen, the loose and unskilled workers and other categories with low and irregular incomes who lead a laborious, semi-criminal existence on the margins of the urban economy.

Origin of the concept

From the content which is given to the "informal sector" concept it is clear that it should be regarded as a new variant of the dualism theories which earlier gained popularity. In Boeke's classical explanation the phenomenon of dualism refers on the one hand to an urban market economy, usually of a capitalistic nature, and on the other hand to a rural subsistence economy mainly characterized by a static agricultural system of production. Boeke's reasoning that this type of segmented society, which originated in a colonial situation, can be explained by fundamental and permanent differences in economic behaviour, has long been dismissed as untenable by many critics. [2]

Less controversial is the assumption of a certain socio-economic duality which originates in a different phasing of development, a process that evokes, or at any rate strengthens, the contrast between modern and traditional, capitalistic versus non-capitalistic, industrial–urban as against agrarian–rural modes of production. Arthur Lewis (1954) and later Fei and Ranis (1964) have used the concept of dualism in this sense to investigate how surplus labour can be transferred from the rural subsistence sector in order to help increase non-agricultural production. These economists see the cities with their modern industries as dynamic centres from which the static character of the rural order, characterized by stagnating agriculture with very low labour productivity, can gradually be overcome. But the assumption that the surplus labour that thus becomes available will be absorbed in the modern sector is not proven. During the last few decades we have seen that expansion of industrial employment opportunities lags far behind the growth of the urban labour force. The urban dualism that is nowadays apparent in many developing countries is not due to any gradually disappearing contrast between a modern–dynamic growth pole and a traditional–static sector which has tenaciously survived in an urban environment, but rather to structural disturbances within the entire economy and society. The low rate of industrialization and the presence of surplus labour are listed as principal reasons why a dualistic system has sprung up in the cities of the Third World. The "informal sector" is therefore said to contain the mass of the working poor whose productivity is much lower than in the modern urban sector from which most of them are excluded.

Differences in interpretation

The over-stereotyped image of the onerous existence led by sizeable groups in the lower echelons of the urban economy is undoubtedly due partly to processes of stagnation or involution which are the root cause of the rapid growth of the "informal sector". However, the idea that this is a source of unproductive labour and loafers, of social isolation if not dislocation and other evils which stress its residual character, does not sufficiently depict reality.

In contrast to this negative evaluation, recent literature shows that activities in the "informal sector" can be economically quite efficient and profitable. The emphasis is then less on actual labour performance and more on the context within which people work. This is an amplification of an urban dualism in which stress is placed not on the nature of the employment but on the mode of production.[3] According to this more positive approach, the distinction formal–informal refers to two economic sectors, each with its own structural consistency and dynamics. Activity in the "informal sector" is characterized, for instance, by low capital intensity, a low level of productivity, a small and usually poor clientele, a low level of formal schooling, intermediate technology, preponderance of family labour and ownership, ease of entrance and, last but not least, lack of support and recognition on the part of the government. In brief, according to a recent survey by the World Employment Programme, the "informal sector" consists of many small-scale enterprises whose labour input is predominantly provided by relatives of the owner (ILO 1976).

It cannot be denied that the introduction of the concept "informal sector" has drawn attention to the nebulous complexity of activities, unorganized, fragmented and divergent in character, with which a large proportion of the population, both urban and rural, has to earn its daily bread. Until recently, research into non-agrarian employment was almost entirely confined to labour in industries and other enterprises with, as ever-recurring themes, the social background of the labour force, their adaptation to the urban and more particularly to the industrial way of life and, of course, work conditions and circumstances in these large-scale economic establishments. The recent shift in focus from the "formal" to the "informal" sector, strongly encouraged by the ILO, has brought an end to the obstinately-held belief that those who do not acquire their incomes in a regular and standardized manner, as is customary in the modern economic sector, have to be regarded as under- or unemployed.

On the other hand, discussion of the "informal sector" seems to give rise to more questions than it has solved. This is due primarily to the lack of precise definition. The concept is taken to cover everything that does not belong to the "formal sector", and it has rightly been pointed out that this gives the distinction a tautological character (see Gerry 1974, 1). The notion of dualism refers sometimes to distinctive employment situations, sometimes to separate economic circuits, and frequently to a combination of the two. To illustrate the latter alternative let me cite Oteiza (1971, 196), who finds it conceivable that:

"the end of the century will see, to an even more pronounced degree, the existence of two labour markets with two very different occupational structures and levels of income, corresponding to two clearly distinctive sectors of the economy—the modern and the traditional sector".[4]

But Oteiza's hypothesis, which is implicitly also to be found in many other essays, that the dichotomy in the two meanings runs parallel, has yet to be proven and can therefore not be taken as a point of departure for empirical analysis.

The vagueness and inconsistency of the definition is said to be due to the fact that the "informal sector" has only recently become a subject of study. On the other hand, it could be posited that the lack of a hard empirical basis was perhaps the reason for the celerity with which the concept has found acceptance. It is noticeable that reports which are based on factual research are often particularly critical of the conceptualization. At any rate, I have come to the conclusion, partly on the basis of research into labour relations in a small town in Western India, that the concept is analytically inadequate. In my opinion, the "informal sector" cannot be demarcated as a separate economic compartment and/or labour situation. Any attempt to do so will give rise to numerous inconsistencies and difficulties, such as will be shown by even a sketchy discussion of social background, size and composition. Moreover, by interpreting the relationship to the formal sector in a dualistic framework and in focusing on the mutually exclusive characteristics, we lose sight of the unity and totality of the productive system. Rather than dividing the urban system into two segments, I prefer to emphasize the fragmented nature of the entire labour market.

Social background of the "informal sector"

Surprisingly, little is known about the relationship between the "informal sector" and social stratification. It seems reasonable to assume that workers in the "formal sector" are mostly recruited from the higher social strata whose educational level is also much higher. Conversely, low social positions and "informal sector" activities are also likely to go hand in hand. This is not much more than an assumption, however. The question of how this social distribution originates is usually left unanswered. On the other hand, the "informal sector" is inevitably seen as connected to urban poverty and to its social determinants, e.g., low incomes, irregular work, inadequate education, a low degree of organization, and other elements from which a lack of security and protection can be inferred.

Various authors have drawn attention to the fact that non-economic aspects have been insufficiently considered in the conceptualization of the "informal sector". It is remarkable, for instance, that many discussions make little or no mention of the extensive social research that during the last few years has been carried out in neighbourhoods where the urban poor congregate. This shows once again that a thorough inventory of existing knowledge based on interdisciplinary research is of more benefit than a proliferation of studies that do not cross narrowly-defined professional borders. Recent sociological and geographical investigations of urban slums in Third World countries have shown that their populations are extremely heterogeneous. Apart from the fact that there is no evidence of an amorphous and disintegrated multitude, it appears repeatedly that the inhabitants of low-income pockets and of shanty-towns in the urban periphery do not form a separate and distinctive social order. Studies of slums show a varied composition and strong and close ties with institutions of the general urban system rather than any deviating pattern of norms and values (see e.g. Brett 1974; Leeds 1969; MacEwen 1974; Portes 1972). The objections made in many recent publications against the definition of slums as locations with specific characteristics and problems are in effect also addressed to attempts to represent the "informal sector" as a clearly distinguishable circuit of the urban economy.

The tendency to consider the "informal sector" as a residue primarily of rural migrants helps to strengthen the image of marginal labour. This emphasis on the rural background is hardly surprising when we consider that the origins of the "informal sector" are attributed to a continuing process of urbanization; i.e. the massive outflow of surplus labour from the countryside. Although these rural migrants indeed form a substantial part of the urban poor, studies based on empirical research have shown in the first place, that in the "formal sector" this percentage is not necessarily much lower (see e.g. Bienefeld 1974, 18–19), and in the second place that a great many of those who earn their living in the "informal sector" were either born in urban areas or have long resided there (see e.g. Gerry 1974, 90–91). There are indications that the rate of urbanization might be gradually declining, particularly in heavily populated countries where the large cities have for many decades been subjected to conditions of extreme scarcity.

The absorptive capacity of the lower levels of the urban economy is anything but unlimited. Cliches regarding shared poverty and employment opportunities notwithstanding, the inhabitants show growing disinclination to take relatives with a rural background into their homes and to help them find their place in the urban economy. The discharge from agriculture continues, but is no longer automatically converted into definitive departure to the cities. Large groups of seasonal migrants wander wretchedly to and fro between town and country, recruited or rejected as need arises (see e.g. Breman 1974, 103–06). In addition to this rural–urban circulation, the seasonal movement of labour within rural areas has lately gained in significance. So far, the literature has shown little interest in these issues, which are also ignored in discussions of the informal sector.

Size of the informal sector

Estimates of the size of the "informal sector" are varied. Moreover, the data supplied for various countries or cities show considerable disparities which cannot be ascribed to actual differences in economic structure. Most authors seem to hold the opinion that half or even more of the populations of the large cities of the Third World should be included in the informal sector, but the varying criteria on which their studies are based preclude any accurate comparison of their percentages.

A major conceptual problem is caused by the fact that the labour forces of the "formal" and "informal" sectors of the economy have different compositions. The use of the term labour force for the "informal sector" may even be misplaced. Not only women, but the old, the young and the maimed are found in this sector, although their working capacity cannot always or sufficiently be put to use. It certainly would be misleading to look upon them as non-working dependents. An analysis at the family level is essential for a proper understanding of the living conditions of the urban poor. Only by assuming that most if not all household members are partially if not entirely absorbed in the labour force can we realize the comparative elasticity with which unemployment, the considerable fluctuations in income and other vicissitudes of daily existence, can be absorbed.[5] The specific character of the "informal sector", typified by fluctuating and discontinuous employment and a gradual transition from employment to unemployment, makes any categorization of labour relations according to current terminology a dubious endeavour. By definition, it seems only possible to measure and enumerate employment in the "formal sector". The complaints made by many researchers that the "informal sector" is disorderly and elusive have to be seen in this light.

Attempts to reduce to the usual variables and components any employment which is non-standardized and non-organized from the point of view of the "formal sector" are mere statistical exercises which cannot do justice to the actual situation. All this may explain why sociological and economic analyses of the labour market are principally if not solely concerned with the "formal sector" of economic activity, but this preference can in no way be justified. Whether our margins are broad or narrow, we must accept that a very large part of the urban multitudes are dependent for their very existence on employment in the "informal sector". If roughly half the populations of the large metropolitan centres where the modern enclaves can be found are employed in this sector, it may safely be assumed that the percentage will be even higher in the smaller towns. If, in addition, part of the rural population can be included in the "informal sector", it might well be asked what significance can be attached to a concept that covers such a large and so little homogeneous section of the labour force.

The composition of the "informal sector"

By definition, most economic activities in the rural areas fall under the "informal sector". This applies not only to trade and handicrafts but also and above all to agriculture. Nevertheless, very few publications give this broader tenor to the distinction formal–informal. The concepts are usually applied solely to the urban system, ignoring rural labour and production relations.

Discussions of the "informal sector" are too often based on the idea that urban production is a more or less independent segment of the national economy, probably due to the fact that most reports are concerned with large cities and national capitals. But although it is easier to show that at the lower levels the urban and rural labour markets gradually merge into each other, thus making a regional analysis essential, it is doubtful whether the situation is any different in the metropoles. The almost exclusive linkage of the "informal sector" to an urban environment entails that the considerable seasonal migration from rural areas to the major cities is underestimated. In discussions of the "informal sector", the significance of this phenomenon of circulating labour is neglected and it will only come to its right if emphasis is transferred to the interchangeability of, rather than the division between, town and country and the concomitant modes of production.

Services

One opinion that is given fairly general credence holds that the "informal sector" is a collection of petty trades and services which, although they provide a meagre existence for poverty-stricken people, are of doubtful economic benefit in terms of actual production. This is typically an interpretation that is based on the "formal sector", and the activities which are almost automatically listed—street hawkers, becak-riders, food sellers, shoeshiners, household servants, beggars, porters, etc.—are also recognizable as those which, seen from the vantage point of the "formal sector", are to be found in city streets. The attention which the ILO in particular has given to the "informal sector" has caused this somewhat negative image to be revised, and various publications have flatly contradicted the sector's asserted parasitical character. A shift in research from services and distribution to productive activities has encouraged a more differentiated view and has moreover stressed that the dichotomy formal–informal cuts right across all sectors of the economy. If the formal–informal division is accepted as valid then it has to be applied not only to personal services, but also to building, trade, manufacture and transport. In other words, if the distinction is at all tenable it cannot logically be confined to certain sectors of the economy or to certain activities. It is concerned much more with the context in which these economic activities originate, than with the manner in which they are carried out.

Self-employment versus wage-employment

Since the original conceptualization by Hart (1973), the informal sector has been seen as almost synonymous with categories of small self-employed who, independently or by enlisting the services of household or family members, try to keep their heads above water. Wage-earning employment, on the other hand, is considered characteristic of the "formal sector" (see e.g. Bienefeld 1974, iii; Hart 1973, 66; McGee 1973). It is probably not coincidental that this contrast is particularly emphasized in studies of African countries. But even if allowances are made for the differences which exist between countries in the nature of economic production and the composition of the labour force, the operationalization of the concepts formal–informal in this way remains open to dispute.

On the basis of my own research in Western India I have ascertained that numerous small shops and one-man firms—the latter particularly in the self-employment sphere, such as those of the free professions—typically bear the stamp of "formal sector" activities. On the other hand it is quite common for small-scale enterprises in the "informal" sphere to employ non-household members. Besides, the content given to the concept of self-employment is somewhat pretentious. It seems rather exaggerated to include, in addition to the owners of small workshops, the shoeshiner, the street barber, the garbage collector or casual wage-labourers as one-man firms in the sense of small entrepreneurs.

The peasant society has long been identified with self-employment of the multitude of small producers, the peasant cultivators, thereby overlooking the various classes in which the agrarian population is divided. Similarly, the fiction has now been introduced of an urban "informal sector" consisting of self-employed who at the most utilize their household members as labour force.

Heterogeneity

The "informal sector" is seen alternately as a form of economic activity or as a reservoir of labour. In both cases, the discrimination from the "formal sector" is emphasized: in the first case the mode of production is stressed, and in the second the characteristics of labour *per se*. But preoccupation with the refinement of this dichotomy has distracted attention from the great variety of activities which make up the "informal sector". Further consideration shows that systematic classification of these activities into one sector is not feasible. The problem is solved to some extent by further subdivision of the urban labour market, while differentiation into three sections is not infrequent (see e.g. Friedman and Sullivan 1974, 388). However, this can only be effective if the dualism concept is abandoned. There is no question of a rift in production or labour relations on the basis of which the urban system can be broken down into two sectors. It is rather a continuum in which borderlines between the composite parts are drawn almost arbitrarily and are also difficult to locate in the actual situation.

Relationship to the formal sector

There are two entirely different views with regard to the relationship between the "informal" and the "formal" sectors.

The existence and continuing expansion of the "informal sector" is accepted in some circles as an inevitable phase in the development process. Emphasis is then placed on the function of the "informal sector" as a buffer zone. Marginal productivity perpetuates the poverty of the urban masses in Third World countries, but economic activities in the "informal sector" provide at least some income and employment, however meagre and irregular, to people for whom even a subsistence level would otherwise be hardly conceivable. But it is not feasible to expect that policies should be oriented towards maintaining inefficient and small-scale economic activities which make use of retrogressive technology. Raising the standard of living of the population demands the fastest possible expansion of the "formal sector".

This can be contrasted by the approach, strongly encouraged by the ILO and at present also by the World Bank, which sees the relationship between the "formal" and "informal" sectors as one of structural inequality (see Emmerij 1974). According to this view, the much praised flexibility, viability and adapted technology of productive activities in the "informal sector" are hamstrung by the much more favourable market conditions which are available to the modern economic sector, advantages which are reinforced by political patronage and government protection. The defenders of this view advocate better attunement and increased complementarity of the two sectors of the urban economy. This would necessitate putting an end to the discrimination against the activities of the "informal sector", which this approach sees as the most promising source of development. At present it sometimes seems that it is an offence to earn a living in this sector (see e.g. Inukai n.d.; Papanek 1975, 10).

Apart from the repeal of discriminatory regulations and various other restrictive and obstructive measures, it is suggested that the government will have to adopt a policy of active stimulation by providing facilities such as credits, managerial knowhow, upgrading of skills, marketing promotion, supplies of raw material, etc., in order to improve the competitiveness of labour-intensive, small-scale activities. Support for entrepreneurial capabilities can be justified by the fact that the "informal sector's" contribution to the national product is much greater than had originally been envisaged and moreover indicates possibilities for accumulation of capital that will allow small enterprises to expand. Such recommendations form part of a policy that attempts to replace the present hypothetical distinction between "formal" and "informal" sectors by a strong linkage intended to bring about harmonious cooperation on the basis of mutual advantage. According to this reasoning, structural inequality can be strongly mitigated, if not entirely abolished, with the aid of especially designed compensatory programmes. Employment for the poor is the motto of this new strategy, which was a central theme of the 1976 World Employment Conference of the ILO. The resolute tone is reminiscent of the many programmes which were drawn up, but not very eagerly executed, on behalf of the small cultivators in Third World countries when it became evident that the agrarian strategy which was introduced at the beginning of the 1970s had almost exclusively benefited the larger, financially better-off farmers. The ILO (1972) report on Kenya, in particular, is written in this spirit and has been strongly and extensively criticized by Leys (1973, 1975).

In Leys' opinion, the points of departure and policy lines of the ILO report are intended to encourage an autonomous local capitalism, divested of the most extreme contrasts but still based on cheap and exploited labour. Research has shown that official programmes and plans which aim at stimulating industry in the informal sector are of little practical use (see e.g. Bose 1974, 3.33–3.35; Gerry 1974, 74ff). Neither can increased aid by the State be expected as long as the political system is dominated by interests which are linked to the "formal sector". The paradox of the situation is that the recommended policy change will inevitably be detrimental to an elite which is responsible for its execution. By ignoring this fact, says Leys, the ILO mission in Kenya was guilty of naivety. As is evident from a later article (Singer and Jolly 1973, 115), the compilers of the ILO report seem to have been aware of this problem, but they sufficed by saying that the government of Kenya had publicly committed itself to a strategy under which the results of economic growth were to be equally distributed. The reference to this statement, which can hardly be taken seriously, illustrates the mixture of optimism, naivety and reservation that is inherent to most reports produced by international bureaucracies or their consultants.

Is the point of departure tenable that there are separate sectors, each of which has its institutional facilities and rationale?

This is the most fundamental difference of opinion in the discussion over the interpretation of structural inequality. Leys is not alone in giving a negative answer. Various other authors have come to the same conclusion on the basis of empirical research. I share their scepticism of an urban dualism in which emphasis is placed on the nature of activities in each individual sector rather than on the relations between the components of the system. According to these critics, the backwardness and impotence of the informal sector is preconditional for the development and progress of the formal sector, while the relationship between the two sectors is expressed in the dependence and subordination of the former on the latter. Research among petty producers in Dakar has caused Gerry (1974) to conclude that these are exploited under the present economic system. Bose (1974) comes to the same conclusion after studying small-scale industries in Calcutta, stating that smallness of scale or inefficient management is not the principal cause of the poverty of those who are employed in the workshops but rather the drain of surplus to larger firms.[6] The inequality between the two sectors of the urban economy, according to Bose, is not very different from the unequal exchange of goods during the colonial period, when not only the economic surplus but also part of what otherwise would have been used for subsistence in the colony was withdrawn for the development of the mother country.

If the distinction formal–informal cannot be seen as a duality, and there is no question of individual markets in terms of production, distribution and consumption, how is the character of the urban system to be defined? In particular, are some modes of production if not autonomous, at least to some degree exclusive of each other?

This issue has been discussed in another framework. Wallerstein (1974) is of the opinion that there is no question of different production systems. Like Frank, although in a more detailed reasoning on the basis of historical data, he considers that there is only one capitalist system which originated in Europe and centuries ago permeated and transformed the world periphery. But to submit that a system of international division of labour exists does not necessarily imply agreement that this is based on a single mode of production. To regard this almost solely as a phase in world history—at present with almost universal validity—gives rise to the danger that widely divergent social configurations, particularly labour relations, which are found in the Third World are brought under one common denominator. I favour an approach such as that outlined, for example, by Bienefeld (1975a, 54), who distinguishes between a capitalist sector which is narrowly linked with the international economy, and a sector consisting of pre- or non-capitalist modes of production. The component parts influence each other and gradually lose their individual identity and independence, so that we are faced with one coherent whole, a system with its own character and dynamics.[7] Instead of applying the concepts formal–informal, we should distinguish in terms of different articulated production relations which can be found within the economic system of Third World countries in varying degrees and gradations.

To return to the literature over the "informal sector", it is noticeable that predictions with regard to the future are rarely optimistic. The dismal prospect is caused by a variety of factors of which the most important are fourfold: first, that as yet the population increase shows little sign of decreasing its present high level; second, that employment in the "formal sector" shows little if any expansion; third, that governments show little inclination to give effective aid to small-scale, labour-intensive industries; and, finally, that the competitiveness of small-scale, labour-intensive industries shows continuous deterioration, resulting in their being ousted from activities whenever these appear profitable for the larger enterprises.

Seen from the viewpoint that the "informal sector" only exists by the grace of the "formal sector", the underdevelopment and backwardness of the former can only be brought to an end by drastic change of the entire economy, including agricultural production. The likelihood of such fundamental change, is difficult to ascertain and would not be the same for each country, but for the short term at any rate it does not seem very feasible. On the other hand, the involutionary trend of continued expansion within an inelastic framework is not coming to an end. How long and how far can those activities which are listed under the informal sector continue? The rift between the extremes is becoming greater (see e.g. Mazumdar 1976; Miller 1971, 221), and various authors mention the growing inequality in income and opportunity within the lower regions of the urban economy (e.g. Friedmann and Sullivan 1974, 401; Papanek 1975, 14).

In most Third World countries, particularly those of Asia, it is probably too late for marginal corrections, and the populist climate no longer exists within which such a policy would fit. Where the capitalist development strategy is still maintained there is little latitude for effective support of small-scale and labour-intensive activities. Moreover, measures which have so far been taken do not appear to be oriented primarily towards structural improvement, but rather to have originated in the fear that the growing tension among the urban poor might get out of hand. In addition to attempts to control the inflow of new migrants by sealing-off the major cities, forced outflow is becoming more frequent.

Groups which are poorly housed and without steady employment—usually called beggars so as to imply that they are "unproductive"—are rounded-up and deported. The "hard State" which has come into being, as shown in many countries of the Third World during the last decade, indicates a policy under which at least 30 per cent of the population will be declared socially and economically superfluous; redundant also in the sense that no measures are taken which would allow them to lead a life of human dignity. The leaders of these countries, according to Friedmann and Sullivan (1974, 405), have to face the following choice: to take the part of those who own the instruments of economic power and to maintain political stability by repressing the poor and their spokesmen, or to take the side of these rural and urban population groups and to bring about an economic system that couples growth with increasing equality. Verbal promises are generous, but when it comes to actual policy implementation it does not seem that this second option is much favoured.

Structure of employment

As I have shown, attempts to conceptualize the "informal sector" encounter problems, arising from the impossibility of demarcating its activities as an isolated sector of the urban economy. The economic system encompasses various modes of production—with labour relations which are more or less attuned to the particular mode—without these being crystallized into independent segments.

In my fieldwork in a district town and its rural surroundings in South Gujarat (India), I initially attempted to divide the local labour market into two levels (see especially Breman 1977). The results of this research show that it is fairly easy to find two extreme categories that oppose each other. On the one hand, those who have to earn their daily bread with the aid of poorly-paid, unskilled, intermittent work which, due to the considerable physical effort involved, is considered of low standing; on the other hand, those in permanent employment for which formal education or trained skills are required—a job with a fairly high and often regular wage which ensures security and social respectability to the worker. However, these profiles are seen most clearly at the extremes of the two poles of the labour force. As the distance between the extremes lessens, similarities in recruitment, working conditions, and bargaining procedures gradually outdo the differences between various categories of labour in this respect; in other words, gradations, rather than watertight divisions. To split the employment system into two sectors is, therefore, to adopt an approach which is over-rigid and too little differentiated.

I have already drawn attention to the fact that various authors try to solve this problem by dividing the labour market into more than two levels. But this concession is not sufficient if it is only intended to indicate the existence of a differentiated horizontal structure. Each sector has its own internal variation, and vertical barriers between the parts of one sector are frequently far more rigid than its horizontal dividing lines. For example, outsiders typically tend to consider various types of poorly-paid, unorganized and unskilled labour as substitutable. Empirical research, however, demonstrates that the labour force threatens to disintegrate into small and fairly independent units—creating a situation which, also for those who operate on the market, is difficult to survey.

It is not unusual for the term "labour market" to be reserved for the structuring of employment in the modern sector of the economy which is characterized by free and mobile labour. Where this is not the case—i.e., where employment conditions are not standardized, relationships are personal, and reaction to fluctuating supply and demand is inflexible—it is said that the market is imperfect, or even, that a labour market simply does not exist. This point of view, advocated by Todaro (1969, 139), for example, means in effect that the employment norm refers to conditions that apply only to a small sector of the total labour force, as Weeks (1973, 62) has rightly remarked.

In my own terminology, the concept "market" should be applied to the entire labour force. The structure of this market is not dualistic, but has a far more complex ranking. This is illustrated by the considerable fragmentation of the labour force, particularly in the lower regions of the urban economy where labour relations are rarely "formal" in the sense stated above.

Does this mean that the labour market is pluralist rather than dualistic? Not if this is taken to imply a great many separate and identifiable sub-markets. If there is a tendency to partition off a sector by excluding "outsiders", this in no way testifies to the presence of closed circuits, each characterized by its own rationale and considerable homogeneity. To take such a rigid compartmentalization as our point of departure would be incorrect for various reasons.

In the first place, the tendency to fence-off a particular field of employment has to be seen as an attempt to monopolize certain occupational roles or activities for social equals in a situation of extreme scarcity. Conversely, attempts are made to penetrate another sphere of work—by establishing a bridgehead and by using various mechanisms and channels to facilitate access from another environment. However, this particularist nature of the labour system should not be equalized with the existence of more or less autonomous circuits.

Secondly, it should be realized that the poor try to increase their security within the urban system by entering into dependency relations with social superiors. In doing so, they accept a wide range of contractual and semicontractual commitments. They have a fundamental claim to a minimal livelihood, to the bare necessities which would enable them to continue to live—a claim which nowadays is no longer duly and completely honoured by the other, stronger, party. Complementary to this expectation of a basic living allowance, posited as a moral imperative, is the willingness on the part of the weaker party to acknowledge infinite accommodation and gratitude, whether this has to be given material or immaterial expression. Work forms part of this obligation and has to be supplied where, when, and to the degree required by the creditor, even if other members of a household or a wider circle of equals have to be mobilized. For this part of the urban population, work is not the basis for a more or less independent existence but the outcome of a comprehensive dependency relationship. This interpretation of labour performance as an element of the social distributive system indicates that employment is not fully crystallized into a separate framework with its own institutional arrangements and consistency. In such circumstances, labour is fluid in character, without any question of differentiated and mutually exclusive sub-markets.

Thirdly, the criteria which are used to distinguish various circuits do not run parallel. It may be very useful to know the differences between regular wage labour, for instance, and self-employment, but this distinction is not necessarily parallel to that between protected and unprotected labour, "formal" versus "informal" activities, organized and unorganized employment, or guaranteed security against insecurity. In other words, these criteria do not cumulate in a clear and consistent stratification.

Labour market fragmentation is the most appropriate term for the situation which I shall describe, and for this exercise I shall also draw on the outcome of team research carried out some years ago in South Gujarat.

Particularism and scarcity

Lack of work is the predominant characteristic of the local economy in Gujarat, also in the urban sector. This naturally has its effects on the structure of the labour market. To start with, there is no question of equal chances for all in the search for work, in terms of acceptability for employment. Many kinds of work have only minimal requirements as regards education and experience, but not all those who meet these requirements have equal access. The extremely skewed distribution of economic opportunity among the various population groups is in no way a new phenomenon. In the past, an important dimension of the social system was the linkage of the division of labour with particular social categories. The fact that membership of a certain caste, region, ethnic group, tribal unit or religious community is still an important factor in the search for employment, causes many people to conclude that the traditional system is still in force, though with some modifications.

I would maintain, however, that the persistence of primordial sentiments is principally due to the situation of scarcity of work and not due to "force of tradition", constancy, and margins for accommodation of a social system that is involved in a process of modernization. The durability of tested loyalties is linked to the advantages offered by such ties under highly unfavourable economic conditions. If employment opportunities are slow to expand and population growth is rapid, the sources of existence will be under pressure, and people are likely to fall back on familiar social mechanisms and make use of them to exert influence and to promote their own interests.

In view of the situation of extreme scarcity, however, it would be a fallacy to think that competition for work on the labour market is absolute. Some economic functions are linked so much to particular groups that penetration by outsiders is almost inconceivable. This closed-shop character of some activities is naturally connected to income, level of education, etc., but it also makes itself felt in other respects. It is too simple to seek the reason for evident cases of self-restraint in cultural inhibition. Apart from the unfamiliarity with the type of work and insufficient knowledge of opportunities, lack of access is one of the most important structurally-determined impediments. The linkage between supply and demand originates in a particularistic fashion, and is part of the reason why the number of applicants for some activities is found to be insufficient even though labour is available in abundance. But it would be rash to conclude that labour market behaviour becomes irrational or imperfect once universalistic norms no longer form the guiding rule.

The particularistic orientation of the labour market does not automatically mean that the higher social classes succeed in monopolizing the most attractive jobs. It is true that their members have the advantage following from their education and contacts, but as other social categories gain access to formal education they are gradually able to penetrate to those jobs that are allocated on the basis of primordial group cohesion. In many countries, some shift in the social distribution is definitely perceptible, although this tendency is hardly likely to be very pronounced in a tight labour market. Nevertheless, it may happen nowadays that younger members of the lower middle classes are educationally equipped for relatively well-paid and highly-qualified jobs. They literally try to buy their way in to the modern sector in an attempt to compensate their lack of influence and protection. In this way, they obtain access to greatly coveted jobs in formal organizations with the prospect of greater security and higher social prestige. These intruders create an outpost through which they try to bring in relatives and other social equals.

Particularistic loyalties are not only found within the same social class. Job allocation is also coloured by patronage relationships, particularly those jobs over which people of high-rank have some say. These people then use their rank to benefit clients in the lower rankings of the social hierarchy. Control over a number of jobs or over licences which are required for certain economic activities can be used to political advantage, economic profit and social prestige. Personal intervention, through the use of protection, occurs both horizontally and vertically on every level of employment and is not tied to favouritism by social elites alone. The ILO (1972, 509–10) Kenya report devotes a separate section to the phenomenon of labour brokerage, involving the figure of the jobber who is particularly concerned with unskilled, unorganized and poorly-paid employment, usually in the form of gang labour.

Mobility

Scarcity not only has its repercussions on the question of who should be considered for which type of work and in what way; it also has its effect on labour mobility. Todaro (1969, 1971), in a model that is as simple as it is naive, assumes that the unskilled workers who migrate to the towns first drift into what he calls the urban traditional sector, and subsequently move on to jobs in the modern sector. This model is a striking example of the assumption that small-scale, labour-intensive activities act as a buffer zone and are carried out by a floating labour force. This way of thinking has various shortcomings. In the first place the rural migrant is elevated to a uniform type, whose mobility is laid down in a completely mechanistic pattern. In practice, however, access to employment occurs at different levels, dependent on socio-economic background, education, availability or lack of protection, etc. Under otherwise equal conditions, determinants of a high ranking in the rural system are converted into advantages over other categories of migrants who, conversely, see their former backward position within the village continued in the urban environment.

In the second place, the idea that in the town it is possible to progress to better-paid and more highly qualified work is largely fictional. Those who join the lower ranks of the urban labour system usually remain there (see also Papanek 1975, 15), and even horizontal mobility is limited. Shortage of work and limited chances to accumulate any capital or to invest in any formal education, can lead to a position of defensiveness in which one's accustomed sphere of activity is protected as much as possible and entrance to it is restricted to those who can appeal to particularistic loyalties—although the success in doing so may vary.

The frequently heard view, that small-scale and non-institutionalized activities are capable of almost unlimited expansion and that newcomers can set themselves up as self-employed with almost no money or without too much trouble and with few tools, because those already present obligingly make room for them, is a dangerous and misplaced romanticization of the hard fight for existence at the bottom of the urban economy. Even the shoeshine-boy, the common example of work which, although it might not provide an opulent standard of living would at least appear to be within reach of any resourceful youngster, is in fact not an open trade at all and working conditions are also more constricted than might be assumed. In an interesting description of this type of streetwork in the Indian town of Patna, Bhattacharya (1969, 167–74) distinguishes between two categories of shoeshiners. Members of the first group have a fixed place of work for which they sometimes have to pay rent to an intermediary who has leased the right to do so from the municipal authorities. These people form a more or less cohesive group, are equipped with proper tools (box with accessories), and demand a fixed sum for their work. The "non-standardized" itinerant shoeshiners, on the other hand, are not organized in a group , have few or only very poor tools, and do not have standard prices. Almost all of them are of the same social class, a low-ranking Moslem community. To gain access, a candidate needs to have connections with a working shoeshiner and sometimes to have been apprenticed to him without payment for a certain period. Only then is the newcomer given the opportunity to rent a shoeshine box, for which he then has to pay the owner a sum equal to half his daily takings. Bonds of this sort often continue almost indefinitely because many younger shoeshiners cannot afford to buy their own material and are, therefore, compelled to rent their boxes from older colleagues or from outsiders.

Examination of the social context of this "informal sector" (see Bienefeld 1974, 21; Temple 1975, 79) shows clearly that access to it is not so easy as is usually assumed. In other respects, too, activities in the sector are closed in character and are typified by dependency relationships which give the concept of "self-employed" a rather dubious meaning.

The difficulty in capturing a place on the labour market and the necessity of doing it within the restricted socio-economic network of which one forms part, does not mean that there is no vertical mobility. Although the road upwards is often blocked, the road downwards is all too easy to traverse. As the inflow to the labour market continues, pressure on the sources of livelihood increases, thus accentuating the competition for work. From one generation to the next, more and more families have to face the problem of consolidating their position in society. Inequality then seems to increase rather than decrease. For example, a particular job nowadays requires a higher level of education than was formerly the case, the access threshold to all levels of employment having been raised during the last few years. This has a socially depressive effect. It is discouraging to have to accept employment of a lower level than one's educational attainments. The consequences for the lower working classes are even more serious. Jobs, which formerly required little if any formal education, now only go to those who have a school-leaving certificate (see e.g. Bienefeld 1974, 15; Breman, 1974, Ch. II), but many households lack the material resources which would enable them to make such a lengthy and ultimately hazardous investment. It is reasonable to assume, therefore, that although more people participate in the education process, their actual performance cannot keep up with the higher demands which are set as a result of the surplus on the labour market. This process of marginalization denies the younger generation access to jobs which are still filled by older, less-educated members of the same family. In these circumstances, we can only conclude that the lower socio-economic groups are mobilized in the urban economy under increasing tensions and under conditions which clearly illustrate the worsening of their overall social and economic position.

Labour reserve and polarization

Do these impoverished masses represent a potential threat to those members of the working population who are employed on a regular and contractual basis, thus enjoying fairly considerable protection and security? Authors who consider that the self-employed and the unorganized workers represent an industrial reserve army are inclined to give an affirmative answer to this question. In their opinion, the presence of what is actually a labour surplus acts as a mechanism which exercises pressure on the wage levels of the regular labour force, hampers their collective action, and generally detracts from the stability of their existence. It is true that many activities of an "informal" nature seem to be redundant or at least would be done away with immediately if employment opportunities in the "formal sector" were to be improved (Dasgupta 1973, 72). But this does not imply that marginal categories in the production process actually represent an industrial reserve army. Such a hypothesis can be rejected without further ado if the distinction between "formal" and "informal" sectors is accepted as valid, in which the non-competitive character of the two circuits of the economy is taken for granted. According to this view, the more educated and specialized workers in the "formal sector", who are recruited on the basis of standard and impersonal procedures, represent an elite, with whose interests the trade unions are exclusively concerned. It is maintained that casual and mostly unorganized workers in the "informal sector" are quite unable to compete with such an elite, and emphasis is sometimes placed on the lack of affinity and substitutability by reference to the unemployable poor; i.e., an approximation to the conception of the lumpenproletariat.

If, contrary to this view, the fundamental unity of the entire production system is emphasized under rejection of the idea of urban dualism, it cannot be automatically hypothesized that the unskilled and uneducated form an industrial reserve army. I have already posited that the employment system is organized on a particularistic basis. The attempt to fence-off particular fields of work is intended to hamper external access, but it also prevents people taking steps in the opposite direction. This contradicts Meillassoux's (1974) assumption of an almost inexhaustible reservoir of free and mobile workers.[8] Moreover, employers and brokers are able to control labour through dependency relationships—wage advances, debts, housing, and other forms of "favouritism". True, the linkage between supply and demand on the labour market is regulated within a single institutional framework, but the channels involved are many and are very often indirectly related to each other.

On the other hand, the fragmentation of the labour market should not be unnecessarily exaggerated. My own research has shown that a surplus of casual labour, which is also characterized by fairly high mobility, exercises a negative influence on conditions in large enterprises, and can increase the tendency to "informalize" labour relations, particularly at the lower echelons (Breman 1974, Ch. III). However, I agree with Quijano (1974) that, in Latin America, as in other countries of the Third World, the expansion of non-agricultural production is no longer dependent on the quantity of available manpower but rather on the quality of the technological improvements which are introduced:

From this point of view, the manpower available in the market no longer constitutes a 'reserve' for those hegemonic levels of industrial production, but an excluded labour force, which as changes in the technical composition of capital progress, *loses in a permanent and not a transitory way the possibility of being absorbed into those hegemonic levels of production*, and especially, in urban–industrial production which has hegemony within the overall economy (Quijano 1974, 418).

In view of the shortage of highly-qualified manpower and the need for stable and continuous relations in large-scale enterprises, there is little chance of an industrial reserve being formed for this sector of the economy. On the other hand, in small-scale workshops, artisan establishments, retail shops, and similar types of activities, people have to work under conditions which are in complete agreement with the classical concept of "exploitation", a situation aggravated by the fact that workers are subject to arbitrary and immediate dismissal. In many cases, relations between employers and workers in these small workshops and enterprises in the distributive sector are standardized, to a certain extent regulated by legal statutes. However, under conditions of a surplus labour market, the unskilled nature of most of the work, the unorganized nature of the work force, and the non-implementation of protective measures, labour relations have gradually become informalized. The hypothesis that an industrial reserve exists at this level thus becomes more acceptable.

I have earlier tried to explain that there is good reason for misgivings on the undiminishing absorptive capacity which is supposed to characterize the lower regions of the urban economy. Adherents of this view consider that mechanisms of shared poverty will make it possible in some malleable fashion to provide a living—however marginal and insecure—for growing numbers of self-employed workers and casual wage-labourers. If this assumption has ever had any validity, this is certainly no longer the case (see Friedmann and Sullivan 1974, 400–01; Papanek 1975, 14). Growing numbers of the urban poor are caught up in a competitive struggle for their mere existence. The tensions to which this gives rise often follow particularistic lines. These are then highlighted as isolated and self-sustaining social and political phenomena without any proper identification of the economic background and its dynamics. During the last few years, conflicts of this nature have become more severe and more numerous in many cities of the Third World, and there is every reason to assume that these conflicts will continue to intensify in the future.

Notes

1. See especially the pioneering works of Hart (1973) and ILO (1972, Introduction, Ch. 13, and Technical Paper No. 22). Hart's paper was originally presented at a conference in 1971, directly influencing some of the authors of the ILO's (1972) Kenya Report.
2. Boeke (1961) provides the most systematic elaboration of his theory, together with critical comments. For a critical appraisal, see also Higgins (1955).

3. Geertz was probably the first to make a distinction within the urban system subdivided between the firm-oriented sector and the *pasar* economy. See also Coutsinas (1975), McGee (1973) and Santos (1971).
4. Without using the terms modern and traditional, Sethuraman (1976, 10–12) gives a similar distinction.
5. See also Bienefeld (1975b, 20). A complicating factor is that all members of a household are not necessarily employed in the same sector. This necessitates a choice between income levels and types of economic activity as the key variable in elaborating the distinction formal–informal.
6. Bose (1974, 4.23–4.24) indicates that "the dominating large-scale oligopolistic sector compels the small units in the informal sector to operate in a different market where the input price is higher and the output price is lower, and the main benefit of the price differential is reaped by the large-scale sector. It also confirms that those whom we often call large industrial houses are, in effect, commercial in nature and earn a major part of their profit by trading goods produced by smaller units. But despite this relationship of what may be called exploitation between the large and the small units, the latter can exist, given the present socio-economic structure, only when they can get the opportunity of offering themselves to be 'exploited' by larger units".
7. Alavi (1975) has gone on to develop the concept of a colonial mode of production.
8. Meillassoux's interpretation is regarded as outdated by other Marxist authors due to the development of a new international division of labour (see Frobel, Heinrichs and Kreye 1976).

References

ALAVI, H. (1975) "India and the colonial mode of production", *Economic and Political Weekly*, Vol. 10, pp. 1235–62.
BHATTACHARYA, S. S. (1969) "The shoe-shiners of Patna", *Sociological Bulletin*, Vol. 18, pp. 167–74.
BIENEFELD, Manfred (1974) "The self-employed of urban Tanzania", *IDS Discussion Paper*, No. 54, University of Sussex, Brighton.
BIENEFELD, Manfred (1975a) "The informal sector and peripheral capitalism: the case of Tanzania", *IDS Bulletin*, Vol. 6, No. 3, pp. 53–73.
BIENEFELD, Manfred (1975b) "Employment and unemployment", in B. Dasgupta and D. Seers (eds.) Statistical Policy in Less Developed Countries, *IDS Communication*, No. 114, University of Sussex, Brighton.
BOEKE, J. H. *et al.* (1961) *Indonesian Economics*, W. van Hoeve, The Hague.
BOSE, A. N. (1974) *The Informal Sector in the Calcutta Metropolitan Economy*, ILO, World Employment Programme, WEP 2–19, Working Paper No. 4, Geneva.
BREMAN, Jan (1974) *Patronage and Exploitation: Changing Agrarian Relations in South Gujarat, India*, University of California Press, Berkeley.
BREMAN, Jan (1977) "Labour relations in the 'formal' and 'informal' sectors: report of a case study in South Gujarat, India", *Journal of Peasant Studies*, Vol. 4, pp. 171–205 and 337–59.
BRETT, Sebastian (1974) "Low income urban settlements in Latin America: the Turner model", in Emanuel de Kadt and Gavin Williams (eds.) *Sociology and Development*, Tavistock, London, pp. 171–96.
COUTSINAS, G. (1975) "Deux circuits de l'economie urbaine: un exemple Algerian", *Revue Tiers-Monde*, Vol. 16, pp. 773–81.
DASGUPTA, Biplap (1973) "Calcutta's informal sector", *IDS Bulletin*, Vol. 5, No. 2/3, pp. 53–75.
EMMERIJ, Louis (1974) "A new look at some strategies for increasing productive employment in Africa", *International Labour Review*, Vol. 110, pp. 199–217.
FEI, J. C. and RANIS, Gustav (1964) *Development of the Labour Surplus Economy: Theory and Policy*, Irwin, Homewood, Illinois.
FRIEDMANN, John and SULLIVAN, Flora (1974) "The absorption of labor in the urban economy: the case of developing countries", *Economic Development and Cultural Change*, Vol. 22, pp. 385–413.
FROBEL, F., HEINRICHS, J. and KREYE, O. (1976) "Tendency towards a new international division of labour: worldwide utilization of labour force for world market oriented manufacturing", *Economic and Political Weekly*, Vol. 11, pp. 159–70.

GERRY, Chris (1974) *Petty Producers and the Urban Economy: A Case Study of Dakar*, ILO, World Employment Programme, WEP 2–19, Working Paper No. 8, Geneva.

HART, J. Keith (1973) "Informal income opportunities and urban employment in Ghana", *Journal of Modern African Studies*, Vol. 11, pp. 61–89.

HIGGINS, Benjamin (1955) "The 'dualistic theory' of underdeveloped countries", *Economic Development and Cultural Change*, Vol. 4, pp. 99–115.

ILO (International Labour Office) (1972) *Employment, Incomes and Equality: A Strategy for Increasing Productive Employment in Kenya*, ILO, Geneva.

ILO (1976) *World Employment Programme: Research in Retrospect and Prospect*, ILO, Geneva.

INUKAI, I. (n.d.) "The legal framework for small-scale enterprise development with special reference to the licensing system", Institute of Development Studies, University of Nairobi.

LEEDS, Anthony (1969) "The significant variables determining the character of squatter settlements", *América Latina*, Vol. 12, pp. 44–84.

LEWIS, W. Arthur (1954) "Economic development with unlimited supplies of labour", *Manchester School of Economics and Social Studies*, Vol. 22, pp. 139–91.

LEYS, Colin (1973) "Interpreting African underdevelopment: reflections on the ILO report on Employment, Incomes and Equality in Kenya", *African Affairs*, Vol. 72, pp. 419–29.

LEYS, Colin (1975) *Underdevelopment in Kenya: The Political Economy of Neo-Colonialism 1964–71*, Heinemann, London.

MACEWEN, Alison (1974) "Differentiation among the urban poor: an Argentine study", in Emanuel de Kadt and Gavin Williams (eds.) *Sociology and Development*, Tavistock, London, pp. 197–228.

MCGEE, T. G. (1973) "Peasants in the cities: a paradox, a paradox, a most ingenious paradox", *Human Organization*, Vol. 32, pp. 135–42.

MAZUMDAR, D. (1976) "The urban informal sector", *World Development*, Vol. 4, pp. 655–79.

MEILLASSOUX, Claude (1974) "Developpement ou exploitation", *L'Homme et la Société*, Nos. 33/34, pp. 55–61.

MILLER, R. U. (1971) "The relevance of surplus labour theory to the urban labour markets of Latin America", *International Institute for Labour Studies, Bulletin*, Vol. 8, pp. 220–45.

OTEIZA, Enrique (1971) "The allocation function of the labour market in Latin America", *International Institute for Labour Studies, Bulletin*, Vol. 8, pp. 190–205.

PAPANEK, Gustav (1975) "The poor of Jakarta", *Economic Development and Cultural Change*, Vol. 24, pp. 1–27.

PORTES, Alejandro (1972) "Rationality in the slum: an essay on interpretive sociology", *Comparative Studies in Society and History*, Vol. 14, pp. 268–86.

QUIJANO, Anibal (1974) "The marginal pole of the economy and the marginalized labour force", *Economy and Society*, Vol. 3, pp. 393–428.

SANTOS, Milton (1971) *Les Villes du Tiers-Monde*, Editions Marie Thérèse Génin, Paris.

SETHURAMAN, S. V. (1976) "The urban informal sector: concept, measurement and policy", *International Labour Review*, Vol. 114, pp. 69–81.

SINGER, Hans and JOLLY, Richard (1973) "Unemployment in an African setting", *International Labour Review*, Vol. 107, pp. 103–115.

TEMPLE, G. (1975) "Migration to Jakarta", *Bulletin of Indonesian Economic Studies*, Vol. 11, pp. 76–81.

TODARO, Michael P. (1969) "A model of labour migration and urban unemployment in less developed countries", *American Economic Review*, Vol. 59, pp. 138–48.

TODARO, Michael P. (1971) "Income expectations, rural–urban migration and employment in Africa", *International Labour Review*, Vol. 104, pp. 387–413.

WALLERSTEIN, I. (1974) "The rise and future demise of the world capitalist system", *Comparative Studies in Society and History*, Vol. 16, pp. 387–415.

WEEKS, John (1973) "Does employment matter?", in Richard Jolly, Emanuel de Kadt, Hans Singer and Fiona Wilson (eds.), *Third World Employment: Problems and Strategy*, Penguin, Harmondsworth, pp. 61–65.

CHAPTER 6

A critique of dualist reason: the Brazilian economy since 1930*

FRANCISCO DE OLIVEIRA

This essay is intended to provide the bases for a reformulation of our understanding of the Brazilian economy, with particular reference to the period after the 1930 Revolution, the phase during which industrialization emerged as the key process. My analysis will focus on *structural transformation* and I will use the term "restructuring" here in its most rigorous sense, to refer to the restructuring and reconstitution of the conditions necessary for the expansion of the capitalist mode of production in Brazil. This analysis neither offers an evaluation of the performance of the system in terms of satisfying the basic needs of the population, nor does it discuss the rate of growth.

The "ethical", "ends rather than means" approach, normally associated with the dualism of CEPAL (the UN Economic Commission for Latin America, ECLA), ignores the fact that the fundamental objective of the system is *production* itself. The secondary objective of the system so appreciated by Brazilian conservative economists, namely consumption, is enmeshed in a vulgar dialectic, just as if the fate of the different parts of society could be analytically reduced to the apparent behaviour of the totality; the commonplace theory of "how the national cake grows".

This study not only examines the economic conditions, but also the political conditions which characterize the system. The transition from one model to another in any system characterized by relations of social domination cannot be understood solely in economic terms. "Economistic analysis" (analysis which isolates economic from political conditions), thus commits a serious methodological error which goes hand in hand with its proponents' refusal to recognize it as ideology.

The present analysis is a contribution to the lively debate on the growth of

*Translated by Chris Gerry from pp. 3–36 and 70–74 of Francisco de Oliveira (1972) "A economia brasileira: Crítica a razão dualista", *Estudos Cebrap*, No. 2 (Oct.), pp. 3–82. This translation is published with the permission of CEBRAP (the Centro Brasileiro de Análise e Planejamento) and of Francisco de Oliveira.

the Brazilian economy.[1]† In this debate, Tavares and Serra (1971) have reintroduced a method long absent from Latin American economic literature, buried under the avalanche of the "CEPAList" model and their work can be thought of as a benchmark and guide for further research. Latin American socio-economic thought of every shade now shows indications of dissatisfaction and willingness to break with the CEPAL style of analysis, in an attempt to recapture an understanding of the general situation. A theoretical approach has been rediscovered after having almost suffocated under the "CEPAList" blanket of "respectability".

Previously, the predominance of "CEPAList" interpretations had allowed the proliferation of Keynesian and marginalist terminology, thereby providing the conditions under which the academic establishment could confer scientific recognition and respectability on marginalist analysis and its policy conclusions. In this way, a large proportion of Latin American intellectuals in the last few decades found themselves on the horns of a dilemma. While denouncing the miserable living conditions of the mass of the Latin American population, their theoretical and analytical efforts were focused on debating the capital–output ratio, national propensities to save and invest, the marginal efficiency of capital, economies of scale and the extent of the market. Thus, unconsciously and apparently against their wishes, was born their strange world of duality, which ideologically presupposed the acceptance of the "vicious circle of poverty" thesis.[2]

The dualistic approach made possible a reconciliation of the "scientific rigour" of marginalist analyses with moral considerations, which inevitably led to reformist proposals. This tendency was more common and more marked in the work of economists than in that of other social scientists. Sociologists, political scientists, and even philosophers managed to partially escape the dualist temptation, and kept as central pillars of their analyses categories such as "economic system", "mode of production", "social classes", "exploitation", and "domination". Nevertheless, the prestige of economics had thoroughly penetrated these other social science disciplines, whose attitudes, in general, became adulatory. For example, the well-known traditional–modern dichotomy is a formulation which, having its roots firmly in the dualistic model, managed to divert a large part of the efforts of sociologists and political scientists into a Rostovian impasse.

The reinterpretation offered in this essay, is theoretically and methodologically entirely opposed to dualism and structuralism. It is absolutely *not* my intention to negate the immense contribution directly made or inspired by the CEPAL model, but precisely to recognize that throughout the last few decades, the CEPAL model has constituted the only valid means of developing intellectual creativity with respect to the debate on Latin American economy and society. Indeed, until recently, critics of the CEPAL model have

---

†Superscript numbers refers to Notes at end of chapter.

neither had nor claimed to have a more adequate theoretical position. The better-known Latin American critics of the model nearly always had the same marginalist, neo-classical and/or Keynesian theoretical credentials, barely hiding the passion for reform and the belief in compromises with the economic, political and social *status quo*, which have long perpetuated Latin American poverty and backwardness. Like parrots, they limited themselves for decades to the repetition of schemas learnt in Anglo-Saxon universities; schemas which contained no critical perspective whatsoever and had no contribution to make to the theory of Latin American society.[3] Thus, in attempting to elaborate here a more fundamental critique of the dualist rationale, I am also recognizing that the critique presented by those "parrots", cannot provide a useful starting point.

Breaking with the "underdevelopment" approach

This essay should not be seen as an attempt to update previous critiques. A break with the concept of "the underdeveloped mode of production" either has to be complete or it offers no solution at all; it merely adds a few more details to the concept of underdevelopment. At a theoretical level, the concept of "underdevelopment" as a particular historical and economic formation, consisting of a formal and polar opposition between a so-called backward sector and a modern sector, cannot be seen as something specific. The type of duality contained within it can be found not only in all systems, but also in all historical periods. Furthermore, this formal opposition in the majority of cases is no more than that. The *real* process is both an organic and symbiotic relationship, a unity of opposites, in which *the "modern" sector reproduces itself and expands on the basis of the very existence of a "backward" sector.*

"Underdevelopment" would therefore seem to be the specific form characterizing preindustrial societies which have been penetrated by capitalism, and are therefore "in transition" towards more advanced and stable forms of capitalism. However, such a formulation ignores the fact that "underdevelopment" is itself a "product" of the expansion of capitalism. In a very few cases in Latin America, the most obvious of which are Mexico and Peru, there was a penetration of anterior, characteristically "Asiatic", modes of production by capitalism. In the majority of cases, Latin American pre-industrial economies were "created" by the expansion of world capitalism as founts of primitive accumulation for the system.

In summary, *the "underdevelopment" referred to here is a capitalist formation and not simply an historical phenomenon.* In order to emphasize the dependency aspects—i.e. the well-known relationships between the centre and the periphery—, the theorists of the "underdeveloped mode of production" have virtually excluded all analysis of the *internal* aspects of the structures and mechanisms of domination corresponding to the specific accumulation processes of countries like Brazil. The whole question of development is seen by them from the point of view of *external* relations, and thus the problem becomes one of opposition between nations, thereby sidestepping (rather than addressing) the fact that *unequal development, even more than being a problem of the opposition between nations, is a problem relating specifically to the opposition between social classes located inside those nations.* The theoreticians of the "underdeveloped mode of production" continue to be incapable, therefore, of clarifying whether it is the internal laws of articulation which determine everything, or whether it is the external laws linking one part of the system with the rest, which determine the overall structure of relations.[4] Shot through with ambiguity, "underdevelopment" is visualized merely as a system which, despite the fact that it can produce a surplus, part of which is appropriated externally, remains incapable of absorbing the other part of its surplus in a productive manner.

In practical terms, any break with the theory of underdevelopment cannot but be radical. It is curious but by no means paradoxical, that the theory of underdevelopment in the last few decades has contributed significantly to the proliferation of *non*-theoretical positions in the debate on Brazilian capitalism. In this way, the "underdevelopment" approach fulfilled an important ideological function in marginalizing questions as to whom Brazilian capitalist economic development was benefiting. With its stereotyped concepts of "self-sustained development", "internalizing decision-making", "national integration", "planning" and "the national interest", the theory of underdevelopment provided the framework in which developmentalism could emerge. Developmentalism deflected both theoretical attention and political action away from the problems of the class struggle, precisely in the period when the objective conditions under which that struggle took place were worsening, due to transformation of the Brazilian economy from its agrarian base to an urban–industrial one. In this way the theory of underdevelopment was the characteristic ideology of the so-called "populist" period. If today, this theory no longer fulfils the role it used to play, it is because the hegemony of one class has been consolidated to such an extent that it no longer needs to hide behind a populist mask.

Capitalist development after 1930 and the process of accumulation

The revolution of 1930 marked the end of one cycle and the beginning of another for the Brazilian economy; i.e. it signalled the end of the hegemony of export-oriented agrarian interests and the beginning of a period in which urban–industrial interests predominate. Though it was 1956 before industry's share in national income surpassed that of agriculture, it is crucial to examine the earlier process by which industrial hegemony emerged. A new correlation of social forces, a restructuring of both the State apparatus and its policies, and the regulation of the use of productive factors, among which labour and its price was the most significant, had two major effects. Firstly, they involved the rewriting of the "rules" which had oriented the Brazilian economy towards agro-exporting activities. Secondly, they involved the creation of the institutional conditions for the expansion of internal-market-oriented activities. In short, this constituted the introduction of a *new mode of accumulation* which was qualitatively and quantitatively different, and which was to depend substantially (though not exclusively) on the growing importance of the internal realization of surplus value. Changing the "rules of the game", which had previously favoured the agro-exporting economy, inevitably meant that this sector's traditional factors of production were penalized both in terms of their costs and their profit-generating capacities. This was done in the case of the coffee sector, for example, by the partial confiscation of profits, and in the case of agriculture in general, by increasing the *relative* cost of loans made to that sector (achieved by making loans to the industrial sector particularly cheap).

In this context, certain features of State intervention came to fulfil very significant roles. One of the most important of these is the regulation of factors of production; i.e. the forces controlling the supply and demand of factors of production in the economy as a whole. In this respect, the regulation of the laws determining the relation between labour and capital has been one of the most important, if not the most important. The so-called "labour legislation" has so far only been studied from the viewpoint of its formal corporativist structure, namely the organization of workers under state tutelage. Most studies have been based on the hypothesis that the establishment of minimum wage levels was unnecessary and artificial as they bore no relation to the concrete conditions of the supply and demand of labour. To Ignacio Rangel, for example, the minimum wage had an institutionally-determined level above that which would have obtained under conditions of "free market" negotiation between workers and capitalists.[5] An argument of this sort both contributes to and endorses the claims made by political scientists about the redistributivist character of the populist regimes of the period 1930–1964.[6] In its economic version, this argument contributed significantly to the way in which Brazil's inflation was theorized and explained, and in the context of the dualist–structuralist model of CEPAL it helped to explain the cumulatively increasing gap between the "modern" and the "backward" sectors.[7]

However, such interpretations have played down the role of "labour legislation" in the post-1930 accumulation process. The role played by the State in creating an internal market was treated in a curiously abstract manner. For example, when it was said that minimum wage-levels were above the levels expected under market conditions, to which market was reference being made? The abstract concept of "the free market" in which the State—by definition—does not interfere, can in no way be a capitalist market, for it is precisely the State's function to institutionalize the rules of the game. Also, it has never been proven that minimum wage levels were above the cost of reproduction of labour power (the most relevant concept for evaluating how "artificial" or "realistic" is a minimum wage level). The labour legislation nevertheless defined the minimum wage very rigorously as a subsistence wage; i.e. a wage capable only of reproducing labour power. The criteria used in the establishment of the first minimum wage level took into account the physical consumption requirements (in terms of calories, protein intake, etc.) for particular workers who would be involved in a determinate type of production, involving a specified intensity of labour, a given degree of psychological commitment, etc. In other words, the minimum wage was seen in very strict terms as being related to the quantity of labour power which the worker would be able to sell. No other criterion whatsoever was used in the calculation of the workers' requirements. Neither in the legislation, nor in the criteria used to establish minimum wage levels, were the gains derived from increases in labour productivity taken into account.

However, even these important aspects are not the decisive ones. The decisive aspect is that *these forms of so-called labour legislation were part of a package of measures designed to pave the way for a new mode of accumulation in Brazil.* In order for this to be achieved, the population in general, and in particular the large numbers which were flowing into the cities, needed to be transformed into a "reserve army". This conversion of enormous numbers of people into such a reserve army, commensurate with the reproduction of capital, was relevant, for two main reasons, to the mode of accumulation to be established and subsequently consolidated. Firstly, it facilitated medium-term capitalist decision-making, by freeing entrepreneurs of the burdens of a perfectly competitive labour market, in which they were forced to compete amongst themselves for access to a strategic factor of production. Secondly, the "labour legislation" had the effect of *equalizing downwards* the price of labour power, rather than effecting the same equalization through an upward shift in selected (already very low) wage levels. This method of equalizing wage-levels downwards caused even skilled workers to be relegated to unskilled levels and thus impeded (contrary to the common assumption) the early formation of a dual labour market.[8] In other words, if wages were to be determined by whatever sort of "free market", it is probable that the wage level would rise for certain categories of skilled workers. The labour legislation, however, introduced a minimum wage which was to be the common denominator of all categories of worker, and in this way the process of accumulation was facilitated rather than impeded.

It might seem legitimate to raise an empirical objection to the thesis just outlined; i.e. that no proof exists that the labour legislation in question actually had the effect of reducing wages. This type of objection is, however, theoretically very weak. In order for accumulation to take place, it was not necessary for the wage levels previously paid to existing workers to be reduced. It was merely necessary for there to be an equalization of the wages paid to *subsequent*, marginal increases in the wage labour force; i.e. the impact only needed to be on average wages. In the case of Brazilian post-1930 industrialization, additions to the labour force often exceed the previous "stock" of workers, and in this way the Brazilian labour legislation achieved its objective without difficulty; i.e. the formation of an enormous reserve army in the interests of capital accumulation. This objective was only *implicit* in the labour legislation, but nevertheless corresponded to the ideological position of the dominant classes. In addition, we can deduce a further argument from the very logic of the system. Had the minimum wage levels been set above the levels obtaining under "free market" conditions (which would of course have increased considerably the remuneration received by labour in the functional distribution of income), a crisis would have ensued because accumulation would have been impeded. However, what in fact happened immediately after the introduction of the labour legislation was the opposite. From that moment onwards the process of accumulation received a massive stimulus, characterizing a completely new phase in the growth of the Brazilian economy.

A second objection to the thesis put forward here could be that, compared with the incomes available in the countryside (in whatever form they might be earned—wages, rents, income from family agriculture, etc.—the minimum wage levels in the cities were undoubtedly higher. Given the massive rural exodus and the arrival of large numbers of people in the cities, this rural–urban income difference facilitated the integration of new arrivals in the urban economy in general, but nevertheless weakened the development of class consciousness among them. The social and political effects of this contradiction are well known, though often exaggerated. However, from the point of view of accumulation, it has never been a factor of particular importance since, even if urban activities (in particular in the industrial sector) pay higher wages than the incomes which can be earned in the countryside, it is principally in terms of the productivity of urban activities that the most favourable conditions for capital accumulation are judged. In other words, the significant relationship is that between urban wages and the productivity of urban (particularly industrial) activities. It is the relationship between wages, profits and/or increases in productivity of urban production (i.e. the rate of exploitation), which will explain tendencies in the accumulation process.

The installation of the new mode of accumulation was not only facilitated by labour legislation, but also by the State regulation of many other factors of production. The State in capitalist society has normally intervened in a number of spheres: by the fixing of prices; by the distribution of profits and losses between the various fractions of the capitalist class; by the deployment of fiscal revenues for either directly or indirectly capital–reproductive objectives; by subsidizing certain spheres of production; and, by engaging in other productive activities on its own account. In this context the State's role is to ensure the reproduction of capitalist accumulation within industry at enterprise level. Such intervention has "planning" characteristics, in the same way as the English State used both the Poor Law and the Corn Laws for purposes of ensuring the transition to a new mode of accumulation. Thus, *the State intervenes in order to destroy the mode of accumulation towards which the economy had been inclined, while simultaneously creating and reproducing the conditions favouring the new mode of accumulation.* In this sense, the prices which had previously ruled in the market are replaced by so-called "social prices" whose function is to permit the consolidation of the "new market"; i.e., until such time as the accumulation process has developed a certain degree of automaticity in reproducing and consolidating the new dominant mechanisms of accumulation. "Social prices" can be established through public finance, or can be quite simply achieved by imposing a different distribution of income, always assuming that these new mechanisms ensure that the capitalist enterprise becomes the most profitable unit of production in the economy as a whole.

In the specific case of Brazil, this was the way in which the State's functions emerged and developed until the beginning of the Kubitschek presidency (1956). By regulating the price of labour in the way already described, by investing in infrastructure, by confiscating foreign exchange from the coffee sector in order to redistribute the available incomes between the various fractions of the capitalist class, by lowering the cost of capital through foreign exchange subsidies for the importation of industrial equipment, by offering industrial enterprises credit facilities at rates of interest which were negative in real terms, and by investing in production (Volta Redonda and Petrobras, for example), the State ensured that resources and income were continually transferred to industrial enterprises, which in consequence began to constitute the new centre of the system.

This "destruction" and "creation" was interpreted both by the Left and the Right as "statism" without the obvious question ever being raised—namely, in precisely whose interests was this being done? However, the process described above does have some formal similarity with the transition from capitalism to socialism. In the period of transition, not only do the automatic economic mechanisms of the previous system *not* operate, but they should not be allowed to operate, since this would impede the implantation of the basis of the new system. For this reason, market mechanisms should be replaced by administrative controls, so that the economy can operate in a *non*-automatic manner. In a period of transition, whether to or from capitalism, all sorts of controls proliferate, not only in the pricing of factors of production, but also in the control of mass consumption. This is perfectly illustrated in the case of Brazilian coffee after the crisis of 1929. Once the automatic laws of the market had been discarded, coffee production operated under conditions of anarchy, at one moment being sharply stimulated, and the very next moment being rigorously constrained. Sudden stimuli followed closely by contractions could have implied significant losses in social terms. Government controls were required precisely in order to permit coffee production to grow *or* diminish in a manner somewhat insulated from market fluctuations. For this reason it was necessary to introduce direct control through the creation and operation of the Brazilian Coffee Institute (the IBC), and to use "social" in place of market prices (the *confisco cambial* or appropriation of coffee-based foreign exchange earnings, was in fact a social price). Even having "socialized" coffee losses, and having, according to Furtado, made the corresponding transfers to the taxpayer, the process could not be termed automatic. Whether business was in general good or bad, the coffee producer could no longer control the conditions of supply and demand for factors of production, and this permitted State allocation of resources to other economic sectors. This was the basic way in which the destruction of the "natural" inclination of the economy for a certain type of accumulation was achieved.[9]

The changing role of agriculture

In the transition to a new mode of accumulation, agriculture developed a very significant and qualitatively distinct (rather than new) function. On the one hand, agriculture oriented towards the production of export crops should not only provide foreign exchange for consumption goods, but also (and perhaps more importantly) for capital and intermediate goods, and hence it is obviously imperative to maintain an active and dynamic agriculture. On the other hand, there is a trade-off between actively encouraging agriculture and giving it no stimulus whatsoever in order to ensure the final destruction of the "old" production and market structures. In the case of Brazil's transition, the world boom and recession had clearly affected the rhythm of accumulation as a whole. However, it seems that an identifiable compromise (or trade-off) was established, albeit with some degree of inherent instability. Clearly, agriculture oriented towards the domestic market had to take into account the requirements of the urban masses, mainly in order to ensure that the costs of foodstuffs and certain raw materials did not increase since, in either case, urban–industrial accumulation would have been impeded. However, the establishment and maintenance of the social stability of the system was fundamental to the creation of a viable process of accumulation for the industrial capitalist enterprise and, in this whole process, the unfettered expansion of the industrial reserve army was crucial.

During the years of transition from agricultural export hegemony to that of urban industrial capitalism, the solution to the so-called agrarian problem was central to the reproduction of the conditions for capitalist expansion. Rather than a single solution, a package of solutions was devised, the three cornerstones of which were as follows:
(i) the availability of an enormous mass of labour power; (ii) the elasticity of the supply of land; and (iii) the role played by the State in bringing together these two factors and making their interrelationships a viable one (through the

provision of infrastructure, and in particular the construction of the railway network). It was a package of solutions whose common denominator was the permanent and horizontal expansion of land occupation with little or no prior capital investment. In short, what was taking place was a type of "primitive accumulation".

The concept of primitive accumulation, as used by Marx, describes a process in which peasant land is expropriated as one of the preconditions for capitalist accumulation. However, in the Brazilian case, the concept requires some redefinition. In the first place, in Brazil the process was one in which *property in land was not expropriated*, since this had already largely taken place in the period during which agriculture passed from its subsistence base to its export crop orientation. What *was* expropriated was the surplus created through the temporary possession of land. In the second place, primitive accumulation did not *only* take place in the genesis of capitalism. Under certain specific conditions, in particular when capitalism develops by exploiting its peripheral zones, primitive accumulation has a structural and not just an organic character. Thus, whether it is "external" or "internal" frontiers which are being opened up, the process is essentially the same. The rural worker clears part of a landowner's property and engages in so-called "subsistence cultivation". During this process the land is given an initial preparation for subsequent *permanent* cultivation, or for the eventual creation of pasture-land, neither of which are for the benefit of the rural worker but for that of the landowner. In this way there is a transfer of "dead labour"; i.e. an *accumulation*, attributable to the value of the crops or other products eventually produced by the landowner, whilst there is a simultaneous *subtraction* of value as far as the original direct producer is concerned, which is reflected in the lower prices of the products of his own labour. This mechanism explains why the majority of foodcrops (rice, beans, maize etc.) which find their way into the large urban market, come from areas of relatively recent settlement, and also why the prices charged for these foodcrops in the urban market have remained very low, and have thereby contributed to the overall process of *urban* accumulation.

In terms of their *raison d'être*, the expansions of external and internal frontiers are inseparable. In the former case, the advance takes place through the progressive encroachment of agriculture on previously uncultivated land, an expansion which takes place alongside that of the transport network, most notably in the Matto Grosso (Centre-West) and Amazonia. In the case of internal frontiers, the rotation of land rather than crops within the *latifundio* fulfils the same role. The secular process which developed in the North-East, for example, is typical of this symbiosis. At the same time as he plants food crops on his newly-cleared plot, the small-scale rural cultivator who "rents" or "sharecrops" on the *latifundio* also plants cotton. The low cost of reproducing his labour power is the variable which makes *all* the commodities he produces commercially viable.

It may seem paradoxical that so-called "primitive" agriculture can compete with an agriculture using the newest inputs such as fertilizers, fungicides, pesticides, advanced agricultural techniques, and above all, mechanization. In abstract terms, it might seem improbable that the costs of such inputs could allow production to be competitive. However, to take a specific case, in the municipality of Irapeva (State of São Paulo) in 1964, maize production was economically more profitable for cultivators using animal traction and very little fertilizer than among those who used tractors, tractor-drawn equipment and large quantities of fertilizer. The former technology was used on small farms of up to 20 hectares, whilst the latter was employed on those having an area of 100 to 200 hectares. The net income per hectare was 12.5 per cent higher on small farms using "backward" methods than on the larger holdings employing "advanced" techniques, despite the fact that those "advanced" techniques yielded almost 60 per cent more output per hectare.[10] This apparently isolated example, relating to a single municipality of Brazil, is in fact valid for the greater part of Brazilian maize production, and is particularly relevant since it applies to São Paulo, where presumably there are a number of conditions which should favour the use of a more advanced agricultural technology. Thus, the combination of an elastic labour supply and an elastic supply of land has permitted continuous primitive accumulation in Brazilian agriculture, giving rise to what Paiva (1968) has called the "mechanism of autocontrol in the expansion of technical improvements in agriculture".

Relationships between agriculture and urban-industrial expansion

The above analysis, presented in a simplified form, has important repercussions, both in terms of relations between agriculture and industry, and in terms of agriculture as a whole. In the first place the analysis emphasizes the importance for the costs of reproduction of urban labour power of ensuring that agricultural production costs do not increase significantly in relation to industrial production costs. Secondly, because of the fall in the real cost of foodstuffs, the analysis explains how a rural proletariat can be (re-)created to fulfil the requirements of the sector which provides commercial crops both for the internal and the foreign markets. As a whole, as long as the rural proletariat-in-formation did not attain the status of a proletariat, the system could successfully ignore the problems of the distribution of property, problems which became critical at the end of the 1950s. Labour legislation was practically non-existent in the countryside and social welfare provisions only existed as rhetoric. In other words, from the viewpoint of agriculture's internal relations, this analysis posits the coexistence of a differentiation of production and a differentiation of productivity. Both were made viable by the maintenance of extremely low costs of reproducing labour power, and consequently, extremely low levels of living for the rural working masses. This then, was the nature of the compromise between industrial and agricultural growth.

If it is true that the creation of "new markets" of an urban–industrial nature demands not only discriminatory but also confiscatory policies to the detriment of agriculture, it is also true that—up to a point—compensation was made, by dint of the fact that industrial growth allowed agricultural and livestock production to maintain their "primitive" patterns based on extremely high rates of exploitation of their labour force. Moreover, it was only after the formation of an urban proletariat that a rural working class began to exist on a significant scale, and of course from the point of view of the production of crops for the internal and external markets, this facilitated and enhanced the overall process of accumulation.

It is probable that in terms of their urban repercussions, the maintenance and expansion of these "primitive patterns" and their combination with new relations of production in the agricultural and livestock sector, were of primary importance. This combined process permitted an extraordinary growth of industry and services. Firstly, it engendered the massive migrations which led to the creation of the urban reserve army, permitting the redefinition of capital–labour relations and thereby broadening the possibilities for industrial accumulation along the lines already described. Secondly, it provided food surpluses at prices determined by the cost of reproduction of rural labour power which, in conjunction with the existing conditions of urban labour supply, had the effect of further reducing urban real wages. In other words, the supply price of urban labour power was basically composed of two elements: (i) the costs of acquiring food,[11] determined by the cost of reproduction of *rural* labour power; and (ii) the cost of goods and services of a specifically urban nature. The existence of an urban "subsistence economy" (to be analysed later) played an important role in forcing down the supply price of urban labour power and consequently real wages, too. However, industrial productivity was simultaneously growing at a rapid rate. When this is combined with the objective conditions under which the labour force existed, and with the prevailing type of State intervention, there existed ample scope for the prodigious accumulation of industrial capital which Brazil experienced in the period 1950–1970. This particular combination of mechanism lies at the root of the Brazilian economy's current tendency towards a marked concentration in the distribution of income.

It should be apparent by now that the scene so far described, has nothing to do with any formal opposition between so-called "modern" and "backward" sectors, however defined. Equally the Brazilian reality can in no way be integrated into the well-publicized thesis of inelastic agricultural supply, constructed on the basis of Chilean conditions, generalized for the whole continent by CEPAL, and repeatedly applied to Brazil in particular by Celso Furtado. Industry never required a significant expansion of the rural market in order to ensure its own viability. Thus, tractor production, promoted and expanded at the same time as the automobile industry was developed, has never really taken off, never achieving a level of production of even 5 per cent of total automobile production. Even the production and consumption of fertilizers, which experienced substantial increases from 1965 to 1970, has not changed the man–land ratio which lies at the basis of the "primitive" agriculture model, but has actually intensified the use of labour power.

Industry has always focused on *urban* markets, not only for reasons of market size and concentration, but basically because Brazil's model of industrial growth allowed its overall development process to become and remain compatible with the necessities of accumulation; i.e. the realization of surplus value. This was growth accompanied by concentration, and it permitted the emergence of the so-called "key sectors". It is not simply a question of the agricultural and industrial sectors experiencing a divergence in their respective levels of productivity, as is suggested by the dualist model, because behind their apparent duality there is a *dialectical integration*. Agriculture fulfils a vital role in permitting the expansion of the system, supplying both the necessary labour power and food surpluses. In other words, agriculture has an important contribution to make in ensuring equilibrium and harmony within the accumulation process at the national level. Also, even though agriculture represents only a very small market for industry, industrial growth redefines the structural conditions of agriculture by introducing new relations of production in the countryside, making commercial agriculture viable, both for the domestic and for the external market, through the formation of a rural proletariat. Far from there being a growing and cumulative isolation of the two sectors, there are considerable structural inter-relations linked directly to the logic of capitalist expansion experienced in Brazil over the last 30 years. The antagonism between Brazilian agriculture and industry is not in terms of the relative levels of development of their respective productive forces, but rather in the sphere of their relations of production.

Reinterpreting capitalist accumulation through industrialization

The establishment of the industrial sector itself is another of the critical aspects of the process. This involves an attempt to make the industrial enterprise the key unit in the system, and to create and consolidate new conditions, such as new market prices, which ensure that the accumulation process consistently favours the industrial enterprise. Orthodox interpretations of the post-1930 industrial "take-off" have often suffered from an exaggerated and simplified reductionism, referring to the process as one of "import substitution". Foreign exchange crises made certain hitherto imported goods more expensive, and in the most extreme periods the non-availability of foreign exchange and the Second World War impeded, even from the physical point of view, access to certain imported commodities. This gave rise to a situation in which demand was either constrained or left unsatisfied. Under such conditions, industrial entrepreneurs were able to establish and consolidate stable and secure markets, protected from competition, which allowed them to sell products with a quality inferior to that characterizing the world market, at higher than world market prices. Subsequently, the adoption of an unambiguously protectionist tariff policy increased domestic demand for products made in Brazil.

CEPAL's dualist model of how the "backward" and "modern" sectors were created essentially consists of the following argument: the imposition of sophisticated consumption patterns from outside led to a weakening of the domestic propensity to save, whilst simultaneously, even though the market and demand for these goods was limited, industry was under pressure to adopt capital-intensive techniques and large-scale production. These options meant that the effects of the employment multiplier were severely constrained, and marked under-utilization of productive capacity and low returns on capital invested became generalized. In the long run, this combination of factors led to a fall in the rates of profit and investment, and consequently also in the rate of growth.[12] Tavares and Serra (1971) have already convincingly demonstrated that the assumptions behind this interpretation are neither theoretically nor empirically valid. In the CEPAL model, the very absence of such analytical categories as "surplus value" is sufficient to explain how, even if its underlying assumptions *are* correct, its one-track-minded conclusions are in error. Thus, for example, it is not only possible to increase relative surplus value but also absolute surplus value, bringing about an absolute decline in real wages and not just a relative decline. Furthermore, profitability can increase even when, in physical terms, capital is not fully used. It is not only surplus value which plays a fundamental role here, but also the monopolistic position of the enterprises, permitting increases in product prices compatible with high unit costs of production.

The "CEPAList" interpretation commonly applied to Latin American industrialization, provides the basis for a half-hearted theory of Latin American integration (ILPES 1967), which benefits the foreign relations of Latin American capitalist economies and, in this guise, also transforms a theory of underdevelopment into one of dependency (Furtado 1971). Thus, we are told that import-substitution industrialization is based on a necessity to consume rather than a need to produce or accumulate. Externally-imposed forms of consumption, when seen in their domestic context, are considered to bear no relation to the existing class structure, or to the distribution of income, and are therefore somewhat unreal in character. In contrast, it is argued that when the production of sophisticated consumption goods for the internal market begins, it creates new classes and changes the pattern of income distribution, thus "perverting" the composition of production and hence recreating the "backward" and the "modern" sectors.

However, the historical experience of South American countries tend to demonstrate precisely the opposite of what is posited above in the "CEPAList" version of underdevelopment theory. Argentina, for example, industrialized in the period 1870–1930 during a phase of increasing integration into the international capitalist economy, dominated by the philosophy of free trade, in periods in which she had ample capacity to import. But who benefited from this? Industrialization always responds to the necessities of accumulation and *not* those of consumption. A large urban population normally consists of an industrial and service labour force, and if it is important to maintain the cost of reproduction of this labour force at a low level in order not to impede investment, it becomes necessary and inevitable that domestic commodities be produced which themselves constitute part of the costs of reproduction of the labour force. The opportunity cost differential between spending foreign exchange in order to maintain a labour force and producing the same commodities domestically, always favours the latter rather than the former option. In the Brazilian case, domestic production consisted initially of predominantly mass consumption rather than durable consumption goods, and not the reverse as is commonly thought. This orientation was made possible, above all, by the wide range of locally-available natural resources.

The fact that the whole process was based upon a model of accumulation which, in its later phase, was to displace the productive axis of the economy towards the manufacturing of durable consumption goods, was *not* due to "the fetish of the consumer durable", nor to any "demonstration effect". Instead, it was due to the *redefinition of capital–labour relations*, to the *enormous expansion of the industrial reserve army*, to the *increase in the rate of exploitation*, and to the *differential velocities at which wages and productivity grew*, thereby reinforcing the accumulation process. Thus it was the necessity of accumulation and *not* that of consumption which determined and oriented the process of industrialization. The phenomenon of "import substitution" was merely the particular *form* of industrialization corresponding to the prevailing foreign exchange crisis. Such a crisis was a necessary, but not a sufficient, condition for the new mechanisms of accumulation to become firmly established.

In the second phase, industry turned towards the production of durable consumer goods, and intermediate and capital goods. The direction taken by industrialization was based more on the necessities of production and accumulation, than of consumption, even though the latter variable was always favoured in the "developmentalist" ideology of the CEPAL— National Development Bank (BNDE) group which provided the bases for the Kubitschek development plans. It is extremely doubtful whether the greater priority which was ostensibly to be given to consumption could have been achieved by producing commodities of a lower quality, but with higher prices, than the corresponding imports. Even at the level of the policy statements in Brazilian development plans it is easy to see that the variable that was emphasized was the *interindustrial effects* of the new sectors of production; i.e. effects on overall production and accumulation.

From the standpoint of the rationale of accumulation, it matters little that national prices for many manufactured goods are higher than those of the same imported products. Indeed, it is "convenient" that many prices are higher because they are transmitted to other sectors of industry, thereby also increasing the average level of prices charged by the so-called "dynamic" branches of industry. From the point of view of accumulation, consumer durable and allied production takes place because the redefinition of capital–labour relations has given rise to a concentration of income which has in turn made possible the consumption of these commodities, reinforcing the process of accumulation. Also, the high level of productivity in the new branches of industry, relative to the growth of wages, produces a "qualitative leap", which itself also reinforces the tendency for national income to be concentrated. What is absolutely necessary is that these high prices are *not* transmitted to those commodities which form part of the cost of reproducing labour power, because this would threaten accumulation. The product-prices in the so-called "dynamic" branches of industry *could* and even *should* be higher than those of the corresponding imported goods, because the realization of an accumulation process based on these very branches takes place *domestically* and not externally. In other words, it only makes sense to talk about competitive prices when products destined for the foreign market are being considered.

As far as the process of Brazilian capitalist development in the 1950s and 1960s was concerned, it was important that coffee's production costs were internationally competitive, but absolutely no importance need be attached to the fact that nationally produced automobiles' prices were two or three times higher than their foreign counterparts.[13] In the context of an extremely inegalitarian distribution of national income, and corresponding to the limited demands of the upper classes, national production of consumer durables, of which the automobile was the archetype, found its market and therefore fulfilled its function in the accumulation process. The associated units and branches of industrial production became the most profitable and vital cornerstones of the system, playing a large part in determining the shape of the economy's future productive structure.

The myth of "tertiary inflation"

The other major element in the urban–industrial equation is the so-called "service sector", a heterogeneous complex of activities whose only homogeneity consists in the fact that they do not result in material goods. The function of such services in the economy has not provided a particularly attractive field for economic analysis, at least to judge by the existing literature.

Colin Clark's now classic work *The Conditions of Economic Progress*, provides the basis for an empirical model which disaggregates economic activities as a whole into three groups, the primary, secondary and tertiary sectors. Analytically, Clark's model has served as a paradigm for judging the contribution of each of these sectors to the gross domestic product. Here, the progressive increase in the relative shares of the secondary (industrial) and tertiary (service) sectors are taken as an index of economic diversification and development. However, Clark's model has also been used in a much more dubious fashion, namely in a manner which has tended to confuse the *formal* relationship between the three sectors with their *structural* relations: i.e. confusing the role which these sectors play within the economy as a whole with the interdependence which they have with respect to each other. Clark's model is explicitly formal–empirical in character, merely indicating the forms taken by the social division of labour in the sequence in which they appear historically. When it is used in order to describe a concrete social formation or mode of production, it becomes necessary to investigate the structural relations between the sectors and the role which each sector plays in the overall structuring of a given mode of production.

The abstract use of Clark's model as a component in numerous analytical exercises within the theory of underdevelopment, has led to a dubious interpretation—what we have previously referred to as the "underdeveloped mode of production" thesis. Here the tertiary or services sector is represented, in terms of its share in the creation of GNP and employment, as something *quantitatively disproportional*. In other words, according to these particular theorists of underdevelopment, the extent to which the tertiary sector is involved in the formation of GNP and in the generation of employment is *more than it should be;* i.e. it is *inflated*. Thus, one of the characteristics of the "underdeveloped mode of production" is this swollen tertiary sector, which consumes a part of the surplus and at the same time constitutes a "dead weight" in the generation of GNP. It must also be pointed out that certain Marxist analysts have contributed to this formulation. For them, most services are in a general sense "unproductive", adding nothing—in terms of value—to the social product. Such an interpretation distinguishes transport and communications services, for instance, from those of an intermediary or commercial nature. Whilst the former are considered productive, the latter are not. In response to such views, the question must be posed *whether commercial and intermediary services do not also represent socially necessary labour within the process of capitalist accumulation.* It would be difficult to sustain the argument that these activities do not constitute an essential part of that process, since they are also components in the reproduction of that commodity which distinguishes capitalism from other modes of production, namely labour power.

The above argument necessarily implies the following question: how do we explain the size of the tertiary sector in an economy such as that of Brazil? Between 1939 and 1969, the share of the tertiary sector in the net domestic product remained constant at between 53 and 55 per cent, while the proportion of the total population which was economically active (i.e. the labour force) grew from 24 to 38 per cent. The tertiary sector absorbed increases in labour force size much more than any other. Such a level of absorption might be attributed on the one hand to the incapacity of the primary sector to sustain its level of labour utilization, and on the other to the incapacity of manufacturing activities (i.e. the secondary sector) to absorb the increases in the labour force.[14] However, the hypothesis which is being presented here is radically different from this: that *the growth of the tertiary sector, in the form which has been observed in Brazil, has increasingly absorbed members of the labour force both in absolute and in relative terms, and forms a part of the urban mode of accumulation commensurate with the expansion of the capitalist system.* The growth of this sector in no way constitutes an "inflation", nor does it constitute a "marginal" part of the economy.

In the expansion of capitalism in Brazil, industrial growth had to be achieved on the basis of a rather poor degree of capitalist accumulation, especially when we take into account that agriculture's contribution to growth was in general based on "primitive accumulation". This means that the growth experienced before the industrial expansion of the 1930s not only provided insufficient accumulation for industrial enterprises, but also did not have the capacity to provide the urban infrastructural base necessary for industrial expansion. Before the 1920s, with the exception of Rio de Janeiro, Brazilian cities (including São Paulo) were hardly more than inward-looking small towns, without the slightest preparation for a rapid and intense industrialization process. However, between 1939 and 1969, manufacturing's share in net national product rose from only 19 to almost 30 per cent, while the proportion of the labour force involved in this sector rose from 10 to 18 per cent. These aggregate data help to illustrate the intensity of Brazilian industrial growth in that period.

In the process of its expansion, Brazilian industry had no pre-existing basis provided by previous capitalist accumulation upon which to rely. As a result, the entire responsibility for capitalist accumulation had to be concentrated within the industrial enterprise itself. However, this would have been impossible without the support of strictly urban-focused services, differentiated from and external to the manufacturing enterprise, and capable of providing the so-called "external economies". Such services were in such short supply that the first wave of industrialization was characterized by an attempt by the manufacturing enterprises to locate all necessary services *within* their own four walls, a process which very soon had to be replaced by a division of labour which stretched *outside* the strictly defined units of production. Soon afterwards, as industrial expansion continued, the process took on a form compatible with the absence of any previous capitalist accumulation which, in other circumstances, would have financed the establishment of these essential services. In the cities, an extensive, horizontal type of growth ensued, characterized by extremely low capital coefficients, in which production relied basically upon abundantly available labour power. There was a resurgence of artisanal forms of production, principally in the so-called "repair and maintenance" workshops of all types. Between 1940 and 1950, the share of production-related services in total employment rose from a little over 9 per cent to almost 10.5 per cent, while services related to individual consumption remained at precisely the same level—just over 6 per cent of total employment. Nevertheless, services related to collective consumption also experienced an increase in their share of total employment, rising from just over 4 per cent to over 5 per cent in the same period.

Between 1950 and 1960, only disaggregated data are available on production-related services, which nevertheless continued to increase their share of total employment, reaching 11.5 per cent by the end of the 1950s. Even though disaggregated data do not exist for the other types of services distinguished above, it is legitimate to assume that these did not increase their share of total employment, since the share of the tertiary sector as a whole remained constant or possibly even suffered a marginal decline.[15] This probably means that the growth of production-related services was primarily responsible, during the period in question, for the growth of employment in the tertiary sector as a whole—a growth which was directly linked to the expansion of industrial activities in Brazil.

In summary then, the phenomenon under scrutiny is not at all one of "tertiary inflation". The size of the tertiary sector in an economy like Brazil, from the viewpoint of its share in total employment, is a question intimately linked with that of urban–industrial capitalist accumulation. Accelerated growth, whose epicentre became the industrial sector, made certain demands on those centres *par excellence* of the new cycle of expansion—the Brazilian cities—namely, the creation of the infrastructure and services not previously available in the urban areas. The intensity of industrial growth, which in the 1930s rose from 19 per cent to 30 per cent of the GNP, *did not permit an intensive and simultaneous capitalization of services,* since this would have involved the service sector in competing with industry for the scarce funds which were available for genuine capitalist accumulation. This contradiction was resolved through the non-capitalistic growth of the tertiary sector. This model has nothing whatsoever to do with the concept of the "swollen tertiary sector", even though descriptively they might coincide. What we are dealing with is *a type of tertiary sector growth which is not in contradiction with the dominant form of accumulation, which is in no way an obstacle to the aggregate expansion of the economy, and which is not a net consumer of surplus.* The justification for denying that the effects of the growth of the service sector have been "negative" from the standpoint of aggregate accumulation, is that its surface appearance of being "over-inflated" or "swollen" actually hides a fundamental mechanism of accumulation. Thus, services performed on the basis of undiluted labour power and remunerated at extremely low levels, permanently transfer to authentically capitalist activities a portion of the value they themselves create. In short, there is a transfer of surplus value to support capitalist accumulation.[16]

Relations between the so-called "backward" and "modern" sectors

Is it so strange to suggest the existence of a symbiotic relation between the "modern" agricultural production of fruit, vegetables and other farm products and their final marketing by mobile street traders in the city?[17] Furthermore, what volume of trade involving specific *industrially-produced* goods, such as razor-blades, combs, cleaning materials and innumerable other small products, is performed by street hawkers in Brazilian city-centres? What is the relationship between the increase in the number of private vehicles on the roads of Brazil and the number of people who offer their services as car-washers? Does any incompatibility exist between the growing volume of car production in Brazil and the proliferation of small workshops devoted to the repair and maintenance of damaged vehicles? How do we explain that all sorts of services related to personal consumption grew in volume precisely when industry was on an *upward* trend (in particular in the creation of additional employment) and when, according to the results of the 1970 population census, an even more unequal distribution of national income was emerging? These types of services, far from being mere excrescences or interstitial activities for the "industrial reserve army", are precisely what the total process of accumulation and capitalist expansion *requires*, contributing to the tendency for income to become increasingly concentrated.[18]

Cities are, by definition, the centres of the industrial economy *and* of services. Urban growth and the "deruralization" of the GNP are consequently nothing more than two sides of the same coin, and in this sense the smaller the share of agricultural activities in the GNP, the greater is the degree of urbanization. Consequently, Brazilian urbanization merely corresponds to the law by which agriculture's share in the total GNP declines historically. However, neither the rising share of industry in GNP, nor that of the secondary sector as whole, can be held entirely responsible for the extremely high increase in Brazilian urbanization. This very fact has led a large number of Latin American and Brazilian sociologists to speak of "urbanization *without* industrialization" or indeed of "urbanization plus *marginalization*". However, the process of urban growth can only be understood within a theoretical framework in which the necessities of accumulation demand a horizontal growth of services, something which has given rise—at the level of superficial appearances—to the so-called "chaos" of Brazilian cities.

It is important not to confuse "anarchy" with "chaos". The "anarchy" of urban growth is *not* "chaotic" at all, when seen in terms of the imperatives of capitalist accumulation. There is at least one aspect of the whole urban phenomenon which we can characterize (perhaps provocatively) as "primitive accumulation"; the individual provision of low-income housing. A not insignificant percentage of working-class urban housing has been constructed by its owners, using days off, weekends, and forms of community cooperation. The housing which has resulted from this process has been constructed essentially by *non-paid* labour; i.e. surplus labour. Even though apparently this surplus labour has not been appropriated by the *private* sector of production, it has nevertheless contributed to the process of increasing the rate of exploitation of the labour force, since its product, namely the private residence, has given rise to an apparent decrease in the costs of reproducing labour power, of which housing-related expenditure is an important and large component. This has consequently depressed the *real* wages paid by enterprises in general. Thus, a process which is apparently a relic of practices commonly found in the "natural economy", but nonetheless taking place in urban areas, is entirely compatible with the process of capitalist expansion, which has as one of the principal bases of its own dynamism the intense exploitation of labour power.

The process described above, seen at its various levels and in its different forms, constitutes the specific aggregate mode of accumulation in Brazil's post-1930 capitalist expansion. This process, despite its obvious inequalities, was nevertheless also a *combined* process, to paraphrase Trotsky's famous words. *It was the product of a relatively poor basis for capitalist accumulation which facilitated industrialization, the post-1930 expansion of the Brazilian economy, and the emergence of the so-called "backward" and "modern" sectors.* This combination of inequalities was by no means an innovation. It has always been present in whatever transformation of systems we care to study. Its "originality" perhaps consists—albeit paradoxically—in the fact that the expansion of capitalism in Brazil emerged out of the introduction of new relations into a pre-existing "archaic" social formation, and the reproduction of "archaic" relations within the new system; i.e. a method of making compatible the overall process of accumulation with what had preceded it. In this transition, the introduction of new relations liberated labour power, which subsequently supported the urban-industrial accumulation process. Meanwhile, the reproduction of certain "archaic" relations actually preserved the accumulation potential which had been created exclusively in the interests of the further expansion of the new system. This process was fundamental to the operation of the system and, in the case of Brazil, took the form of a radical transition from a situation in which accumulation was based almost exclusively on the foreign sector, to one in which the domestic sector tended to become once-and-for-all, the focal point for the realization and expansion of surplus value. The system tended inexorably towards the concentration of income, property and power, and ostensibly corrective and/or redistributive policies were transformed into a Promethean nightmare in which the very tendencies condemned in the public rhetoric were, in fact, exacerbated.

A pause for political reflection: bourgeois revolution and industrial accumulation in Brazil

We reject the demand for global generality implicit in the "underdeveloped mode of production thesis" because it is evident that Brazil's history and the economic process in which it has been involved since the 1930s have certain peculiarities; i.e. a certain "*individual* specificity". Though the process can be understood in a general way as that of a capitalist economy in expansion, this expansion does not repeat or reproduce *ipsis literis* the classical capitalist model of the more developed countries; neither in structural terms, nor in terms of the effects produced by the process. Thus, right from the outset, we must take care not to use the "classicism" of the Western model as a "structural rule".

Acceptance of the fact that what we are dealing with here is indeed the expansion of a capitalist economy, derives from a recognition that the basic relations within the system since the 1930s, from the standpoint of owners and non-owners of the means of production (i.e. buyers and sellers of labour power), have not changed. The system continues to be one based upon the realization of profit. Given Brazil's insertion into and membership of the capitalist system, the forms taken by its structural transformation since the 1930s have been based upon possibilities defined within the economy itself. In other words, the existing relations of production contained the possibility for the overall restructuring of the system, *thereby enhancing the tendencies towards a capitalist restructuring, even when the international division of labour and the world capitalist system opposed this process.* This hypothesis diverges from the basic interpretation of the dependency theorists, which only allows internal restructuring to take place when both internal and external tendencies are synchronized and in harmony.

With regard to the internal articulation of the social forces involved in the reproduction of capital, only one question remains to be resolved—that of the replacement of the rural propertied classes at the top of the national power structure by the new bourgeois class of industrial entrepreneurs. At this turning point, the working classes in general had no real option. Even the attempted revolution of 1935 reflected more a moment of indecision on the part of the old and newly-emerging upper classes than a determined strategy by the working classes. However, from the viewpoint of Brazil's relations with the rest of the capitalist world, the situation was completely different.

The crisis of the 1930s created a vacuum throughout the capitalist system, but no real alternative to the restructuring upon which Brazil was to embark. Later, the Second World War impeded this restructuring, strengthening the role of economies like Brazil as suppliers of raw materials. The world emerged from the War with the crucial problem of how to reconstruct the economies of the defeated countries. One of the aims of this reconstruction was to block the expansion of socialism in the industrialized countries—an expansion which was also taking place on the periphery. This reconstruction diverted resources which, under other circumstances (according to Prebisch), might have been channelled towards the non-industrialized countries of the capitalist system to transform the pre-War international division of labour. The reconstruction of the devastated economies of Germany, Japan, and their former allies had industry as its strategic focus. The international trading of manufactures between industrial nations in the capitalist system was to guarantee the viability of this strategy. The role of the non-industrial countries in the international capitalist division of labour was—at least for the foreseeable future—to continue to be suppliers of raw materials and agricultural products.

In these circumstances, the expansion of capitalism in Brazil was fundamentally characterized by an internal dialectic involving a struggle between antagonistic social forces. The determinants of this process were to be the possibilities available for transforming the mode of accumulation, the structure of power, and the form of domination. If this process failed, the alternative prospect was stagnation, and reversion to an economy oriented towards primary exports. Caught between the hammer and the anvil of these two possibilities, a bougeois revolution emerged in Brazil. It took the political form of populism, and this is one of the peculiar traits characterizing the expansion of Brazilian capitalism.

As opposed to the "classic" bourgeois revolution, the replacement of the Brazilian rural propertied classes by the new bourgeois class of industrial entrepreneurs did not require a *total* rupture in the system, neither for socio-political nor for structural reasons. In the case of Brazil, the crisis centred upon the country's relations with the rest of the capitalist world, while in the "classical" model the crisis was to be found within society and the economy itself. In the European model, the hegemony of the rural propertied classes was *total*, and it paralysed all development of the productive forces because the "classical" economies were not party to any system which could allow them access to the capital goods which they needed for their expansion. These economies had to produce the required capital goods themselves, or there would be no expansion of capitalism; i.e. no expansion of the system of generalized commodity production. Thus a rupture had to take place at all levels and in all spheres. In the case of Brazil, the rural propertied classes exercised only a partial hegemony, in the sense that they maintained the economy's external relations, which allowed them to retain the same patterns for the reproduction of capital which had served as the basis for the primary-exporting economy. With the collapse of these external relations, this partial hegemony was isolated from its material base. The rural propertied classes found themselves in a vacuum. However, it was not for this reason *ipso facto* that the industrialization process based on import substitution somehow "automatically" emerged. The key precondition was that a new mode of accumulation be identified and implemented, so as to begin to replace accumulation based on the export of primary products. For such a change to take place, it was necessary that appropriate relations of production came into being beforehand.

Populism constituted a comprehensive mechanism by which this process of "adjustment" was achieved, in the first instance by establishing new material and ideological relations between the "archaic" and the "new". As has already been shown, this populism was corporativist and had as its principal function the creation of new forms of capital–labour relationship so as to consolidate the internal sources of accumulation necessary for the restructuring. Labour legislation provided the means of achieving this. Thus, at the same time as the necessary conditions were created for accumulation to be reoriented towards an industrialization strategy, a labour legislation devoid of any *economic* "distributivist" tendencies (Weffort 1966) emerged as the turning point in the forging of a class alliance. The nascent industrial bourgeoisie needed to win the support of the urban working classes in order to politically liquidate the old rural propertied classes. This alliance was not simply the outcome of mass pressure from below, but was necessary for the success of the industrial bourgeoisie's strategy to see that there was no reversion to the pre-1930 situation after the Second World War, when coffee prices were rising alongside the prices of other agricultural and mineral raw materials. Thereafter there was a long period in which apparently contradictory policies coexisted. The State penalized export production, while recognizing that agricultural and livestock exports—being the country's only sources of foreign exchange—still constituted the cornerstone of Brazil's import capacity. This contradiction was further complicated by the fact that the State needed to transfer resources on a continuous and expanding scale to the industrial enterprises which were to be the motive force behind the new strategy of expansion.

Populism's most profound political impact was to definitively change the power structure, transfering hegemony to the new bourgeois class of industrial entrepreneurs. However, this whole process took place under generally adverse international conditions (even when export prices were high) and therefore one of its structural prerequisites was the maintenance of conditions for the reproduction of agricultural activities. This was to avoid totally excluding the rural propertied classes either from the power structure or from the benefits of the system's expansion. In return, labour legislation had no impact on agrarian relations of production, thereby preserving a type of "primitive accumulation" which is nevertheless highly compatible with the aggregate expansion of the economy in its new orientation. This "structural pact" or alliance has preserved distinct modes of accumulation within specific sectors of the economy, though not in an antagonistic relationship as commonly assumed in the CEPAL model. It is on this basis that the rural population has continued to grow, even though it is a declining proportion of the total population.

The internal dynamic of the Brazilian "model" of economic development

It is due to the preservation of distinct modes of accumulation that unambiguously capitalist forms of production have not totally penetrated the rural areas, but on the contrary, have actually contributed to the maintenance of typically non-capitalist forms of reproduction. This is the first "peculiarity" of the Brazilian model, because in opposition to the predictions of the "classical model", the progress of Brazilian capitalism has not required the complete destruction of the old mode of accumulation.

A second peculiarity or "individual specificity" can be found in the restructuring of the Brazilian urban–industrial economy, in particular in the relative share of the manufacturing and tertiary sectors in total employment. This has already been discussed in terms of the limited degree to which the manufacturing sector could create employment for the absorption of the new labour force and the consequent so-called "inflation", or more properly the "adaptation" in size, of the tertiary sector. In the first place, as has already been shown, variations in the growth of manufacturing employment have been to a large extent conjunctural. In the second place, the fastest employment growth in services linked to personal consumption (the so-called "inflation") has occurred when the growth of employment in the manufacturing sector has been accelerating. My aim here has been to demonstrate that the growth of these two sectors, in the specific forms observed in the period since the 1930s, illustrates the structural conditions for the expansion of capitalism in Brazil. In this sense, certain aspects of the "individual specificity" of Brazil can be adduced and compared with the corresponding predictions of the "classical" model.

It is useful at this point to look again at Brazilian history. During the colonial period and most of the nineteenth century, slavery constituted an obstacle to industrialization, to the extent that the cost of reproduction of slaves was an *internal* cost of production. Thus, early on, the progress of industrialization meant that a series of attempts had to be made to "expel" the cost of reproduction of the slave from the cost of production. In other words, contrary to the predictions of the "classical" model, (i.e. that it was necessary to absorb or internalize these "peripheral" relations of production), in Brazil it was necessary to *create* a "periphery". In this context, the manner in which the economy of the country was inserted into the international capitalist division of labour is decisive and therefore has been used to justify a whole range of interpretations—most notably those of Celso Furtado. The fact that this process of "expulsion" and "creation" was so lengthy, from the abolition of slavery until the 1930s, derives from the fact that the process of insertion under scrutiny here favoured the maintenance of certain "slave-patterns" within existing relations of production. It was to be a crisis at the level of the productive forces which obliged this pattern to change.

Post-1930 institutions, among which those involved with the so-called labour legislation are probably the most important, have fulfilled the role of "expelling" the cost of reproduction of labour–power from the industrial enterprise. While in the previous pattern of Brazilian industrialization enterprises often completely dominated a single area (company towns, workers' suburbs etc., providing housing, commercial and social services, and even food supplies), the new pattern has transferred such expenditures *outside* the units of production. In the process of "expulsion", the minimum wage has been a *maximum* obligation imposed on the enterprise, enabling it to concentrate all its potential for accumulation on the expansion of output.

Industrialization, by virtue of its "lateness' in the case of Brazil, has taken place at a time when accumulation has been facilitated by the existence of an immense reservoir of "dead labour" (in the form of technology) on the international market, ready to be transferred to countries still in the process of industrialization. As a result, the process of capital reproduction has "jumped" several stages, among which probably the most important is the lengthy period required for the price of labour power to become sufficiently high to force the introduction of labour-saving technology.

This "jumping" of stages, reinforced by the labour laws, has permitted vast increases in the productivity of investment. Seen in this way, the problem is not so much that industrial growth has not provided employment as that, by accelerating the process of industrialization, the distribution of income between capital and labour has become irreversibly, and even more widely, divergent. For the price of labour power to increase in a manner which would have steadily reduced the gap between these two types of income, it would have been necessary for the demand for labour to grow several times faster than the labour supply. Furthermore, because the large-scale acquisition of capital goods (made possible by accumulated technological advances) occurred at a "premature" stage of accumulation, it has impeded the internal circulation of capital. Among other consequences this has lowered the impact of the investment multiplier below the level which would have accompanied an exclusively *internal* realization of capital. It is obvious that one of the multipliers affected in this case is that of direct and indirect employment. The historical rationale of late industrialization thereby takes on a *structural* form, giving to the secondary sector in general, and industry in particular, a much larger share of the gross domestic product than of the proportional distribution of the labour force.

In terms of the dimensions of the tertiary sector, it is possible to identify further historical and structural reasons for the "specificity" of capitalist expansion in Brazil. Historically, late industrialization tends to require a social division of labour which is more differentiated because of the high degree of "modernity" (i.e. use of advanced technologies) in industry. Furthermore, all types of modern services complementary to industry and commonly encountered in the mature capitalist economies, are required. This demand comes into conflict with a structural constraint—the amount of funds available for accumulation, particularly as these have to be shared between industry and services. The solution is found by causing services to grow *horizontally* with virtually no capitalization, on the basis of the labour power and organizational talent of thousands of pseudo-proprietors who, if the truth be known, do nothing more than sell their own labour power to the principal production units of the system. This sale of labour power is mediated through a bogus conception of property on the part of the small proprietor. The real relationship consists of the *transfer* of those costs corresponding to services outside the internal costs of capitalist production. This very process is then transformed into priorities for the institutions which would mould the accumulation process in Brazil. Thus, with the sole exception of EMBRATUR (the Brazilian government's Tourist Development Company), there is no case in which legislation to promote capitalist development or the actions of government departments gives priority to the service sector in the concession of credit, the exemption from import taxes on equipment, tax incentives, the provision of discriminatory tariffs, or the capital formation process.

For many years, both general economic policy and the specific policies of the various government and public sector departments, have always considered that the requirements of the service sector can be satisfied with levels of capitalization far below those normally applied to industry. Such policies result from governmental attitudes regarding the abundant supply of labour, which not only constitutes a guarantee, but also a *motivation*—that services not only *can*, but also *should*, be established and maintained so as to utilize abundant cheap labour.

The complex of relations which has determined industrial expansion established, from the very outset, an enormous gap between the shares of capital and labour in the benefits arising out of increased labour productivity. This widening disparity has accelerated the growth of services—both those related to production and those involved in catering to the demands of personal consumption. A vast range of service activities has sprung up throughout the cities as a result of the growth and spread of urban population. Such services have been stimulated by the impact which the process of industrialization has had on consumer demand, leading to a proliferation of small grocery shops, more specialized shops, markets, repair activities, and salons for personal services (such as hairdressing and photography). These activities, with the workers' suburbs and shanty-towns as their centres of gravity, have been oriented towards satisfying the basic requirements of those with relatively low levels of purchasing power. As a result, the low wages of their clienteles have determined the earning capacity of these pseudo-petty-proprietors, establishing pockets of interdependent subsistence within the low-income sections of the population. The low level of these earnings represents the marketing costs which have been "expelled" from industry's own production costs, thereby aiding the drive for accumulation which has taken place in the industrial hub of the Brazilian system.

Thus, we can see that the strategic element in defining the complex of economic relations as a whole is constituted by the type of relations of production which are established between capital and labour in industry. In the "classical" model, this strategic element tends to be "exported" to the rest of the economy. Far from corresponding to this model, the Brazilian experience—and that of many other underdeveloped countries—shows that with fully capitalist relations of production in the strategic, industrial sector of the economy, there is a tendency towards the perpetuation of non-capitalist relations of production in agriculture and the development of non-capitalist patterns of reproduction and appropriation of surplus in services. The reasons for this tendency are primarily historical, but very soon they are transformed into a structural rationale.

The particular specificity of such a model lies in the creation and reproduction of a sizeable periphery in which *non*-capitalist patterns of production relations predominate. These patterns constitute both the forms and the means whereby this periphery supports and sustains the growth of the unambiguously capitalist sectors of the economy. In turn, over a long time-scale, this growth guarantees the continued viability of the structures of domination and the reproduction of the capitalist system.

Notes

1. This essay was written as an attempt to reply to much of the interdisciplinary research (and the resulting conclusions) undertaken by my colleagues at CEBRAP on the socio-economic aspects of Brazilian capitalist expansion. The essay has benefited enormously from the very special atmosphere which characterizes the institution, and which has permitted authentic intellectual debates to take place. I would like to express my gratitude to the following CEBRAP staff members for their contributions to and criticisms of this piece of work: José Arthur Gianotti, Octávio Ianni, Paul Singer, Francisco Weffort, Juarez Brandão Lopes, Boris Fausto Fábio Munhoz, and Regis Andrade. I would also like to thank Caio Prado Jr. and Gabriel Bolaffi, both of whom participated in the seminars which discussed the ideas contained in the present essay. For any errors and omissions, I am, of course wholly responsible.
2. A typical case would be that of Prebisch's denunciation of a system of international trade which gave rise to deteriorating terms of trade for Latin American economies. This *should*

have provided a starting point for an extension of our theory of imperialism, but no such initiative was taken, and thus the result was clearly in the *reformist* mould. Industrial nations were ostensibly to reform their own behaviour, increasing the prices they paid for Latin American exports, and reducing the prices they charged for their own exports to Latin America. This was also the fundamental thrust of the UNCTAD conferences' policy conclusions—namely, a profoundly ethical but equally ingenuous proposition.

3. None of the anti-CEPAL conservative economists in Latin America has made a *theoretical* contribution to the debate: their work is characteristically casual and unsystematic, arguing at one moment from one point of view, and the very next moment defending the opposite position.

4. Cardoso and Faletto (1970) have elaborated a theory of dependency whose fundamental postulate is the recognition that the specificity of underdevelopment is to be found in its very ambiguity, since this dependency is the mechanism which articulates internal interests with the rest of the capitalist system. In this respect, Cardoso and Faletto have departed from the CEPAL model, in which external relations are seen as operating *against* overall national interests, inasmuch as the two authors have recognized that dependency is "an articulation of the interests of specific classes and social groups *within* Latin America, with those of classes and social groups outside". Hegemony, in their theoretical framework, emerges as the result of common interests which are themselves determined by the international division of labour at the level of the world capitalist system. Their formulation, in my opinion, is much more correct than that of the CEPAL orthodoxy, even though they do not attach sufficient importance to the possibility (both theoretical and empirical) that capitalism *might* expand in countries like Brazil *even when* the international capitalist division of labour is unfavourable to that expansion. In my view, the expansion of capitalism in Brazil since 1930 illustrates this point very clearly.

5. "Thanks to this (labour legislation), the pattern of wages became relatively independent of the conditions created by the presence of an industrial reserve army" (Rangel 1963, pp. 44–45).

6. Political scientists who have written on this topic certainly did not fail to notice that the sort of "domination" embodied in Brazil's labour legislation can work in the interests of capitalist expansion, particularly when the urban masses in general come to play a key role in the political restructuring which permits industrialization subsequently to take place. However, this correct analysis has led to the erroneous conclusion that, once supported by the masses, these labour laws gave groups an increased share in the benefits arising out of increases in productivity. But the facts in no way support this conclusion. Though the populist régimes could perhaps be termed "redistributivist" in other (i.e. political) respects, in terms of the way in which "redistribution" is used here (i.e. how the benefits of increased productivity are distributed) they were far from being 'redistributivist".

7. According to CEPAL the "artificial" levels at which the minimum wage was set, led to a premature increase in the fixed capital component of capital. This led to increasingly "capital-intensive" investments which reduced the employment multiplier associated with new investment. Consequently, the capital–output ratio declined, the market shrank, and the long-run profit-rate dropped, as did ultimately the overall rate of growth. In the CEPAL view, this complex process as a whole had the effect of exacerbating the dual nature of the economy. However, it has not been demonstrated empirically that there was, in fact, a disproportionate amount of "capital-intensive" investment in the overall structure of investment. In theoretical terms, the error of the CEPAL formulation lies partly in the fact that investments were defined over-rigorously *only* as those undertaken in the industrial sector. In addition, no account was taken of the effect of international relations on the aggregate production function; i.e. that these relations had allowed only a very fragile basis for accumulation to be established in Brazil, mainly through the impact of the very high level of absorption of foreign technology (i.e. "accumulated labour" or "dead labour", originating abroad).

8. An interesting question here is why the labour legislation under scrutiny had found its inspiration in the juridical forms characterizing Italian corporativist (fascist) law. But, unfortunately, this point has only ever been studied from the standpoint of the Brazilian State *at the time when the laws were promulgated*, and not in terms of what preceded or succeeded their enactment. The Brazilian State was undoubtedly authoritarian, but at the same time it

was *in transition* between the hegemony of the rural propertied classes and that of the industrial bougeoisie. The role played by the State in providing a "bridge" between various pre-capitalist economic forms (particularly in agriculture) and the emergent industrial sector, has barely been studied. Corporativist law is the means by which the two sectors were, in fact, made compatible. It destroyed the potential duality between the "archaic" and the "new" by *unifying* the two. The persistence of this duality, as far as the setting of urban wage levels is concerned (especially in industry), could actually have damaged the viability of the nascent capitalist industrial sector.

9. The growth in the State's degree of intervention necessarily implies the extension of the "machinery of state"; i.e. of the bureaucracy and of the technocratic sphere. In the "transitional" phase, the growth of these two aspects of the State apparatus was derived from a differentiation taking place within the social division of labour *at the level of the economy and society as a whole*. In contrast, more recently, and in particular as from the early 1960s, this same expansion was determined much more by a differentiation of the social division of labour *at the level of the State itself*, since by this time in the economy at large, a considerable degree of self-sustaining growth had already been restored through the establishment of the "new market" and "new laws".

10. The data were drawn from Ettori (n.d.) and have been recalculated by Paiva (1968).

11. Between 1945 and 1965, the general index for wholesale food prices rose from 22 to 3,198, while that of industrial products rose from 52 to 5,163. There data lead us to reject CEPAL's argument that agricultural production costs constituted an obstacle to the creation of a viable market for industrial products (data from *Conjuntura Econômica*, cited by Paiva 1966).

12. This type of analysis is also found in Furtado (1971). For a more complete elaboration of the model and its most radical conclusions, see also Furtado (1966).

13. But the situation is, of course, different, if these automobiles are *exported*. In this case, products must be competitively priced, and this is why, by 1970, the Brazilian government was subsidizing manufactured exports to the tune of 40 per cent of the f.o.b. prices. Such exports, however, are of minimal importance to the accumulation process in general. In the majority of cases, they constitute a *destruction* (or loss) of surplus at the aggregate economic level, despite the fact that such exports can provide excellent profit-making opportunities at the level of the individual unit of production.

14. Many of the attempts to theorize the so-called "inflation" of the tertiary sector have focused on specific historical or political conjunctures. In the 1950–1960 period, for example, there was a relative slowing-down in the growth of industrial employment, and this provided an empirical basis for an attempt to generalize the "tertiary inflation" thesis. However, analyses of Brazil's 1970 population census indicate that the rate of increase in industrial employment in the period 1960–1970 was almost double that of the previous decade. Moreover, this doubling of the rate of employment expansion took place at a time when the much-publicized *destruction* of artisanal production, in the wake of the expansion of manufacturing industry, was no longer occurring to any significant extent. Indeed, in the period in question, gross and net rates of employment–expansion were becoming increasingly convergent.

15. The decade 1960–1969 was to see the share in total employment of those services related to individual consumption grow to exceed that of production-related services. Their respective shares in the third quarter of 1969, were 15.3 per cent and 13 per cent. This incredible expansion in "personal" services has traditionally been characterized as evidence of the "dumping" of labour currently surplus to the requirements of the capitalist market, and yet it took place precisely when the secondary sector as a whole (and industry in particular) was recovering its dynamism with respect to employment-generation (i.e. reasserting itself as the leading force in employment generation).

16. All variants of orthodox analysis—the "inflated tertiary sector", the "lumpenproletariat", neo-Malthusianism, and neoclassical marginalist views—when applied to the problem of the changing composition of urban employment, are opposed to this idea. Such a proposition is incompatible with ideological prejudices, and with the poor arithmetic of those who seek to increase *per capita* income through birth control. It is also opposed to those who describe "leakages from the system" or "imperfections in the optimum allocation of factors"—grossly over-optimistic theorists who compare today's "darkness" with the "golden dawn" of the future, when the system will be able to "distribute" that which, today, it must keep concentrated in few hands.

17. In the 19 March 1972 issue of the leading Brazilian newspaper, *O Estado de São Paulo*, there
was a statement by the President of the Rural Union of Small Farmers of São Roque, which
clearly illustrated this relationship. He described a crisis in fruit production which had taken
place after an excellent harvest, saying that the prohibition of street-hawking and selling of
fruit by the Prefecture of São Paulo had dealt a completely unexpected and massive blow to
local fruit producers, since street sellers were *absolutely essential* to the process of fruit
marketing. Without the six hundred or so fruit-sellers, there had been a complete collapse in
the fruit distribution system, and producers had been forced to bear the losses, while the
populace had gone without fruit, despite its legislated low price. The fundamental lesson here
is that the producers suffered losses which were derived not from the price level, but from the
prohibition of street-selling. There was no way in which street sellers could themselves have
raised prices, with the result that the losses incurred (i.e. the portion of the producers' incomes
which was *not* realized) could be attributed to the fact that the street sellers' labour had not
been available. In this example, the mechanism by which the transfer of value takes place can
be seen very clearly.

18. Certain strictly *personal* services (rendered directly to the final consumer, or even taking place
within the family itself) are characterized by disguised forms of exploitation which play their
own part in the process of accumulation. For such services to be rendered *outside* the family,
there would have to exist an infrastructure base which the city has yet to make available.
Equally, the provision of such services presupposes a capitalist accumulation which does not
exist on the appropriate scale. Household laundering of clothes could only be replaced by
industrial launderies (as far as costs are concerned) if the latter could emulate the low wage
levels paid currently to domestic servants. The chauffeur who drives the children of the
wealthy to their schools could only, realistically, be replaced by an efficient system of public
collective transport. Compared to the average North American, a middle-class Brazilian with
an equivalent money income, has a much higher standard of living and a much wider pattern
of consumption. The availability of family-level personal services, based upon the
exploitation of mainly female labour, is a particularly significant factor in explaining such
international contrasts.

References

CARDOSO, Fernando Henrique and FALETTO, Enzo (1970) *Dependência e Desenvolvimento na
América Latina*, Zahar Editores, Rio de Janeiro.

CLARK, Colin (1957) *The Conditions of Economic Progress*, Macmillan, London.

ETTORI, O. T. (n.d.) "Aspectos económicos da produção de milho em São Paulo" (unpublished
ms.).

FURTADO, Celso (1966) *Subdesenvolvimento e Estagnação na América Latina*, Civilização
Brasileira, Rio de Janeiro.

FURTADO, Celso (1971) "Dependência externa e teoria económica", *Trimestre Económico*,
Vol. 38 (2), No. 150.

ILPES (Instituto Latinamericano de Planificación Económica y Social) (1967) *La Brecha
Comercial y la Integración Latino-Americana*, Siglo XXI, Mexico City.

PAIVA, R. M. (1966) "Reflexoes sobre as tendências da produçao, da produtividade e dos preços
do setor agrícola do Brasil", *Revista Brasileira de Economia*, Ano 20, Nos. 2–3.

PAIVA, R. M. (1968) "O mecanismo de autocontrole no processo de expansão da melhoria técnica
da agricultura', *Revista Brasileira de Economia*, Ano 2, No. 3.

RANGEL, Ignacio (1963) *A Inflação Brasileira*, Tempo Brasileiro, Rio de Janeiro.

SINGER, Paul (1971) "Força de trabalho e emprego no Brasil, 1920–1969", *Cadernos CEBRAP*,
No. 3.

TAVARES, M. da Conceiçao and SERRA, José (1971) "Más allá del estancamiento: una discusión
sobre el estilo del desarrollo reciente de Brasil", *Trimestre Económico*, Vol. 38 (4), No. 152.

WEFFORT, Francisco (1966) "Estado e massas no Brasil", *Revista Civilização Brasileira*, Ano 1,
No. 7.

SECTION III

The exploitative coexistence of large and small in a single system

"Craftsmen who produce for a market are often in the clutches of moneylenders, of suppliers of raw materials, of middlemen who purchase and market their product, or of a single person who performs all these functions simultaneously. Earnings of craftsmen are often lower than those of unskilled wage laborers, and loans from moneylenders are used, as in agriculture, mainly for consumption purposes."

(Gunnar Myrdal 1968, *Asian Drama*, 1101–02)

"Child workers in Bombay's 'unorganized' construction industry . . . work alongside their parents, digging earth, carrying headloads of mud and mortar, preparing the mortar, removing the debris, straightening, cutting, bending and shouldering iron rods. . . . Contractors recruit the workers from drought-stricken villages."

(Sumanta Banerjee 1979, *Child Labour in India*, 17)

"What stands out about the so-called 'informal sector' is that it denotes primarily a system of very intense exploitation of labour, with very low wages and often very long hours, underpinned by the constant pressure for work from the 'reserve army' of job seekers. . . . The economic activities (and inactivities) it comprises . . . provide goods and services at a very low price, which makes possible the very high profits and wages of the 'formal sector'."

(Colin Leys 1973, "*Interpreting African Underdevelopment*", 426)

Introduction

The four essays in this section consider the ways in which small enterprises may be incorporated into the capital accumulation mechanisms of large corporate and State enterprises, the degree to which small enterprises are exploited by outside interests, and the extent to which such enterprises exploit their own labour force. The main focus is on the mechanisms establishing "dependency" through moneylending, the rent of premises or equipment, monopolistic supply of raw materials, and monopsonistic acquisition of the goods and services produced. This is linked to an examination of subcontracting ("putting out work") from large to small enterprises, and of the use of commission selling and piecework arrangements as means to "disguise" a wage-working relationship (see Bromley and Gerry 1979, 6; Gerry and Birkbeck 1981).

The relatively large numbers of small enterprises working in many branches of economic activity, combined with the strongly individualistic and somewhat petit bourgeois attitude often characteristic of small-scale entrepreneurs, tends to produce intense competition. Such competition combines with the pressures of middlemen, moneylenders, and larger firms offering subcontracts, to pare down margins and prices to such a low level that the small enterprises can only continue to operate if they intensively use very cheap labour, and if they avoid investing in the sorts of premises, equipment and facilities which would ensure healthy, pleasant and safe working conditions. The result, in many cases, is a "sweat-shop"—a small manufacturing or repair establishment where people work long hours in overcrowded, unsanitary and dangerous conditions, and where much of the work is often performed by women and children because they are considered cheaper and more docile than able-bodied men. In other cases the result is the small individual or family enterprise—a workshop, shop, market stall or street stall where the individuals involved work long hours, often exposed to the elements and to possible theft or assault, and frequently lacking the certificates and licences required by the authorities.

The situation of small enterprises and their relations with larger enterprises are best understood in terms of the relationships between labour and capital on both the global and national scales. In competitive situations with considerable fluctuations in consumer demand, capital has three major alternative strategies to hold down labour costs in order to increase profits and market shares (see Portes and Walton 1981, 55–56). The classic strategy in the more highly industrialized countries has been technological innovation, using new equipment and production line techniques to increase labour productivity. A second and alternative strategy is to seek cheaper labour, contracting from such groups as women, the young, ethnic and cultural minorities, and legal and illegal immigrants. There is a continuous quest for cheap, docile labour, and a series of legal measures are taken so as to ensure a high labour turnover, to avoid paying for costly social welfare benefits, insurance and pension schemes, and to prevent the formation of powerful trade unions. The third alternative is to transfer production to enterprises with cheaper labour, either within the country or in other countries which are renowned for their cheap, "well-disciplined" labour forces. In some cases these enterprises may be wholly or partly the property of the large capitalist enterprise which is transferring production (see e.g. Grossman 1978–1979; Siegel 1978–1979), while in others they are subcontractors owned by interests separate from those of the major enterprise, but under contract to perform specific tasks or to provide specific goods for the major enterprise.

International subcontracting is an increasingly significant aspect of the emerging global division of labour (see e.g. Berthomieu and Hanaut 1980; Germidis 1981), with productive activities being located according to the comparative advantages of the countries concerned, and with multinational companies deliberately choosing to operate through quasi-autonomous subsidiaries or through smaller local firms. Such decisions reflect the nervousness of many large companies about the possibilities of strikes or expropriation if they establish their own factories in other countries, and also their concern to achieve the maximum flexibility in their operations by adjusting the volumes and sources of subcontracted supplies according to fluctuating levels of demand and the relative prices of alternative subcontractors.

Of even greater significance than international subcontracting is subcontracting within individual countries. Under certain sets of market conditions and of technological, legal and institutional circumstances, direct investment by large enterprises may be the most efficient means for them to increase their profits. Such direct investment is most likely to take place when market and general economic conditions are in a state of sustained expansion, and when there is a stable and strong government willing to use repressive measures to restrain the trade union movement and to hold down workers' real incomes. When some or all of these circumstances do not prevail, indirect investment may occur through quasi-autonomous subsidiaries, or there may be subcontracting to "outside" firms and individuals. Such subcontracting not only transfers much of the work to smaller enterprises, but also transfers to them most of the risk inherent in unstable market conditions. A vivid example of such subcontracting in most Third World countries can be found in the construction industry, and particularly in the construction of offices, apartment blocks and housing estates. In such activities the major construction companies usually rely very heavily on subcontracted small firms and "foremen/contractors", who provide both specialized services such as plumbing and electrical work, and also gangs of unskilled labourers with no "direct relationship" to the company organizing the construction (see e.g. MacEwen Scott 1979; Stretton 1979).

Subcontracting relationships between large and small enterprises are paralleled by the various intermediate employment relationships between the two polar extremes of "career wage-work" and "career self-employment". These intermediate relationships can be collectively described as "casual work", and they are characterized by the lack of even a moderate degree of stability and security of income and work opportunities (see Bromley and Gerry 1979, 5–11). This does not mean that all casual workers change occupation, or even change job, with great frequency, but rather that they are continually faced with considerable risks which may force them to change occupation in order to survive.

Casual work can be crudely divided into four broad, and occasionally overlapping ideal type-categories, which, if put in order of increasing dissimilarity from career wage-work are: "short-term wage-work", "disguised wage-work", "dependent work", and "precarious self-employment" (which grades into "career self-employment", the other extreme of the continuum). These four categories can be described as follows:

1. *Short-term wage-work:* This is paid and contracted by the day, week, month or season (so-called casual labour), or paid and contracted for fixed terms or tasks, with no assurance of continuity of employment, for example "on probation", "for a specific one-off job", or as "peak period assistance". Short-term wage-work is recognized as wage-work in law, but it carries relatively few of the benefits to the worker which are associated with career wage-work (redundancy pay, sickness benefits, family benefits, insurance, pensions, holiday pay, special bonuses, etc.) The employer normally provides short-term wage-workers with most or all of their equipment, raw materials and other inputs, and in most cases short-term wage-workers work on the employer's premises at specific times, and for specific periods, as defined in a verbal or written contract of employment.

2. *Disguised wage-work:* In this case, a firm or group of firms regularly and directly appropriates a fixed proportion of the product of a person's work without that person legally being an employee of the firm or group of firms. For example, many firms utilize "outworkers" for manufacturing and repair operations; workers who work in their own homes performing specific productive functions in return for a payment

predetermined by the firm for each task or piece—a form of off-premises work which is not defined as "employment" in most countries, but rather as a type of subcontracting. Similarly, many manufacturing firms, wholesalers and insurance companies retail through commission sellers, vendors who receive an agreed sum as their commission for each sale, and who only sell the products of one firm or of a few related firms. A more sophisticated form of commission selling is "franchising", which is of great importance in North America and Western Europe (especially in the "fast food" business—e.g. Kentucky Fried Chicken), but which is not yet significant in the Third World. In this system a large firm (the "franchisor") "sponsors" a number of quasi-independent entrepreneurs (the "franchisees"), who establish and run businesses according to a standard model prescribed by the franchisor. The franchisor supplies raw materials, service delivery techniques, packaging, decoration and advertising, and sometimes also training, credit, equipment and buildings, and the contract between franchisor and franchisee prescribes a system of payments and reumerations including a more-or-less fixed commission on sales (see Ozanne and Hunt 1971; Sklar 1977). "Outworkers", "commission sellers" and "franchisees" can all select their own working hours as long as they bear in mind the need to obtain a subsistence income and to maintain a good relationship with "the firm".

3. *Dependent work:* In this case, the worker is not in open or disguised wage-work, as there is no wage payment or fixed commission, but is dependent upon one or more larger enterprises for credit and/or the rental of premises or equipment. The credit and/or rental arrangement provides a mechanism for the appropriation of part of the product of the worker's labour, and the opportunity to work is dependent on its continued availability. Typical examples are the carpenter who works in rented premises and buys the necessary equipment with a loan, and the taxi driver who operates someone else's vehicle keeping any earnings over-and-above a fixed rental and running costs. A further example is the street trader who normally sells products bought from a specific wholesaler because only that wholesaler will allow credit on the purchase of merchandise. The key differences between dependent work and disguised wage-work concern the relationship between appropriation and production. In dependent work appropriation is through the payment of a fixed sum of rent and/or interest by the worker, agreed prior to the onset of production, rather than through the operation of a fixed margin of commission. Thus, in dependent work the worker is not usually constrained by fixed prices and proportional deductions, and there is no necessary relationship between the amount of appropriation and the amount of production.

4. *Precarious self-employment:* In this case the worker has two major characteristics; considerable instability of income and insecurity of

work opportunities (i.e. the work is casual), and self-employment (i.e. working independently, doing a job without engaging in open or disguised wage-work or in dependent work). Most self-employment is clearly precarious, both because of the sharp fluctuations in environmental and economic circumstances which characterize the work opportunities involved, and because of the worker's lack of protection against loss of work opportunities through such natural and man-made disasters as drought, fire, accidents at work, and arbitrary closure by order of local officials. Self-employed workers must, of course, rely on inputs provided by others, on the receipt of outputs by others, and on a system of payment in goods, services or money. However, the keys to their self-employment are that they have a considerable and relatively free choice of suppliers and outlets, and also that they own their means of production.

The above typology of social relations of production and appropriation in casual work is not only useful in examining the employment of individual workers, but also in examining the structuring of firms and the relationships between smaller and larger enterprises. Thus, small enterprises based on family labour, partnership or wage-labour, may develop relationships with larger firms which are similar in type to those developed between individual workers and firms providing them with opportunities to work. For example, if a male welder employing two assistants on his own premises agrees to produce metallic structures for a larger firm on a continuing basis, receiving the raw materials from that larger firm and being remunerated at a fixed price for each finished structure that he produces, then both his small firm and by inference he himself, are converted into disguised wage-workers of the larger firm. Indeed, large firms who are unwilling to take on extra activities and contract extra wage-workers onto their own payroll may establish a whole cluster of relationships with smaller enterprises. There may well also be further subcontracting by subcontractors of the larger firm, so that a whole hierarchy of indirect relations of production is established forming an archipelago of inter-related economic activities centred on a particular large firm. It is in this context of partially decentralized production that the full significance of casual work and subcontracting can be appreciated as a means by which the owners of capital can increase the diversity and profitability of production without substantially increasing their own long-term commitments. Casual workers and small enterprises are used to carry much of the burden of risk in unstable and insecure situations, being incorporated into the economic system when extra labour and production is advantageous, and being excluded from the same system when they are no longer needed.

All of the issues discussed so far in this introduction are further explored in A. C. Lewin's major essay, "The dialectic of dominance" (Chapter 7), covering economic, social and political issues relating to capital–labour relations and the significance of small enterprises on the global scale. His approach is particularly innovative in the consideration of the ideological and cultural underpinnings of petty production, the media manipulation of petty producers, and the processes of class formation which affect those working in small enterprises.

Lewin's wide-ranging analysis is followed by three detailed case studies of specific economic activities in individual countries: John Harriss on engineering in Coimbatore, South India (Chapter 8); Chris Gerry on the sale of gambling opportunities in Cali, Colombia (Chapter 9); and a collective essay by the Anti-Slavery Society on Morocco's carpet industry (Chapter 10). Harriss provides an in-depth analysis of subcontracting in manufacturing activities, covering the sorts of enterprises and issues which are most frequently taken into consideration in existing small enterprise promotion policies in Third World countries. In sharp contrast, Gerry examines disguised wage-working in a little-studied but relatively important group of service occupations—the sale of tickets for State lotteries and for "numbers games" organized by private companies. His essay raises numerous issues relating to labour exploitation and to the role of the State as "disguised employer", regulator of employment relationships, recipient of tax incomes, organizer of lotteries, and agent in the redistribution of income, wealth and public services. The final essay, by the Anti-Slavery Society, provides a description and analysis of manufacturing sweat-shops with mainly female child labour, covering both small and medium-scale enterprises and also considering the international marketing factors which determine competitiveness on the broader scale.

The four essays in this section provide ample food for thought regarding the role of government in regulating small enterprises. "Exploitation" is revealed as a major issue, both *of* and *within* small enterprises, and this exploitation is shown to be reproduced on both the international and the national scales as a major factor underlying the "competitiveness" of small enterprises. In many cases, if small enterprises raise their prices and profit margins so that their workers can earn more and can afford to work less hard, they lose their competitive edge and production either ceases to take place or is shifted to other firms within the country or in foreign countries. In other cases, however, the "hyper-exploitation" of labour in small enterprises reflects little more than the greed and inhumanity of the petty entrepreneurs who run those enterprises. Governments are therefore placed in a triple dilemma: how much to simply ignore labour exploitation and to promote economic activity in all scales of enterprise because it contributes to total production and consumption?; how much to attempt to regulate export production, foreign investment and international subcontracting within the country, given that negative controls may reduce the exploitation of local labour, but that they may also reduce national competitiveness and lead to a shift of production to other countries?; and, how much to regulate working conditions and labour use in small enterprises, given that such enterprises are both numerous and difficult to enumerate, that controls require considerable effort and expenditure, and that such regulation is highly susceptible to corruption?

References

BANERJEE, Sumanta (1979) *Child Labour in India*, Anti-Slavery Society, London.

BERTHOMIEU, C. and HANAUT, A. (1980) "Can international subcontracting promote industrialization?", *International Labour Review*, Vol. 119, pp. 335–49.

BROMLEY, Ray and GERRY, Chris (1979) "Who are the casual poor?", in Ray Bromley and Chris Gerry (eds.) *Casual Work and Poverty in Third World Cities*, Wiley, Chichester, pp. 3–23.

GERMIDIS, D. (1981) *International Subcontracting: A New Form of Investment*, OECD (Organization for Economic Cooperation and Development) Development Centre, Paris.

GERRY, Chris and BIRKBECK, Chris (1981) "The petty commodity producer in Third World cities: petit-bourgeois or 'disguised' proletarian?", in Frank Bechhofer and Brian Elliott (eds.) *The Petite Bourgeoisie*, Macmillan, London, pp. 121–54.

GROSSMAN, Rachel (1978–79) "Women's place in the integrated circuit", *Southeast Asia Chronicle*, No. 66, and *Pacific Research*, Vol. 9, No. 5–6, joint issue, pp. 2–17.

LEYS, Colin (1973) "Interpreting African underdevelopment: reflections on the ILO report on Employment, Incomes and Equality in Kenya", *African Affairs*, Vol. 72, pp. 419–29.

MACEWEN SCOTT, Alison (1979) "Who are the self-employed?", in Ray Bromley and Chris Gerry (eds.), *op. cit.*, pp. 105–29.

MYRDAL, Gunnar (1968) *Asian Drama: An Inquiry into the Poverty of Nations*, Pantheon/Random House, New York.

OZANNE, Urban B. and HUNT, Shelby D. (1971) *The Economic Effects of Franchising*, United States Senate, Select Committee on Small Business, 92nd Congress, First Session, Washington D.C.

PORTES, Alejandro and WALTON, John (1981) *Labor, Class, and the International System*, Academic Press, New York.

SIEGEL, Lenny (1978–79) "Orchestrating dependency", *Southeast Asia Chronicle*, No. 66, and *Pacific Research*, Vol. 9, No. 5–6, joint issue, pp. 24–27.

SKLAR, Fred (1977) "Franchises and independence", *Urban Life*, Vol. 6, pp. 33–52.

STRETTON, Alan (1979) "Instability of employment among building industry labourers in Manila", in Ray Bromley and Chris Gerry (eds.), *op. cit.*, pp. 267–82.

CHAPTER 7

The dialectic of dominance: petty production and peripheral capitalism*

A. C. LEWIN

Employment and unemployment in Third World cities have been the subjects of a wide-ranging debate which began in the early 1950s and has gained momentum in recent years. Whereas in its initial phase the discussion centred on the issues of labour surplus and its absorption, in recent years the focus of scientific attention has turned to the structure and role of the "informal sector" or "petty production" in the urban economy and the post-colonial State.

The following discussion is an attempt to summarize both the empirical evidence and the theoretical positions of diverse authors, to compare the available evidence and to discuss its implications, identifying some of the weaknesses of the various arguments. It also endeavours to discern the *objective* role and functions of petty production within the context of peripheral capitalism and the neo-colonial State and to throw some light on the social forces involved.

Informal sector or petty production: some comments on the nature of the debate

Issues of rural–urban migration, labour force composition and employment policy in the Third World have been the subject of considerable scientific attention and debate for nearly half a century.[1]† The measurement of potential labour availability and of labour productivity started when colonial governments were confronting problems of labour shortage, and these issues have been complemented in more recent, post-colonial times by a growing concern with urban underemployment (however defined) and unemployment,

---

*An original essay prepared especially for this book in cooperation with Dr. D. Peukert, University of Essen, Germany.
†Superscript numbers refer to Notes at end of chapter.

related to the increasing out-migration from rural areas. The following topics have received particular attention since the mid-fifties:

— labour surplus transfer from subsistence economy to productive employment (Lewis 1954);
— labour supply and measurement (Weeks 1971);
— employment and unemployment, definition and quantification (Jolly, de Kadt, Singer and Wilson 1973);
— the identification of "traditional" versus "modern" sectors, and the subsequent distinction between "formal" and "informal" sectors of the urban economy (Hart 1973).

The neo-classical and liberal paradigm of a two-sector model, has been the subject of an on-going debate and criticism which need not be recounted here (Bromley and Gerry 1979; Sethuraman 1981). Nevertheless, and for the sake of the following discussion, it may be useful to summarize the arguments of several scholars who loosely may be labelled as radicals, and who have made a more fundamental attempt to identify the role and status of the "informal sector" in the capital-labour process of underdeveloped economies.[2] Despite substantial differences in approach, methodology and conclusions, the hypotheses and theory evolved indicate a common matrix and a consensus based on the Marxist approach. The concepts involved may be outlined as follows:

a. The "informal sector" represents, in fact, a subordinate mode of production understandable only within the larger framework of capitalist relations of production, extraction and surplus appropriation, and their articulation in the countries of the Third World.
b. The term "petty production" (including the production of both goods and services) does not refer to the size of operations but rather the subordinate pre-capitalist mode of production and its relative position *vis-à-vis* the dominant capitalist mode of production. Implicitly (and for some authors explicitly), petty production is a transitional mode which is either gradually dissolved and replaced by dominant capitalism or is being itself transformed into capitalist production.
c. However, as opposed to the highly developed capitalist countries, petty production continues to persist in the underdeveloped ones and is even promoted by dominant capitalism, which prefers to extract surplus value by means of subcontracting. Thus, the costs and risks of capitalist production are transferred to—and shared by—the proletarianized petty producers who eventually become disguised wage labour (sub-contractees, outworkers, etc.).
d. This process of differentiation of capital–labour relations cannot be explained in terms of a polarity replacing the formal–informal sector duality, but rather as a continuum or "ensemble" (Gerry 1979) which is

governed by a dialectical, rather than a simple, functional relationship. Petty production does not exist simply to serve dominant capitalism, and there are constellations under which dependence may be mutual (Portes 1978).

e. The objective function of petty production *vis-à-vis* dominant capitalism is to lower the variable capital costs of capitalist production through the production of cheap wage-goods and to hold down industrial wages, facilitating reproduction and accumulation. In the wider context of underdevelopment, petty production provides cheap consumer goods and services to masses of the population, thereby setting in motion an indirect process of surplus appropriation (mainly in the sphere of circulation), where subordination also takes place.

f. The petty producers are not a homogeneous and static mass of the urban or the working poor. Rather they represent a heterogeneous societal formation which can be heuristically disaggregated by form and degree of ownership of the means of production and of subordination to capital. The different positions of the petty producer (proprietor) and his labourers *vis-à-vis* the capitalist mode of production suggest a process of class formation and differentiation which may lead to the growth of a petty *bourgeoisie* amongst the subordinated producers. At the other pole of the disaggregation, the parasitical "lumpenproletariat", with non-functional or disfunctional relations with capitalism, can be located.

Although the "petty production theory" and its empirical evidence have carried serious debate beyond the gross over-simplifications of dualistic analysis, a number of weaknesses, deficiencies and contradictions need to be scrutinized carefully in an attempt to further evolve the theoretical framework. A critical assessment proves somewhat difficult as the implicit conclusions do not always reflect the authors' convictions. Furthermore, some of the basic issues discussed below have been considered by various scholars, though without attributing to them the significance which they deserve. The following points and arguments will thus require further elaboration:

a. Practically all the theoretical assumptions made are based on empirical surveys of one sphere of petty production in a single country. Attempts to compare the results inter-occupationally and cross-culturally are conspicuous by their absence, so that comparable phenomena are not used to verify the generalizations produced. The degree of capitalist penetration and its particular mould in the context of underdevelopment are, however, essential for the understanding of the relative size and significance of petty production and of the processes affecting it in a given situation.

b. Terminology and concepts such as capitalism, pre-capitalism and petit bourgeois are used indiscriminately. Although the widely recognized concept of peripheral capitalism is acknowledged by some of the radical authors (e.g. Gerry 1979; Portes 1978), the application and implications of the theory for the study of petty production are largely neglected. One cannot escape the impression that the "capitalisms" in the core and in the periphery are treated alike, as equal instruments of domination.

c. Consequently, the complexity and contradictions of the peripheral capitalist mode of production and reproduction, the intricate composition and the role of social forces and social relations of production, the instruments and apparatus of domination and subordination, and the significance of deformed pre-capitalist relations of production, are either neglected or at best described but not analysed.

d. The historical perspectives of peripheral capitalist penetration and domination, its transformation under conditions of post-colonialism, the ensuing contradictions and their articulation, are essential for the understanding and interpretation of the universe of petty production and its dynamics. Whereas a number of scholars have recognized the significance of historical processes and describe some of their attributes (e.g. King 1977), fundamental political–economic evaluation of the texture within which petty production unfolds and of its historical dimensions is usually either absent or superficial.

e. Capitalist domination in the periphery is exercised through a complex of alliances among hierarchically interacting dominant and subordinated societal formations and social forces, reinforced and reproduced by the repressive and ideological apparata and their instruments of domination. Surplus appropriation in the periphery occurs not so much at the level of capitalist production of goods as in the sphere of circulation, through a chain of interrelated and subordinate intermediaries and agents essential for the assertion and reproduction of the structure's dominance. The position and role of petty production in the process of "subordinate" surplus appropriation and *vis-à-vis* the various social forces which comprise the vertically interacting alliance, have not yet received the attention they deserve. Instead, and despite assertions to the contrary, a new deterministic dichotomy of capitalist versus petty production has been produced—an undifferentiated and sometimes simplistic polarity where the "objective laws of history" dictate a progressive process of subordination, transition and proletarianization of the petty producers (e.g. Gerry 1980).

f. Class formation and consciousness are the sum of the individuals' and groups' experiences, and their reproduction and interrelationships at both the cultural–symbolic and the economic–structural levels. Although labouring takes on different specific forms and meaning in different societies, there are some similarities in the articulation of social relations of production under peripheral capitalism which may help to explain the class "position" of petty producers. The penetration of monopolistic capitalism does not destroy the vertical, patrimonial hierarchy of pre-capitalist social formations, but rather deforms their social relations to serve a particular mode of domination. Vertical orientation and transmuted traditional values, with their symbolic expressions and accumulated experience, continually reproduce themselves through a dialectical process of resistance-adaptation to cultural and ideological domination. In turn, this process contributes to the shaping of a contradictory consciousness of the petty producers and their labourers.

An understanding of the complex issues of "class" identity among petty producers cannot be obtained from the application of vacuous blanket terminology such as "underemployment" and "petite bourgeoisie". Instead, it must derive from a concrete and unprejudiced investigation of individualistic relations and conditions of production, of the implications of patrimonial social relations, and of the instruments and role of cultural–ideological domination. The critical arguments voiced here are not intended to discredit the petty production theory and its conclusions regarding the role of petty production *vis-à-vis* the dominant capitalist mode of production. They are rather aimed at proposing a more differentiated and complex framework for research and discussion, placing much greater emphasis on the theory of peripheral capitalism.

Capitalist and petty production in the periphery: the theory and the evidence

Fundamental to the understanding and interpretation of societal processes under peripheral capitalism are the external conditions affecting the occurrence, constitution and articulation of social forces and determining also the degree to which contradictions prove inevitable. Neither the asymmetric penetration of the dependent periphery by monopolistic (core) capitalism, nor the means by which it asserts its dominance, are merely economic. They are also expressed through the manipulation and control of socialization and the communications media (cultural imperialism), and of the political, military and legal systems (political imperialism). Even more notably, they are expressed through the orientation of economic reproduction in the periphery to the requirements of the core-metropolis: economic imperialism and dependent reproduction (Senghaas 1974).

Societal formations in the periphery are distinguished by diverse modes of production, hierarchically related to each other and functionally dependent on the requirements of the dominant, dynamic, capitalist pole of the periphery. The modes and relations of production which fall outside the dynamic pole of capitalist production are neither capitalist nor pre-capitalist, but can only be described as mixed forms. They need to be examined in terms of their subordinate location and role, not only *vis-à-vis* the dominant capitalist mode, but also in terms of their significance for societal processes and formations.

The structural heterogeneity of the periphery is a fundamental character-istic of a society which did not develop out of its own autonomous dynamics, but through dependent reproduction of various social forces. The penetration of capitalist relations of production in their economic and cultural–ideological manifestations has, however, remained partial, due to the particular trajectory of the dominant core-capital. It has affected and deformed other modes and relations of production, which have been subordinated to the capitalist mode and made dependent on its particular requirements. Thus, the size, composition, structural attributes and forms of subordination of petty production can only be understood as a function of the peripheral capitalist economy. However, the nature, mode and dynamics of capitalist penetration and domination in the periphery are subject to heteronomous forces and influences, and are by no means the same throughout the Third World.

The reproduction of social formations under peripheral capitalism is determined by their orientation towards the core. The dominant local social forces which have emerged prior to, in the course of, or after formal independence, are economically, socially and culturally dependent on, oriented to and allied with those of the core. Despite real conflicts of interest among various segments of the dominant local formations (landowners, commercial–industrial interests, political–bureaucratic élites, the military, etc.), and implicit or explicit contradictions between local and foreign dominant forces, such formations represent an alliance of interests main-tained through a complex system of bonds and the exercise of economic, social and cultural–ideological dominance.

Historically, it is possible to distinguish between colonial and post-colonial direct extraction and transfer, and the more recent period of indirect monopoly-dominance through import-substitution dependent on technology and capital goods supplied by the core-metropolis. A further variation of indirect dominance is indicated by the "privileged subcentres" (e.g. Brazil, Taiwan, Philippines and South Korea).

A basic and highly generalized picture of the historical changes affecting forms of subordination of petty production suggests that the colonial restriction of commodity production to raw materials, combined with the import of industrial products from the metropolitan core (particularly clothing and footwear, basic consumer goods and beverages), brought about the decline of artisan production. This process has gained momentum with the "import substitution" policy adopted by most Third World countries, and it has been reinforced further by the introduction and diffusion of capital-intensive advanced technology under the monopolist control of multinational corporations (Quijano 1974). As a result, the marginalized and finally redundant petty commodity producers are forced into the army of casual workers who seek employment in petty commerce and services, and in construction and other day-labour (see Bromley and Gerry 1979).

While this picture may hold true for most cases, it is not *per se* adequate to elucidate the diverse variables affecting capitalist penetration and their impact on petty production. The trajectory of capitalist growth and production in the periphery may be determined by such factors as:

a. Types and volume of primary export goods produced (agricultural monocultures, minerals and other natural resources), and the level of concentration and nationalization in production.

b. Fluctuations in world market prices and their impact on GDP, balance of payments, etc.

c. Capital inflow due to the cash remittances of labour employed abroad (e.g. Pakistan, Turkey) or to sizeable foreign aid programmes (e.g. Tanzania, Bangladesh).

d. The share of GDP which is actually spent on consumption and its restrictions (e.g. by expenditures for armaments).

e. The structure and role of public-sector production.

f. The expansion and stabilization of the consumer market in the post-colonial State, and particularly the evolution of new social formations (e.g. cash crop producers, public-sector employees, professionals, intermediaries, blue-collar workers, and small entrepreneurs).

g. The degree of orientation and inter-relationships with the "old" colonial core or "new" core-metropoli.

Capitalist penetration and domination in the periphery is by no means harmonious and homogeneous. It is rather characterized by contradictions resulting from the competition for markets, resources and privileges among the various fractions of dominant capital aided by their local allies. To some extent, structural contradictions are inherent to peripheral capitalism, where the grossly ineffective, vertically hierarchical bureaucracy (repressive apparatus), essential for the maintenance of dominance, simultaneously undermines or impedes the national and impersonal decision-making process of monopoly capital.

The common image of dynamic and aggressive capitalist expansion in the periphery and the gradual elimination of petty production needs thus to be carefully examined and scrutinized on the basis of available empirical evidence for the individual regions and countries. Comparison suggests that capitalist (capital-intensive and technologically advanced) investment in predominantly import-substituting consumer-goods industry may also be stimulated or restrained by the following political–economic and market factors, in addition to those already mentioned:[3]

a. Existing policy measures to encourage foreign investment, including cheap credits, concessions, monopolies, tax holidays, free profit repatriation and other incentives.

   b. Competition with other established monopolies, and particularly multinational corporations, for similar markets and products.
   c. Market structure, size and loopholes (macro-economic determinants).
   d. Risk minimization: inflationary trends, fluctuations and seasonality of demand, changes in tastes, etc.
   e. Availability of physical infrastructure for the production and distribution network on the national level and for communication (advertising).
   f. The ultimate profitability consideration, whereby investment in the periphery is justified only when returns are significantly higher than in the core (Amin 1974).
   g. Costs of labour (including fringe benefits), advanced technology, and sophisticated distribution (circulation) mechanisms.
   h. Bureaucratic and political constraints: bureaucratic inefficiency, tightening government control, radical unionization of the skilled labour force, and agitation of radical political parties and progressive social forces.
   i. Actual or envisaged political instability.

Depending on the particular constellation and impact of such variables, as well as the degree of dominant capitalist penetration, a cross-cultural comparison may indicate that there are whole spheres and regions where direct competition and the elimination of petty production do not take place, either because dominant capitalism is not inclined to invest or is incapable of competing. Although generalized statements are of little use in considering non-comparable development paths, some examples may help to illustrate the argument:

   a. There are a whole range of consumer goods which are not conducive to capital-intensive production in particular situations (e.g. footwear, ready-made clothing) and are either ignored by dominant capital or subcontracted to petty producers.
   b. In a large number of countries (e.g. Indonesia, Bangladesh, Nigeria and Egypt), hardware and other household goods are produced out of waste materials or a mixture of waste and imported, semi-processed materials (e.g. aluminium sheets), which are compatible with industrial products or are even cheaper and more durable. The same may apply to other "basic-needs" articles and a variety of spare parts for vehicles and machinery which are unavailable locally (due to import restriction, outdated models etc.) or are too costly (Papola 1978).
   c. Many forms of traditional artisan production, such as the manufacture of jewellery and ornaments (gold and silver—which are a major form of accumulation and investment), folk-weavings, furniture, and tools for peasant agriculture, continue to prevail throughout the Third World and are not conducive to capital-intensive production.
   d. In the spheres of commerce and personal services, the direct penetration

of dominant capital is relatively weak, though there are numerous processes of subordination through such mechanisms as subcontracting, piecework and the manipulation of credit. Impersonal distribution networks such as supermarkets and discount warehouses are of almost no significance outside the major cities of most Third World countries. Despite higher prices, small and petty traders offer the advantages of small quantities, the possibility of credit, long hours, vicinity to the consumer's residence or place of work, and social communications through gossip and the exchange of information (Tokman 1978).

e. Large and nationalized construction companies are rarely found in the context of underdevelopment, due to the risks involved, market fluctuations and the low rate of return on investment in equipment. Instead, piecework is usually (chain) subcontracted—a practice also found in the core capitalist countries (Stretton 1979). In addition, however, a large number of independent masons, bricklayers, plumbers, electricians, etc., are engaged in the construction of squatter (unauthorized) dwellings and are not related to the capitalist construction sector (e.g. Clinard 1966).

f. In the realm of transport, capitalist companies and enterprises, whether public or private, rarely replace the multitude of often antiquated taxis, jitneys, rickshaws and similar transport which are less packed, quicker and often independent of fixed routes, while prices do not differ substantially. As in most of the other branches mentioned above, transport operators are usually in relations of dependency, the nature of which is still to be examined.

g. Repair and life extension, predominantly of industrial articles, plays a significant role in societies characterized by extremely uneven income distribution and low earnings. The momentous increase in the number of petty repairers and workshops during the last two decades (e.g. Moir 1978; Papola 1978) betrays not only the decreasing employment opportunities in other spheres of petty production, in industry and in the public sector, but also the downward proliferation of "luxury" consumer goods.

The notion that the avenues open to expansion by petty producers are those not yet profitable for capitalist production (Bromley 1978b; Gerry 1980), or that when a remunerative market has been identified and tested by petty producers, it will be taken over by multinational capitalist industry (Bienefeld 1975), is therefore not universally applicable and depends on a complex of factors and market-demand elasticities in a given situation. It can be assumed further that the oil crisis, which has seriously affected most of the Third World, may slow the path of capital-intensive investment and production and eventually stimulate and revive petty production.

The above discussion and arguments do not deny the dominance and expansion of monopoly capitalism. Where competition between capitalist and petty production takes place, the latter will be driven out of the market and its operators marginalized. The role and significance of petty production are, however, to be sought in the sphere of the social relations of production essential for the exercise and maintenance of the structure of dominance, rather than in the polarity of capitalist versus petty production.

The dialectic of dominance

The subordination of petty production by dominant capital and its role in the process of surplus appropriation have been the subjects of both empirical study and theoretical discourse.[4]

The central and generally-accepted paradigm suggests that by providing cheap consumer goods and services, petty production gives dominant capital an accelerated rate of surplus appropriation and profits which are transferred to the core, constituting a drain of resources from the periphery. This mode of surplus appropriation applies not only to the relatively small labour force engaged by capitalist (import substitution) industry, but indirectly to the entire market and consumption mechanism in the periphery, which is essential for the reproduction of capitalist dominance.[5]

Based on empirical studies, several (and to some extent corollary) determinants of the mode of subordination/surplus appropriation by dominant capital were identified. These include: implicit subordination via labour processes (the reserve army theory), indirect subordination through the market mechanism, and direct subordination and surplus appropriation through capital–labour and production relations.

The reserve army theory suggests that, as a result of rationalization and the introduction of capitalist relations of production in agriculture, the surplus rural labour force is expelled and forced to seek wage-employment in the cities. Being unable to find more than casual work, it is marginalized predominantly in the sphere of circulation-distribution (petty trade) and performs the task of a "reserve army of labour" which suppresses wages in the capitalist sector (Quijano 1974). This theory has been challenged by a number of scholars who have analysed the structure of wage determination in the capitalist sector and proved that both the growing specialization as a result of technological advancement and capital intensity, and the complex mechanism of wage determination (government–employers–unions), make the "reserve army" redundant in the considerations of dominant capital (Portes 1978). Not yet analysed, however, is the respective role of job-seeking casual labour in the sphere of circulation–distribution, personal services and, to some extent, also petty manufacturing and repair, where little or no skill–education is required and the competition for jobs tends to increase. Likewise, the role of casual labour circulating between wage–employment and petty production, and especially its function in "regulating" the labour market, requires a more profound study and explanations which have not been offered by current research.

Indirect subordination of petty producers by dominant capital and the related processes of surplus appropriation take place through the actions of a complex network of intermediaries at the levels of supply and circulation, aided by the "regulating" functions of the State. Thus, the asymmetric symbiosis of peripheral capitalism and the structure of indirect subordination and dependence are reflected in the following elements of the system: the monopolization of inputs supplies for petty manufacturing and services; the limits placed on access to credit, skills and technology; the dependence on the growth of imports or of local capitalist industry to ensure an adequate supply of semi-processed and waste materials, and of ageing equipment to repair; the regulation of distribution through import controls, licences, incentives and concessions intended to benefit the dominant capitalist interests; and, finally, the direct harassment of petty producers so as to limit the range and scale of their activities and to create something of the image of the "city beautiful" favoured by local élites.

Direct subordination involves control over the means of production and production processes through the labour process—i.e. the subordination of labour to capital (Bose 1978; Gerry 1979). In the realm of commodity production, and equally in the sphere of such services as recuperation (e.g. sifting through garbage to find industrial raw materials such as scrap metal and paper) and the retail distribution of mass consumer goods, dominant capitalist enterprises may subcontract specific tasks to petty producers or outworkers, rather than assume production directly. Such subcontracting may take place for any or all of the following reasons:[6]

a. To spread fixed capital costs between petty production and capitalist enterprise. The means of production are owned or hired by the petty producers, and such costs as repair and maintenance, interest, and amortization are also borne by them.
b. To transfer social costs to the petty producer and to evade factory legislation.
c. Because minimum wage regulations need not be observed, and costs of labour can be reduced through piece-wages and outwork.
d. Because prices can be manipulated and even depressed, particularly when inputs or loans have been provided by the capitalist enterprise.
e. To adapt to market instability, insecurity and fluctuations, so that the costs of intermittent production (and unemployment) can be transferred to the petty producer.
f. Because petty producers may specialize and acquire expertise in particular production processes, especially those of a very labour-intensive nature.

In an attempt to illustrate capital–labour relations, the subsumption of labour to capital, and the process of class formation, Gerry (1980) has identified the following five categories, which will be discussed below: "direct" wage employment; reserve (circulating) army of labour; "disguised" wage employment; "pure" self-employment; and the "residuum" (open unemployed). Significant as this typology is, it has notable limitations, resulting from the inadequacies of the theorem employed to interpret the mechanism and apparata through which social relations are reproduced and to identify social processes and levels of interaction of various social forces under peripheral capitalism.

An unbiased reading of the sparse, though highly instructive and rich evidence, reveals that relations of production, subordination and surplus appropriation hardly ever are formed directly between the capitalist enterprise and the petty producer. They are rather filtered through a complex network of intermediaries,[7] vertically hierarchized and functionally inter-related, in what seems to be an invisible alliance of social formations which help to reproduce peripheral capitalist dominance. In order to examine the nature of this alliance and the role of such intermediaries, themselves subordinated to the dominant social formations, some general observations on the articulation of the various social forces, and on their reproduction and interaction under peripheral capitalism, are necessary.

Capitalism in the periphery is a product of historical processes and developments determined by the particular mode of penetration of the periphery by the core and the modes of extraction and surplus appropriation. These, in turn, have given rise to, and have shaped, the various social formations and forces, distinguished by diverse modes of production which are hierarchically related to each other and functionally dependent on the requirements of dominant capitalist production. The nature of capitalist dominance in the periphery cannot, however, be explained in terms of economic penetration and hegemony alone. It rather needs to be examined in the light of the historical and social processes, conditions and experiences which have instigated the emergent social forces and which determine their means of material and cultural reproduction, their articulation, coalescence and alliances, as well as their differentiation and contradictions. Thus, capitalist dominance and reproduction in the periphery does not take place in a vacuum or through ambiguous capital–labour relations, but rather through hierarchical and symbiotic interaction of the prevailing social forces. Its means of self-assertion and reproduction are vertical–patrimonial social interaction and the resulting economic dependence, reinforced by the instruments of the repressive and cultural–ideological State apparata.[8]

In attempting to determine the nature of patrimonial hierarchies, one enters upon treacherous ground, considering the variability and heterogeneity of their manifestation. Loosely they may be described as the transformation and deformation of pre-capitalist traditional systems and rules of personal exchange. In a society without a national–capitalist market, domination can be exercised only through hierarchical personal relations and exchange. The economy builds on graded ownership rights and extra-economic appropriation, but also on a common sense which may bestow on each person or element in the process of production and distribution a variety of traditional rights. In such an economy, production relations are personal and highly diversified, and corrective measures are needed to redress deviations whenever they occur. Of course, the notion of this economic order does not exclude extreme exploitation. However, personified reciprocal bonds, based on a common sense which represents a type of "moral economy", will reassert the obligations, rights and duties in relationships such as those between patron and client (Thompson 1971).

In the process of capitalist penetration in the periphery, the personal form of interaction and domination is gradually replaced by a capitalist system which functions through an anonymous and "rational" market (to borrow Weber's terminology). Yet, while and because pre-capitalist production relations are replaced or transformed from above, the social relations of personal exchange must be retained, reproduced and instrumentalized to enable capitalist dominance and hegemony. This does not mean that pre-capitalist social relations and their mode of reproduction in the periphery remain intact. Rather, they are either depleted and ritualized, even though they may continue to retain a symbolic value, or they may be valorized through the adaptation of new meanings and experiences.

Vertical–patrimonial interaction is consummated through a complex personal exchange of both material and non-material benefits, services and obligations, which ultimately helps to secure the structure of capitalist dominance. Its main vehicles are the class and non-class alliances and linkages, both within and between social classes. These stretch and transmute from the allies and direct beneficiaries of (foreign) dominant capital (managers, the bureaucracy, the military, merchants, landowners and local industrialists), to the "old" and "new" middle classes (Poulantzas 1977) and the multitude of low-paid white- and blue-collar workers and petty producers, and down to the "residuum" of day-labourers and job-seekers who are tied by contradictory bonds of resistance–adaptation and expectations–aspiration to the patrimonial hierarchy.[9]

It would be erroneous, however, to conceive of the patrimonial interaction and linkages as a smoothly organized, functional mechanism. The deformed vertical network is the framework within which conflicting and competing interests, themselves an expression of inherent contradictions, can be articulated and resolved. The individual and the group (or social formation) are subject to persistent pressures and demands which act to determine and modify the decision-making process and its implementation. Yet, the emergent contradictions and the conflicting interests rarely articulate themselves explicitly. They rather affect the status and position of the parties involved indirectly, through a network of coalitions, alliances and patronage relationships which enhance the invisible mechanism of dominance.

The vertical orientation and identification of the individual and the social formation are not determined by economic considerations alone. Indeed, in the periphery, even more unambiguously than in the core, capitalist dominance is maintained, reinforced and reproduced through the closely interacting instruments of the ideological and repressive apparata which shape both individual and collective orientation maps. The significance of the ideological–cultural apparatus for securing economic and political domination, deferential orientation and benign alliances with the core, cannot be underestimated. Its channels of suggestive and explicit articulation and dominance are not only the educational system and the mass media or the communication network as a whole, but also the various forms of social, socio-political and socio-cultural movements, organizations and clubs, including informal groups where the mechanism of cultural–ideological penetration is far more complex. The values and norms induced and spelled thereby are symbolically and ritually reproduced at the level of the daily experience, behaviour, conduct and attitudes of the individual and the group. The market economy, modernism, nationalism, "progress" and their somewhat coarser manifestations such as Levi jeans, "soap operas", chewing-gum and transistor radios, all stand for upward mobility, status and security. These "benefits" can be valorized as "attainable" aspirations, thus enabling unequivocal and acquiescent identification with the system *per se*. Where formal qualifications such as education are absent, symbolic values and gestures may often compensate, allowing for illusion of mobility and the endurance of hardships and humiliation.

Empirically observed, the politician, the planner, the senior bureaucrat, the junior trade-inspector and the policeman, may all sincerely believe that the street vendor and the old marketplace are public nuisances, health hazards and an insult to the progressive image of their skyscraper city. This conviction is, of course, independent of the direct material benefits (land speculation, participation in wholesaling enterprise, contracts, bribes and confiscated goods) that such people may secure, each at their own level, and which in turn, may help to reconfirm that conviction. The acquisition of a transistor radio by the casual worker, on the other hand, serves not only an illusory perception of upward mobility but also as a concrete means of accumulation for social security. In case of emergency, sickness or dire need, it can be sold quickly.

Culture is not just learned passively. It is also an active response of the individual and the group, reproduced and enriched through their daily experience. The penetration of imported ideology and culture does not take place in a vacuum. It confronts, challenges and ultimately dominates the deformed, pre-capitalist cultures of the ethnic or affinity group, the caste or the urbanized rural community.[10] This process of partial subjugation is not passively accepted nor does it presuppose the gradual rejection of autochthonous culture either, as has been suggested by several scholars (e.g. Amin 1974). For the masses of urban petty producers, low-paid white- and blue-collar workers and employees, the casual workers and the marginalized job seekers, this autochthonous culture offers a particularly creative guideline and an orientation map for the subjective consciousness in a contradictory social situation which, at the level of appearance, is dominated by rational, impersonal, capitalist norms of demeanour.

Cultural heritage is, nevertheless, far from being a static subject of identification, even though rituals may be applied in a coercive and obligatory manner. The individual and the group interpret and reproduce diverse elements or paradigms both consciously and subconsciously, according to their immediate (material and immaterial) requirements and depending on the situations in which they find themselves. Constituents of the intrinsic culture are being rejected, supplemented or reinterpreted through the reflection of daily experience at work, at home, in the market, among friends and at leisure. Norms, values, rituals and symbols are continuously readjusted to urban life, even though they may seem invariably and conservatively to persist at the level of appearance and articulation.[11]

The sub-culture which emerges in the process of adaptation articulates the fundamental resistance of the subordinated social formations to the dominant culture and, indeed, to the rationale of impersonal and anonymous capitalist dominance, which largely functions beyond and past the limits of their experience. Resistance not only enables a demarcation from an alien culture and a retreat to a private world where identity can be found and retained, but also helps the subordinated to preserve their human dignity in the face of enduring oppression.

At the same time, and in the process of finding their role and identification, the subordinate social formations are forced into a dependent position, and then adapt and integrate themselves into the existing social system through their resistance. The subordination and the penetration of the cultural and political life of the subservient social formations by the dominant ones plays a decisive role in this process. This dialectic of resistance and adaptation cannot be clearly disaggregated. The same instruments (e.g. the voluntary associations) and identical modes of conduct—for example in leisure behaviour and neighbourly mutual aid—embody aspects of both resistance and adaptation. Objectively, they ultimately serve the mechanism of deferential vertical orientation and thus also subordination in the hands of dominant social forces.

How does this discourse relate to petty production and its role in peripheral capitalist relations of production? It has been suggested that peripheral capitalist dominance can only be secured through the maintenance of a deformed patrimonial interaction, reinforced through the instruments of the repressive and ideological apparata. However, the structure of dominance, and thus also of surplus appropriation, can be preserved and protected only as long as access to means of accumulation and reproduction are restricted by the dominant social formations (from top to bottom). The cultural–ideological hegemony supplemented by the repressive State apparatus is not in itself a sufficient instrument, since the aspirations valorized cannot be stretched indefinitely without material compensation.

The acquiescence and the upward orientation of the subordinated social formations and groups can only be guaranteed if a limited access to means of appropriation (and thus also reproduction) is made available on all levels of the hierarchy. This equivocal "surplus" appropriation takes place in the sphere of circulation rather than in the production of goods, and it is conducted retrogressively by various social formations which are integrated into the patrimonial hierarchy. Thus, if the backwards and forwards linkages of the petty producer are examined, a whole network of intermediaries and "parasites", themselves in a subordinate position, can be identified. These may include:

a. The government officials who trade with import licences for raw or semi-processed materials and equipment, the importers, wholesalers, warehouse owners and smaller shopkeepers who supply the petty producers and through whose "appropriation" the prices of means of production have increased threefold in the course of transfer.

b. The landlord or owner of means of production who charges rent, the broker who charges intervention fees (e.g. for procuring a trade licence), the junior municipal inspector, the army officer and the policemen who demand bribes or benefit from the confiscation of the goods of the unlicensed producer.

c. The distributors, owners of "formal" shops, brokers on behalf of the factory, transporters and others who underpay the petty producers, appropriating thereby part of their potential earnings.

These patrimonially interacting but often competing networks perform the essential function of reproducing the trajectory of economic, political and cultural–ideological dominance, which ultimately enables the capital drain from the periphery to the core (Marini 1974). Despite being grossly ineffective and costly, the vertical–patrimonial hierarchy and its mode of appropriation are not replaced by a more efficient capitalist system. This, not only because it does not really endanger the interests of dominant social formations, but rather since its survival is indispensable for the exercise of dominance.

As a result of the patrimonially interacting networks, petty production performs a key (and not a transient) role in reinforcing the reproduction of various social forces essential for the maintenance of peripheral capitalist dominance. This may be done either directly or indirectly, through the appropriation of surplus on various levels of the hierarchy and by various agents. These agents are both integrated with and subordinated to the dominant social forces through economic dependence and cultural–ideological bonds. Whether they recognize and acknowledge their subordinate position or not is immaterial. By virtue of their cumulative experience, cultural–ideological heritage and orientation, as well as their economic dependence and reproduction process, the subordinate "appropriating" social formations are objectively allied to the dominant ones. Rejecting or challenging the reciprocal–patrimonial network implies not only alienation from the immediate environment but also from the "self" which is reproduced through the reflection of the environment in the "self".

Whereas petty production can be regarded as essential for the reinforcement and reproduction of peripheral capitalism, the role of the "residuum", including those engaged in illicit services and activities, is far more complex. Objectively these people are the victims of peripheral capitalist penetration, its contradictions and the resulting marginalization process. A closer examination may indicate a significant function for various sub-groups, so that some may constitute a "reserve army", particularly for commercial and service enterprises, and others may help to justify or reinforce the ideological–cultural and repressive apparatus. Thus, for example, prostitution is not only an innate consequence of a high urban male to female ratio resulting from rural to urban migration (see e.g. Bujra 1978–1979; N. Nelson 1979), but also an instrument of cultural–ideological dominance which reasserts the role of the family, male chauvinism and the image of machismo, and which helps to ensure the docility, "respectability" and subservience of most female wage-workers. Similarly, in the grey area between legality and illegality, smuggling, drug-pushing, liquor distilling, traffic with stolen goods and petty crime are welcome sources of "surplus appropriation" for "respectable" intermediaries and representatives of the repressive apparatus. In addition, they can serve as safety valves for unarticulated despair and frustrations which otherwise might find their outlet in riots and disorder. These safety valves are used and controlled by the repressive apparatus, always allowing for some flexibility within the context of patrimonial interaction. At the same time, the threats of crime and disorder produce fear among the "respectable citizens" which, in turn, legitimates the repressive apparatus. It might also be worthwhile noting that the image and thus also the status of the "outcasts" is not necessarily negative. They often articulate the resentment of the subordinate social formations and their resistance to oppression.

The above exploration of the function of petty production is not an attempt to deny the process of social differentiation under conditions of peripheral capitalism, but rather to demonstrate its complexity. The relative positions and composition of social forces in the periphery depend on a variety of factors, such as the composition of pre-colonial social forces, the mode and degree of capitalist penetration, the conditions affecting the spread of capitalist relations of production, and the development and changes of ownership and proprietorship of means of production. These, as well as a host of others, affect the composition and functions of petty production in the periphery, and their interrelations and effects need to be studied concretely in specific countries and situations.

Social formations and political consciousness

On the basis of recent research, it has been suggested that the majority of petty producers are progressively "proletarianized" (Gerry 1980), whereas a small minority of those who own the means of production have the material basis for a "bourgeois" consciousness (MacEwen Scott 1979) and gradually are being transformed into petty capitalists. The hypothesized "proletarianization" process takes various forms, such as: (a) subcontracting for commercial–industrial capital; (b) domination by commercial capital without subcontracting; (c) organization of petty producers by the State; and (d) temporary wage employment whenever the petty producer is unable to retain his self-employment.

The very nature of labour force composition and processes of peripheral capitalism casts doubt upon the validity of the "proletarianization/transition to the bourgeoisie" concept of the petty producers in both an objective and subjective sense. In a situation where the majority of the active urban labour force are not factory workers but rather low-income white-collar employees, messengers, petty traders, manufacturers and repairers, etc., one has to look into the social processes which determine orientation and consciousness, rather than search for vague concepts which suggest that the mass of petty producers are gradually sinking into the "proletariat". Objectively, the relative position of petty producers vis-à-vis dominant capital does not substantially differ from that of other subordinate social formations. It is determined by the prevalence of a large segment of low-paid white-collar employees and the small size of factory labour, which seldom exceeds 15–20 per cent of the urban labour force. Status perceptions may vary considerably, depending on the actual or symbolic access to and identification with instruments and values of dominance. The socially divisive effects of differences in income and living conditions, however, are often blurred by common socio-cultural experience.

The orientation maps and consciousness of urban petty producers are shaped by diverse factors and patterns of interaction, which determine reactions to situations of extreme inequality. Thus, for example, the valorization of both urban and rural identity may have cultural–ethnic as well as material roots. Ownership or claim to land in the village often fulfils the function of old age and unemployment security thus making possible a rural–urban circulation which situationally compartmentalizes the consciousness of the migrant (Bujra 1978–1979). Similarly, corporate identity, exercised through ethnic, caste or other urban associations and socio-cultural networks, not only offers the opportunity for gaining and articulating status, but also serve the ends of social security (mutual aid, sickness, burials, etc.), functioning as a point of reference in an impersonal urban situation (Peattie 1970).

The consciousness of the petty producer is affected by his isolated and individualized conditions of production no less than by his affinity and affiliation with urban associations and networks. These conditions are usually characterized by non-industrial time and work discipline, by the continuum of labour and leisure, and by the resulting, personally experienced and perceived social interaction and linkages. The patron–client bond with suppliers or buyers, often materially enhanced through loans, favours and protection, is also replicated in the daily or sporadic contacts with the bureaucracy, police, political bosses, etc., and reinforces the personal–vertical orientation of the petty producer.

Equally important to understanding the orientation of the petty producer is the role of the ideological apparatus and particularly the mass media. The suggestive promises of "success" and "upward-mobility" symbols in the educational system, the media and roadside advertising, raise expectations and aspirations which enable the individual to cope with the extreme situation of destitution, and which justify and reproduce deferential attitudes. The expectations that "hard work and a bit of luck" or "a windfall gain" may help the "breakthrough" can largely explain deferential and acquiescent attitudes towards the existing social order. "Successful" petty producers provide a model for the aspirations of their workers and the poor, thus reinforcing the ideology of mobility via individual initiative. Repeatedly-told "success stories" are an essential element of mitigating potential antagonism and of exalting adaptation. The exploiting intermediary is not regarded as such, but looked upon as a positive model and a proof that money can be made (Birkbeck 1978). By virtue of his success, his access to information, and as a result of the client's dependence, the intermediary or employer often functions as a natural leader and protector of his client's workers. Conflicts and antagonism are not likely to emerge as long as consensus regarding the rights and duties of each party and the fair remunerations which can be expected is maintained.

The consciousness of petty producers and, for that matter, the subordinate poor, may be shaped further by the high rate of labour circulation and by the lack of obvious socio-cultural, ethnic and economic distinction between the successful producer, his workers and the rest of the community. The prospects of securing income by means of individual initiative outside the capitalist economy encourages frequent mobility from wage-to self-employment and vice-versa. This circulation necessarily affects the attitudes of both wage-labour and the self-employed, and results in a lack of clear distinction between the two. The petty producer does not clearly distinguish between wage- and self-employment, but regards both as a response to an urban situation (Bujra 1978–1979).

Divisions and distinctions between the petty producer and his workers, or other petty producers which he may exploit, are blurred not only by vertical–clientele relationships and sometimes by ethnic (affinity) relationships, but also by the absence of difference in life-style, living conditions, clothing, behaviour, etc. The successful petty producer often works with his labourers under the same conditions and shares their life-style. Even where conditions of extreme exploitation prevail, the petty producer will not be viewed as a villain as long as the socio-cultural consensus is maintained. Rather he will be seen as someone who exercises his rights and as an object with which to identify. Both his workers and the community in which he lives (e.g. the squatter) will consider him a natural leader and a patron who may be approached in case of distress. The redistributive obligations of the petty producer enhance his position and enable him to exercise social-political influence and sometimes also control. It would be wrong, however, to view the patrimonial interaction and the "consensus" between the successful petty producer and his workers or community as harmonious and benign. The tensions resulting from the contradictions between the proliferation of peripheral capitalist market forces and the deformed patrimonial interaction, necessarily affect the social relations of production and are likely to produce resentment. Reaction to exploitation is circumscribed, however, by the limited cumulative experience of the worker. The individual (rather than collective) articulation of resistance usually takes the form of a continual change of jobs.

Complex social relations of production, patrimonial interaction and upward orientation, affinity to socio-cultural urban networks, working experience, and a host of other factors are likely to produce an integrative rather than a militant response to the exploitative situation. This is typically articulated in the ultimate hope of the unsuccessful petty producer, as well as the factory worker and the low-paid white collar employee, to accumulate sufficient savings to open a small business (Peace 1974; Williams 1974).

Recognition of the sources of deprivation and its attribution to a system of exploitation needs to be concretely, subjectively and collectively experienced before it can be translated into horizontal interaction and solidarity. Since the petty producer cannot and does not identify the subordinate intermediary as the immediate exploiter, but rather as a positive object of identification and imitation, he is not likely to recognize the sources of his deprivation and poverty. The more indirect causes of destitution, namely the rich, the factory owner, the dominant bureaucracy and the peripheral capitalist system as a whole, do not lie within his daily and cumulative experience. They remain ambiguous despite being visible, and cannot be translated into immediate action, though such action could take place *vis-à-vis* the immediate exploiter (e.g. organizing a boycott to force him to pay higher prices). The rich and powerful are therefore perceived as vague and equivocal exploiters and a subject of resentment, envy or hate, but not as concrete opponents who represent a societal system and who need to be confronted (see e.g. Peace 1974; Sandbrook and Arn 1977).

A cognitive process resulting in solidarity and collective action, is occasionally articulated in the form of populist movements, sometimes led by charismatic personalities, or by means of "senseless" outbursts and violence against individuals and property. More often, solidarity of the subordinate will be manifested in the face of a concrete danger such as bureaucratic harassment and repression. The common objective of the interest group, frequently led by the immediate exploiter himself (the intermediary), is to reach a compromise and restore a *modus operandi* (Birkbeck 1979). Similarly, acts of rebellion and violence are usually aimed at presenting and satisfying several demands by means of pressure on individuals, such as politicians, administrators and tax collectors. As soon as these are accepted or partially fulfilled, the movement will tend to disintegrate (Williams 1974). Such cases of violence against individuals in leadership positions illustrate the nature of movements, rebellions and acts of solidarity aimed at restoring an equilibrium which has been distorted and deformed by the penetration of capitalist relations of production. The rich and the powerful are expected to look after the interests of their clients as well, and a failure to do so is viewed as a betrayal of the "sons" by their "fathers" (Williams 1974, 133).

At the level of the "residual" labour force, or the "outcasts", cognitive processes affecting their orientation maps and consciousness are bound to find a more distorted and disintegrative articulation. Lack of access to the mechanism of integration and to the instruments through which the dominant apparata function (education, language, bureaucratic procedures and systems, rituals, etc.), will *a priori* drastically restrict the opportunities and options open to them. Such factors are accentuated by extreme poverty, the lack of legal rights and protection, and the impact of generalized economic instability, establishing patterns of mobility between income opportunities, and consequently a process of uprooting from an early age onwards. As a result, even if the opportunity arises, the outcasts are unlikely to take steady and often repetitive jobs which require time and work discipline. Usually their chances of finding a permanent employment are meagre, as they lack the necessary identification papers and certificates, "decent" clothing and the "right" social networks.

Lack of access to and experience with the mechanism of dominance and its operations strongly affect the conduct and behaviour of the outcast. In the case of a male, for example, in his childhood and youth he may resort to begging, physical violence and illicit activities in order to survive. His individual resistance to the deprivation and subordination which he sees but does not understand, is shaped by objective conditions and such skills as the ability to run away quickly or to break locks. Later on, and after having experienced the heavy hand of the repressive apparatus, his resistance will turn integrative–adaptive. Utilizing the social networks he has established meanwhile (a substitute for the dominant–formalized ones), the outcast will engage in unstable peripheral occupations as the opportunity arises. An attempt towards accumulation and a petty entrepreneurial activity often involves tremendous risks, as he may not only lack the know-how and the social network with suppliers and customers, but also the essential self-discipline. Although he may establish permanent social relationships with his immediate environment, these remain extremely vulnerable and insecure. The ingenuity which he might have shown in his youth while trying to secure some livelihood will give way to apathy and acquiescence, reinforced by under-nourishment, susceptibility to disease and the burden of feeding a family. Resistance and deference will continue alternately to guide his orientation map and mode of behaviour; yet he remains largely unaware of the forces which determine his fate.

The prospects

While the term "informal sector" has been rejected because of its connotations, rather than as a semantic exercise, the extension of the paradigm "petty-commodity" or "subordinate mode of production" to embrace the universe of the subordinate social formations is no less problematic. Neither a set of multiple variables nor an attempt to disaggregate activities can procure tangible and absolute criteria for definition, and it may justifiably be asked whether these criteria are needed at all.

Petty production is an adaptive response to an asymmetric and symbiotic capitalist penetration. Its objective function and modes of operation and articulation can only be elucidated in the context of its relative position in the periphery, namely, to enable the reproduction of social forces essential for the maintenance of dominance. Petty production therefore must be viewed not as a sequestered phenomenon, but as a subordinate mode of production reciprocally linked with the dominant one through vertically-oriented and interacting social networks.

Heuristically and empirically, however, a disaggregation of activities and a situational or cross-cultural comparison of branches may prove useful, both for the purpose of discerning the mode and social relations of production, and its constraints and potentialities, and for avoiding misleading generalizations based on small samples and single branches. Typology by branch or activities usually involves such categories as: production of consumer and other goods (disaggregated by type), transport, construction, trade (disaggregated by permanency of location), repair and life extension, and various personal services (including illicit ones). Historically or dynamically conceived multivariate criteria may comprise: mobility and access, skill acquisition, accumulation and scale of operations, backward and forward linkages (dependency, subordination and appropriation), labour relations and the use of technology.

A generalized description of the labour processes affecting urban employment and petty production is more-or-less as follows: The expulsion and migration of rural workers and the accelerated rate of natural population increase, have led to the growth of the urban labour force seeking employment. Capital-intensive (import-substituting) industry, and the public and large-scale private tertiary sectors, are incapable of absorbing more than a small share of the job-seekers. Consequently, an increasing share of the growing labour force have to look for their livelihood in activities defined as petty production or casual labour. Due to inherent disadvantages of petty production as compared with capitalist production, and the dependence of the former upon the latter's rate of growth, accumulation can hardly take place and petty production stagnates or exhibits involutionary trends (Bienefeld 1975; Quijano 1974). These are also produced and reinforced by growing competition and by the existence of a reserve army whose availability acts to depress wages.

While the above paradigm may prove valid when generally applied and on the macro-economic level, there may be significant local variations. Although the scanty data available do not justify absolute statements, it may be suggested that the structure, nature and anticipated trends of petty production in a given country and situation will be shaped by factors such as:

a. The degree of capitalist penetration and the development of capitalist infrastructure.
b. The mode, types and volume of primary product extraction.
c. The size of import-substitution industry and the downward proliferation of its products.
d. The size of the market (population) and purchasing power.
e. The structure of the dominant local social formation and its historical development, ownership of means of production, forms of capital accumulation and consciousness.
f. The size, historical roots and traditions of petty production.

These closely interlinked, and interacting macro-economic factors and their impact need to be carefully examined in a given situation before conclusions regarding petty production on the micro-economic level can be reached. Although demand for the commodities and services of the petty producers are bound to lag behind supply because of inherent inequalities in income distribution and the growth of the marginalized labour force, external as well as internal changes may promote (or destroy) specific branches of petty production. These, may involve structural changes such as the expansion of the urban middle class, with its consumption patterns, as well as fluctuations in GDP and its distribution–proliferation as a result of booms (or slumps) in the price of primary products or of changes in foreign aid. Severe deficits in balance of payments, as well as the aspirations of an increasingly conscientious local dominant formation, may restrict the growth of foreign-owned import substitution industry, while at the same time local industrial investment may be constrained by various factors. The oil crisis and its devastating effect on the balance of payments in most Third World countries may enhance this trend and further restrict investment in import-substitution industries as well as the import of "luxury" consumer goods.

A survey of petty production conducted by the author in Dacca in 1979, has shown that specific branches or production lines may prosper or deteriorate as a result of numerous and seemingly unrelated factors. Thus, for example, labour migration to the Middle East and government incentives to stimulate investment by the repatriated migrants, have led to a voluminous import of cheap gold from the Middle East (prior to the mid-1979 "gold rush"). The gold is sold to members of the goldsmiths guilds who re-export it in the form of jewellery through smugglers to India, where gold is a scarce commodity which fetches much higher prices due to strict governmental control and trade restrictions. This has led to a relative, though probably short-lived, prosperity for a not insignificant number of goldsmiths and smugglers.

On a much broader "Third World" scale, import restrictions and the trade with import licences, as well as the underdevelopment of local industry, have stimulated the growth and prosperity of a number of branches of petty production, such as readymade garments, household goods (consumer durables) and light engineering. Other petty production enterprises, such as those making soap, have often been able to hold on to their market despite competition of capital-intensive industry, whereas a whole range of traditional products and producers are doomed or already have disappeared from the market. The reasons for this are not always to be found in capitalist competition but also in such factors as changes of tastes, themselves a result of the "modernization" and "sophistication" of an urban middle class which benefits from the inflow of foreign aid.

Petty producers are often subject to cut-throat competition (sometimes literally so), both from capital-intensive enterprise and from other petty producers working in the same branch of production. However, such competition does not necessarily mean the destruction of petty production or severe involutionary trends, and capital-intensive production does not expand uninhibited in every situation. Furthermore, internal competition in specific branches of petty production may be restricted by producers' guilds or associations (which may nonetheless serve as instruments of exploitation or surplus appropriation), by spatial concentration of producers (e.g. in markets or courtyards), and even more so by limited access to investment capital, skills and circulation networks. Precapitalist social relations of production, which also regulate competition, are distorted by the introduction of an impersonal capitalist market, but they continue to persist because they are essential for the maintenance of dominance.

The processes or prospects of accumulation and the ensuing involutionary tends also require more differentiated observations. It has been suggested above that accumulation by petty producers is impeded mainly by surplus appropriation through intermediaries in the sphere of circulation, by the mode of subordination, and by general market conditions. On the micro-economic level, accumulation prospects may also be controlled by various objective and subjective determinants. Objective determinants involve factors such as the location of the enterprise in relation to its market, sources of inputs and access to physical infrastructure (e.g. water and electricity). Subjective determinants relate more to the cumulative experience of the petty producers and their access to means or instruments of reproduction, which are monopolized by the dominant social formation.

The notion that the "successful" petty producer will tend to become a "petty capitalist" (Gerry 1980) still requires close and careful examination from the producer's standpoint. It may be suggested here that transition to "petty capitalism" (presumably capital-intensive production) is restricted not only by lack of access to technological and managerial skills, but also by the economic and cultural–ideological networks of dominant social formations, and by the social relations of production. The introduction of impersonal and rational capitalist relations of production in the course of transition to "petty capitalism" distorts and transforms the vertical–patrimonial interaction between the petty producer and his workers. This, in turn, implies an alienation of the petty producer from his environment and "self-understanding".

Though a few petty producers may gradually shift to capital-intensive production, most tend to invest horizontally in commercial and speculative projects in order to maintain vertical social interaction with their workers. Thus, for example, the petty production survey in Dacca identified several cases where identical petty enterprises manufacturing the same products are owned by the same person. When asked why they do not concentrate production in one enterprise, most of them answered that direct control would become impossible. From their point-of-view "rational" production can only be secured by personal relations of production.

The object of this discussion is not to establish some universal "truth", or to anticipate growth or involutionary trends of petty production, but rather to indicate the complexity and variability of the dynamic processes and their articulation. Therefore any attempt to evaluate the trajectory of petty production in a given situation presupposes not only a macro- and micro-economic analysis but also, and particularly, an insight into the socio-cultural circumstances under which this mode of production occurs.

The conclusions reached by radical scholars are inherent in their polarity paradigm, Any assistance to petty producers "tends to be selective, helping a minority . . . and reinforcing the essentially marginal position of the majority . . ." and ". . . any real changes cannot be made in the situation of poor casual workers without transforming the whole socio-economic system within which they work (Bromley and Gerry 1979, 11). How such a transformation can take place has been the subject of debate for more than a decade (see e.g. Armstrong and McGee 1968; Nelson 1970). It is now usually agreed that the urban poor in general and the petty producers in particular are unlikely to take the initiative on their own (Waterman 1975). Furthermore, it has been observed, rightly, that the approach of radical scholars does not allow for any recommendations and solutions which may reinforce an existing repressive political structure or reaffirm its existence, regardless of whether these solutions may alleviate poverty or increase employment (Moser 1978, 1056).

This paper has endeavoured to discuss some of the complex societal processes which take place in the Third World and result in a continual process of differentiation and structural transformation. In the course of the differentiation process, progressive and liberal social forces will emerge and attempt to articulate themselves, coalesce with each other and disintegrate again. Some progressive or liberal people or groups will passively reject the social system under which they live, while others organize themselves in political and voluntary organizations. In a number of Third World countries such organizations, whether radical or not, have initiated programmes and projects such as literacy, conscientization and organization of rural workers, mutual aid societies and others.

In alliance with other social forces, including professionals, disillusioned bureaucrats, trade-unionists, enlightened clergymen, teachers and students, both progressive and liberal–democratic, political and voluntary organizations may articulate a challenge to the existing regime and become a driving force towards social transformation. Simultaneously, these voluntary, church and other organizations may initiate projects to organize the poorer petty producers, casual workers and other groups of the poor. Employment and income-generation programmes can be geared towards both low-income petty producers and job-seekers such as the unemployed, school-leavers and dropouts, women and casual labourers. They can involve various elements such as:

a. Small loans, procurement and marketing services (particularly the introduction of new products) as well as technological and skill upgrading for petty producers and their protection *vis-à-vis* the authorities.
b. Vocational training for unemployed youths and women (training cum production), and post-training aid so that they can establish themselves in employment.
c. Skill-upgrading training for casual workers with the aim of improving their market chances.
d. Integrated urban development programmes such as squatter improvement, where an employment element can be introduced.

The type and elements of such programmes and the forms of conscientiz-ation and motivation involved depend on the individual cases and conditions. Although they are neither likely to commence a radical social transformation nor to solve the problems of petty production, they may contribute to the alleviation of urban unemployment, particularly if they can be expanded gradually. The same might be true for some types of governmental and semi-governmental programmes. For some observers this goal may seem quite insignificant; for the persons affected it may mean a lot.

Notes

1. For interesting case studies see Berger (1974), Grillo (1973), and Wilson (1972).
2. See e.g. Birkbeck (1979), Bose (1978), Breman (1977), Bromley (1978b), Bujra (1978–1979), Gerry (1976, 1979), Rusque-Alcaino and Bromley (1979) and Stretton (1979).
3. See Levitt (1976), Lewin and Peukert (1977), MacEwen Scott (1979) and Moser (1978).
4. See the studies cited in Note 3, and also El-Hakim (1977), Hake (1977) and King (1977).
5. This model has recently been questioned and modified; see e.g. Kitching (1977), Phillips (1977).
6. See Bienefeld and Godfrey (1976), Birkbeck (1978, 1979), Bromley (1978a, 1978b), Gerry (1979), Lewin and Peukert (1977) and MacEwen Scott (1979).
7. The term "intermediaries" is used heuristically only in this context and needs to be empirically disaggregated in a given situation. "Intermediaries" comprise a vast network of importers, suppliers and buyers, contractors, brokers, government officials who issue licences, etc. They are often related to one another through diverse mechanisms. Despite being ideologically–culturally allied with the dominant social formations, they are economically dependent on those formations.
8. The term "vertical–patrimonial interaction" applies to all pre-capitalist societies and is merely an empty phrase if intended to denote social system of exchange, as often suggested by liberal sociologists of various schools (see e.g. Eisenstadt and Roniger 1980). In the context of this article the term is used to describe distorted, and often symbolically articulated, social interaction, which is shaped by the tensions created between the penetration of capitalist social relations of production and the deformed pre-capitalist relations.
9. There is little point in trying to identify a rigid vertical social hierarchy, as it will inevitably prove useless and contradictory. The individual's perception of his status may help to explain the argument. Thus, in diverse contexts and in different situations, he may identify himself with different formations and, in fact, belong to heterogeneous social networks of a dissimilar status and functions. His position in the production process or the ownership of means of production, will hardly help to explain his status (whether actual or symbolic) as an instrument of access to social and material means of reproduction.
10. More than by any study, this challenge and domination is vividly documented in Ousmane Sembene's films (e.g. *Xala* and *The Mandate*), and in such works of contemporary African literature as Achebe (1971), Ekwesi (1963), and Mwangi (1973).
11. Here I have followed Favert's (1967) critique of the naive anthropology and his warning that claims based on status-group affiliation must be analysed in terms of the actual function which such claims perform in a given social situation or system.

References

ACHEBE, Chinus (1971) *Things Fall Apart*, Heinemann, London.
AMIN, Samir (1974) "Accumulation and development", *Review of African Political Economy*, No. 1, pp. 9–26.
ARMSTRONG, Warwick and McGEE, T. G. (1968) "Revolutionary change and the Third World city: a theory of urban involution", *Civilisations*, Vol. 18, pp. 353–77.

134   A. C. Lewin

BERGER, E. L. (1974) *Labour, Race and Colonial Rule: The Copperbelt from 1924 to Independence,* Clarendon Press, Oxford.
BIENEFELD, Manfred (1975) "The informal sector and peripheral capitalism: the case of Tanzania", *IDS Bulletin,* Vol. 6, No. 3, pp. 53–73.
BIENEFELD, Manfred and GODFREY, Martin (1976) "Measuring unemployment and the informal sector: some conceptual and statistical problems", *IDS Bulletin,* Vol. 7, No. 3, pp. 4–10.
BIRKBECK, Chris (1978) "Self-employed proletarians in an informal factory: the case of Cali's garbage dump", *World Development,* Vol. 6, No. 9/10, pp. 1173–85. Reprinted in Ray Bromley (ed.) (1979) *The Urban Informal Sector: Critical Perspectives on Employment and Housing Policies,* Pergamon, Oxford.
BIRKBECK, Chris (1979) "Garbage, industry, and the 'vultures' of Cali, Colombia", in Ray Bromley and Chris Gerry (eds.) *Casual Work and Poverty in Third World Cities,* Wiley, Chichester, pp. 161–83.
BOSE, A. N. (1978) *Calcutta and Rural Bengal: Small Sector Symbiosis,* Minerva, Calcutta.
BREMAN, Jan (1977) "Labour relations in the 'formal' and 'informal' sectors: report of a case study in South Gujarat, India", *Journal of Peasant Studies,* Vol. 4, pp. 171–205 and 337–59.
BROMLEY, Ray (1978a) "The urban informal sector: why is it worth discussing?" *World Development,* Vol. 6, No. 9/10, pp. 1033–39. Reprinted in Ray Bromley (ed.) (1979), *op. cit.*
BROMLEY, Ray (1978b) "Organization, regulation and exploitation in the so-called 'urban informal sector': the street traders of Cali, Colombia", *World Development,* Vol. 6, No. 9/10, pp. 1161–71. Reprinted in Ray Bromley (ed.) (1979), *op. cit.*
BROMLEY, Ray and GERRY, Chris (1979) "Who are the casual poor", in Ray Bromley and Chris Gerry (eds.) *Casual Work and Poverty in Third World Cities,* Wiley, Chichester, pp. 3–23.
BUJRA, Janet M. (1978–1979) "Proletarianization and the 'informal economy': a case study from Nairobi", *African Urban Studies,* No. 3 (Winter), pp. 47–66.
CLINARD, Marshall B. (1966) *Slums and Community Development,* Free Press, New York.
EISENSTADT, S. N. and RONIGER, U. (1980) "Patron-client relations as a model of structuring social exchange", *Comparative Studies in Society and History,* Vol. 22, pp. 42–77.
EKWESI, Cyprian (1963) *People of the City,* Heinemann, London.
EL-HAKIM, S. M. (1977) "The role of the family, kinship and rural–urban migration in the processing of solid waste in Cairo", *African Development,* Vol. 2, No. 2.
FAVERT, Jeanne (1967) "Le traditionalisme par excés de modernité", *Archives Européenes de Sociologie,* Vol. 8, No. 1, pp. 71–93.
GERRY, Chris (1976) "The wrong side of the factory gate: casual workers and capitalist industry in Dakar, Senegal", *Manpower and Unemployment Research,* Vol. 9, No. 2, pp. 17–27.
GERRY, Chris (1979) "Small-scale manufacturing and repairs in Dakar: a survey of market relations within the urban economy", in Ray Bromley and Chris Gerry (eds.), *op. cit.,* pp. 229–50.
GERRY, Chris (1980) "Petite production marchande ou 'salariat deguise'? Quelques reflexions", *Revue Tiers-Monde,* Vol. 21, No. 82, pp. 387–403.
GRILLO, R. D. (1973) *African Railwaymen: Solidarity and Opposition in an East African Labour Force,* Oxford University Press, London.
HAKE, Andrew (1977) *African Metropolis: Nairobi's Self-Help City,* University of Sussex Press, Brighton.
HART, J. Keith (1973) "Informal income opportunities and urban employment in Ghana", *Journal of Modern African Studies,* Vol. 11, pp. 61–89.
JOLLY, Richard, DE KADT, Emanuel, SINGER, Hans and WILSON, Fiona (1973) "Introduction", to their (eds.) *Third World Employment: Problems and Strategy,* Penguin, Harmondsworth, pp. 19–23.
KING, Kenneth (1977) *The African Artisan: Education and the Informal Sector in Kenya,* Heinemann, London.
KITCHING, Gavin (1977) "Modes of production in Kenya", *Review of African Political Economy,* No. 8, pp. 56–74.
LEVITT, K. (1976) "New approaches to national economic accounting in developing countries with a large foreign trade sector", *IDS Bulletin,* Vol. 7, No. 3.
LEWIN, A. C. and PEUKERT, D. (1977) *Afrika: Informeller Sektor und Probleme und Perspektiven städtischer Beschäftigungspolitik,* Friedrich-Ebert-Stiftung, Bonn.
LEWIS, W. Arthur (1954) "Economic development with unlimited supplies of labour", *Manchester School of Economics and Social Studies,* Vol. 22, pp. 139–91.

MacEwen Scott, Alison (1979) "Who are the self-employed?", in Ray Bromley and Chris Gerry (eds.), *op. cit.*, pp. 105–29.

Marini, Ruy Mauro (1974) "Die Dialektik der Abhängigkeit", in D. Senghaas (ed.) *Peripherer Kapitalismus: Analysen über Abhängigkeit und Unterentwicklung*, Suhrkamp, Frankfurt.

Moir, H. V. J. (1977) *The Jakarta Informal Sector*, National Institute of Economic and Social Research, Indonesian Institute of Science, Jakarta.

Moser, Caroline O. N. (1978) "Informal sector or petty commodity production: dualism or dependence in urban development?", *World Development*, Vol. 6, No. 9/10, pp. 1041–64. Reprinted in Ray Bromley (ed.) (1979), *op. cit.*

Mwangi, Meja (1973) *Kill Me Quick*, Heinemann, London.

Nelson, Joan (1970) "The urban poor: disruption or political integration in Third World cities?", *World Politics*, Vol. 22, No. 3, pp. 393–414.

Nelson, Nici (1979) "How women and men get by: the sexual division of labour in the informal sector of a Nairobi squatter settlement", in Ray Bromley and Chris Gerry (eds.), *op. cit.*, pp. 283–302.

Papola, T. S. (1978) *The Informal Sector in an Urban Economy (Agmedabad)*, Giri Institute of Development Studies, Lucknow.

Peace, Adrian (1974) "Industrial protest in Nigeria", in Emanuel de Kadt and Gavin Williams (eds.) *Sociology and Development*, Tavistock, London, pp. 141–67.

Peattie, Lisa R. (1970) *The View from the Barrio*, University of Michigan Press, Ann Arbor.

Phillips, Anne (1977) "The concept of development", *Review of African Political Economy*, No. 8, pp. 7–20.

Portes, Alejandro (1978) "The informal sector and the world economy: notes on the structure of subsidized labour", *IDS Bulletin*, Vol. 9, No. 4, pp. 35–40.

Poulantzas, Nicos (1977) "The new petty bourgeoisie", in A. Hunt (ed.) *Class and Class Structure*, Lawrence and Wishart, London.

Quijano, Anibal (1974) "The marginal pole of the economy and the marginalized labour force", *Economy and Society*, Vol. 3, pp. 393–428.

Rusque-Alcaino, Juan and Bromley, Ray (1979) "The bottle buyer: an occupational autobiography", in Ray Bromley and Chris Gerry (eds.), *op. cit.*, pp. 185–215.

Sandbrook, R. and Arn, J. (1977) *The Labouring Poor and Urban Class Formation*, Occasional Monograph Series No. 12, Centre for Developing-Area Studies, McGill University, Montreal.

Senghaas, D. (1974) "Elements einer Theorie des peripherer Kapitalismus", in D. Senghaas (ed.) *Peripherer Kapitalismus: Analysen über Abhängigkeit und Unterentwicklung*, Suhrkamp, Frankfurt.

Sethuraman, S. V. (ed.) (1981) *The Urban Informal Sector in Developing Countries: Employment, Poverty and Environment*, ILO, Geneva.

Stretton, Alan (1979) "Instability of employment among building industry labourers in Manila", in Ray Bromley and Chris Gerry (eds.), *op. cit.*, pp. 267–82.

Thompson, E. P. (1971) "The moral economy of the English crowd in the eighteenth century", *Past and Present*, No. 50 (Feb.), pp. 76–136.

Tokman, Victor E. (1978) "Competition between the informal and formal sectors in retailing: the case of Santiago", *World Development*, Vol. 6, No. 9/10, pp. 1187–98. Reprinted in Ray Bromley (ed.) (1979), *op. cit.*

Waterman, Peter (1975) "Third World workers: an overview", *Working Papers of the Centre for Developing Areas Studies*, No. 9, McGill University, Montreal.

Weeks, John (1971) "Does employment matter?", *Manpower and Unemployment Research in Africa*, Vol. 4, No. 1. Reprinted in Richard Jolly, Emanuel de Kadt, Hans Singer and Fiona Wilson (eds.) (1973), *op. cit.*

Williams, Gavin (1974) "Political consciousness among the Ibadan poor", in Emanuel de Kadt and Gavin Williams (eds.) *Sociology and Development*, Tavistock, London, pp. 109–39.

Wilson, F. (1972) *Labour in the South African Gold Mines, 1911–1969*, Cambridge University Press, Cambridge.

CHAPTER 8

Our socialism and the subsistence engineer: the role of small enterprises in the engineering industry of Coimbatore, South India*

JOHN HARRISS

Durairajan owns a large workshop (officially a "medium-sized factory"), producing a range of small machine tools. The workshop has a partially-automated foundry section, sheet-metal and machine shops and it employs altogether about 200 people, most of whom receive provident fund and other benefits, and who are union members. Not long ago more were employed in the workshop, but it is now Durairajan's policy not to replace men who leave, whilst he is also encouraging some of the experienced workers from the machine shop to leave and to set up their own small workshops. He has helped those who have agreed to do this by selling them second-hand machinery at its book values, and by giving them orders for work. It is this that he refers to, jokingly, as "Our Socialism!", or the "sharing out" of the prosperity of his firm. Whether or not this pattern of paternalistic sub-contracting does mean prosperity for the men who set up small workshops and undertake "jobwork" for Durairajan is a question we consider. Durairajan himself certainly benefits, for—according to his own account—by splitting up his machine shop he has been able to reduce the costs of production of the small drilling machines for which his company first established its reputation, through lowering labour costs and by cutting down overheads. Those who undertake "jobwork" for Durairajan receive materials and the specifications for the parts they undertake to make; and the parts are quality controlled on their return. The jobworkers are paid only for the work which is found satisfactory, and the costs of materials wasted on parts which are found not to pass the quality control are deducted from their total payments. Durairajan finds that

*An original essay prepared especially for this book.

137

he can get certain types of work done more quickly and more carefully in this way. He had benefited at the same time by having got rid of some workers who, whilst having valuable experience and skills, were also leading union members and at least potential "trouble-makers". Durairajan is one of the many industrialists of Coimbatore who talks spontaneously of the problems of controlling labour (although he has actually had only one quite serious strike in the 25 years in which his firm has been running). By splitting up a formerly more integrated process of production Durairajan has achieved a number of objectives, relating to labour and costs and control over the labour process, whilst retaining some of the advantages of economies of scale, as in the purchase of raw materials.

In addition to assisting the establishment of jobwork units Durairajan has also set up two new small workshops of his own, though they are both nominally owned by other family members, and he says that it is now his policy to set up more such "ancillary" units. Because they will not be unionized, labour problems will therefore be averted, and wage costs may be brought down. The level of taxation, via central exercise, may also be reduced. He says that it is only in this way that he can continue to compete with manufacturers of small drilling machines in North India. Meanwhile he is developing more sophisticated products in his main workshop.

> Durairajan's concern about the control of labour is also reflected in his use of contract labour for the operation of his foundry and for the cleaning of castings (fettling). In his view ". . . the efficiency of labourers is in inverse proportion to their strength"—and those who are employed on a contract basis, through a labour contractor who agrees to undertake a particular operation, can easily be dismissed. Foundry work is generally almost unskilled, and fettling is unskilled, but Durairajan fears that if foundry workers became permanent employees they would come to demand the same levels of payment, increments and bonuses as the more skilled machine shop, sheet-metal workers and fitters. Besides, "moulding sections"—foundries—are notorious throughout Coimbatore as the centres of "labour trouble" in the engineering industry, as they were in Britain in the 19th century (Samuel 1977).

Durairajan's story is a paradigmatic example of tendencies which characterize the engineering industry in Coimbatore. This paper is concerned with the pattern of ownership of small enterprises, with indirect forms of labour use (as in the subcontracting arrangements developed by Durairajan), and with the employment in the engineering industry of casual, temporary or contract workers (generally with "non-specific" labour use, using Bienefeld and Schmitz's terminology[1]†). The paper examines the circumstances which have given rise to the pattern that is observed and considers some of its

†Superscript numbers refer to Notes at end of chapter.

implications. It thus takes up questions about the role and function of small-scale enterprises in economic development—an issue which has been brought into debate by the controversy over the concept of "the informal sector" (see Bromley ed., 1979; and especially the papers by Moser and by Tokman in that volume).

Context: the engineering industry of Coimbatore

The state of Tamil Nadu in south-eastern India, and its capital Madras, have lagged behind only Maharashtra and Bombay in Western India, and Bengal and Calcutta in the east, in terms of their shares of the industrial economy of the country. Industrial development in the state has been subject to the same sluggishness which has characterized industrial growth in the country as a whole since the mid-1960s (with the exception of a brief period during the Emergency). There is evidence too, showing that the rate of growth of employment in manufacturing has lagged behind such growth of investment and of productivity as there has been (Kurien and James 1979). The extent of foreign ownership is controversial, but may have been increasing in India as a whole, in spite of such celebrated affairs as the expulsion of Coca-Cola and of IBM in the recent past. There is also a good deal of evidence of increasing monopolization, which seems sometimes to have been assisted by the legislation which is intended to control it (see e.g. Mitra 1977; Patnaik 1972; Shetty 1978).

Coimbatore, in southwestern Tamil Nadu, is a city with a 1981 population of about 750,000, second (though by a long way) to Madras in terms of population and industrial importance. It is situated in a semi-arid but intensively cultivated region in which commercial cotton growing rose to prominence in the last century. An important cotton spinning industry was then established, really only after the First World War, and mainly by powerful landowners who also cultivated and traded cotton. The industry still dominates the city and provides about half of registered manufacturing employment; and it was the demands of cotton spinning and the money of the most important mill owners which gave rise to the engineering industry for which Coimbatore is also well known. Coimbatore's basic metal industries were first established to supply the cotton mills: foundries for the casting of iron and other metals, and aluminium rolling mills; engineering industries manufacturing textile machinery, light machine tools and prime movers; and metal fabricating industries, originally the manufacturing of structures for factory building, but latterly including also the manufacturing of consumer goods such as steel furniture and aluminium and stainless steel vessels. Another important stimulus was supplied by the agricultural interests of the first industrialists and their demand for water lifting equipment for use in cultivation in the dry region of Coimbatore. The manufacture of electric motors and pumps, for irrigation and domestic water supply, remains a major section of the engineering industry of the city, and the manufacture of electric motors has in turn given rise to other industries requiring their use. Finally, another important section of the engineering industry is the manufacturing of accessories for the automobile industry (such as filling station equipment), first established by two men from the same dominant group of landowner-traders, who moved into transport operation rather than into cotton spinning.

Table 1 shows that the engineering industries (Nos. 33–37 of the National Industrial Classification) dominate in terms of the numbers of registered units of production (that is units registered as "factories" under the terms of the Factories Act), and that registered "small-scale industries"[2] (units registered as such with the Directorate of Commerce and Industry) are also heavily dominated by engineering. The great majority of the largest units of production—factories as they were defined by Marx—as well as the most important employers of labour, are still those in the cotton textile industry. The engineering industry on the other hand is predominantly organized on the basis of small units of production—the great majority of them "workshops", in the sense that they are characterized by detail work and specialized skills. They are places of *manu*-facture, in contrast to the *machino*-facture which characterizes the factories of Coimbatore.

The data on which this analysis is based come from field studies of a sample of 15 relatively large factories (drawn from the 53 registered factories employing more than 50 people in categories 33–35—engineering), and of a further sample of 175 small enterprises (workshops). Many of the workshops in Coimbatore are not registered in any way, and the individual researcher lacks the resources necessary to conduct a comprehensive census to locate these establishments so as to define a population for sampling purposes. The approach adopted to sampling workshops, therefore, had something of a Heath Robinson character. Data were collected from a 10 per cent random sample of the 902 registered "small-scale industries" in categories 30 (rubber and plastic products) and 33–35 (engineering), and from 85 unregistered workshops drawn from a survey of occupations in five contrasting slum areas of the city, and from interviews in another part of the city characterized by large numbers of workshops (where I lived for almost ten months in 1980).

The sample of 175 small enterprises (workshops), both registered and unregistered, can be divided into three groups: (1) units which are registered with the Factories Inspectorate under the Factories Act, and which are registered as "small-scale industries" with the Directorate of Commerce and Industry—henceforth "factory-SSIs" (32 units); (2) all units which are registered as "small-scale industries" with the Directorate of Commerce and Industry—henceforth "SSIs" (90 units); and, (3) units which may be described as falling within the "unorganized sector" in the sense that they are neither registered with the Factories Inspectorate nor with the Directorate of Commerce and Industry—henceforth described as unregistered small units (85 units). The first two groups *do* overlap, but it seems to be useful to present

TABLE 1. *Registered factories and small-scale industries of Coimbatore, 1979 (Coimbatore Taluk data)*

Branch of industrial production	Number of registered factories[1] Size of units—numbers employed						Percentage of all employment in registered factories[2]	Number of registered "small-scale industries"[3]
	10–20	21–50	51–100	101–500	over 500	Total		
20–21 Food products	23	9	3	1	1	37	3.0	15
22 Beverages	0	0	1	1	0	2	n	13
23 Cotton textiles	25	33	17	25	35	135	49.0	0
24 Other textiles	3	0	0	0	0	3	n	0
26 Hosiery and garments	1	3	0	0	0	4	n	16
27 Wood products	16	5	0	0	0	21	n	33
28 Paper products and printing	41	11	3	2	1	58	1.8	119
29 Leather products	1	1	1	0	0	3	n	16
30 Rubber and plastic products	33	11	4	3	0	51	2.0	85
31 Chemicals and chemical products	9	9	1	0	0	19	3.8	72
32 Non-metallic mineral products	16	6	0	0	2	24	3.4	67
33 Basic metals	68	55	9	6	1	139	8.8	244
34 Metal products	30	17	0	4	0	51	3.4	261
35 General machinery and parts	88	58	18	12	3	179	17.5	312
36 Electrical machinery	12	13	5	6	0	36	2.6	181
37 Transport equipment	12	10	5	7	1	35	3.4	36
38 Other manufactures	3	1	2	0	0	6	n	20
Others	5	5	3	0	0	13	n	0
Total	386	247	72	67	44	816	100.0	1490

n = negligible (the sum of all the n's is 1.3 per cent).
[1] "Factory Industry" here refers to units which are registered under the Factories Act with the Factories Inspectorate. According to the terms of the Act this should be all units employing ten or more people and using power; or all units not using power but employing twenty or more people.
[2] These data, showing the percentage of all those employed in registered units who are employed in a particular industrial group, were taken from the records of the Factories Inspectorate in Coimbatore.
[3] These are the numbers of units registered as "Small-scale industries" with the Directorate of Industry and Commerce.

the material in this way because the defining characteristic of each group represents a different relationship of small enterprises to the State.

Ownership and financing of small enterprises

It is striking that the "factory-SSIs" are most commonly units which have been started by those with managerial and professional backgrounds. The unregistered small units, on the other hand, are more likely to have been started by workers or artisans, and those which do belong to managerial or professional people are often merely side-businesses or businesses which have been started only recently. The significance of this observation is that former

TABLE 2. *Ownership of workshops in the Coimbatore sample*

Type of entrepreneur	"Factory-SSIs"		"SSIs"		Unregistered small units	
	No.	%	No.	%	No.	%
Worker–artisan	8	25	50	56	56	66
Manager–professional (including industrialists and traders)	21	66	31	34	20	24
Agriculturalist	3	9	7	8	3	3
Others	0	0	2	2	6	7
Total	32	100	90	100	85	100
Incidence of multiple ownership	21	66	35	39	16	19

managers/professionals are more highly educated than worker–artisan entrepreneurs and come from wealthier and higher caste backgrounds, and they generally enjoy much easier access to the cheap institutional credit now being made available to "small enterprises" (see Table 3). They are also more likely to be able to raise funds through the fixed deposits of friends and relatives, since they mostly come from close-knit, relatively affluent caste communities. More of the worker–artisan entrepreneurs come from lower ranking communities and do not have a network of well-placed caste fellows and kin on which to draw, though even they very rarely come from the lowest ranked caste communities (in Coimbatore dominantly Pallans and Chakkiliyans, both of them "untouchable" groups). These differences in access to financial resources exercise an important influence upon the possibilities of survival, and even more upon the possibilities of expanded reproduction, of the different units. All of the registered "SSIs" have experienced expansion and accumulation, and so have almost all of the unregistered small units which belong to managers or professionals. Only

TABLE 3. *Financing and growth of workshops in the Coimbatore sample*

	Original finance		Finance for further investment	
	"SSIs"	Unregistered small units	"SSIs"	Unregistered small units
UNITS WHICH HAVE RECEIVED INSTITUTIONAL FINANCING (as % of totals)				
Worker–artisan entrepreneurs	13%	7%	88%	50%
Manager–professional entrepreneurs	38%	29%	95%	50%
UNITS WHICH HAVE USED CHIT-FUNDS OR PRIVATE FINANCIERS (as % of totals)				
Worker–artisan entrepreneurs	13%	25%	25%	25%
Manager-professional entrepreneurs	0%	5%	5%	10%

UNITS WITH A RECORD OF ACCUMULATION (up to 1979–1980)	"SSIs"	Unregistered small units
Median date of start	1970	1973
Worker–artisan entrepreneurs	100%	47%
Manager–professional entrepreneurs	100%	85%

about half of the unregistered small units belonging to former workers have experienced expansion and accumulation (see Table 3). This difference may be due in part to the fact that the unregistered units are generally of more recent origin, but it is unlikely that the greater difficulty which worker–artisan entrepreneurs experience in raising loans from formal credit sources, and their greater reliance on informal credit at higher interest rates, does not play a large part in explaining the differences between the two groups. The point is strengthened when we note that worker–artisan entrepreneurs who have received assistance from formal credit sources, have more often than not had access only to a limited overdraft facility.

Prominent among the unregistered small units which have not experienced any expansion are the tinkers (making galvanized iron vessels), welders, aluminium and gun-metal casters, a manufacturer of aluminium vessels, some turners owning their own lathes, and carpenters who make patterns for moulding. These are all activities which require rather little capital, which operate in highly competitive markets (where the cheap consumer goods are concerned) and in which there are difficulties over the supply of raw materials to very small producers.

A note on big capital and small enterprises, and on "multiple ownership"

"Small enterprises" are not necessarily owned by "small capitalists", and among the 90 units in our survey of registered "SSIs" and entitled thereby to access to the facilities made available by the State for the encouragement of such industries (see Kurien 1978; Tyabji 1980), were four units directly owned by factory owners with interests also in the "monopoly" sector. Textile mill owners entered the pump and motor industry at an early stage, for example, and they have also sometimes set up workshops, registered as "SSIs" for the manufacturing of spares for textile machinery. There are other industrialists who own groups of "SSIs", though the ownership of the different units is made to appear different by what the industrialists call "benami" registrations, whereby a unit is registered in somebody else's name, usually wife or child. In such groups the value of capital invested in plant and machinery and the numbers of those employed in all the units put together may be equivalent to the levels of so-called "large-scale industry". Five of the "SSIs" in the sample of 90 belong to industrialists of this kind, who, by their own accounts of their decisions, have found the arrangement advantageous in terms of diversification and flexibility, and particularly in the interests of labour cost and control. These factors appeared to be of greater importance than the incentives of cheaper credit and the possibility of reduced taxation, offered to "SSIs".

In addition to these big industrialists' multiple holdings, however, "multiple ownership" (the ownership of several units by the same individual(s)) is a much more general feature of the ownership of "SSIs" in Coimbatore. Among the 32 "factory-SSIs" for example, there are 21 which belong to people who also own other enterprises, numbering 41 in all, so that the sample of 32 provides entry to a group of 73 small production units. Although there are nearly 1500 registered "SSIs" in Coimbatore, there are probably only just over half as many real "owners" of such units. As with the ownership of several units by big industrialists, the reasons for multiple ownership of "SSIs" include advantages of diversification (extending the range of electric motors and of types of pumps manufactured, or adding a new product altogether) and of complementarity (as when the owners of a small foundry add on a machine shop). Most frequently, however, multiple ownership of these kinds of units reflects various forms of "splitting", where a single workshop is registered as two or more separate companies, or where, as is often the case with the manufacturing of steel furniture in Coimbatore, an industrialist owns several units of a very similar type so as to avoid having to pay higher levels of sales tax or central excise. These various reasons for multiple ownership are interwoven with considerations of labour cost and control.

As might be expected, the incidence of multiple ownership among unregistered small units is lower (it occurs in about one-fifth of cases), and only in two cases is more than one other unit involved.

Small enterprises, subcontracting and linkages

Durairajan's story, which is paralleled in some other of the larger enterprises in the engineering industry in Coimbatore, illustrates the possible roles of subcontracting between large and small units, or between workshops and petty commodity producers or factories and workshops. By "subcontracting" we refer to those arrangements whereby:

> The party offering the subcontract (parent firm, enterprise or company) requests another independent enterprise . . . to undertake the whole or part of an order it has received instead of doing the work itself, while assuming full responsibility for the work *vis-à-vis* the customer. Subcontracting differs from the mere purchase of ready-made parts and components in that there is an actual contract between the two parties setting out the specifications of the order (Watanabe 1971, 54).

Durairajan subcontracts work in just this way, mainly the machining of parts, to small workshops and to petty producers. The pattern of subcontracting relationships entered into by enterprises in our sample, both those registered as "SSIs" and the unregistered small units, is shown in Table 4. It will be seen that in both cases almost half the units have subcontracting relationships with large-scale industries; most commonly with the big textile mills, with L. G. Balakrishnan Brothers (who are the manufacturers of a range of products, mostly related the the automobile industry, and on some of which they hold a monopoly position in the market), with the Lakshmi Machine Works, with Textool, and with the Bharat Heavy Electricals Ltd. (in the town of Tiruchirapalli, just over 100 miles away).

Almost all the "factory-SSIs" which are engaged in sub-contracting obtain their own raw materials, whereas over half of the unregistered small units which are sub-contractors for big factories are engaged in "jobwork", working on materials supplied by the parent firm, for labour charges. Some of them are tied to a single parent firm, as Durairajan's former workers are mostly tied to him, relying on his firm for both orders and assistance.

Subcontracting has been seen as a dynamic aspect of industrial growth and Watanabe (1970, 1971) and others have drawn attention to its positive role in the industrial development of Japan, whilst pointing out that ". . . the lack of cooperation between large and small enterprises remains conspicuous in developing countries" (Watanabe 1970, 573). It has been argued that "if the government takes appropriate measures to ensure prompt payment and other

TABLE 4. *Subcontracting and linkages of workshops in the Coimbatore sample*

	"Factory-SSIs"	"SSIs"	Unregistered small units
SUBCONTRACTORS			
Not "tied" using own materials			
— for big factories	13	24	13
— for small units	0	8	10
job-work			
— for big factories	0	} 4	12
— for small units	0		2
"Tied" using own materials			
— for big factories	1	4	2
— for small units	0	1	1
— for a trader	0	4	4
job-work			
— for big factories	1	1	7
Total subcontractors	15 (47 %)	46 (51%)	51 (60%)
LINKAGES			
Subcontractors	15	46	51
Producers of parts or finished goods on order from the factory sector	7	10	3
Producers of parts for other small units	3	4	3
Producers of finished goods	7	30	28
Total units	32 (100 %)	90(100%)	85(100%)

fair trade practices, subcontracting can be a most effective means of stimulating industrial activity by small entrepreneurs and promoting small enterprises, without sacrificing economies of scale" (Watanabe 1970, 574). In his study of Indian industry in the 1950s, Rosen (1959) found that subcontracting was little developed, and he, like Watanabe, argued that government should encourage its development in the interests of industrial "efficiency" (by reducing under-utilization of capacity in large plants, for example) and of the growth of small enterprises. Others, however, have been less sanguine about the prospects for the development of small firms under these conditions of linkage with large-scale factory enterprises (see, for example, Gupta's report on subcontracting in the automobile industry in the town of Bursa in Turkey; 1980). Watanabe too refers to the possibility of the exploitation of subcontractors by parent firms when the conditions of prompt payment and fair trading practices are not fulfilled—as they evidently were not, for example, in the case of small firms supplying British Leyland in Coventry in the 1970s. According to Friedman (1977), a good many such firms were made bankrupt as a result of delays in payments from British Leyland.

What is the role of subcontracting in the engineering industry of Coimbatore, and what are its implications for the reproduction of small enterprises, workshops and petty producer units? Does the kind of subcontracting system developed by Durairajan provide opportunities for establishing independent units of production or does it only set up those whom we might call "subsistence engineers"?

It is suggested that large enterprises may benefit from subcontracting arrangements in various ways: (a) by saving capital; (b) by saving labour costs; (c) by diversifying the product range without sacrificing economies of scale in the main production lines; (d) by taking advantage of the subcontractors' specialized technology; (e) by increasing adaptability to market fluctuations. It is further suggested by Watanabe (1970, 554) that in Japan the first two considerations have been most important while in Europe and America the last three have been more significant. In the case of Durairajan's system, and those of other firms like his, factors (b), (c) and (e) are all salient, though we have seen that, at least according to their own accounts, the factor of labour control and cost was most important for the capitalists concerned. This is not necessarily true in general of subcontracting in Coimbatore, for if we consider the work in which small units of production are engaged as subcontractors we find that a number of specialized activities are performed. Among the registered "SSIs" the provision of specialized work, with its associated capital savings for the "parent" firms, may be a more important factor than that of labour costs. The foundries in this group, for example, do specialized work—principally shell castings, used in making cylinder heads in the automobile industry. Here the big parent firms (in the "monopoly" sector)—several of them located in North India—make use of the specialized knowledge and the intensity of supervision in their subcontractors' units, thereby making capital savings for themselves in what is a fairly tricky and potentially costly operation. The conditions of subcontracting among the unregistered small units are less clear-cut, though in their case too, the provision of specialized work—plastic parts, gun-metal and aluminium castings, electro-plating, and glass-fibre tanks—remains important. Those subcontracting and jobwork units which undertake machining or produce ordinary rough castings, however, fall rather into the Durairajan pattern. Here the parent units save capital and labour costs, though the use of subcontractors may make diversification possible and increase their adaptability to market fluctuation.

The argument against the view that subcontracting can be means of promoting industrial growth depends on a demonstration that it yields situations of unilateral dependence and exploitation (e.g. Gupta 1980). This argument does not appear to be valid in the case of the engineering industry of Coimbatore, when we consider that in our sample of 32 "factory-SSIs", 12 of them started out as subcontracting or jobwork units and have either progressed to manufacturing on their own accounts (eight cases) or have experienced quite rapid and substantial growth. Eight of the workshops which are not registered under the Factories Act have similarly progressed from origins as jobwork units. But the circumstances of the linkages between small enterprises and factory industry are certainly such as to place the smaller units at a substantial disadvantage, and most of the subcontractors, and indeed the owners of firms supplying parts or finished goods to large-scale industry, reported cash flow problems, as they have to give extended credit (commonly 30 days) to the firms they supply, while often having to pay on delivery for raw materials themselves. They face credit constraints in these circumstances in particular (like the subcontracting firms in Coventry discussed by Friedman). They are also subjected to raw materials costs squeezes, because of the inflationary situation and especially because of recurrent raw materials shortages. In 1980 both coke and pig iron were often scarce and available only at black market prices, but at other times mild steel bars and steel sheet, aluminium and raw plastic have all been in short supply. It is usually impossible for subcontractors to pass on unanticipated cost increases to the parties they supply.[3] The jobworkers are insulated from some of these difficulties, but many of them experience difficulty in making the transition from jobwork to production on their own accounts. The implications of Durairajan's "socialism" therefore, are not clearcut; and whether or not a man can pass through the stage of being a "subsistence engineer" depends crucially upon the extent to which he has access to finance, which hangs, in turn, upon his education and upon his social background. There must be many small workshops and petty labour units which fail within a relatively short space of time, though we have no means of establishing what the proportion is.

Studies of industrial development in Japan have drawn attention not only to the quantitative importance of small units and of subcontracting, but also to its special qualities. In Japan "shitauke", or "subcontracting" implies something more than is given in the definition we cited earlier:

> First the relative sizes of the contractor and the subcontractor are important: the former is larger than the latter. Second, the business relationship between the two parties is continuous, although it is not established as such by law or by contract and can be interrupted during a depression. Third, as a consequence of the first and second features . . . a paternalistic relation exists between the two. . . . While the contract is usually concluded by tender in European and American subcontracting, it is not so in Japan, where subcontractors are generally attached to a single parent company (Watanabe 1970, 551).

It is believed that this particular kind of relationship between units has been beneficial because it has reduced the barriers to entry of new firms, and references are made to some enormously successful Japanese firms which started out as subcontractors. Surveys have shown for example, that among

Japanese engineering enterprises employing fewer than 300 workers over 70 per cent are subcontractors, and that 20–30 per cent are "tied" subcontractors—working for a single parent firm only.

Data from the random sample of 90 "SSIs" in Coimbatore show that just over 50 per cent of such small enterprises are subcontractors, and data for the sample of 85 unregistered small units show that 60 per cent are subcontractors. But only 11 per cent of the former sample and 16 per cent of the latter are "tied" subcontractors. It seems then, that while subcontracting in engineering in Coimbatore is quite extensive—a fact which may suggest, incidentally, that there has been considerable development in India in this regard since Rosen wrote in the 1950s—it is still neither so well-developed, nor developed in the same way that it was at an earlier stage in Japan. There is some evidence, however, in the history of enlightened paternalism of the principal founding director of the textile machinery firm, Textool, of the kind of influence upon industrial development reported from Japan. Many of the units originally set up to supply Textool soon became independent manufacturing concerns.

Small enterprises and the conditions of labour

According to industrialists themselves, major reasons for the kind of "multiple ownership" of small enterprises which we reported above are their beliefs that this represents a way in which they can protect themselves against the effects of unionization and exercise greater control over labour, while also reducing labour costs directly by avoiding the provisions of the factories legislation. The same factors affect decisions to subcontract work. What then are conditions of labour like in the small enterprises of Coimbatore?

Among the 32 "factory-SSIs", 19 of them employ both "permanent" and "temporary" workers (who are also called "helpers"), and in these units, on average, about one-third of the total workforces are people employed on a temporary basis and paid daily wages. Another six units employ mainly or entirely "permanent" workers, four units are operated entirely by contract labour, and the remaining three units employ only daily paid labour. In seven of the 32 units, employees receive neither Provident Fund nor Employees' State Insurance, though in all of them more than 20 people are employed, and workers should be entitled to both of these benefits. In another 11 units workers do not receive Provident Fund, when they should under the terms of the relevant Act. Even registration under the Factories Act, therefore, is not a strong guarantee of "permanent" status for workers, or a guarantee that they will receive the benefits to which they are entitled.

In *none* of the 85 unregistered small units do workers receive these benefits, though in as many as seven of them they should do. The owners of these units evade the legislation by splitting their enterprises into what are only nominally separate units, or by employing contract workers. Though the courts have ruled that contract workers should be covered by the Employees' State Insurance Act of 1948, its provisions are easily evaded.

The wages received by workers in registered "SSIs" are not always or necessarily lower than those of workers in big factories, though rates are generally lower in the unregistered small units. Lower labour costs in small enterprises are primarily the result of avoidance or evasion of legislation concerning the payment of benefits, and of the widespread employment of younger, less qualified men, and sometimes of women and children (Harriss 1980). Amongst the employees of small foundries, steel furniture manufacturers and manufacturers of plastic components and plastic bags, in particular, there are quite large numbers of boys and of women. Many women are employed in the grime and sweat of the small foundries for a wage of four or five rupees per day.[4]

Finally, it is striking that the general level of wages in the engineering industry as a whole is considerably lower than it is in the spinning mills. There are workshops in which the whole process of production depends to a great extent upon the skills of the best turners. Yet their wages of Rs 15 or 16 per day are five or six rupees lower than those received by many permanent mill workers. This difference reflects the fact that the engineering industry is mainly operated on a workshop basis, with a weakly unionized or non-unionized labour force.

Only ten of the registered "SSIs" have unions, seven of them organized by the Coimbatore and District General Engineering and Mechanical Workers' Union, the principal union in the engineering industry, and affiliated to the CITU.[5] The three unregistered small units which formerly had unions (none of them is unionized now) are all ones which should be registered under the Factories Act but in which the owners have managed to avoid registration by using contract labour or part-time workers. Nine of the registered "SSIs" and five of the unregistered small units have seen strike action more serious than short bonus disputes, which are almost an annual ritual in many firms. But it is usually not very difficult for the owners of engineering firms to control their workers—and some of them said as much in casual remarks—given the small size of most units and the paternalistic relationships within them encouraged by industrialists. The larger firms in the industry, which we also surveyed, have experienced much more serious labour disputes than the small enterprises. But even in them, managements hold the upper hand (sometimes by making use of informal networks of "trusties"—caste fellows, or other clients—to forestall trouble).

Conclusions

Small enterprises are a prominent feature of the industrial landscape of Coimbatore, especially in the engineering and plastics industries. In these industries small units are rather strongly linked, forwards and backwards, with the large-scale factory sector.

With the principal exceptions of some small plastic moulding shops which use re-cycled plastic scrap, and of small foundries which use a high percentage of scrap metal, these units rely for their most important raw materials on the big-capital factory sector: pig iron, coke, mild steel bars, steel sheet, aluminium, copper wire, raw plastic, and chemicals for electro-plating. Most of these commodities are produced in a few large plants, many of them in the public sector, but the smaller units in particular are placed at a serious disadvantage, as their owners and managers seek to obtain supplies on the black market. This usually cuts deep into their profits, and is one of the causes of the rather high mortality which is believed to be characteristic of such units, for neither subcontracting workshops nor producers of finished goods can easily and quickly pass on their increased costs to their customers. The same feature of the industrial economy of India helps to account for the continuing attractiveness of trading in industrial raw materials as opposed to, or in addition to, manufacturing (see Streefkerk 1978).

A rather high proportion of small enterprises (50–60 per cent) is of units which are directly linked with big-capital factories as subcontractors, obtaining their own materials (in a majority of cases) or as jobworkers. A minority of these workshops and petty producers are "tied" subcontracting or job-working units. Another quite large group of workshops is of producers of parts or finished goods on order from big-capital factories; and there are others which are indirectly linked with big-capital factories as subcontractors or producers of parts for workshops which do have direct links. In all, as many as two-thirds of the small-scale units in these industries may have forward linkages of the kind described with big-capital factories.

The subcontracting and product linkages between small-scale units and factories in Coimbatore are not homogeneous, and there is a good deal of variation in the extent of subordination and exploitation which is involved, depending of course, upon the bargaining power of different units. Some of them have bargaining power by virtue of providing specialized services, and others by virtue of having secure access to finance. A majority have seen accumulation and expansion. Of course, we have no means of knowing how many units have failed, so that it would be unwise to present a very rosy picture of the possibilities for "growth" of small-scale industrial enterprises in general; but equally it would be wrong to deny the possibility of expansion altogether. These possibilities exist within the broad constraints of the dependence of subcontracting units upon the firms for which they work, which include the kinds of cash flow problems also confronted by subcontracting units in the British car industry as these have been described by Friedman.

Prominent among the reasons for the persistence of small-scale forms of production is the interest of large-scale capitalists (the owners of factories and of large workshops) in the control of the labour process, and in the reduction of labour costs—as we observed in the account of Durairajan's activities with which we began, and as is reflected in the pattern of ownership of small units.

We may note that few of the objectives *claimed* for the policy of encouraging "small-scale" production by the State, are fulfilled: "SSIs" are *not* decentralized (see the work by Saha on Bihar, 1980; and note the concentration of Tamil Nadu's "SSIs" in Madras and Coimbatore), and they do not seriously dent the concentration of economic power, when, as we have seen, they serve the interests of big capital as markets and as suppliers of important services—not the least of these being that of labour control. They are instrumental, perhaps, in increasing employment, though evidence on the capital/labour ratio in "small" as opposed to "large-scale industry" in India is equivocal (Subramaniam and Kashyap 1975). But this employment is generally on terms which are very favourable to capital, given the lower labour costs and lower levels of unionization in "small industries". Satisfaction of the equity objective claimed for the policy of encouraging small-scale production is therefore doubly doubtful: access to the benefits made available by the State to "SSIs" is skewed strongly in favour of those who are already relatively favoured, while the employment that "SSIs" provide is frequently of a very exploitative kind. The one objective claimed for the policy which probably has been satisfied is that of "democratizing" ownership—given that this objective was (fairly explicitly) to widen the bourgeois base of the regime. The objectives *claimed* for the policy of encouraging "SSIs" may, anyway, be much less important than the interests served by it—which include those of big capital as much as those of small capitalists.

Notes

1. The terms "non-specific" and "indirect" labour use are taken from Bienefeld and Schmitz (1976) who define them in opposition to "specific" and to "direct" labour use. "Specific labour use . . . involves, as a primary objective, the raising of productivity of specific workers /and/ is therefore closely connected with stable labour force /though/ it is not synonymous with that character" (Bienefeld and Schmitz 1976, 10)—and it is associated with the creation of internal labour markets. "Non-specific" labour use refers to the employment of unstable, easily replaceable labour. The term "indirect labour use" refers to labour which is employed at one or more removes, as in forms of subcontracting. Bienefeld and Schmitz propose the hypothesis that there has been a shift in many capitalist enterprises in the periphery towards specific labour use, accompanied by the employment of unstable, easily replaceable labour in other parts of the production process; and that indirect use of labour is one important means of controlling and co-opting labour while continuing to extract surplus value.
2. The category of registered "small-scale industries" refers to units which are registered as such for purposes of State promotional programmes, and which are defined as units employing not more than Rs 1,500,000 of capital invested in plant and machinery. For discussions of policy towards "small-scale industry" see Kurien (1978) and Tyabji (1980).
3. Attempts by the State to administer the supply of scarce raw materials may only exacerbate the situation for small producers (see Van der Ween 1973).
4. Average 1980 exchange rates were around Rs. 18 to the pound sterling and Rs. 8 to the U.S. dollar.

5. The CITU is the Confederation of Indian Trade Unions affiliated with the Communist Party of India (Marxist).

References

BADEMLI, R. R. (1977) "Distorted and Lower Forms of Capitalist Industrial Production in Underdeveloped Countries: Contemporary Artisan Shops and Workshops in Eskisehir and Gaziantep, Turkey", Unpublished Ph.D. dissertation, Massachusetts Institute of Technology, Cambridge, Mass.

BIENEFELD, Manfred and SCHMITZ, Hubert (1976) "Capital accumulation and employment in the periphery: a programme of research", *IDS Discussion Paper* No. 98, University of Sussex, Brighton.

BROMLEY, Ray (ed.) (1979) *The Urban Informal Sector: Critical Perspectives on Employment and Housing Policies*, Pergamon, Oxford.

FRIEDMAN, A. (1977) *Industry and Labour*, Macmillan, London.

GUPTA, S. C. (1980) "Subcontracting between factories and workshops: a case study of automotive industry in Bursa, Turkey", Unpublished M.Sc. dissertation, Middle East Technical University, Ankara.

HARRISS, John (1980) "Urban labour, urban poverty and the so-called informal sector", *Bulletin, Madras Institute of Development Studies*, October, pp. 491–512.

KURIEN, C. T. (1978) "Small sector in new industrial policy", *Economic and Political Weekly*, Vol. 13, No. 9, pp. 455–61.

KURIEN, C. T. and JAMES, J. (1979) *Economic Change in Tamil Nadu: A Regionally and Functionally Disaggregated Study*, Allied Publishers, Bombay.

MITRA, A. (1977) *Terms of Trade and Class Relations*, Frank Cass, London.

MOSER, Caroline (1978) "Informal sector or petty commodity production: dualism or dependence in urban development?", *World Development*, Vol. 6, No. 9/10, pp. 1041–64. Reprinted in Ray Bromley (ed.) (1979) *op. cit.*

PATNAIK, P. (1972) "Imperialism and the growth of Indian capitalism", in Owen, Roger and Sutcliffe, Bob (eds.), *Studies in Imperialism*, Longman, London.

RAJ, K. N. (1976) "Growth and stagnation in Indian industrial development", *Economic and Political Weekly*, Annual Number, February 1976, pp. 223–36.

ROSEN, G. (1959) *Industrial Change in India: Industrial Growth, Capital Requirements and Technological Change 1937–1955*, Asia Publishing House, London.

SAHA, S. K. (1980) "Industrial policy and locational dynamics of small-scale enterprises in India: A case study of small-scale metalworking firms in the Chotanagpur region of Bihar". Paper presented at a Seminar on Industrial Location Research organized by the Industrial Activity and Area Development Study Group of the Institute of British Geographers, held at the LSE, 9 May 1980.

SAMUEL, Raphael (1977) "Workshop of the World", *History Workshop*, No. 3 (Spring), pp. 6–72.

SHETTY, S. L. (1978) "Structural regression in the Indian economy since the mid 1960s", *Economic and Political Weekly*, Annual Number, February 1978, pp. 185–244.

STREEFKERK, H. (1978) *Lichte Industrie in een Kleine Indiase Stad*. Amsterdam.

SUBRAMANIAM and KASHYAP (1975) "Small-scale industry: a trend report", in *A Survey of Research in Economics, Vol. V*, Indian Council of Social Science Research, Delhi, pp. 75–112.

TOKMAN, Victor E. (1978) "An Exploration into the nature of informal–formal sector relationships", *World Development*, Vol. 6, No. 9/10, pp. 1065–75. Reprinted in Ray Bromley (ed.) (1979), *op. cit.*

TYABJI, N. (1980) "Capitalism in India and the Small Industries Policy", *Economic and Political Weekly*, Special Number, October, pp. 1721–32.

VAN DER WEEN, J. (1973) "Small-scale industries in Gujarat State", Unpublished Ph.D. dissertation, Cornell University, Ithaca, N.Y.

WATANABE, S. (1970) "Entrepreneurship in small enterprises in Japanese manufacturing", *International Labour Review*, Vol. 102, pp. 531–576.

WATANABE, S. (1971) "Subcontracting, industrialisation and employment creation", *International Labour Review*, Vol. 104, pp. 51–76.

CHAPTER 9

Wagers and wage-working: selling gambling opportunities in Cali, Colombia*

CHRIS GERRY

"My father used to say that formerly . . . the lottery in Babylon was a game of plebian character. He recounted . . . that barbers sold, in exchange for copper coins, squares of bone or parchment adorned with symbols. In broad daylight a drawing took place. Those who won received silver coins without any other test of luck. The system was elementary, as you can see."

(Jorge Luis Borges, *The Lottery in Babylon*)

Anyone walking through the central square of Cali, Colombia's third largest city and capital of the Department of Valle,[1]† can hardly avoid noticing that the major commercial activity for most of the day is the selling of lottery tickets. Though the number of lottery ticket sellers (*loteros*) varies from morning to night and from day to day, on average they make up at least three-quarters of the total number of people engaged in open-air commerce in the square. Peak selling occurs on Wednesday afternoons, with about 100 *loteros* active in the square; this is due to the fact that the local lottery (*Lotería del Valle*) is drawn that day, and the tickets for the following week's draw become available. On other weekdays, numbers range from as many as 95 to as few as 40, depending upon the time of day and the lottery being drawn that day.

Moving away from the city centre, the preponderance of stationary *loteros* diminishes, except in established selling areas such as markets, large shopping centres and office blocks. *Loteros* are still to be found in the suburbs, though more dispersed and often working a specific route rather than selling from an established location. In Cali, as in many other Third World cities, the sale of

---

*An original essay prepared especially for this book and based upon fieldwork conducted in Cali in 1977 (the ethnographic present throughout the text). The author is grateful to Libardo Amaya for fieldwork assistance, to the U.K. Overseas Development Administration for financing the research as part of a broader project on the street occupations of Cali, and to the Regional Office of SENA in Cali for their invaluable support. For their helpful comments and criticisms based on local knowledge, he is indebted to Max Nieto (Universidad del Valle) and Ray Bromley. It should be emphasized, however, that the author is wholly responsible for the content and conclusions of the paper, and that no institutional viewpoint is being expressed.
†Superscript numbers refer to Notes at end of Chapter.

lottery tickets is very visible and relatively widespread. But precisely what sort of occupation is it?

In popular folklore and social scientific analysis lottery ticket sellers appear as almost lumpenproletarian figures. In part this springs from the fact that, as sellers of "gambling opportunities", they have been identified paradoxically with the threat of fraud and the promise of windfall gain. This characterization applies to virtually all workers in the "gambling sector", whether they are active in the legitimate State lotteries or in the numerous forms of the "numbers racket" which lotteries have spawned. Such street-sellers are also identified with yet another mechanism by which the infinitesimal savings of the poor can be channelled into the coffers of the wealthy. These characterizations will remain little more than prejudice and speculation until considerable and detailed analysis is undertaken to ascertain the extent to which such sellers are, in fact, "lumpenproletarian", "marginal", or pariahs, or indeed, the extent to which they are relatively ordinary members of the urban self-employed. This short paper summarizes the results and conclusions of one such empirical study. It proceeds from the hypothesis that neither the "lumpenproletarian" nor the "ordinary self-employed" characterization is likely to reflect the reality of *loteros* or similar sellers of wagers, and that the real situation faced by such urban workers is much more closely connected with broader processes of capital accumulation and labour exploitation than is commonly assumed.

Street-selling of any variety has been characterized most frequently as "self-employment"—the commercial sector's counterpart to the artisanal form of production. However, the apparently quite reasonable assumption that almost all such individuals are self-employed, has been challenged recently (see e.g. Bromley 1978). The present paper argues along similar lines that, although lottery ticket sellers and allied vendors in the "gambling sector" are apparently own-account, autonomous workers, their conditions and relations of production are nonetheless characterized by an extremely deep-rooted and well-defined subordination to capital. Such relationships may be so influential (whether in commercial or directly-productive activities) that the supposedly self-employed producer or trader would be more accurately characterized as a *disguised wage-worker* (Bromley and Gerry 1979, 5–11; Gerry 1980; Gerry and Birkbeck 1981). The term "disguised wage-working" is not a conceptual innovation, but just shorthand for Marx's own analysis of the "formal and real subsumption of labour under capital" (Marx 1976, 1019–38) applied to the conditions of contemporary underdeveloped capitalist economies.

However, to return to the specific case of vendors in the gambling sector of Cali, research has shown that extremely complex relations exist between: (i) State charitable institutions (*Beneficencias*), such as that which operates Cali's "own" *Loteria del Valle*); (ii) the *loteros* who sell the tickets of this and other lotteries; (iii) the gambling public; and (iv) the producers, distributors and consumers of *other* wagers (e.g. the "numbers game" or *chance*, horse-racing bets, raffles and prize draws). State-sanctioned and -operated lotteries in Colombia have spawned a "parasitical" counterpart, called *chance*, which in general appeals to poorer sections of the gambling public, and which is operated by small capitalist enterprises through their separate networks of street-vendors. *Chance* relies on the winning number generated by an official lottery, and provides an additional example of disguised wage-work. Like lottery, the selling of *chance* tickets is based upon ambiguous capital–labour relations, which have been the focus of significant syndicalist responses in recent years by the representatives of the *chanceros* who link the private companies with the gambling public.

The fundamental relationship between *chance* and the lottery is as follows: the winning lottery ticket number of the week (for example, ticket 2345) provides a number of winners whose tickets correspond exactly to that number or its permitted permutations. The last three numbers of the winning ticket (345) are used by the *chance* companies as the winning *chance* number. If a customer has selected the three numbers in the right order, the maximum dividend is paid. If a permutation, the last two numbers, or just the last number, have been guessed, then smaller dividends are paid according to the size of the original investment. The *Beneficencia* receives no fee from the *chance* companies for the privilege, and the latter are consequently thought of as parasites by the former, and are accused of not only making profits to the detriment of public charities, but also of stealing clients from the *loteros* and thereby reducing their earnings. Similar parasitism exists between Colombia's two major horse-race organizers and the myriad off-course betting agencies in every town and city.

Employment, earnings and income distribution in the lottery

Cali's gambling public tends to favour its "own" *Loteria del Valle*, a tendency which is perhaps accentuated because "outside" lotteries must pay a "tax" to the *Beneficencia del Valle* for the privilege of selling in Valle. As a consequence of this and the fact that the basic prices of different lotteries vary considerably, the income-levels and distribution of a *lotero*'s regular and irregular clientele will be the principal factors determining his sale of particular lotteries' tickets. An additional complication is the variation in the ratio between the cost of the ticket and the magnitude and number of prizes from one lottery to another.

The channels through which the public receive their tickets and through which *loteros* distribute their wares are summarized in Figure 1. The *Beneficencia del Valle* and the Cali-based agencies of other lotteries distribute their tickets mainly to registered wholesale agencies, who subsequently reach the gambling public through street-level wholesalers in Cali's central square and through retail *loteros*. Tickets are sold to agencies and street-level wholesalers at bulk-discount prices, and only the former and a few of the latter

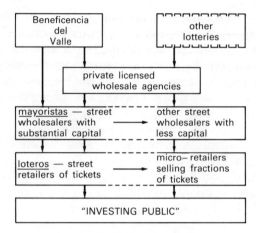

FIG. 1. Distribution channels for
lottery tickets in Cali.

are in a position to purchase the requisite quantity to secure such a discount. Since the majority of tickets reach the "lottery public" through the hands of the street-level retailer (*lotero*) at a price fixed by statutory decision, it is not surprising that *loteros* have been characterized unambiguously as self-employed retailers. However, the reality is more ambiguous since the fixed selling price means that competition between *loteros* is restricted to the uphill struggle to find the best location, the most stable clientele, and the "luckiest" sequences of ticket numbers which will ensure high and stable sales.

Wholesalers' prices are virtually invariable and margins are fixed by cartel arrangements; this implies that the *lotero*'s earnings are, in fact, nothing more than a fixed percentage commission on the level of sales achieved. Thus it would not be inappropriate to identify *loteros* as one of the more humble forms of so-called commission agents. No real distinction exists between a commission agent and a wage-worker earning a piece-rate, except that the former term is usually applied to subjectively "higher status" purveyors of services (e.g. insurance) or *indirect* purveyors of goods (the travelling salesman looking for new orders), rather than to those involved *directly* in the production of tangible commodities.

These conclusions, drawn from the specific examination of *loteros*' working conditions and relations in Cali can, in principle, be expanded to provide a more general set of conclusions relating to the employment of labour, in particular in less developed capitalist economies. Whether producer of commodities in a factory, or purveyor of services on the street, regardless of whether the form of payment is a time-rate, piece-rate or "commission", workers are often subjected to a temporary or even permanent "externaliz-ation" by the capitalist enterprises which control their basic working relations and conditions. This means that capitalist enterprises can make significant temporary or permanent reductions in costs by forcing a section of their "employees" (whether formally recognized as such, or not) to accept an increasing share of the costs of reproducing their own labour power (see e.g. Wolpe 1972 on South Africa; Oliveira's essay, which appears as Chapter 6 of this volume; Gerry and Birkbeck 1981). Capitalist enterprises, when faced with fierce local or foreign competition, and/or with general or local crises of accumulation, can insulate themselves to some extent by working temporarily or permanently with a certain amount of labour which is simultaneously wage-labour in form, but self-employed in law, custom and, inevitably also in ideology. Such an arrangement can permit the transformation from primitive accumulation to a more dynamic and permanent process of, say, industrial capital accumulation, or may be employed in such a more defensive manner in order to sustain early accumulation impulses in the absence of significant political power. In either case, a dependent, small-scale, apparently pre-capitalist sector persists and even expands *outside* the formal boundaries of capitalist enterprise, and yet its form and trajectory of growth is subordinate to and determined by the accumulation requirements of organized, large-scale capital (see Chapter 6 of this volume, by Francisco de Oliveira).

On first inspection, lottery ticket sellers may not seem to fit easily into the framework outlined above; however, a more detailed analysis of their current situation indicates that the *lotero–Beneficencia* relationship is no exception to this general trend. State lotteries have experienced declining sales due to the diminishing real incomes of large sectors of the population, increased unemployment and underemployment, as well as competition from other sorts of gambling. In such circumstances the strategy adopted by the *Beneficencias* has been to increase both the price of lottery tickets and the prizes for winning numbers. However, the fact that the *Beneficencias* have been able to both "hold their retailers at arm's length" and keep the average *lotero*'s commission as low as possible, while at the same time mollifying the *loteros*' professional associations with subsidies, has contributed to the stabilization of lottery incomes and profits, despite generally unfavourable market and economic conditions. The subsidies nevertheless constitute a smaller contribution to *loteros*' welfare than would be the case if retailers were contractually employed by the *Beneficencia del Valle*, since under these circumstances they would receive a more comprehensive package of insurance and welfare provision.

Ironically, the subsidies paid by the *Beneficencia del Valle* to the *loteros*' union federation have been used to provide members with *private* medical and educational facilities, while the principal role of lottery surpluses has been the provision of funds for extending *public* health services and other social facilities. In 1977 the *Beneficencia del Valle* had a total income of 192.8 million pesos (equivalent to about five million U.S. dollars), 76.5 per cent of which was derived from lottery operations (147.5 million pesos—the net income after deducting expenditures on prizes, tickets, advertising etc.). The remaining 23.5 per cent came from a levy on horse-racing bets, and income on the property of the *Beneficencia*—a cinema, a restaurant, various buildings rented out, and interest on capital invested. Of the total expenditure of the *Beneficencia* (also 192.8 million pesos), 75.2 per cent—a sum fractionally smaller than the total income from lottery—was on the infrastructure and running costs for public health services and other social welfare institutions (e.g. kindergartens and old folks homes). The remaining 24.8 per cent was divided between the running costs of the *Beneficencia* (10.6 per cent), real estate investments to generate future income (7.8 per cent), and a transfer of funds to the 1978 budget (6.4 per cent).

A striking characteristic of lottery ticket sellers in the past has been their physical handicap. Though most of the older *loteros* are handicapped in some way, the ranks of street retailers have been swollen in recent years by an influx of able-bodied men, women and youths. This influx mainly results from the problems of worsening structural unemployment and underemployment, and the particularly serious impact this has had upon new entrants into the labour market. So what sort of income can a *lotero* expect?

On the basis of fieldwork surveys conducted in Cali,[2] it appears that approximately one-third of the *loteros* working there[3] earn an amount equivalent to or less than the official minimum wage (59 pesos per day worked—equivalent to 1.55 U.S. dollars—in June 1977).[4] These *loteros* are mainly micro-retailers and small-scale suburban sellers, with a smaller number of part-time or intermittently active sellers drawn from the student and frictionally unemployed population. A further one-third of the total *lotero* labour-force in Cali are city-centre vendors earning up to double the official minimum wage, while the remaining third are the more prosperous *loteros* who earn up to five times the minimum wage.

Loteros who have joined one of the professional associations have been encouraged to see themselves as the élite, professional majority in their chosen occupation, as opposed to the street urchins, students and other "unprofessional" elements who also sell tickets. Some unionized *loteros* even likened themselves to public employees, and felt that one of their associations' major objectives should be to win recognition of this status from the *Beneficencia del Valle* in the first instance and ultimately from all lottery authorities. The conception of the *lotero* as an unrecognized public employee has been rejected by the *Beneficencias*, which claim that the retailers work *with* rather than *for* them. This situation is further confused by the fact that "technically", *loteros* in Cali, for example, only work "with" the *Beneficencia del Valle* on one day each week—namely the day on which the lottery is drawn and new tickets are issued—since this is when most sales are made. On the other days of the week, it is the other *Beneficencias* "with" whom the *loteros* are working, since the former's tickets are being sold. Even so, the *Beneficencia del Valle* indirectly draws benefit from *loteros'* endeavours on these other days, since it receives a tariff from the other *Beneficencias* permitting them to sell their tickets in Valle through Valle's own "self-employed" distribution system.

Under strong moral, professional and ethical pressure from the *Beneficencias* to moderate their claims for better levels of commission and/or larger subsidies, the *loteros'* associations have been content to accept an annual 10 per cent rise in the subsidy given by the *Beneficencia del Valle*, despite the fact that inflation has been running at around 35 per cent per annum over the same period. This is strangely timid and complacent behaviour: the *loteros'* leaders have always been quick to point out that inflation and increasing claims from members for benefit-payments were placing their finances in jeopardy. In addition, it is perhaps surprising that *loteros* have never employed the strike weapon in support of claims for better conditions and remuneration, despite the obvious leverage this threat could exert. As long as the relationship between the *lotero* and the *Beneficencia* is defined by the latter as non-contractual, the *Beneficencias* will continue to reap the rewards of a form of work which gives them all the economic advantages of wage employment and the productivity levels usually associated with piece-rates, while the disadvantages of wage-labour (in terms of militancy and upward pressure on wage-cost) can be obviated through the simple application of legal definitions and distinctions. Put another way, the *lotero* is a wage-worker on a piece-rate when it serves the interests of the *Beneficencia*, but a self-employed "external" commission agent when the burden of labour costs is to be apportioned. The *lotero* is thus self-employed to the extent that he or she is forced to bear a greater or lesser share of the costs of reproducing his or her labour-power as a result of the prevailing relations of production between the *Beneficencias* and the ticket sellers.

In summary, as suggested above, the average *lotero* is a relatively low-income, highly dependent worker, dominated by producer and wholesaler cartels. The *lotero* is free to decide where, when and how long to work within the limits provided by inter-retailer competition, and has a degree of flexibility in determining the range of merchandise offered to the public. Nevertheless, ticket prices are effectively fixed both with respect to suppliers and buyers. Furthermore, because of the daily drawing of the various lotteries, the *lotero* cannot play one supplier off against another, nor readily concentrate on selling just one's lottery tickets. In these respects, the *lotero* is an unrecognized or *disguised* wage-worker, maintained as such by the *Beneficencias* in order to diminish their own burden of labour cost and the effect it might have on the potential rate of accumulation of funds for social infrastructural investment and/or other forms of (re)distribution.

The accumulation generated by the lottery system operates simultaneously in at least two ways, differentially benefiting several relatively distinct sections of the population of Valle. First, Colombian *public* hospital services (the main beneficiary of Departmental *Beneficencia* disbursements) cater specifically to the urban and rural poor. In contrast, purchasers of lottery tickets range from bourgeois and middle-class buyers who will purchase whole tickets, on the one hand, to the urban poor who can only afford to buy "fractions" (shares in whole tickets) on the other hand. Thus the net income from lottery operations is redistributed in a mainly downwards direction. The power of the lottery and its prize-winning potential is used in preference to purely fiscal methods in order to transfer funds from private speculation (it being rather difficult to say whether lottery ticket purchases are current consumption or savings!) to the lowest rung of medical provision.

Second, despite the mainly downward redistribution of the net income from lottery operations, there are some significant horizontal and upwards transfers of lottery ticket buyers' "speculative funds" to paying the running costs of the *Beneficencia* and financing its capital investments. These transfers principally benefit the middle- to upper-income staff of the *Beneficencias*, the constructors and users of luxury real estate, and a variety of banking and other financial interests.

Disguised wage-working in the "numbers game"

Colombian Presidential decree number 537 of 28 March 1974 prohibits all raffles and draws of a continuous nature which have money prizes. Nevertheless, Valle and several other Colombian Departments have legalized *chance*, a game which falls unambiguously into this very category. The game is a derivative of the American "numbers game" and came to South America via Costa Rica. In Valle, *chance* has become fully institutionalized in the sense that it is both popular with the lower-income strata of the "gambling public" and has become a minor source of revenue for the departmental government.

In Cali, selling *chance* tickets is seen by many as a low status occupation, all the more so since *loteros*, lottery ticket wholesalers and the *Beneficencia del Valle* accuse *chance* of stealing the very bread out of their mouths. *Loteros*, themselves the object of middle class scorn and opprobrium, view the *chanceros* and the companies for whom they work as the lowest form of parasite. Other more influential sections of the community, such as the police, still see *chance* as a suspicious activity, despite the fact that the majority of current *chanceros* did not enter the profession until after it had been legalized. The police openly claim that *chanceros* act as fences for stolen goods; it is probably more accurate to say that fences sometimes use *chance* as a "front" for their principal activities.

As in all prejudiced generalizations, there is a grain of truth in these characterizations. Many of the entrepreneurs (rather than the sellers) who operated illegal *chance* games before the law was changed, were well-known to the police for their involvement in a wide range of inter-locked criminal activities. In addition, the now-dominant *chance* companies have both apocryphal and real "mafia" connections with drugs trafficking, prostitution and organized crime, as well as with legitimate commercial and industrial activities elsewhere in the country. Finally, there *is* a degree of overlap between the clientele of the State lottery and that of *chance*, though competition is likely to be of marginal importance in influencing lottery revenues and the incomes of *loteros*. Nevertheless, the prejudices commonly articulated by *loteros* against *chance* deserve further comment.

Chance companies (rather than the street sellers through whom they reach their clientele) do have a case of parasitism to answer. The *chance* losers contribute mainly to the private capitalist accumulation of the *chance* companies, and in 1977 these companies contributed only about 14 million pesos (equivalent to slightly over a third of a million U.S. dollars) in licence fees and taxes to Valle's departmental administration—less than a tenth of the amount contributed by the lotteries to the *Beneficencia del Valle*. The funds paid by the *chance* companies to the departmental administration are not canalized to the *Beneficencia*, even though it is the lotteries' winning numbers which provide the basis for *chance* gambling, and even though the *Beneficencia*'s main objective is to finance health services for the urban and rural poor from which most *chance* gamblers are drawn. Instead, the funds paid by the *chance* companies contribute to general departmental expenditures, and particularly to the servicing of the departmental government's large public debt.

Though parasitism exists to the extent that both the urban poor and the *Beneficencias* lose out, while the *chance* companies accumulate on the basis of someone else's labour and someone else's lottery, it is extremely difficult to quantify the extent and impact of the parasitical relationship. Declining popular purchasing power, heightened structural unemployment and underemployment, accompanied by a worsening real distribution of income, have been instrumental in reducing lottery sales and have probably damaged *chance* revenues too. However, the extent to which former lottery clients have shifted to *chance* is unlikely to be significant, since there are substantial differences in the potential winnings between lottery and *chance*, and the latter also places limits on the amount of money that can be invested. In attempting to maintain the level of earnings derived from lottery sales, the *Beneficencias* have tended to increase both ticket prices and prizes, thereby heightening the already substantial degree of market segmentation.

Since its legalization in Valle in 1971, *chance* activities have become progressively more concentrated in fewer hands: by 1977, more than half of the companies originally registered had disappeared. Failed *chance* entrepreneurs have been commonly absorbed into surviving companies as employees, agency managers and *pachangueros* (suburban collectors).[5] There are now only 11 companies operating in Cali, and the top six control almost three-quarters of the total *chancero* labour force in the city and two-thirds of that in Valle.

The concept of disguised wage-working is even more appropriate to the relationship between *chanceros* and the *chance* companies than it is to that between the *Beneficencias* and the lottery ticket sellers. Though *chanceros* also do not have the legal status of employees, they are *registered* with a particular company, and are paid a commission by that company of up to 25 per cent of the value of their sales. For those selling *chance* in the more peripheral districts of the city, the cost and delay involved in personally delivering the day's receipts and collecting the corresponding commission at the company's central office, can be avoided—at a cost—by dealing with the company's local collector, who receives 5 per cent of the *chancero*'s daily takings as his own commission. The *panchangueros*, or local collectors, each deal in this way with as many as 15 or 20 suburban sellers, and actively operate as "scouts" for successful *chanceros* currently working with other companies. It is advantageous for a *chance* company to have a stable, experienced and profitable caucus of sellers in prominent locations; thus the *pachangueros* are often authorized to offer shopkeepers special inducements to allow *chance* to be sold from their premises, and to proffer "transfer fees" to high-turnover *chanceros* to encourage them to defect from their current company's service.

There are numerous other relations, often of an ill-defined, personal and paternalistic nature, which link the *chance* company to the street sellers. *Chance* entrepreneurs provide financial and other assistance on a discriminatory basis to well-behaved, reliable and/or successful *chanceros*. Short-term loans and even gifts are quite common, and have the effect of continuously undermining the welfare provision established by the *chanceros*' own (unrecognized) trade union, and fostering individualistic rather than collective responses to labour–capital relations. Many companies also operate a voluntary savings scheme in which *chanceros* opt to receive 5 per cent less than the normal commission on a daily basis, receiving the accumulated sum at the end of the month. While this has clear benefits for the sellers, it simultaneously provides the company with an interest-free expansion of circulating capital— no small advantage in the precarious operations of a gambling enterprise! The savings scheme further acts as a means of tying sellers to the company, particularly when it is a means to pay off previous loans provided by the company. It also protects the company to some extent from the "poaching" of *chanceros* by other companies.

In these ways, the typical *chance* company can create and maintain a labour force which has many of the characteristics of wage-labour, and few of the disadvantages as seen from the company's viewpoint. Ironically, the methods used by the companies to consolidate the subordination of *chanceros* to this peculiar form of money capital, are characteristically *pre*-capitalist and quite similar to the methods used by medieval merchants in the subordination of rural craftsmen, or by master craftsmen in their exploitation of apprentice and journeyman alike. However, rather than taking place during the transition from feudalism to capitalism, these relations characterize an accumulation process which is firmly situated within an economy and society dominated by capitalism. The use of apparently pre-capitalist mechanisms of labour control and exploitation is entirely compatible with the attempts by weaker sections of the domestic bourgeoisie and petite bourgeoisie to secure a satisfactory process of accumulation, within a relatively restricted range of accumulation possibilities.

The situation of *chanceros* is further complicated by the fact that, unlike *loteros*, about half of them normally combine the sale of *chance* tickets with some other substantial earning opportunity, such as newspaper vending or the street-retailing of confectionery or cigarettes.[6] It can be seen from Table 1 that *chance*, which may be unviable as a single occupation, becomes a very useful and supportive activity when combined with other occupations, particularly other forms of selling. Since the micro-retailing of *any* commodity (whether "good" or "service") in a Third World economy usually involves proportionately more waiting-to-sell than actual selling, the judicious combination of a variety of articles to sell can have a considerable impact upon the level of turnover achieved, and the income derived from what is a highly competitive sphere.

TABLE 1. *Activities with which* chance *selling is combined in Cali,* 1977

	Percentage of *chanceros* interviewed
Chance combined with no other activity:	40
Chance combined with:	
Newspaper selling	25
Off-course horse-racing bets	14
Street retailing (e.g. ice-cream, cold drinks, etc.)	8
Housework (*chance* sold from home)	5
Studying (*chance* earnings to subsidize education)	5
Tailoring	3
Total	100

Chanceros earn incomes approximately equal to the minimum wage (59 pesos per day in mid-1977) from their ticket sales, in addition to their earnings from any complementary occupation they might have. Over three-quarters of the 63 *chanceros* interviewed earned less than 100 pesos a day from ticket sales. Though the stability of *chance* earnings is an important factor in determining the overall economic position of *chanceros*, the requisite data are very difficult to collect. Nevertheless, some tentative conclusions can be drawn from two data sources which, though incomplete, are closely corroborated by more qualitative data provided by the fieldwork.

First, a detailed interview with a secondhand bookseller and *chancero* provided data not normally available. The *chancero* had meticulously kept a record of all his day-to-day earnings from ticket sales and, though he was unwilling to hand over the records due to a sneaking suspicion that he was

TABLE 2.*Variability of* chance *earnings: bookseller–chancero, Cali, 1977*

Level of daily receipts	No. of days in the month				
(pesos) (of which income constitutes 25 %)	normal month 1	normal month 2	bad month	good month	average of four months
201–300	—	1	—	—	—
301–400	3	1	7	1	3
401–500	9	9	12	7	9
501–750	11	8	5	12	9
more than 750	—	3	—	5	3
Total	23	22	24	25	24

dealing with tax officers rather than social scientists, he gave access to a selection of data corresponding to subjectively-assessed "good", "normal" and "bad" months in terms of *chance* earnings. Day-to-day variability of *chance* earnings is considerable, irrespective of whether the month was deemed "bad" or "good" by the *chancero*. On the other hand, the distinction between "bad" and "normal" monthly earnings was much less marked than that between "normal" and "good" earnings.

A second source of data originated in a suburban *chance* agency, where the manager allowed the daily receipts of a few of his *chanceros* to be recorded and analysed, before his head office over-ruled his decision and refused further collaboration. The data indicate that the most variable incomes (whether measured on a monthly or daily basis) are those of both the lowest and the highest earning brackets. Such a conclusion is only superficially surprising, since it is to be expected that the two tails of a roughly normal distribution of *chance* earnings would be characterized by the enhanced influence of luck, on the one hand, and scale on the other. The peripheral suburban *chanceros* operate on such a minute scale that an external shock of minor proportions will often have a disproportionately large destabilizing effect on the level of earnings. More successful *chanceros* with favourable selling locations, with larger clienteles and consequent turnover, and perhaps with the possibility of supplementing their earnings with *pachanguero* activities, will probably be operating with higher stakes and with a more volatile clientele.

Whereas lottery ticket sellers in Cali have several trade unions or professional associations, some of which date back to the 1930s, the emergence of collective action among *chanceros* is rather recent. The only *chanceros'* union was founded in 1975 and since then has had as one of its main objectives the securing of employee status with respect to the *chance* companies. The results have been disappointing, though predictable. A Ministry of Labour and Social Security investigation in 1977 concluded that the list of employees provided by the *chance* companies corresponded neither in terms of names nor numbers to the list of members provided by the union. Nevertheless, if *chanceros* are *de jure* self-employed commission agents working only "in conjunction with" *chance* companies, their real social and economic relations with these enterprises are very close to those of the classic piece-rate wage-worker. Some additional support to this contention is given by the fact that the Department of Valle taxes *chance* companies not according to profits or turnover (which are more normally taxed on an individual basis) but on the number of sellers which the company has registered.[7] The objective situation of *chanceros* is masked by legalistic definitions and existing employment practices which themselves reflect a more fundamental reality—the necessity of relatively weak domestic capital to minimize labout-costs and their associated social overheads.

Conclusion

This paper has summarized the results of a detailed study of worker–enterprise relations in the "gambling sector" of a Colombian city. The general theoretical conclusion is that it should not be assumed that those working on the street, in apparently "marginal" or "informal" occupations, do so in virtual isolation from the processes of capital accumulation which characterize the "modern" urban and national economies. Such workers are not outside the capitalist labour market, and somehow immune from the strategic and tactical decisions made by capitalists and/or the State. Their exclusion from capitalist labour markets and the laws of capitalist accumulation is only apparent, though "appearances" and the class-based definitions which enshrine them, play an important ideological role in support of capitalist interests. The relations outlined in this paper not only characterize the "exotic" occupations such as lottery ticket sellers, garbage scavengers (see Birkbeck 1979) and prostitutes, but also the many directly productive activities normally associated with the "informal sector" (Gerry 1980).

Detailed analysis of such occupations shows that the mechanism by which they are incorporated into the process of capitalist accumulation involves the reproduction of working relations which combine increasingly capitalist forms of exploitation with persistently petit-bourgeois, individualist levels of consciousness. Thus the law defines disguised wage-workers as "self-employed", the enterprises which dominate and exploit them are able to optimize their current levels of accumulation, while trade union representatives rarely if ever attain even a syndicalist level of struggle. The distributional and redistributional effects vary considerably: disguised wage labour in the lottery sector has both a horizontal and a downward redistributional impact, while in *chance*, the impact is to favour the already rich at the expense of the poor, as well as to drain resources from an already "leaky" system of basic health finance. Despite the variable distributional effects, the mechanism of disguised wage employment has been widely used by relatively weak domestic capitals to ensure that a larger than "normal" share of the costs associated with capitalist accumulation are borne by labour itself.

Notes

1. The principal territorial/administrative unit in the Republic of Colombia is the Department (*Departamento*). Of the 22 Departments in Colombia, Valle (formally known as Valle del Cauca) is one of the most populous.
2. Detailed interviews were conducted with 18 *loteros*, and the income data subsequently corroborated in numerous other interviews in various parts of the city.
3. FEDELOVAL, the lottery ticket sellers' Departmental Union Federation, claimed that there were just over 600 unionized *loteros* in Cali in 1977, and that non-unionized *loteros* constituted only 20 per cent of all sellers. This would give a total number of sellers of 730. Assuming a lower level of union membership (say only 50 per cent) would give a total of 1,200 professional *loteros*. An informed guess would suggest that an additional 40 per cent could be included for temporary, part-time and unregistered juvenile sellers, giving a final maximum labour force of almost 1,700 loteros.
4. If this is related to a 30-day working month, it would give a monthly wage of 1,770 pesos ("equivalent" to about 47 U.S. dollars). Colombian employers commonly limit payment to the 5 or 6 days a week which are actually worked, which would result in minimum monthly wages of either 1,278 or 1,534 pesos. *Loteros*, of course, advance the money (or acquire credit facilities) to buy the tickets which they subsequently sell, and only "repay themselves" from what they receive on the days they actually work.
5. *Pachangueros* derive their name from *pachanga*, a slang term for a dancing *fiesta*, and are so called because they "dance" from one *chancero* to another collecting money for the *chance* companies.
6. The sample of *chance* sellers interviewed in this way numbered 63. Additional qualitative interviews were conducted with many more *chanceros*, and the information they gave generally corroborated the conclusions drawn from the more limited sample.
7. Since 1977, and partly in response to the charges of "parasitism" discussed in this essay, two major administrative changes have been made to more effectively supervise and tax *chance* companies. First, Departmental Decree no. 2037 of 20 December 1978 formally transferred the responsibility for printing *chance* tickets from the companies to the Departmental Treasury as from 2 January 1979. Since then tickets have been printed on "security paper" and sold to the *chance* companies at a standard price (one peso per ticket in 1979) to cover both printing costs and a direct tax on *chance* sales. This replaced the previous indirect taxation on numbers of "registered" *chance* sellers and substantially increased government revenues from *chance*. Second, because of National Law No. 1 of 11 January 1982 legalizing *chance* at the national level and transferring the right to regulate it to the *Beneficencias*, on 1 July 1982 the responsibility for printing *chance* tickets in Valle, taxing *chance* and using the tax revenues has been transferred to the *Beneficencia del Valle*. Despite the many advantages of this new system (fraud and forgery control, additional revenues from gambling, a direct support to health services for the poor, greater customer confidence, and a government "seal of approval" for *chance*), it has exacerbated the ambiguity of *chanceros'* working relations by further "distancing" them from formal or legal employee status, while doing nothing to increase their "autonomy" with respect to their companies.

References

BROMLEY, Ray (1978) "Organization, regulation and exploitation in the so-called 'urban informal sector': the street traders of Cali, Colombia", *World Development*, Vol. 6, No. 9/10, pp. 1161–71. Reprinted in Ray Bromley (ed.) (1979) *The Urban Informal Sector: Critical Perspectives on Employment and Housing Policies*, Pergamon, Oxford.

BROMLEY, Ray, and GERRY, Chris (1979) "Who are the casual poor?", in Ray Bromley and Chris Gerry (eds.), *Casual Work and Poverty in Third World Cities*, Wiley, Chichester, pp. 3–23.

GERRY, Chris (1980) "Petite production marchande ou 'salariat deguisé'? Quelques reflexions", *Revue Tiers Monde*, Vol. 21, No. 82, pp. 387–403.

GERRY, Chris, and BIRKBECK, Chris (1981) "The petty commodity producer in Third World cities: petit-bourgeois or 'disguised' proletarian?", in Frank Bechhofer and Brian Elliott (eds.), *The Petite Bourgeoisie*, Macmillan, London, pp. 121–54.

MARX, Karl (1976) "Appendix" to *Capital, Volume 1*, Pelican and New Left Books, London.

WOLPE, Harold (1972) 'Capitalism and cheap labour power in South Africa: from segregation to Apartheid", *Economy and Society*, Vol. 1, pp. 425–56.

CHAPTER 10

Child labour in Morocco's carpet industry*

ANTI-SLAVERY SOCIETY

In March 1975, following reports of large-scale employment of children in carpet factories in Morocco, the Anti-Slavery Society sent a small team to investigate the situation. The team found that children aged from 5 upwards were permanently employed, some for up to 12 hours a day and often in very bad conditions. They noted that the children were not directly employed by the factory owners, but worked for an intermediary—a *maalema*[1]† (craftswoman/supervisor)—who was herself paid on a piecework basis by the factory owners. The team also noted the increasing demand for Moroccan carpets, the large number of girls not attending school and the consequent ready supply of cheap labour.

Feeling that this situation was detrimental both to the small girls involved and to the well-being of the whole country, the Society sent the team's report to the Moroccan government on 8 May 1975 and urged it to take steps to improve the working conditions of these girls. The Moroccan government replied to the Society at the beginning of 1976. Pointing out the existence of legislation protecting all workers, including those in carpet factories, it stressed that the employment or apprenticeship of children under 12 was illegal. It accepted that in "a few" establishments these laws were not strictly applied, and it stated its intention to investigate the firms mentioned and ensure that in future the laws were obeyed. The government felt that the fact that "a few" employers did not obey the laws should not lead to the hasty conclusion that such practices were widespread. The unfavourable publicity that would result from publishing what they considered was not an objective

---

*Extracts from a longer report with the same title, published by the Anti-Slavery Society, London, in 1978. The report is based on fieldwork conducted in Morocco in 1977, and all its descriptions and factual statements relate to 1977 and the preceding years. Though few grounds for optimism were noted in 1977, it is possible that the conditions described have changed for the better since then. Because of this, all descriptive material based on the field research is presented in the past tense. This essay is published here with the permission of the Anti-Slavery Society.
†Superscript numbers refer to Notes at the end of the chapter.

study would, they felt, be prejudicial to Morocco's "considerable efforts" in this field.

The Anti-Slavery Society therefore waited a further year and in March 1977 sent out another small team to see to what extent the situation had improved. This Arabic-speaking team visited 62 private premises and 17 state centres in 17 cities and towns throughout Morocco. They found that the situation, far from having improved, had worsened. The custom of employing young girls under the legal age of 12 was even more widespread.[2] Hours of work often far exceeded the legal maximum and paid annual holidays, medical visits and the official minimum salaries were hardly ever provided.

The Moroccan carpet industry

The Moroccan carpet trade has always played an important part in the economy of the country, where several regional styles have developed. In the early and mid 1970s, however, it won an increasing share of the export market. In 1972, carpets accounted for 53.8 per cent of craft exports. In 1973, this figure had risen to 72.2 per cent, to drop back again to 59 per cent in 1974. In terms of value in Moroccan dirhams (DH),[3] however, the rise was steady: 58.7 million in 1972, 81.7 million in 1973, 88.9 million in 1974, and 113.1 million in 1975.[4] With this increase in production there was a consequent increase in the industrialization of an activity that was originally carried out in small workshops. Many companies began to work solely for export, operating large factories in several different towns.

Government policy has been to give all possible aid to exporters of rugs. Wool has been imported duty free ("temporary importation") on condition that it is exported in the form of rugs. Export duty and certain taxes have been waived.

West Germany has been the greatest importer of Moroccan rugs and acts as redistributor throughout Europe. Many firms the team visited were booked far into the future with West German orders. By all accounts the trade was booming in the 1970s, especially as labour legislation and resulting higher prices put other competing countries out of the market. Algeria used to be the most important rug producer in North Africa but it was said that, with nationalization of the carpet firms, their prices had risen. Most Moroccan manufacturers considered that Morocco had attained first place for North African rugs and many did not hide the fact that low labour costs had made Moroccan rugs highly competitive. In Iran, for instance, legislation had forbidden the employment of children under 14 and this had considerably raised the cost of Persian rugs.

Many of the firms visited were companies with interests throughout Morocco. Many new factories were planned by the factory owners interviewed. At the same time the Moroccan population was growing faster than its educational system and one-and-a-half million girls did not attend primary school. These girls provided an obvious source of cheap labour to factory owners.

A decline in standards in rug making was also clearly noticeable. Regional-style rugs were made anywhere in the country as well as in their reputed place of origin, officially stamped in the town of the head office of the firm, not where they were made, and shipped out in bulk. The tradition of the craftsman had been replaced by the mass-production factory. Another unpleasant feature was the contrast between the well-appointed head office of a rug factory and the dark, cramped, back-street premises of its scattered workshops.

Child workers, *maalema* and conditions

With Morocco's carpet industry booming and fortunes being made rapidly by the factory owners, child workers had an important place in the scheme of things. In only eight of the 62 private premises visited were little girls not actually seen at work—and three of these premises were head offices of companies which employ children elsewhere. In 28 factories/workshops at least one-third of the employees were under 12, sometimes as many as three-fifths. These children were often only 8, 9 or 10 years old.

Hours were long: two factories visited worked a 72-hour week; five worked 60–64 hours a week. Half of those from which information was obtained exceeded the 48-hour legal maximum for a week's work for *adults*. Wages were meagre, with so-called apprentices earning nothing. An annual holiday with pay—laid down by the law—was almost totally unknown.

In many of the factories visited the children looked undernourished and overworked. While most factories and workshops had lavatories and running water, working conditions were often poor, with bad lighting, poor ventilation, and crowded looms.

On a less industrialized scale, a few of the small rug-making workshops provided an agreeable contrast. Although employing young girls, they nevertheless offered pleasant surroundings and a more friendly atmosphere than the large factories where several hundred girls were under the strict control of older women or male overseers.

Government establishments too were characterized by their good working conditions. The premises were generally modern and well laid-out. The 48-hour week was universally respected in the 14 establishments from which information was obtained. Indeed, a week of less than 40 hours was worked in four of these centres. More than half the working force of three State centres was made up of children under 12. In this respect the State did not abide by its own legislation, for even apprentices under 12 were illegal. Yet one centre said its apprentices could start as young as 8. In six other State centres a number of under-12s were seen while in seven there were no children under 12.

It was clear that as long as primary school remained inaccessible to so many children, especially girls, this situation would continue. It should not be forgotten, moreover, that thousands of Moroccan families were very poor and that these small girls' wages were an important element in their survival. Parents played into the hands of the factory owners in their desire to see their daughters bringing in even a small sum of money. It should be remembered, too, that an adult working man's minimum legal wage was also very small. Furthermore, the exploitation of children was not limited to rug factories: small boys worked long hours as apprentices in a number of crafts and trades and no legislation whatever existed to protect domestic help—often a child of 9 or 10. Compulsory primary education would have put an end to all this, but was obviously not feasible in the short term.

In general, a rug-making loom was worked by a team of four to eight girls. Larger looms—able to make rugs 5 metres wide—could accommodate more people, while it was not uncommon in smaller workshops to find a loom being worked by only one or two girls. One girl or woman was responsible for each loom. The workers stood or sat on a bench, sometimes raised as the work progressed, knotting with one hand and cutting off the wool with a pair of scissors or a knife with the other. The rug's design was drawn on squared paper and stood beside each loom.

The girls worked with great speed and dexterity. The amount each loom produced in a day depended of course on the number of workers, the complexity of the design, the thickness of the wool and the amount of beating given to each line of weft. One square metre a day of simple design was about the maximum for a team of five or six.

The person responsible for each loom was sometimes an older girl or an experienced woman. However, in many factories the basic organization of production was a system which was a relic of the old craftsman–apprentice structure. A qualified craftswoman, a *maalema*, supplied her own team and was paid for the work they produced. In turn, she paid her workers as she saw fit.

Originally, the *maalema* worked in her own home, with as many looms as she could manage but rarely exceeding three or four, with up to 20 workers. Many of her workers were apprentices, waiting their turn to become *maalema* and set up on their own. Sometimes these unpaid apprentices were lodged, fed and clothed by the *maalema*, who might take a personal interest in their well-being. On other occasions the apprentices were little more than slaves—it all depended on the character of the *maalema*.

The transfer of this system to the factory was prejudicial to the children but convenient to the factory owners. The employer paid the *maalema* per square metre worked and had no further responsibility towards the children. He did not know who they were, how old they were, or whether they stayed one week or several years. The *maalema* had every interest in squeezing the maximum amount of work out of her charges, to whom she paid the minimum possible rate. She had absolute control over these children and could recruit and discharge them as she liked.

In four of the big factories visited, *maalema* were responsible for engaging and paying the children. This also was the case in two government centres and in the majority of the smaller workshops. In three equally large factories it was said that the *maalema* system was definitely not used. The wages paid by the employer to the *maalema* depended on the square metres worked by her team. In the four factories/workshops where information was obtained, the salaries ranged from 15 to 30DH a square metre, equivalent to one or two days' work. In the two state enterprises, 25DH was recorded.

Where the workers were paid a daily wage, this varied from 2DH to a maximum of 6DH, with the average around 4DH (women and girls). In only one establishment were the workers paid as much as 12DH a day. "Apprentices" usually got nothing, or a maximum of 1DH a day (a 500-gram loaf of bread cost 0.60DH). In one case apprentices had to bring presents to the factory manageress. Overtime working slightly increased the day's pay.

Some apprentices in State concerns got nothing. Others were paid 2 or 3DH a day. Qualified workers in State enterprises sometimes got as little as 2.50DH a day, sometimes as much as 5DH and once 200DH a month was noted. This is not taking into account those "true" cooperatives where the workers shared the profits.

Local attitudes to child labour

Employers were generally reluctant to let visitors see working conditions in the factories or to discuss the children working for them. On many occasions entry to the loom area was strictly forbidden and doors firmly shut. There was an obvious desire not to draw attention either to the numbers of girls employed or to their ages. Many factories were completely anonymous. This was particularly so of small workshops working for a large company. Hidden away in back streets or poor districts, they were only identified by the noise coming from them.

Two employers, however, spoke with warmth of the beneficial effects of their factories in supplying work to needy families. One employer of a smallish concern was said to be "like a father" to his workers. The overall impression was nevertheless one of indifference to the children. No employer was willing either to discuss the wages he paid his workers or how well off a *maalema* was compared to other salaried workers.

The companies had no difficulty in finding children to work for them. Many factories were near *bidonvilles* (shanty towns) or in poor districts of the towns. Parents, too, were keen to see their daughters working. Some Agadir parents felt happy that their girls were "out of mischief" and under supervision.

Another mother begged a small workshop to take on her child as she was "impossible" at home.

Some parents liked to inspect the premises where their daughters worked, but the majority were only too glad to have extra money coming into the house, even a few dirhams a day. A father spoken to said conditions where his two daughters worked were bad and the money poor, but it was obviously better than nothing.

In some of the smaller workshops seen, working conditions were undoubtedly better than in the children's home. This was invariably true in the State craft centres. In addition, families were pleased to have the girls learning a useful craft. Moroccan parents were generally ambitious for their sons but tended not to seek schooling for their daughters. One father told the first team: "What use is school to a girl? She doesn't learn anything useful and she doesn't earn anything. She is expected to marry and that is her future".

The girls themselves often spoke with great freedom and frankness if given the chance, even inside some of the most factory-like premises. It was easier, nevertheless, to talk to the children outside the factory. One girl said she would not be doing the work if she could have been at school, while another said earning money was better than going to school. Many said the work was "good" and only one said it was hard. The majority were reluctant to say how much they earned—except for apprentices who were eager to insist that they got nothing at all for their work. A few girls said the pay was "good".

In some premises visited, discipline was too severe to allow visitors to talk to the girls or even to see them at work. *Maalema* and male overseers were quick to reprimand idle, chatting girls. The workers in most establishments were lighthearted despite the poor conditions.

An inquiry into the family situation of a number of girls working in one rug factory revealed that in the majority of cases there were as many members of the family not working as working. In other words, the wages of the child worker, small as they were, were an important supplement to the family's resources. The fathers of these children were generally employed, while the mother and younger brothers and sisters remained at home.

The situation of orphans or semi-orphans working in rug-making or embroidery workshops was said by many people to be disquieting. Cases were mentioned where the girls were virtually slaves, but no specific information concerning these cases was obtained.

Five examples of private factories and workshops visited

The following cases have been selected from the 62 described in the full report. They are considered a fairly typical selection, excluding both the very worst and the very best.

Tapis, Anowar, Mekouar et Ben Lamlil, Fez

Hours of work (72-hour week): 0700–1900 (shut Sunday)

These premises displayed no name and little information was available since the manager was busy in the upstairs office. A male employee said there was no mid-day break. At least 100 girls were at work in a large room, many of them under 12. The looms were packed close together and the light from the small windows had to be supplemented by electricity. The ceiling was very low and the workshop stuffy.

Société Artisanale de Tissage de Tapis (SAAT), Kenitra

Number of workers: 400.
Hours of work (54-hour week): 0800–1200 and 1400–1900 (shut Sunday).

This factory was clearly identified and easy to find. A large room, well-lit with overhead daylight and high roof, contained some 60–70 looms, packed close together. There were three to eight girls per loom. A total of 182 women and children were counted and at least three-fifths were under 12. Many were said to be only 6, 7 or 8 years old.

There was a certain amount of dust but conditions, though factory-style, were otherwise reasonable. The girls sang at their work and were ready to talk. Discipline did not seem too strict, although the girls worked with great rapidity. There was no summer holiday; the girls could go off—they were "easily replaceable". Only a few male workers were regular employees and received steady wages. The girls were taken on by the *maalema* responsible for each loom, and she paid them as she thought fit. One girl said in French that she was "well paid". Another informant said the older girls were paid 5–6DH a day.

The owner, Mr. Lyazghai, was vice-president of the Chambre de Commerce Artisanale in Rabat. He was pleased to show off his factory and said he had three others, each of the same size, and employed a total of 1,400–1,500 workers, with 260 looms. He had started eight years ago when there were no such factories in Kenitra. Now there were 30 other rug-making concerns in the town, all as important as his. He imported his wool from France (12 tons per month and 4–5 tons of cotton). He said he had just received an order for 500,000 square metres from West Germany and had orders that would take him up to the end of the year.

Mr. Lyazghai explained that Moroccan carpets were now the best for quality and price and that factories such as his did a lot of good for the country and were particularly beneficial in bringing work to the region. He said that low labour costs were instrumental in making Moroccan carpets highly competitive in the European market, "where trade unions and high wages make such an activity impossible".

16 rue Derb el Bahia, a small workshop in Marrakesh

One loom with eight girls, two under 12, was squeezed into a corner of a shop. The shop was popular with tourists. The eight workers took at least two, sometimes three to six days to finish a square metre, depending on complexity of design. Apart from a good toilet, conditions were poor. There was no fresh air and lighting was by electricity. The hours of work were 0800–1200 and 1400–1800, though the cashier said with great frankness that if they had orders to fulfil they doubled the hours.

Douar Ain Itti, another small workshop in Marrakesh

In a private house in this very poor district, 11 girls were working on a rug. A young *maalema* explained that there used to be 30 workers but that the figure had dropped recently.

The workers were from three families. They worked all day but not Friday and had one month's holiday in the summer (unpaid). They worked for Dar Si Said (the State craft cooperative). The *maalema* had been trained there and the design for the rugs were supplied by Dar Si Said. They were able to make all kinds of rugs and the *maalema* said she was paid "a little" for her work. The room was small and badly lit. One child was only 6 years old.

13 Bab Sebta, Salé

Neighbouring craftsmen pointed out this entirely anonymous establishment as being a rug-making concern. A young Moroccan who opened the blue-painted door said it was only the workshop, and the owner turned out to be Berbère Carpet in Rabat.

Thirty looms were counted in this very crowded, low-roofed room, though there could well have been double that number. At least 120 girls were counted, the great majority very young. It was lit by daylight overhead but conditions were otherwise bad.

State-run establishments

Government-sponsored handicraft cooperatives existed in many Moroccan towns. They were generally housed in modern buildings and tourists were encouraged to visit them. They were principally sales outlets but craftsmen could usually be watched at work on the premises. It was originally hoped that these cooperatives would help the craftworker to compete in an increasingly industrialized world. It seemed (*Lamalif*, No. 86, February/March 1977), however, that they had not been entirely successful: of 113 cooperatives existing in 1972, only 72 were still active and of these only 45 were actually engaged in production.

It should be borne in mind that these cooperatives were not groups of producers working together to share costs and benefits: they were simply undertakings run by the State on commercial lines, with the workers receiving some sort of remuneration for their work. Each cooperative was a semi-autonomous body, with its own hours of work, system of recruitment, remuneration and prices.

It was not surprising that conditions varied, from the strict *maalema* system at Azrou, with the children engaged and paid by her, to the more relaxed atmosphere at Chichaoua or Tetuán. Working conditions were generally better and hours of work shorter than in the average factory, a fairly typical case being the following:

Ensemble Artisanal, Marrakesh

Hours of work (42-hour week): 0800–1200 and 1500–1800 (shut Sunday). Display centre open 0830–1200 and 1430–1900.

This modern and attractively laid-out Moroccan-style centre, with stucco work, glazed tiling and fountains, was inaugurated on 8 March 1977 and had been functioning since October 1975. A wide variety of craft goods were on sale on the premises, but the workshops for the craftworkers were housed apart. Many tourists were present, buying, watching the weavers at work or taking photographs.

The weaving workshop was large, well-ventilated, well-lit with large windows looking on to an open courtyard. Some 20 girls were at work but not all 14 looms were in use. Generally two or four girls worked a loom, occasionally six. At least six or seven of the girls were no more than 10 years old, others were about 14 or 15 and one could have been as old as 20. No adult women were present, nor could any *maalema* be seen. The children spoke with great freedom. All except one were from Marrakesh. All said they enjoyed the work and they certainly seemed quite carefree. They had one month's unpaid holiday in the summer. There appeared to be no discipline.

Conclusions and recommendations

The use of child labour in carpet factories in Morocco violates basic human rights and domestic legislation. Yet, the employment of children has expanded rapidly with the growth of the industry.

Moroccan labour legislation represents on paper a genuine desire to safeguard the welfare of the worker. The Moroccan government, in its reply to the Anti-Slavery Society dated 14 January 1976, emphasized that workers in craft enterprises were fully covered by this legislation. It therefore remains a matter of some surprise and concern that such a wide gap existed between the theory and the practice. The Moroccan government may have considered it desirable to enact legislation which, though unenforceable, might have helped to raise standards eventually by educating public opinion. Nevertheless, it is surely undesirable to present to the outside world a series of laws that are largely disregarded.

A principal cause of and excuse for violation of labour regulations was the employment by factory owners of *maalema* or *maitresses*: women who, having graduated from the looms, were made responsible for the recruitment, training, supervision, administration, discipline, and, if they so wish, dismissal of the girl-workers. Some *maalema* were as young as 17. The system was formerly standard practice when rugs were made in private houses and when treatment of the workers varied from benevolent paternalism to slavery. Transferred to the factories, though labour could be lawfully recruited only through a state employment office, the system provided a means whereby factory owners could, if the law was not enforced, avoid all contact with their workers. Though government-owned factories generally conformed with the law in regard to recruitment and in most respects set a high standard, the *maalema* survived in a few state factories as well as in most of those in the private sector. The eradication of this system was considered to be a necessary—and practicable—first step towards reform of working conditions. Its elimination would have meant that factory owners could no longer excuse themselves from direct responsibility for their workers.

The Anti-Slavery Society recognizes that a remedy for the exploitation of children in carpet manufacturing cannot be found in isolation from broader social and economic issues. However, the employment of children aged from 8, or even less, to 12 years, for as long, in some instances, as 72 hours per week, often for no pay at all, should not be tolerated in any country. The very good conditions in most Moroccan government factories gave grounds for hope that the situation in private factories could be improved.

Notes

1. *Maalema* is used here for both singular and plural.
2. When the ages of children are not specifically stated, "very young" is used in the text to mean they are about 7 or 8. "Young" means aged between 8 and 12.
3. The approximate exchange rate in April 1977 was 4.5DH to the U.S. dollar.
4. Source: Direction de l'Artisanat.

SECTION IV

Physical and legal constraints: the heritages of town planning, municipal government and policing

"The colonial world is a world cut in two. The dividing line, the frontiers are shown by barracks and police stations. In the colonies it is the policeman and the soldier who are the official, instituted go-betweens, the spokesman of the settler and his rule of oppression. . . . The settler's town is a strongly built town, all made of stone and steel. It is a brightly lit town . . . a well-fed town . . . a town of white people. . . . The town belonging to the colonized people, or at least the native town . . . is a place of ill fame, peopled by men of evil repute. They are born there, it matters little where or how; they die there, it matters not where nor how. It is a world without spaciousness; . . . huts are built one on top of the other. The native town is a hungry town, starved of bread, of meat, of shoes, of coal, of light. It is a town of niggers and dirty Arabs. The look that the native turns on the settler's town is a look of lust, a look of envy."
(Frantz Fanon 1968, *The Wretched of the Earth*, 37–40)

"Mexican immigration over the border is a good thing. It's a good thing for the illegal immigrants, it's a good thing for the citizens of the U.S., but it's only good so long as it's illegal. That's an interesting paradox to think about. Make it legal and it's no good. Why? Because so long as it's illegal the people who come do not qualify for welfare, they don't qualify for social security, they don't qualify for all the other myriads of benefits that we pour out. . . They take jobs that most residents of this country are unwilling to take. . . They're hard workers, they're good workers—and they are clearly better off. . . . They vote to cross the border with their feet, on their feet, or in any other way they can."
(Milton Friedman 1978, "What is America?", 9–10)

Introduction

Government policies towards small enterprises can be divided into two major groups: the constraints (regulation, restrictions, sanctions or negative controls—see e.g. Fitzpatrick 1980, 164–97; Mitnick 1980; Wilson 1974); and, the supports (promotion, incentives or positive controls—see e.g. Harper 1977; Neck 1977; World Bank 1978). Throughout history constraints have predominated over supports, and even in those countries where the most positive and enlightened policies have been adopted towards small enterprises, this is probably still the case. This section focuses on governmental constraints on small enterprises, examining the heritages and contemporary practice of town planning, municipal government and policing in terms of how they restrict the numbers, activities and profitability of such enterprises. In Section V supports are examined, focusing on how assistance can be delivered to small enterprises, how they can gain access to credit, technical training, government contracts and public services, and on the extent to which all forms of support are necessarily selective, increasing the degree of differentiation between the various types and sizes of small enterprise.

The imposition of constraints on the operation of small enterprises may respond to nine major types of governmental concern:

1. The creation and preservation of the city-beautiful

The desire to produce an orderly, zoned, tranquil "Garden City", with relatively low population densities, a strict separation of housing from both manufacturing and commerce, smooth traffic flows, and a general lack of congestion. Such cities correspond to a particularly Euro–American, opulent, compartmentalized, and colonial or neo-colonial mentality (see King 1976, 1980), yet they are still widely recommended by Western-trained town planners. It is very dubious whether such an urban development model can be viable in the Third World and outside the most elegant upper-income residential neighbourhoods, yet there is a continuous attempt to impose such a model over large urban areas. It leads to frequent persecution of economic activities in residential areas (workshops, shops, etc.) and of all forms of small enterprise which can cause congestion (para-transit and street traders).

2. Developmentalism

This is an ideology and value system which is characteristic of dominant élites in many Third World countries, and which consists of an almost obsessive belief in the desirability of "modernization" and "progress" coupled with a strong belief that these objectives can be achieved by imitating the features of the countries which are considered to be the most "modern" and "progressive" (most commonly and notably, the United States). Such attitudes produce a form of economic growth and sociocultural change which is achieved mainly by imitation of countries which are perceived to be more developed, rather than by local innovation and self-reliance. They lead to the neglect and eventual persecution of economic activities which do not fit their image of "development", most notably such petty service occupations as street, market and shop selling, para-transit, and the recuperation of waste materials. The requirements of these occupations are ignored in the design of the urban environment, new facilities such as public retail markets are simply not provided, and opposing technologies are deliberately promoted through such investments as supermarkets, mass transit systems and garbage incinerators (see Bromley 1980, 1981).

3. Public safety and the prevention of public nuisance

For example, preventing the sale of unhygenic or polluted food and drink, severely controlling the manufacture and distribution of fireworks and other explosive and inflammable goods, and insisting that taxis, buses and other public transport vehicles are regularly checked for faults which could cause accidents.

4. The protection of those working in small enterprises

Such protection not only covers the dangers which could threaten the general public (explosion, fire, etc.), but also specific dangers to individual workers (faulty and unguarded machinery, stairs without handrails, etc.) and general working conditions which could lead to long-term deterioration of physical or mental health (poor lighting, continuous loud noise, excessively long working hours, the employment of children, etc.).

5. The creation and maintenance of the governmentally-desired socioeconomic order

In such actions the government overtly supports certain social groups, economic interests and moral values against the real or potential threat posed by other groups, interests and values. For example, small enterprises may be restricted as a means of protecting larger enterprises engaged in similar economic activities, the enterprises of particular ethnic, cultural or political groups may be penalized as part of some negative discriminatory policy (see e.g. Dinwiddy 1974, 20–31), or specific occupations may be persecuted in order to impose a moral standard (e.g. prostitution, usury, or the sale of gambling opportunities).

6. Containment intended to give the impression of prohibition while deliberately not taking the steps needed to achieve elimination

This case applies when activities are prohibited and persecuted, but when persecution is deliberately restrained so that the activity can continue on a limited scale. It is an expression of double standards on the part of government, the best-known case probably being the attitude towards illegal immigration expressed by Milton Friedman in the second quote at the beginning of this section (for more details on this case, see Portes and Walton 1981, 53–59). Similar attitudes are often taken to the regulation of street trading, where sanctions are imposed to restrict trader numbers and to "defend" prestigious areas, but where there is no real intention to eliminate the activity because of the power of larger-scale enterprises which distribute through street traders and of public opinion which condemns violent repression against small-scale entrepreneurs providing a public service (see Bromley 1978). Another form of containment occurs when official licences are mandatory in order to operate a specific type of enterprise, and when bureaucratic documentation requirements and delays are made especially onerous so as to deter applications and to ensure that most of the applications which are made are either rejected or interminably delayed.

7. The creation of regulatory employment

All governmental activities have a tendency to respond to Parkinson's Law, continuously creating new tasks and generating the requirement for additional personnel. In political systems of a strongly clientelistic nature, there are also strong pressures on the government to generate new jobs for political supporters and for the friends, relatives and hangers-on of leading politicians and administrators. A major area for such task- and job-generation is the regulation of small enterprise, where all too often it is assumed that no special skills are needed, and where there are ample opportunities for petty corruption.

8. Taxation

Many registration and licensing procedures are primarily intended to define the population which should be taxed for pursuing a specific economic activity, and often these procedures include an element of taxation through the payment of fees. Providing tax income is used to benefit the poorer majority of the population, taxation is both a useful and a necessary process in any social formation. When carried to extremes, however, the taxation of small enterprises can become a deterrent to the operation of such enterprises, establishing an additional mechanism of persecution.

9. *The prevention of commercial malpractices*

This area of concern requires a wide-ranging system of inspections and sanctions designed to deter such obviously anti-social practices as the sale of defective, stolen and contraband goods, the deliberate giving of short weights and measures, the sale of adulterated and falsified products, and the use of forged money.

The constraints which governments can apply as a result of some or all of these concerns vary considerably in nature, intensity and apparent "legality". Sometimes they imply nothing more than the deliberate neglect of small enterprises and the adoption of policies which favour larger-scale enterprises (national and foreign) with credits, technical assistance, duty-free imports, export subsidies and other forms of support. In most cases, however, they imply a mixture of bureaucratic regulation through registration, licensing, inspection and taxation procedures, with "policing" and the application of violence, arrest, imprisonment, confiscation of documents or goods, closure of premises, or fines. Though "policing" is the best general term for the latter range of activities, it is important to recognize that in many countries and contexts such functions are performed not only by the regular police force, but also by municipal inspectors and police, and/or by members of the armed forces.

Both constraints and supports can be divided into two major groups in terms of the way in which they are applied: "discretionary" and "non-discretionary". These two groups have been defined by Myrdal (1968, 904) as follows:

> If their application involves an individual decision by an administrative authority with power to act at its own discretion, they are considered to be *discretionary*. If the application follows automatically from the laying down of a definite rule, or from induced changes in prices, the imposition of tariff duties or excise duties, or the giving of subsidies to a particular branch of industry without the possibility of discrimination in favour of particular firms, the controls are presumed to be *non-discretionary*.

Myrdal goes on to suggest that, in substantial parts of the Third World, the scarcity of administrative personnel with both competence and integrity makes discretionary policies difficult to apply effectively, and makes reliance on them hazardous in both practical and moral terms.

Both bureaucratic regulation and policing tend to be very partial and selective in their coverage, and as a result, their use tends to be highly discretionary in character. In some cases this represents a deliberate "containment" policy in which the objective is to limit through the application of penalties rather than to eliminate altogether. More often, however, incomplete coverage is mainly a reflection of the complexity of the procedures and laws involved, the large numbers of highly dispersed small enterprises to be constrained, and the shortage of adequate bureaucratic and policing personnel, transport and equipment. All too often regulations are numerous, issued by a wide variety of different authorities, overlapping, and conflicting, creating a situation in which the great majority of small enterprises contravene a variety of regulations. In such a situation, law enforcement has more of the character of "selective victimization" of a few offenders amongst many, than of any real administration of justice. This produces a highly discretionary form of enforcement, even though the law may be framed in terms of the total prohibition of certain activities and practices, and is therefore non-discretionary in character.

The practical problems involved in policing small enterprises are well illustrated by the case of street traders in the city of Cali in Colombia, where several hundred pages of municipal and police regulations specify in great detail where and under what conditions street trading may take place. In reality, however, the great majority of the municipal inspectors (from three different municipal departments), the police and the soldiers who are supposed to enforce these regulations neither know them to any great extent nor have easy access to the key reference books. Furthermore, very few of the policing personnel have completed much more than basic primary education, and most of them earn substantially less than the amount which is estimated by the National Statistical Department (DANE) to be necessary to adequately house, feed and clothe a family. The overall result is that there is considerable overlap between the different departments dealing with street traders, and the actions of one department frequently contradict those of another. Complaints about policy brutality and corruption are frequent, and some officials even run neighbourhood "protection rackets" charging each trader a daily or weekly sum in return for the promise of unhindered business operation (Bromley 1978, 1163–64).

Myrdal (1968, 945) asserts that "whenever discretionary power is given to officials, there will tend to be corruption", and he goes on (p. 952) to indicate that:

Corruption is one of the forces that helps to preserve the "soft state" with its low degree of social discipline. Not only are politicians and administrators affected by the prevalence of corruption, but also businessmen and, in fact, the whole population. . . . Of particular importance is the fact that the usual method of exploiting a position of public responsibility for private gain is by threat of obstruction or delay. Where corruption is widespread, inertia and inefficiency, as well as irrationality, impede the process of decision-making and plan fulfilment.

Of course there is some corruption in all countries, but there is clearly more corruption in some than in others. The significance of corruption varies considerably between different spheres of activity, but there can be little doubt that it is especially notable in the bureaucratic regulation and policing of small enterprises. This is a reflection of the dispersed small-scale and labour-intensive nature of such bureaucratic regulation and policing, and also of the low priority accorded to such activities by most governments—demonstrated by the relative shortage of personnel, equipment and funds allocated to such activities, and by the poor quality and low salaries of most of the personnel involved.

Even if the real or potential corruption of bureaucratic regulation is ignored, small enterprises are severely affected by bureaucratic delays and by the time and expense required to keep up-to-date with the regulations, to visit officials, to complete standard procedures, and to appeal against unfavourable official decisions. In relation to the proprietors of large enterprises, petty entrepreneurs are at a grave disadvantage in terms of information, access to officialdom, capacity to wait for decisions, and capacity to pay for specialized messengers, queue-standers, agents and lawyers. These problems are well summarized by Adams (1959, 149), who indicates that:

> Small business is peculiarly vulnerable to strangulation by regulation. It is often incapable of coping with (1) the time, cost, and red tape inherent in the administrative process; (2) the use of the administrative process as a weapon of competitive harassment; (3) differential or discriminatory standards followed by the regulatory authority; (4) regulatory re-trictionism and suppression of competition; and (5) undue identification between regulators and regulatees. These handicaps are only illustrative of a more basic problem, *viz.* the inability of small business to battle on two fronts. . . . A small firm may be able to surmount the challenges of the market place, and yet be unable to withstand a hostile regulatory bureaucracy. It may win the battle of managerial efficiency and market rivalry, only to be destroyed by "administrative expertise".

The four essays in this section cover a wide range of constraints on small enterprises, ranging from the general context of the urban environment (Chapter 11, by Emilio Pradilla and Carlos Jiménez), to the comparative international analysis of regulatory measures (Chapter 12, by J. S. Eades), and to specific case studies of regulatory bureaucracy and policing in Jakarta (Chapter 13, by Dennis J. Cohen) and in Johannesburg (Chapter 14, by C. M.

Rogerson and K. S. O. Beavon). All of these essays confirm the essentially repressive nature of most bureaucratic regulation and policing of small enterprises, reinforcing socio-economic inequalities and impeding the upward mobility of petty entrepreneurs. This repression is a major element in the explanation of why "detailed observations of 'informal sector' activities always reveal great vitality, considerable technological developments, and every sign of responsive and adaptable growth, while the larger picture remains one of seemingly endless perpetuation of the sector and its problems" (Bienefeld 1975, 73).

Pradilla and Jiménez's "Architecture, urbanism and neocolonial dependence" is an extract from their path-breaking book with the same title, written in Spanish and presenting a Marxist interpretation of the urban economy under peripheral capitalism. It provides a general analysis of "urban development" processes, the role and organization of the construction industry, the role of architect/designers, the significance of mass-produced and so-called "self-help" housing, urban renewal, and land and property speculation. Using Colombian examples, it also illustrates some of the capitalist pressures to create the "city-beautiful", with consequent demands for the persecution of street occupations and the "developmentalist modernization" of transport and commerce.

Eades' essay on the State regulation of small enterprises presents a comparative analysis of the regulatory process using Papua-New Guinea, West Africa and Singapore as case studies. His analysis relates the economic structure of the country, its form of insertion into the international economy, the heritage of colonialism, and the strength and characteristics of the contemporary State, so as to produce a general interpretation of the factors influencing both the nature of regulatory legislation and the ways in which it is enforced.

Cohen's "The people who get in the way" is a remarkably perceptive analysis of the situation of the urban poor in early-1970s Indonesia, explaining both how and why squatter settlements, street traders and a wide range of other small enterprises are subjected to official persecution. The regulatory processes of Jakarta are placed in a national context, and the nature of official regulation is specifically related to the characteristics of the régime holding power at the national level. In turn, these characteristics are related to recent history and national political processes, so as to set contemporary policies within a broader framework of conflicting ideologies and power relations.

Finally, Rogerson and Beavon's "A tradition of repression" provides a detailed case study of official regulation of street trading in Johannesburg. It analyses an extreme case of social, economic and spatial segregation, and the deliberate persecution of non-white entrepreneurship. While extreme, however, a reading of the quote from Frantz Fanon at the beginning of this section, combined with a glance at Eades' analysis of Papua-New Guinea or

Cohen's analysis of Jakarta, will show that such segregation and persecution are reflections of a much more generalized set of colonial and neo-colonial socio-economic processes affecting much of the Third World.

At their worst, the rhetoric and policy prescriptions of "modernization" and "progress" are simply articulations of the class interests of local and foreign élites. Their implementation protects such interests from intrusion and competition by other groups, ensures them a substantial and docile labour force, provides for their continued enrichment, and intensifies a dependent and transplanted development model. Small enterprises are likely to be tolerated and even mildly supported if they fit in with these interests, but deliberately obstructed or persecuted if they do not.

REFERENCES

ADAMS, Walter (1959) "The regulatory commissions and small business", *Law and Contemporary Problems*, Vol. 24, pp. 147–68.

BIENEFELD, Manfred (1975) "The informal sector and peripheral capitalism: the case of Tanzania", *IDS Bulletin*, Vol. 6, No. 3, pp. 53–73.

BROMLEY, Ray (1978) "Organization, regulation and exploitation in the so-called 'urban informal sector': the street traders of Cali, Colombia", *World Development*, Vol. 6, No. 9/10, pp. 1161–71. Reprinted in Ray Bromley (ed.) (1979) *The Urban Informal Sector: Critical Perspectives on Employment and Housing Policies*, Pergamon, Oxford.

BROMLEY, Ray (1980) "Municipal versus spontaneous markets? A case study of urban planning in Cali, Colombia", *Third World Planning Review*, Vol. 2, pp. 205–32.

BROMLEY, Ray (1981) "From Calvary to white elephant: a Colombian case of urban renewal and marketing reform", *Development and Change*, Vol. 12, pp. 77–120.

DINWIDDY, Bruce (1974) *Promoting African Enterprise*, Croom Helm, London.

FANON, Frantz (1968) *The Wretched of the Earth*, Grove Press, New York.

FITZPATRICK, Peter (1980) *Law and State in Papua–New Guinea*, Academic Press, London.

FRIEDMAN, Milton (1978) "What is America?", *The Sohioan*, Vol. 50, No. 1, pp. 8–11.

HARPER, Malcolm (1977) *Consultancy for Small Businesses*, Intermediate Technology Publications Ltd., London.

KING, Anthony D. (1976) *Colonial Urban Development: Culture, Social Power and Environment*, Routledge & Kegan Paul, London.

KING, Anthony D. (1980) "Exporting planning: the colonial and neo-colonial experience", in Gordon E. Cherry (ed.) *Shaping an Urban World; Planning in the Twentieth Century*, Mansell, London, pp. 203–26.

MITNICK, Barry M. (1980) *The Political Economy of Regulation*, Columbia University Press, New York.

MYRDAL, Gunnar (1968) *Asian Drama: An Inquiry into the Poverty of Nations*, Pantheon/Random House, New York.

NECK, Philip A. (ed.) (1977) *Small Enterprise Development: Policies and Programmes*, Management Development Series No. 14, International Labour Office (ILO), Geneva.

PORTES, Alejandro and WALTON, John (1981) *Labor, Class, and the International System*, Academic Press, New York.

WILSON, James Q. (1974) "The politics of regulation", in James W. McKie (ed.) *Social Responsibility and the Business Predicament*, Brookings Institution, Washington D.C., pp. 135–68.

WORLD BANK (1978) *Employment and Development of Small Enterprises: Sector Policy Paper*, World Bank, Washington D.C.

CHAPTER 11

Architecture, urbanism and neocolonial dependence*

EMILIO PRADILLA AND CARLOS JIMÉNEZ

The process of production of architectural, urban and other physical works is adjusted to the general form of the capitalist process of production, with its concrete characteristics within a social formation being determined by the particular form of insertion and relationship of the capitalist mode of production to the elements of other modes of production. The raw materials for this process of production are the so-called construction materials, from bricks and cement to electrical wiring and sanitary artefacts, lifts etc. The tools used range from the trowel and the spirit-level directly handled by the construction worker, to the cranes, bulldozers and giant concrete mixers that are directly linked to the large factories producing enormous prefabricated pieces or even entire housing units.

It should be pointed out, however, that in capitalist countries in general, and particularly in those countries that are subjected to the conditions of neocolonial dependency, the régime of production of these objects lags behind that of social production in general insofar as it employs petty manufacturing or even precapitalist forms of production on a large scale. A similar situation exists in the production of constructional materials, where there are small artisanal workshops which act as "contractors" producing wooden pieces, metal frames, tiles and bricks, and where the various forms of over-exploitation of labour-power survive, such as payment by piecework, a working day of 12 to 16 hours, and child labour. All this survives no matter what labour legislation exists, alongside the large monopolies producing cement, concrete and prefabricated elements where the more developed forms of capitalist production are present.

This situation of backwardness also appears in the actual construction process itself where manufactured forms of production are employed—above

---

*Translated by Rod Burgess from pp. 47–63 of Emilio Pradilla and Carlos Jiménez (1973) *Arquitectura, Urbanismo y Dependencia Neocolonial*, originally published by Ediciones SIAP, Planteos, Buenos Aires. This translation is published with the permission of SIAP (the Sociedad Interamericana de Planificación) and of Emilio Pradilla.

all in the construction of individual houses. This involves more or less limited groups of workers operating within a rudimentary division of labour and working with manual tools—a process whose fundamental driving element continues to be human labour power, and which continues to rely on the individual skills of the direct worker. However, the growing tendency for the prefabrication not merely of the elements of an architectural work, but of the entire work itself, indicates the way in which the industrial labour form—which implies the progressive displacement of man by machine—is penetrating this sector.

In dependent neo-colonial countries the survival of these precapitalist forms in construction activities is explained by a double reason. On the one hand the limitation on the capacity to import machinery and equipment that is determined by the low availability of foreign exchange funds affects construction activities, as it does all activities in the productive sector. In these conditions, and given the absence of a local producer sector for machinery and equipment, the construction sector has to work with relatively rudimentary means of production. On the other hand, the absence of competition on the world market, given the lack of mobility of the goods produced, permits the massive utilization of unskilled labour power whose wage levels are maintained below those current in the remaining branches of industry. This labour power is not able to obtain employment in industry, where the demand for hands is restricted by structural factors already mentioned. It therefore sells itself at a price equal to or even below the minimum legal wage for short periods of time, under arbitrary contract conditions (where they exist), and at the margin of any possibility for union organization given its limited numbers and the limited duration of its contractual period.

All these facts permit the entrepreneur to overexploit the worker, and to obtain high profit margins that are increased by the process of permanent inflation. This is also the source of the attraction that construction exercises on capital that is not reinvested in the industrial sector.

It is not accidental that the Colombian State, amongst others, seeks a solution to the crisis that affects the accumulation and reproduction of capital through massive action in the entire construction sector (housing, road networks, means of collective consumption etc.). This much is revealed in the emphasis put on the construction sector as a key sector in the "Four Strategies" of the 1971–1974 Development Plan and the enormous sums of money invested in "urban renewal" projects. Equally as unaccidental is the rapid process of monopoly concentration of capital in this sector, and the recent appearance of large "savings and housing finance" corporations which unite finance capital, national and foreign bank capital, property capital, and the monopolies controlling urban landed property. Capital and the State in this way seek to reopen the process of accumulation through the expansion of the very sector in which the over-exploitation of the working class is the easiest to achieve (see Pradilla 1974, 27–42).

The relatively low level of development of the productive forces in the sector as well as the labour relations that are dominant in it, place the construction worker in an ambiguous situation in relation to workers in the industrial sector: dispossessed of his means of production and forced to sell his labour-power in conditions of over-exploitation, the productive régime into which he is inserted still requires his particular skills and insists that his labour-power becomes the fundamental motor of this process. As a kind of proletarian–artisan, he is even talked about in terms of a division of labour that has been copied from the old artisanal and manufacturing forms: masters and apprentices.

In those situations where the process has taken on the form of large scale industry, it is more obvious that the direct worker is a worker in the fullest meaning of the word. And it is equally as clear that in both cases it is he who is the producer of the surplus labour that is appropriated by others and in the existing conjuncture, it is on him that the "development" policies of neo-colonial capital depend.

The role of the architect-designer in the construction sector

The most common form of activity of the architect–designer is that of controlling the productive process as the designer of the work to be realized, and hence as the moulder of the final form of the product, or as the direct supervisor of the work in progress, or as both. This common form assumes different particular forms in agreement with the relationship that is established between the architect–designer and the "client" or owner of money-capital and/or the means of production invested in the realization of the work.

1. When he lacks the means of production and simply acts as the technical agent in the design and direction of the process, whether it be for an individual owner, a capitalist owner, or the State. In this case he is an indirect productive worker independently of the fact that his remuneration takes the form of a wage or appears in the form of "professional fees".
2. When he owns the means of production and realizes and controls the constructive process for an individual owner, for a capitalist or for the State. In this case, which almost always assumes the form of a contract at a fixed price, the designer–builder not only directs the productive process, but also appropriates a part of the surplus value produced by the worker, leaving the remaining part to the owner of the money-capital invested in the process, and to the other fractions of capital who participate in its realization as a commodity. Obviously when he is the owner of money-capital he will appropriate the quantity of surplus value corresponding to that of the investor–capitalist in the distribution since

he is acting as a capitalist owner. His participation in the distribution of surplus value will increase if he is the landowner, if he commercializes the product etc., until the point arrives when he appropriates its totality, this being the case with the property and financial monopolies that have developed in recent years.

It is necessary to emphasize the fact that the level of development of the productive forces in the construction sector has a direct influence on the design itself insofar as the design tendencies that emphasize the poetry of formal creation are consistent with the precapitalist forms of production that survive within developed capitalism, but which have a far greater importance in dependent capitalism. The preferred fields of action of this type of design are in the construction of individual houses—i.e., "unique" use-values that are valorized by the "semi-artistic" labour of the workers, and in prestige works for monopoly capital or the State. Both of these are charged with a clear ideological-symbolic content that the designer simply reproduces. In these cases the spontaneous form and lack of rationality of the product, as well as the employment of expert direct workers, are a prior condition for the existence of the activities of the "creators" who are obliged to materialize their personal "genius" in brick and cement.

On the other hand, the rationalist tendencies of design clearly correspond to the régime of production of large-scale industry, in which the determination of costs, the calculation of investment, profits and above all assembly-belt production for a large market constitute themselves into demands that progressively restrict the creative "genius" of the designer. It has been a rather sad truth of history that the development of capitalism has assassinated our old and glorious master of design with his "artistic" dreams.

We have already spoken of the State as a "client" of the builder–designer. As a "client" the State acts in three particular ways:

1. As a capitalist by appropriating from the labour put in by the construction workers. This is the case in the construction of so-called "social interest" housing where the State assumes a multiple role as an industrial, commercial and finance capitalist as well as that of a rentier. In this way the State will use surplus-value in the form of profits or of interests, in order to hand it over to the builder to pay the bureaucracy for its services or to "capitalize" it, all this being the fruit of the exploitation of the worker. It acts in a similar way when it realizes investments in public services which are sold to their users in the form of "convenient monthly quotas" that simultaneously include the profits and interests on the capital invested and the rents on the land occupied. Talk of making public services "profitable" is far from accidental.
2. As a general administrator of society to the benefit of capitalist interests. By investing the funds derived from taxing all social agents (the State budget) in public services and infrastructure that are "necessary for

economic development", the State will realize a regressive distribution of income. This is to say that it will collaborate in the process of capitalist accumulation because the works which constitute "the general conditions of production and circulation", such as roads, water-systems, sources of electrical energy etc., will not be undertaken by individual capitalists because of their low rate of profitability, even though they are indispensable for the process of reproduction of capital. Whilst for capital they constitute the means of realization and reproduction, for the wage-earner they represent a greater reduction in his wage.

3. As an instrument for the reproduction of the social relations of production (and in particular property relations) and the relations of class domination when the responsibilities of the State include such works as schools, official buildings, barracks etc. In this case architectural and urban physical works take on an inseparable dual character: on the one hand they become the material supports of the repressive or ideological apparatuses through which the State dominates society in the name of capital and reproduces its ideology; and on the other hand they provide the material supports of the means of life necessary for the maintenance and reproduction of the labour-power of the working-class, employees, and even the bourgeoisie itself (e.g. education, health, culture etc.). The State does not deduct the cost of these works from the profits of the capitalists (indeed they contribute to an increase in these profits) but rather from the wages of the workers, in this way making them pay for the means that assure their own slavery.

The designer, in carrying out his technical practice is thus an instrument in the service of the relations of production ruling in society. His practice is compromised by capital both in economic terms where it serves as an instrument in the exploitation of wage labour that is employed in construction, and in ideological terms where it acts as an often very efficient means for the reproduction of bourgeois ideology. Such ideology is contained not only in the function of the work, but also in the very form that the designer gives it in order to satisfy his client and the eternal glory of his personal genius.

Having exposed the nature of the process of production of object-works and the role of the agents who participate in it, we can now ask the question: Why are these objects produced? For what purposes are they produced? We shall insist on emphasizing that they are obviously produced to satisfy the needs of individuals or society, whether these needs grow out of a man's stomach, or out of his own imagination or fantasy. It has always been this way from those historical periods when each individual made his own clothes, utensils and tools up to the present day when the production of objects is undertaken through a complex division of labour. However there is a difference: the objects produced today do not satisfy the personal needs of those that produce them, but rather the needs of others; i.e., they do not have a use value for the producer, but only for others. They are produced for exchange, and they acquire the commodity form. As this form, objects then have the dual character of use-values and exchange-values.

Where are these objects exchanged—on the local, national or world market. However, they cannot be compared as useful objects in their natural form, since a vanilla ice-cream as a useful object has nothing to do with a piece of toilet soap, even if both are valued at the same sum of money. What makes it possible to compare two objects that are so dissimilar is their unique shared quality: the fact that they are products of human labour—not the concrete labour of the ice-cream or soap maker which is impossible to compare, but rather that of the general, comparable abstract labour that is shared by all forms of human labour—the expenditure of muscles, nerves and brain.

The essential value of a commodity is this abstract labour—its magnitude, the quantity of abstract labour contained in it, and its measure of labour-time. What we are dealing with here is not the time that each skilled or unskilled worker uses up, but rather the average time employed in society for its production: that is to say the *socially necessary time* to produce this commodity in a specific country and at a determined historical moment. In this way the capitalist market does not confront things, but rather producers through things: the exchange value of objects triumphs over their use value and all the objects produced are produced for exchange—they are commodities.

Architectural or urban objects do not escape this general law of capitalism: they are produced for exchange and he who does not dispose of money—the produce of the sale of the commodities that he produces or of the sale of that particular commodity that is labour-power—is not able to buy them on the market. As the bourgeois economists put it: if there is not *solvent demand* there is not the production of houses or anything.

This law is equally as valid for housing as it is for the services that the State produces. Proof of this lies in the fact that whilst thousands of houses remain empty for long periods of time, thousands of poor families lack houses and minimum services and live overcrowded in inner-city tenements and slums. If capitalist production had as its object the satisfaction of individual and social needs, logic would demand that it must produce housing and services for all those families that need them. The capitalist produces houses only if there exist buyers who are capable of paying the price that *he* fixes for his product, and which logically includes his profit.[1]† This is the ultimate reason for the "housing problem" which though it affects all social classes, affects the working-class and the unemployed most of all, making it impossible for them to accede to the supply of housing offered. In this way the myth of the "social" function of the private construction of urban, architectural and housing objects is exploded. However, we should make it clear that we are not dealing

---

†Superscript numbers refer to Notes at end of chapter.

with the particular "ill-will" of housing constructors but rather with *the general law of the capitalist production of commodities*. For a capitalist it matters not whether the commodities whose production guarantees the reproduction of his capital and the increase in his profits takes the form of housing, basic foodstuffs, perfumes, pornographic articles, napalm bombs and weapons, or pious engravings. To forget this is to forget the reality of capitalism and to live in the fallacious world of bourgeois ideology.

Is it valid to apply this law to self-building? Let us see. There are two types of self-building: that of the "shanty" miserably built to satisfy the vital need for shelter, without designers, with throwaway materials, and with a heavy investment of family labour, and that of bourgeois and petit-bourgeois housing built by an architect, with "first-class" materials and with the utilization of wage-labour. In the second case the commodity relationship is established in the construction process through the purchase of the commodities used in it (including labour power). In both cases, however, the fact that they are products of human labour and are inserted into dominantly commodity relations means that both the "shanty" and the luxury mansion can be converted into commodities, independently of the fact that they may have been produced for the use of the owner and not directly for exchange.

The designer then participates as a technical agent or capitalist owner in the production of commodity objects and not simply in the production of useful objects or "art-objects". His direct determination by the system of relations of production/productive forces, and by the class structure can be identified in two areas: on the one hand by the conditions ruling in the production of objects, and on the other by the form in which the owner of capital seeks to introduce his products on the market for a determined social class. This conditioning is not only present in terms of the function that this object must fulfil, but also in its form and dimension. In this way the myth of the "free and neutral designer" is exploded.

We can now see why the formal and dimensional reply given by the designers of housing ranges from the burrows that the State constructs in its "self-built units for the least favoured classes", to the gilded palaces of our bourgeois neighbourhoods. The consumption capacity of an individual for architectural objects depends in part on the social production that he succeeds in appropriating for himself, and this part is determined by his relation of ownership or non-ownership to the means of production i.e., it is given in terms of social class, though it is achieved through the mediation of the "distribution of income".

The designer works at the heart of the class division of society, and if we are to be honest, at the side of his bosses, the capitalists. He carries out the same mission when his technical practice is put into service in the construction of the locations for the ideological or repressive apparatuses of the bourgeois State. Finally, it can be said that the urban designer acts in the same manner when, despite his good intentions, he becomes an instrument in the general programming of the urban segregation of the classes and the strategy of the maintenance of that "urban disorder" which is nothing more than the sacred and inviolable order of private free enterprise. This urban disorder then is an expression of the liberty of capital—a reflection in space of the anarchy reigning in the capitalist market—that the bourgeoisie defends with blood and fire as the highest achievement of "individual dignity".

This liberty obviously has two faces: the liberty of the capitalist to exploit the dispossessed, and the liberty of the dispossessed to be exploited, to develop their own misery and to die of hunger where they want. These rights of the exploited, however, encounter one limitation—they are to be exercised only where they do not offend the sight or the smell of the bourgeoisie and the petite bourgeoisie in its service. The urban designer respects and improves on the fine spatial delimitation for the exercise of these rights, by zoning our cities and by defining through the use of indices and codes the spaces where the liberty of the one or the other can be developed.

The urban designer is also working for capital when he designs "urban renewal" zones and road plans, because in this function he is programming: the uprooting of the exploited classes that live in these areas; the recuperation of the land by speculative landed and property capital; and the mechanisms through which this capital appropriates the ground rents generated by the new investment in roads and services.

To conclude we shall reply to a question that rises out of this discussion: what social class does the designer belong to? Using a definition of social class as the "effect" of the totality of the structures of the mode of production, or social formation, on the social agents that support it (an organization that is determined in the last instance by the relations of production and economic structure—see Poulantzas 1972, 75 and 98), we can thus affirm that:

Those who own the means of production and/or invest money capital in the production of objects of design, exploiting the paid labour force (or who employ other designers and assistants as wage earners in the production of the same design), belong to the bourgeoisie proper or the petite bourgeoisie.

The designers who sell their labour power to the State, to property capital or to other designers, in exchange for a wage, are located in the highest social stratum of the wage-earners. However a series of factors conspires to place them objectively in a social category in the service of capital—the technocracy. These include: the fact that they act as technical agents and docile instruments of capital in the exploitation of building workers; the profound domination exercised by bourgeois ideology on the general components of "design ideology", and its consequent reproduction in design practice and teaching; and, the political support that these designers generally give to the bourgeoisie and its State.

In short, irrespective of the intentions and consciousness of the designer, design as a technical practice is in the service of capital in its activity of exploiting wage-labour and dominating society in general.

"Vulgar" urban and architectural ideology: an instrument of class domination

The world of commodities has rapidly been integrating all urban and architectural objects; including the natural elements considered suitable by speculative capital for increasing the advantages of its specific commodity. From the "natural" relation that is established between the designer and capitalist producers in construction activities, and at the heart of this fabulous world of consumer objects, there has arisen an urban and architectural ideology skilfully manipulated by the sellers of housing that both serves to create new consumer needs and to continue to reproduce the general ideological values of bourgeois society. In this way individuals are enslaved in a certain form of consumption and are convinced on a day-to-day basis that their "liberty and happiness" depend on the perpetuation of the economic and political domination of the bourgeoisie. As a simple, particular region of bourgeois ideology, this architectural and urban ideology, injected daily in small doses through the radio, cinema, television and the press, supports and transmits the social relations that characterize bourgeois society; private property, family, individual privacy, social differentiation etc.

A simple collation from the advertisements in three Colombian newspapers that were picked at random from a large pile is significant in helping us to see how these values are transmitted and reproduced.[2] Thus we read in a three-quarter page advertisement: "In Modelia, Fernando Mazuera and Co. Ltd., has seven responses to your demands for *your own house:* in *styles,* in prices, and in *tastes.* Fernando Mazuera has seven responses to your demands; one and two storey houses from 290,000 to 370,000 pesos, *different* facades, *different* distribution yet the same quality: a fabulous location and a magnificent day and night transport service, a neighbourhood without equal of more than 3000 *families like your own,* with all the services of a "modern city" . . . A few days later we read "we are not selling an apartment, *we are selling a different life* . . . Torre Panorama" . . . and, "in the *exclusive* Carrera 10° 97-27, alongside a beautiful park, . . . the house you have always dreamed about". We have here then, the "dream world" that is the result of the marriage of design, speculative capital and publicity: the private ownership of the house—the "divine gift" that guarantees security—at least while the monthly quotas are being paid and with them the profits, the rents and interests of the capitalist: the family—a particular family whose unity is structured around patrimony and inheritance; the differentiation of each family according to its tastes but amongst "families that are the same as yours", i.e., of the same social class; "a different life" that is to be achieved through monthly repayments and the gift of two or three electrical household appliances that will fill housewives with joy. We have here the same "dream world" that promotes "Marlboro" cigarettes, the "popular car", the beauty queens, transistor radios and this or that political message—all draped with naked women; commodities to be used in the same way as a French perfume. This opium of the desires is aimed at the exploited classes who are submerged in unemployment, starvation, disease and overcrowding with the aim of producing the dream that makes them forget their exploitation.

The capitalist State is equally as bound by the same language. If, for example, the ICT (*Instituto de Crédito Territorial*, the Colombian Government's national public housing agency) changed its publicity message from "A house for every Colombian" to "A house for every Colombian family" (the absurdity of the former is obvious), then the content of this publicity remains the same: the private and individual ownership of property in housing. The maximum security that the State gives to Colombians thus consists of 20 years of monthly fret and worry over their repayments, and the permanent threat of eviction through incapacity to pay.

But the ideological message is not only transmitted through the publicity for housing, it also reaches us through the "qualities" of other architectural and urban objects: in the *beauty* of the parish church that pierces the sky with its tall steeple and makes us believe in the other life—in paradise—and reminds us that the prize of resignation to the poverty of this world is "that the poor will be kings in heaven"; the *solidity* of our barracks and jails that fills us with healthy patriotism making us feel safe as Colombians in our national honour as well as in our property, and makes us forget the repression that is exercised over the popular masses, and the unemployment and misery that are the origins of delinquency; the *majesty* of our skyscrapers that like phallic symbols cut the blue of the firmament and relate to us the successes of this aviation company, or that national or foreign beer, textile or petrol company—the "beauty" that is offered to the eager eyes of "all the people" though it is a product of the hunger of the workers and their families, whose strikes have been broken by labour legislation, the legal counter-pleas of the bosses, and the use of "available force". These are some examples of the ideology transmitted by architectural works that can only with difficulty be concealed by the "theories" of architectural design and form, and by discourse on "the aesthetic content of symbols" and "the contrast between the horizontality of volumes and the verticality of the elements of the facade".

The last example (at least in this essay if not in reality) of the use of vulgar urban ideology as an instrument of class domination arises out of the ruins of the inner city tenements and shacks destroyed by the bulldozer that announce the passage of a new avenue. "Urban Road Development" and "Urban Renewal" have as their goal the eviction, through reason or force, of the inner-city inhabitants from their central residential locations that allow them to survive through crime, street commerce, the sale of lottery tickets etc., and the presentation of this process as works of development, modernization, and beautification. Beneath this phraseology is hidden the character of these projects as true weapons for the reconquest of the urban centre by monopoly capital and the State. Several months after the remains of their former houses have been swept away in the advance of the reconquest of the urban centre by capital, it is not uncommon to find the victims of this very process standing in delight in front of the iron and steel towers, and their windows stuffed with the luxury goods that they have never been able to consume. Often, as victims of their own lack of consciousness, they can be seen applauding the beneficiaries and promoters of this process of the private monopoly appropriation of an urban centre, that in fact was created by their own efforts (see Pradilla 1974, part IV).

The last residue of the neutrality of the artist-designer or technical planner dies here, in the extensive and complete field of vulgar architectural and urban ideology—part of bourgeois ideology in general. He has helped to create this ideology in his collaboration with capital and advertising, and he reproduces it on a daily basis in marble and bronze, aluminium and glass, asbestos and cement blocks, and over a more lengthy period, in his works or through his students in the university education system. All this is objectively marginal to the operation of individual will, since every technique and every technician is in the service of the dominant relations of production in the society in which he develops his particular practice.

Notes

1. In Colombia, for example, the industry concerned with the construction of housing and architectural and urban objects has experienced an accelerated process of monopoly concentration which follows the general tendency of dependent neo-colonial capitalism, and which characterizes its market as oligopolistic. In these conditions the producers can freely fix the price of their products, relatively marginal to the play of supply and demand. The permanent presence of people producing houses under almost artisanal conditions with high costs of production, and the shortage of housing generated by the demographic growth of the cities, makes it possible for these monopolies to obtain super-profits by fixing their prices inside their costs of production. The ICT, the State agency that constructs "social interest housing", is nothing more than a State capitalist monopoly that controls the market of the highest stratum of the working class, and low-paid employees, which is not catered for by private industry.
2. *El Tiempo* (Bogotá): 21 May 1972, p. 7A; 17 June 1972, p. 12C; 8 Oct. 1972, p. 78. All italics are the author's own.

References

POULANTZAS, Nicos (1972) *Poder Político y Clases Sociales en el Estado Capitalista*, Siglo XXI, Barcelona.
PRADILLA, Emilio (1974) "La política urbana del estado colombiano", *Ideología y Sociedad* (Bogotá), No. 9, enero-marzo.

CHAPTER 12

If you can't beat 'em, join 'em: State regulation of small enterprises*

J. S. EADES

"After twenty-five years of effective town and country planning . . . we find that the main distributive effect was to keep the poor, or a high proportion of them, poor" (Hall, 1972, 267; cited in Simmie 1974, 149).

The criticisms of the planning process made by Simmie and others apply not only to the advanced industrial societies, but also to the cities of the Third World. Here, too, the decisions of the burgeoning planning profession are often regressive, and this in a situation where the existing income differentials between rich and poor are even greater. Particularly badly hit by planning decisions in many instances are people operating small enterprises and especially those involved in marketplace trade (see e.g. Marris 1961; Gamer 1972; Bromley 1980, 1981). Markets tend to attract the attention of planners disproportionately: not only because large concentrations of traders give rise to the sorts of problems of access, transportation, public health and noise with which the planners feel particularly competent to deal, but also because they are relatively easy to administer and regulate compared with more dispersed forms of economic activity. However, planning processes are only one aspect of the wider relations between small enterprises and the State, and it is with these wider relations that this paper is concerned. It is obvious that the degree of control over small enterprises claimed by, and actually exercised by, the State varies widely both in time and place, from *laissez faire* tolerance to outright repression. What I seek to do here is to explore some of the major factors affecting this variation in three widely contrasted Third World settings: Papua-New Guinea (PNG), West Africa and Singapore.[1]† These three cases encompass some of the major variations in the economies of the Third World; from the settler-dominated plantation economy of PNG to the indigenous cash-crop producers of West Africa and the growing industrial

---

*An original essay written especially for this book.
†Superscript numbers refer to Notes at end of chapter.

sector of Singapore. They also encompass major variations in the attitudes of the State towards small enterprises—from comparative acceptance in, say, Nigeria or Ghana, to the more rigorous control exercised in Singapore and the outright hostility of colonial PNG. But the types of small enterprises to be discussed are broadly similar in all three instances: they involve limited capital, are labour-intensive, and are carried on "quasi-independently" by men, women or children, either on their own or with the help of the family, kinsfolk, friends, or other sources of labour. Most of the discussion relates to marketplace trade, though many of the points raised apply to other types of enterprise as well.

The discovery of, and subsequent debates about, the nature of small-scale economic activity in the Third World in the last few years have successfully highlighted and clarified a number of issues. It is generally accepted now that earlier dualistic approaches over-stressed the autonomy of small enterprises and obscured the nature of their links with capitalism, both in terms of flows of goods, services etc., and through their functions in the reproduction of labour power for capitalist enterprises (for a summary, see Moser 1978). Because of these variable links, the superficially simple category of the "self-employed" should be divided into a variety of groups, ranging from relatively independent operators to "disguised proletarians" (Gerry and Birkbeck 1981), totally dependent on, and providing cheap inputs and services for, larger capitalist firms or State enterprises. The penetration of capitalism has had powerful, if variable effects on pre-existing patterns of economic activity, some of which persist, or have even been intensified, in interaction with capitalism. All this can be taken as read. What cannot be taken as read, however, is the precise nature of "capitalism", "the State", or "articulation" in each concrete instance. The transition to capitalism is a very different process in different areas, and the nature of precolonial links with the world economy had a profound effect on capitalist development during and after the period of colonial rule. Similarly, the State, as a system of political and legal organization, is also the result of a complex interaction between capitalist and indigenous forms of economic organization, and is not simply explicable in terms of the "capitalist mode of production" in some general sense. Here I want to focus on two aspects of the State: (1) a corpus of enacted legislation shaping the development of trade and other small-scale economic activities; and (2) a social organization of officials responsible for the day-to-day enforcement of this legislation. As we shall see, there is considerable variation in both these areas in the three case studies discussed here.

Papua-New Guinea[2]

The main features in the peculiar development of Papua-New Guinea compared with other countries in the Third World are as follows: a precolonial social structure consisting of small-scale societies with cross-cutting ceremonial exchange networks as the bases of production and distribution; a form of colonialism involving the establishment of settler plantations as the basis of the export economy, leaving large areas of traditional society relatively untouched, except for those, mainly the men, who were drawn into wage-labour through inducement or coercion (Fitzpatrick 1978); a limited urban structure, in which the capital, Port Moresby, constituted by far the largest town (Levine and Levine 1979); a pattern of urban administration which drew rigid boundaries between the various racial and ethnic groups in the urban population; and, relations between the colonized and the colonizers marked by exploitation and antagonism. Capitalist penetration of the hinterland took place very late, and it was left to the colonial State to take the leading part in policies which provided labour and land for the settlers and expatriate firms. The antagonism between the settlers and the natives which resulted from the level of coercion and exploitation created a siege mentality among the Australian colonists, who responded by regulating in minute detail the lives of the PNG natives in town.

The two most serious sets of legal constraints imposed were on freedom of movement and freedom of economic activity. Harsh vagrancy laws made it an offence for a native to be in town for more than four days without either a job or an official permit. Having "sufficient means of support" was usually defined in terms of employment by a European. A native employee could not have another person staying in his quarters without his employer's permission. There was a curfew and natives on the streets after 9.00 p.m. were liable to arrest. The courts had the power to return a convicted vagrant to his or her home area. Freedom of association was further curtailed by the laws relating to recreation, drinking and gambling (Fitzpatrick 1980, Ch. 6).

Economic activity by the Papua-New Guineans was also curtailed. The country has never had a "bazaar economy" (Geertz 1963), and even now, the hordes of street traders and small shops that flourish in most cities in the Third World are absent in urban PNG (Levine and Levine 1979, 127; Fitzpatrick and Blaxter 1979). Markets exist, but the locals deal mainly in local foodstuffs, while the trade in manufactured goods is in the hands of outsiders, mainly Europeans but with some Chinese. Ironically, legislation originally introduced to protect Papua-New Guineans from unscrupulous foreign traders has functioned to protect unscrupulous foreign traders from Papua-New Guineans (Fitzpatrick 1980, 191–92). Rules were imposed in the capital which restricted mobile traders from trading within 800 yards of fixed premises selling similar goods, effectively barring the street trader from the central urban areas. The granting of licences was similarly restricted and, even if the traders could get licences, there was a daunting series of standards which had to be met, and which limited the kinds of trade they could pursue. A good example is the small-scale trade in cooked foodstuffs which flourishes in most Third World cities. In PNG metropolitan standards have been applied to regulate this trade: the Trading with Natives Act of 1946 requires for the selling of meals "potable water from a reservoir tank of at least ten gallons capacity which shall be fitted within the body of the vehicle" with "an approved pumping apparatus". Of course, many Third World countries have a mass of regulations concerning trade inherited from the colonial period, but which they seldom enforce. In PNG on the other hand, the bureaucracy for their enforcement is quite large and efficient, thanks partly to pressure from European enterprises to make sure that the law is upheld (Fitzpatrick 1980, 195).

If entry to trade is barred for the average Papua-New Guinean, so are some of the other common forms of small-scale enterprise. Bar ownership is out. PNG natives have been allowed to drink since 1963, but access to alcohol has only been provided in large centrally located bars, which have proved to be centres of social disorder. Transport ownership is also heavily regulated, and the legislation was initially designed to protect foreign bus companies. Housing construction is also restricted by a similar mass of public health standards, which mean expensive housing. The result has been the proliferation of illegal, and therefore insecure, squatter settlements.

The result of all this is a deep and comprehensive domination of much of the economic life of towns by settler and metropolitan interests which has survived the dismantling of some of the more restrictive legislation in the 1970s. The lack of a strong indigenous entrepreneurial tradition and precolonial market economy, coupled with the exploitation of the territory by settler interests, led to the growth of legislation designed to support settler interests against those of an emergent local commercial class. The resulting colonial State in PNG was authoritarian, efficient, and inaccessible to the mass of the local people. In the development programmes initiated in the 1960s by the Australians, as a response to pressure from the United Nations, some of the more obviously discriminatory legislation was repealed, and the formation of a local middle class to whom power could be eventually entrusted was encouraged. However, much of the old legislation remains on the books, and it is sporadically enforced. The economy is still dominated by foreign capital, and to the PNG police a native seen on the streets after 9 o'clock in the evening is still a potential vagrant.

West Africa[3]

The contrast between PNG and West Africa is striking. In West Africa, long before the colonial period proper, various forms of currency, markets, and a network of long-distance trade had developed. In some instances, for example the kola trade between the forest and Northern Nigeria, it was the long-distance traders who took new economic initiatives in the colonial period (see e.g. Cohen 1966; Hogendorn 1970). Second, the nature of European involvement in the economy was generally different. In the 19th century the abolition of the slave trade had led to the growth of the "legitimate" trade in palm oil (Coquery-Vidrovitch 1971; Law 1977b), but the production and transport of this was still under the control of local political leaders. West Africa until the middle of the 19th century was quite literally the "white man's grave", and by the time that medical technology and political interests stimulated the European powers to bring the interior under effective political control, production of cash crops such as cocoa had already spread to the interior, and was firmly under indigenous control (see e.g. Berry 1975; Hill 1963). When the colonial, and later the post-independence, State began to exploit the agricultural sector more intensively, it was through the medium of marketing boards rather than through direct control of production (Bauer 1954; Beer and Williams 1976; Helleiner 1970). With the exception of the Ivory Coast (Campbell 1978), there were few settler plantations, and the indigenous development of cash crops, which in PNG only appeared in the 1960s, had occurred in West Africa by 1900. Early expatriate involvement in West Africa was therefore essentially mercantile. The major profits were to be made by shipping out locally-produced export crops, and by shipping in European manufactures. With the establishment of colonial rule, this trade became concentrated in the hands of a few major European companies, and by 1930 three of them (the United Africa Company, the Compagnie Française de l'Afrique Occidentale, and the Société Commerciale de l'Ouest Africain) controlled between two-thirds and three-quarters of West Africa's overseas trade (Hopkins 1973, 199). Smaller European firms were progressively absorbed or driven out of the market, as were African merchants, who were more vulnerable to downturns in trade. The most serious competition for the Europeans came from Levantine merchants (Bauer 1954; Winder 1962).

Colonial administration in West Africa thus took a form rather different from that in PNG, and the legal and administrative framework which developed served different interests. There were proportionately fewer European settlers, and there was less need for direct coercion to encourage the locals into the labour market: what coercion there was was generally to provide labour for the administration or the mines, rather than the agricultural sector (see e.g. Asiwaju 1976; Thomas 1973). There was also less need to protect settler interests against local competition. While administration in the French colonies generally took a more centralized form, the British aim was to administer as cheaply as possible, to provide a law-and-order framework in which the large companies could operate profitably. This could only be done with the compliance of the existing political authorities, and where centralized states existed, their institutions were adapted and incorporated into the British administrative system, the ideology being one of indirect rule (Crowder and Ikime 1970). This created a local political class with access to substantial resources which could be invested in enterprises, including trade, or in education. The categories of the wealthy and the educated coincided more and more. The large companies increasingly relied on local traders to carry out small-scale collection, bulking, bulk-breaking and retailing functions, which they could perform more cheaply than could the companies themselves, and in some cases company employees were set up as independent dealers (Hopkins 1973, 277–78). Thus both the administration and the firms depended on an infrastructure of local initiative which allowed a wealthy and politically active group of traders and educated clerks to develop at an early date. Increasingly this group demanded a role in decision-making at the local and national levels, and by the 1950s they had begun to achieve it.

In the 1950s came the start of local party politics, and the new political class consolidated its position in the next two decades. In the British colonies, this was possible through their access to the funds which had been accumulated through the commodity marketing boards. Some of the funds were invested in basic infrastructure or the expansion of the education system. Other funds found their way into the pockets of the party faithful, through loans, through dummy corporations which diverted State funds into party coffers, or through contracts allocated to party supporters for projects of dubious productivity. But not all these funds were frittered away unproductively. Politicians, civil servants and the military have all invested heavily, either on their own account or through their relatives, in property, in transport, in commercial farming, in trade or in contracting. The scale of these enterprises ranges from the grandiose—Tahir (1976) cites examples of Kano businessmen in the early 1970s with six-figure annual incomes—to the marginal, with minor officials starting enterprises little more secure than those of the average trader or artisan.

The attitude of the State towards the trader has always been ambivalent. The success of the colonial enterprise (particularly in the British colonies) was seen to depend on the stimulation of demand for European goods, which implied unrestricted trade. On the other hand, trade has, since the 19th century, been one of the few obvious sources of revenue at both the local and national levels, whether this revenue was derived from import and export taxes, market dues and licence fees, or through other forms of direct and indirect taxation. In the post-independence period, relations between the trader and the State have been complicated in a variety of ways, given the vagaries of the economies of the West African countries.

Some economies, like those of the Ivory Coast, buoyed by French capital, or Nigeria, buoyed by the oil revenues, have been able to expand. Others like those of Ghana or Guinea, faced with declining export revenue, the loss of metropolitan confidence and the withdrawal of foreign capital, have been stagnant or in decline (Johnson 1978; Killick 1978). The weakness of these economies has led to a black market developing, both in imported goods and currency, as the governments have severely restricted imports to conserve foreign exchange. Smuggling has become an endemic and uncontrollable problem. Goods in short supply are smuggled in and imported goods are smuggled out, as traders cash in on the difference between the official and black market exchange rates. Despite occasional arrests and harassment, the large numbers of traders involved, the wide-open borders, and the susceptibility of the customs officials to bribes, all make adequate control impossible. In both instances the government has intervened in marketing to supplement or, in the case of Guinea, to replace the private trading sector. The failure of this has merely compounded the problems of shortages, smuggling and the black market (Berg 1968).

The ability of the market traders to circumvent government regulation is also well demonstrated over the question of price controls (Killick 1973). These were introduced in both Ghana and Nigeria in the 1960s and early 1970s in an attempt to reduce the cost of living in the face of high rates of inflation, government austerity programmes and falling real income levels. They were applied to manufactured goods, both imported and produced locally. The results fell short of expectations, and tended to exacerbate the existing problems. As the price control officials joined the police and the customs in harassing the market traders, many kinds of goods vanished from the open market, and sources of supply became even more erratic. Major beneficiaries included the clerks of the large wholesale stores, who were able to extort a payment from traders in return for supplying any goods at all, and the rich wholesalers, who could afford the costs of maintaining sources of supply, of hoarding goods against a price rise, and of keeping themselves out of trouble with the law. These costs they passed on to the retail traders and the consumers, and it was the poorer retail traders who were the most likely to be arrested by the authorities for a breach of the regulations. Because of the vertical integration of the market, the poorer traders are unable to take direct action against the wholesalers, for fear of harming their own sources of supply (Williams 1974). In Ghana, after 1972, the job of enforcing the price controls was transferred to the police and army, who gave the work low priority. Killick (1978, 290) concludes that the exercise had little impact on inflation, and in terms of income distribution it was actually retrogressive, benefiting the wealthy.

The wealthy have also tended to benefit from the supply of, and demand for, market stalls. Strategically located stalls in the major urban markets of West Africa are a lucrative resource. With the connivance of market officials, there are many illegal transfers of stalls at inflated prices, and it is the wealthier traders who have the resources and contacts to accumulate stalls in their own names in the first place. The legal stall rentals represent a net transfer of resources from the traders to local government: the amounts paid by the traders usually exceed the expenditure by the State on facilities, as anyone who has visited the latrines of a large Nigerian or Ghanaian market, or waded through the puddles which accumulate in the rainy season, will have realized (see Sada and McNulty 1974, 163).

It is also the wealthy who have gained most from the indigenization measures introduced in Nigeria and Ghana in the late 1960s and early 1970s.

In 1968–1970, the Ghana government restricted large sections of enterprise, including small- and medium-scale trade, to Ghanaian citizens (Killick 1978, 30). These measures were aimed principally at the Lebanese and Indian traders who occupied positions in the market between the large European companies and the local African traders, and many of them were forced to sell up and leave. Nigeria carried out a similar exercise in 1972–1975 (Collins 1975; Turner and Williams 1978). Not only Asian traders were affected. Measures taken in Ghana in 1969–1970 to force foreign nationals to comply with the immigration regulations resulted in the mass exodus of nationals from other West African countries (Peil 1971), many of them, like the Yoruba from Nigeria, involved in trade (Eades 1975; Sudarkasa 1975). In all these cases it was the wealthy who were able, through their access to capital, to take over these niches in the markets, helping to provide the political class with an economic base.

Thus, the types of regulation attempted by the State over trade in West Africa have tended to follow well-defined patterns: indirect control through fiscal policy, import regulation and price control; direct control through licensing and market fees; and, increasing State intervention in the market and restriction of the activities of non-nationals. Unlike PNG, or for that matter, Singapore, there has been little systematic attempt to regulate where traders may or may not operate, and the streets in many towns are literally lined with traders. Other traders operate from within the house, invisible to the agents of the State. What is characteristic, however, is the sporadic enforcement of the controls which have been instituted.

Legislation has thus provided a good deal of discretionary power for the agents of the State. Whether or not they invoke it depends on how they see their own interests. When salaries are low, and the inflation rate is high, they may well decide that regular payoffs from the traders are preferable to over-zealous enforcement of the law. This sporadic enforcement acts in favour of the wealthy, who are able to afford the bribes to stay in business, and who have most to offer in other ways to State officials. But there is a further complicating factor in the relationship between traders and the State. The officials of the State are often part-time businessmen themselves, and if they are not, their wives or close kin almost certainly are. Where official incomes are falling in real terms, such linkages are vital. For the lower-paid formal sector employee, self-employment offers the only real chance of increased income: the role model is not the senior bureaucrat but the self-made cash man, with his houses, his shops and his vehicles (see Peace 1979), and they are accumulating the capital to get out of the formal sector as quickly as they can.

Thus, the agents of the State are ambivalent towards the legal and administrative apparatus they are employed to uphold. It serves as a source of discretionary power, but this is valued not for itself, but for the income which it can generate. Thus, much of the legislation relating to small enterprises fails to be enforced, largely because the agents are either closely connected to the sector through affinal or kinship links, or are actual or potential small-scale businessmen themselves.

Singapore[4]

In terms of the rest of the Third World, Singapore is extraordinary. First it is a city State, and therefore has few of the problems of rural–urban migration and economic imbalance that are so significant in other countries. Second, it has achieved a very high rate of economic growth, and in two decades has become a major industrial centre. The economy grew at an annual rate of 10 per cent per annum in the 1960s, rising to 13 per cent in the early 1970s, before the 1973 oil crisis (Goh 1972, ix; You and Lim 1972, 2). Third, the government has carried out urban renewal and housing programmes on a massive scale, and more than two-thirds of the entire population has been rehoused, mainly in government flats (Gamer 1972; Hassan 1977; Yeh (ed.) 1975). This housing programme has contributed to the success of the population control programme, which has reduced the increase from an average of 3.9 per cent per annum between 1957 and 1962 to 1.3 per cent in 1975 (Wong 1980, 20). All these factors have to be taken into account when considering the position of the small-scale sector in Singapore compared with its counterparts elsewhere.

Historically, Singapore was a colonial port and naval base, established in the early 19th century, and handling much of the trade of the Malayan peninsula since then. The population came to consist predominantly of Chinese groups, with Malay and Indian minorities, and in time there developed an English-educated and bilingual élite which dominated the professions and the administration. Singapore joined the Malaysian Federation in 1963, but was forced out in 1965, and has been a small, independent State ever since.

The early 1960s were times of considerable political tension. The ruling party, the People's Action Party (PAP) divided, and the left-wing faction, consisting mainly of Chinese-educated members with strong links both with the trade unions and the poorer areas of the island, formed an opposition with considerable grass-roots support. The government responded firmly: opposition leaders were detained, and opposition organizations, including some market traders' associations, were banned. It was against this background that Singapore joined the Malaysian Federation to neutralize the threat from the left within a wider political framework. With the help of the civil service the PAP developed alternative lines of political communication based on local committees which coopted local communal leaders and businessmen (Chan 1976).

The resulting system of government has been described as a peculiar form of democratic socialism, characterized by a unique blend of one-party authoritarianism, bourgeois liberalism, devout anti-communism, State welfare, unbridled free enterprise and Chinese chauvinism (Buchanan 1972, 19). The general leadership style is directional and paternalistic. As one of Wong's informants lamented: "The People's Action Party has been transformed into merely an action party: when they tell us to walk, we walk, and when they tell us to run, we run" (Wong 1980, 42). Over local community issues—street lighting, drains, roads and bus shelters—the local committees can obtain results. In shaping or affecting the long-term government strategy for the country as a whole, they have little power or influence.

In recent years the major government policies have included building up the industrial base of the economy and rehousing the population. In the 1950s and 1960s industrialization had been seen as the solution to the problem of providing jobs for the growing population, then growing more rapidly than it is now, in a period when the rift with Malaysia, the confrontation with Indonesia and the run-down of the British military presence were all threatening the historical bases of the economy. The government pursued this policy in collaboration with the multinationals, who were provided with sites, infrastructure, and a cheap, well-educated and well-disciplined English-speaking labour force. The trade unions were firmly under the control of the State. As might be expected, this package appealed to those companies looking for new markets and ways of reducing labour costs, and Singapore's industrial base has flourished—so much so, that now the problem is one of a labour shortage.

Ministers realized that if labour could be diverted from other sectors of the economy, this shortage could be partially alleviated (Wong 1980, 247). Restricting entry to market trade was an obvious possibility, in view of the fact that the profitability of the sector made it attractive, even to the skilled workforce. The urban renewal programme played a part in controlling the labour force, in that many of the older markets were demolished and their traders relocated in new markets near the new housing. Many traders were badly hit as their clienteles were scattered, and they looked for other work. Another way of controlling the number of traders has been through the licensing system. In the 1970s the policy was to restrict licences to the over-40 age group and the disabled, and to persuade the younger able-bodied workers to seek work in industry or construction. Other aims were to restrict the number of licensed traders, and to locate the entire hawker population off the streets, either in public markets, or in the dwindling number of private ones. The number of licensed traders fell from nearly 50,000 in 1968 to 25,000 in 1978 (Wong 1980, 246). The reaction of the traders has been ambivalent and fragmented. The 1970s were a boom period in the markets, with standards of living and levels of turnover both increasing. The government's policy of restricting entry to trade protected existing traders from competition. But with no possibility of effective political organization which could challenge the general direction of policy at the top, the traders have been left to negotiate with the State in small groups for the best deal which they can obtain in the face of urban renewal.

Initially therefore the nature of the trading sector in Singapore resembled that in West Africa. Entry to the market was easy, and the colonial rulers were content to leave the bulk of the trade in the capable hands of the Chinese communities. As in West Africa, the attitude of the administration towards small-scale trade was at times ambivalent. While welcoming enterprise, they restricted traders' movements on the grounds of hygiene, noise, obstruction of the traffic and so on, and established systems of official markets and licences. The major divergence between the two cases came in the 1960s, with the government of Singapore committed to rapid industrialization, and having the resources and the political autonomy to carry this through. A corollary of this policy has been the need to control access to the small-scale sector. These policies have been successful, in contrast to similar policies pursued elsewhere in the Third World, owing to a number of factors. First there is the small size of the country and the lack of a large rural hinterland. This has made it possible for the government to control migration, and it has also made it far easier for the government to coordinate and carry out their policies effectively than would have been possible in a larger geographical area. The administrative and security systems are the most efficient in South-East Asia.

Second, Singapore's location in relation to regional and world markets, and its success in attracting foreign capital, have meant that the government has been able to deliver the goods in terms of job creation and rising living standards, and these factors have tended to reduce the level of political opposition despite the leadership style of the régime.

Third, there is the element of class differentiation. The political and administrative ruling group, educated in English-medium schools and colleges, has become largely detached from the kinds of particularistic relationships which bedevil the implementation of State policy in other parts of the Third World. This separation has been facilitated both by the urban policies, and by the rising living standards. Local communities and the extended family have been largely broken up, and kinship and communal links are less significant in finding jobs or making ends meet than in poorer countries. The result is a political transformation which goes far beyond anything to be found in the other two cases. The obvious point of comparison in West Africa is Ghana under Nkrumah, where similar rhetoric and a political system which was also dominated by a single party at the top, produced much less by way of a transformation at the bottom. In Singapore, the political class has been committed enough to the system in a material sense to achieve such a transformation. Corruption in the administration is rare, and socialization into the values and ideals of the ruling group through the education system is extremely efficient.

The dynamics of variation

These three cases illustrate a wide variety of State policies. In PNG an administrative "hard line" made entry to the small-scale sector difficult until the 1960s, and the dead weight of existing legislation, still invoked by settler interests, continues to make difficulties for would-be businessmen. In West Africa, entry to the market is generally easy, and the existing legislation is enforced sporadically, partly owing to the large numbers of people working in small enterprises and the limited resources of the State, and partly owing to the close links between State officials and small enterprises. In Singapore, a generally accommodative approach by the State towards small enterprises in the colonial period gave way in the 1960s to the subordination of their interests to the requirements of the industrialization programme. If the agents of the State in Singapore are intent on controlling the sector, the agents of the State in West Africa are usually intent on joining it.

But why this variation? In the brief sketches earlier in the paper, four sets of factors would appear to be crucial: the presence or absence of a well-developed division of labour, coupled with specialization of production and inter-regional trade in the precolonial period; the presence or absence of a settler community involved in primary production; the nature of the links with the surrounding region, and particularly with a rural hinterland; and the nature of integration into the world economy in the 20th century.

In the case of West Africa, both the Saharan and Atlantic trade routes developed early, and the trade in slaves, horses, gold and guns gave a considerable impetus to processes of State formation (e.g. Law 1977a; Goody 1971; Wilks 1977) and to the development of local markets and urban centres (Meillassoux (ed.) 1971). Thus colonialism was imposed in an area with many large-scale political units and with a well-developed urban hierarchy and marketing system. A further factor was the presence on the coast of acculturated creole groups who acted as middlemen in the trade with the interior, in the absence of large-scale European settlement. Thus, in the development of cash crops from the 19th century onwards, production and transportation were in the hands of local people: both the production of cash crops and the lower levels of the marketing system have remained in indigenous hands, despite the increasing control of the higher levels of trade and cash crop marketing by the multinationals and the State.

In Papua-New Guinea, in contrast, integration into the world system came later. Politically the area was fragmented, and the large-scale States and systems of interregional trade that were a feature of West African social organization did not exist here. European exploitation of the area took the form of plantation agriculture in the absence of an indigenous cash crop industry. Settler interests became entrenched in both political and economic life, with the results outlined above.

The case of Singapore is more complex. The Chinese migrants who formed the majority of the population came from complex societies which provided them with the skills to organize and control small-scale trade. But the complexity of the division of labour and the process of class differentiation went much further than in West Africa. Singapore's regional rather than national role as a commercial centre and military base meant firstly the emergence of a large bilingual group which came to dominate the political system. Secondly it meant the separation of this group from the kinds of family relations which in West Africa continued to underpin political and economic life. All these processes have been accelerated by the absence of a rural hinterland: political and geographical separation from the Malayan peninsula allowed Singapore to control its population growth and concentrate its development efforts in the industrial sector, at a time when this suited the requirements of foreign capital, and the firm control exercised by the English-educated ruling group was reinforced by the comparative success of these policies.

These brief case studies have implications for the meaning of general concepts such as capitalism, articulation and the State. It is, for instance, clear from the West African case that the present situation is not simply the product of interaction between a precapitalist and a capitalist mode of production about which it is possible to generalize outside the specific historical context. The precapitalist social structure was itself the product of 300 years or more of involvement in international trade, and in that period not only the local political economy, but also the nature of European capitalism, developed out of all recognition. Similarly, "articulation" involves a continuous process of interaction and modification which is also historically specific.

Similar considerations relate to the notion of the State. I have suggested here that two aspects of the State can be investigated empirically—the legislation which it produces and the social organization of its agents, both their relations with each other and with other groups in the population. A body of law is created over time which reflects political and economic conditions in historically specific periods. How and why this legislation is invoked in later periods, when conditions have changed, depends on the interests of, and relations between, the new interest groups which have emerged. Three variants of this process are found here. In West Africa the overlap between the social networks of those working in small enterprises and the agents of the State is considerable, and the body of legislation is invoked partially and sporadically. In Singapore the degree of overlap is increasingly limited: while small enterprises can win concessions on minor issues, the main thrust of State policy, to control and restrict such enterprises, is carried through with great energy and rigour. Finally, in PNG, the settlers rigidly controlled local economic initiative through residential and administrative segregation. Thus the degree of control over small enterprises is greater when the degree of overlap between the social networks of the small-scale entrepreneurs and the agents of the State is minimal, and where rigid enforcement is monitored by a powerful interest group anxious to avoid any erosion of its dominant position in the economic and political system.

Notes

1. In writing this paper I have been largely dependent on the help and advice of Peter Fitzpatrick who, but for pressures of time, would have co-authored it. I would also like to thank Charlotte Wong who introduced me to the Singapore material. Neither of them bear any responsibility for the form of the paper or its conclusions.
2. The main source drawn on for this section is Fitzpatrick (1980, Ch. 7). Other discussions of the "informal sector" in PNG can be found in Fitzpatrick and Blaxter (1979) and Norwood (1978).
3. For general surveys of economic development and the development of trade in West Africa, see e.g. Bauer (1954), Hopkins (1973) and Meillassoux (1971).
4. In this section I have drawn on Wong's study of Bukit Timah (1980). Other studies of the economy and markets of Singapore are contained in Buchanan (1972) and Yeung (1977). On urban development see Gamer (1972), and on political development see Turnbull (1978) and George (1973).

References

Asiwaju, A. I. (1976) *Western Yorubaland under European Rule 1889–1945*, Longman, London.
Bauer, P. T. (1954) *West African Trade*, Cambridge University Press, Cambridge.
Beer, C. F. and Williams, Gavin (1976) "The politics of the Ibadan peasantry", in Gavin Williams (ed.), *Nigeria: Economy and Society*, Rex Collings, London.
Berg, Elliot J. (1968) "Socialist ideology and marketing policy in Africa", in Reed Moyer and Stanley C. Hollander (eds.), *Markets and Marketing in Developing Economies*, Richard D. Irwin Inc., Homewood, Illinois, pp. 24–47.
Berry, Sara S. (1975) *Cocoa, Custom and Socio-Economic Change in Rural Western Nigeria*, Clarendon Press, Oxford.
Bromley, Ray (1980) "Municipal versus spontaneous markets? A case study of urban planning in Cali, Colombia", *Third World Planning Review*, Vol. 2, pp. 205–32.
Bromley, Ray (1981) "From Calvary to white elephant: a Colombian case of urban renewal and marketing reform", *Development and Change*, Vol. 12, pp. 77–120.
Buchanan, Ian (1972) *Singapore in Southeast Asia*, G. Bell and Sons, London.
Campbell, B. (1978) "Ivory Coast", in John Dunn (ed.), *West African States*, Cambridge University Press, Cambridge.
Chan, H. C. (1976) *The Dynamics of One Party Dominance*, Singapore University Press, Singapore.
Cohen, Abner (1966) "Politics of the kola trade", *Africa*, Vol. 36, pp. 18–36.
Collins, P. (1975) "The policy of indigenization: an overall view", *Quarterly Journal of Administration*, Vol. 9, pp. 137–47.
Coquery-Vidrovitch, Catherine (1971) "De la traite des esclaves à l'exportation de l'huile de palme et de palmistes au Dahomey, XIXe siècle", in Claude Meillassoux (ed.), *The Development of Indigenous Trade and Markets in West Africa*, Oxford University Press, London, pp. 107–23.
Crowder, M. and Ikime, O. (1970) "Introduction", in M. Crowder and O. Ikime (eds.), *West African Chiefs*, Ife University Press, Ife.
Eades, J. S. (1975) "The growth of a migrant community: the Yoruba in Northern Ghana", in Jack Goody (ed.), *Changing Social Structure in Ghana*, International African Institute, London.
Fitzpatrick, Peter (1978) "Really rather like slavery: law and labour in the colonial economy in Papua New Guinea", in E. L. Wheelwright and K. Buckley (eds.), *Essays in the Political Economy of Australian Capitalism, Volume 3*, Australia and New Zealand Book Company, Brookvale.
Fitzpatrick, Peter (1980) *Law and State in Papua New Guinea*, Academic Press, London.
Fitzpatrick, Peter and Blaxter, Loraine (1979) "Imposed law in the containment of Papua New Guinean economic ventures", in S. B. Burman and B. E. Harrell-Bond (eds.), *The Imposition of Law*, Academic Press, London, pp. 115–26.

GAMER, R. E. (1972) *The Politics of Urban Development in Singapore*, Oxford University Press, London.

GEERTZ, Clifford (1963) *Peddlers and Princes*, University of Chicago Press, Chicago.

GEORGE, T. S. (1973) *Lee Kwan Yew's Singapore*, André Deutsch, London.

GERRY, Chris, and BIRKBECK, Chris (1981) "The petty commodity producer in Third World cities: petit-bourgeois or 'disguised' proletarian?", in Frank Bechhofer and Brian Elliott (eds.), *The Petite Bourgeoisie: Comparative Studies of the Uneasy Stratum*, Macmillan, London, pp. 121–54.

GOH, K. S. (1972) *The Economics of Modernization and Other Essays*, Asia Pacific Press, Singapore.

GOODY, Jack (1971) *Technology, Tradition and the State in West Africa*, Oxford University Press, London.

HALL, Peter (1972) "Planning and the environment", in Peter Townsend and Nicholas Bosanquet (eds.), *Labour and Inequality*, Fabian Society, London, pp. 261–73.

HASSAN, Riaz (1977) "Public housing", in Riaz Hassan (ed.), *Singapore: Society in Transition*, Oxford University Press, London.

HELLEINER, G. K. (1970) "The fiscal role of the marketing boards in Nigerian economic development, 1947–1961", in Carl K. Eicher and Carl Liedholm (eds.), *The Growth and Development of the Nigerian Economy*, Michigan State University Press, East Lansing, pp. 119–55.

HILL, Polly (1963) *Migrant Cocoa Farmers of Southern Ghana*, Cambridge University Press, Cambridge.

HOGENDORN, J. S. (1970) "The origins of the groundnut trade in Northern Nigeria", in Carl K. Eicher and Carl Liedholm (eds.), *The Growth and Development of the Nigerian Economy*, Michigan State University Press, East Lansing, pp. 30–51.

HOPKINS, A. G. (1973) *An Economic History of West Africa*, Longman, London.

JOHNSON, R. W. (1978) "Guinea", in John Dunn (ed.), *West African States*, Cambridge University Press, Cambridge.

KILLICK, Tony (1973) "Price controls in Africa: the Ghanaian experience", *Journal of Modern African Studies*, Vol. 11, pp. 405–26.

KILLICK, Tony (1978) *Development Economics in Action*, Heinemann, London.

LAW, Robin (1977a) *The Oyo Empire c. 1600–c. 1836*, Clarendon Press, Oxford.

LAW, Robin (1977b) "Royal monopoly and private enterprise in the Atlantic trade: the case of Dahomey", *Journal of African History*, Vol. 18, pp. 555–77.

LEVINE, Hal B. and LEVINE, Marlene W. (1979) *Urbanization in Papua New Guinea*, Cambridge University Press, Cambridge.

MEILLASSOUX, Claude (ed.) (1971) *The Development of Indigenous Trade and Markets in West Africa*, Oxford University Press, London.

MOSER, Caroline (1978) "Informal sector or petty commodity production: dualism or dependence in urban development?", *World Development*, Vol. 6, pp. 1041–64. Reprinted in Ray Bromley (ed.) (1979), *The Urban Informal Sector: Critical Perspectives on Employment and Housing Policies*, Pergamon, Oxford.

NORWOOD, H. C. (1978) "Papua New Guinea needs a strong informal sector", *Yagl-Ambu*, Vol. 5, pp. 61–72.

PEACE, A. J. (1979) "Prestige, power and legitimacy in a modern Nigerian town", *Canadian Journal of African Studies*, Vol. 13, pp. 265–94.

PEIL, Margaret (1971) "The expulsion of West African aliens", *Journal of Modern African Studies*, Vol. 9, pp. 205–29.

SADA, Pius O. and MCNULTY, Michael L. (1974) "Traditional markets in Lagos: a study of the changing administrative processes and marketing transactions", *Quarterly Journal of Administration*, Vol. 8, pp. 149–65.

SIMMIE, James (1974) *Citizens in Conflict*, Hutchinson, London.

SUDARKASA, N. (1975) "Commercial migration in West Africa with special reference to the Yoruba in Ghana", *African Urban Notes*, Series B, Vol. 1, pp. 61–103.

TAHIR, I. A. (1976) Scholars, Sufis, Saints and Capitalists in Kano, 1904–1974. Unpublished Ph.D. thesis, Cambridge University.

THOMAS, R. G. (1973) "Forced labour in British West Africa", *Journal of African History*, Vol. 14, pp. 79–103.

218   J. S. Eades

TURNBULL, C. M. (1978) *A History of Singapore, 1819–1975*, Oxford University Press, London.
TURNER, T and WILLIAMS, Gavin P. (1978) "Nigeria", in John Dunn (ed.), *West African States*, Cambridge University Press, Cambridge.
WILKS, I. (1977) "Land, labour, capital and the forest kingdom of Asante", in J. Friedman and M. Rowlands (eds.), *The Evolution of Social Systems*, Duckworth, London.
WINDER, R. B. (1962) "The Lebanese in West Africa", *Comparative Studies in Society and History*, Vol. 4, pp. 296–333.
WONG, Charlotte H. S. (1980) The "Little Businessman" of Bukit Timah: A Study of the Economic, Social and Political Organization of Traders in a Market Complex in Singapore. Unpublished Ph.D. thesis, University of Kent, Canterbury.
YEH, S. K. (ed.) (1975) *Public Housing in Singapore*, Singapore University Press, Singapore.
YEUNG, Yue-man (1977) "The marketing system in Singapore", in Yue-man Yeung and C. P. Lo (eds.), *Changing South-East Asian Cities: Readings on Urbanization*, Oxford University Press, Singapore.
YOU, P. S. and LIM, C. Y. (eds.) (1971) *The Singapore Economy*, Eastern University Press, Singapore.

CHAPTER 13

The people who get in the way: poverty and development in Jakarta*

DENNIS J. COHEN

Hijau, green, pervades the country of Indonesia and its capital city of Jakarta.[1]† It is the vibrant green of ripening rice fields in the countryside and on the outskirts of the city—the symbol of life, sustenance and regeneration. *Hijau* is also the colour of force and power in Indonesia. For some that force and power is life and sustenance. For many it offers the hope of political regeneration, but for others it is a frightful force. *Kemeja hijau*, green shirts, is the Indonesian army, the new lords of the Indonesian State.

Soldiers came in the middle of the afternoon. They were neither expected nor unexpected. They came. In their wake they left nothing but ruins and rubble—the remains of a community which had been built by poor people out of the leftover garbage of the city's economy. The squatters had had enough time to gather their few belongings and leave their houses. They stood in a tight sullen knot to the side of the road. They said nothing. They offered no resistance as the *Team Penertiban* proceeded to tear down their cardboard houses and burn the materials which had provided a minimum of shelter against the elements.

These soldiers of the *Team Penertiban* are an élite force of the Jakarta city administration. They enforce the recent laws against squatters, pedlars, and illegal immigrants to this closed city. The "Team" takes care of the people who get in the way of development. They are the enforcing arm of a political élite desperate to find a way to improve the material conditions of the city and the country. This élite is attempting to build a modern country, a metropolitan city, a just and prosperous society, but all of these poor people keep getting in the way. They will not stay in their villages. The come to Jakarta to seek work that does not exist. In the process they continue to overload an already desperate

---

*Reprinted from *Politics*, Vol. 9, No. 1, May 1974, pp. 1–9, with the permission of the author and of the editors and publishers of the journal, the Australasian Political Studies Association.
†Superscript numbers refer to Notes at end of chapter.

219

situation. It is very difficult to build a metropolitan city under such circumstances. It is even more difficult to create an image of a metropolitan city. The pedlars, the squatters, the *becak* (pedicab) drivers—all of these poor people keep getting in the way.

Understandably the "Team" is impatient. The fires do not burn fast enough. The rubble is pushed down the bank into the canal which is already choked with litter and pollution. The squatters are questioned by soldiers. Those who can produce resident's cards are left alone. The few who cannot are taken away. Satisfied that this particular blight has been removed from the city landscape the "Team" jumps back into their trucks and jeeps. They leave. The squatters hesitantly return to the site of their former community. There is nothing left, but there was really nothing there in the first place. By that night most people have set up camps on their former house sites. The home fires burn brightly. Within three days the community has been rebuilt. It is undistinguishable from the collections of shacks and shelters which had been obliterated by the "Team".[2]

This non-confrontation between the rulers and the ruled, the rich and the poor, the modernizers and the people who get in the way, is symbolic of the problems facing all Jakartans and all Indonesians. The imposition of order from above through the *Team Penertiban*[3] is like trying to build a castle out of dry sand. The structure invariably reverts to its original state. Those at the top of society become more and more frustrated as their new structures slowly dissolve, while the majority of Indonesians simply go on with their lives basically cynical and uninspired by the building that is going on around them.

This majority of Indonesians in Jakarta are the subject of this essay. They are the low income residents of the capital city.[4] While they do "get in the way" of development from one perspective, they are intimately involved in development from another. They do not participate, yet their lives cannot help but be affected in the long run by the building around them. The nature of development and politics in Indonesia and Jakarta cannot be fully understood without including the perspective of this low income group. Although they now have little to say about planning, they figure prominently in the final long-range results.

The situation of urban low-income people in society

In order to understand the perspective of low-income people in Jakarta, one must first understand their social, economic and political situation in the wider social context. The problem of the low income group and their position in urban society is not simply a municipal problem. It is a reflection of the national economic dilemma which faces Indonesia today. The immediate effects, like all parts of the economy, are centred in Jakarta. As Clifford Geertz (1963) has demonstrated, the colonial economic system inherited by the present government resulted in an involuted economy in the rural areas.

Jakarta has always been the centre of a more dynamic Westernized economy because of its linkages to the metropol-Holland, and to the world. The dual economies have never been truly separate. This is most evident today in the midst of efforts to develop the economy. While involution in the rural areas allowed a greater number of people to live on a fixed amount of land, the standard of living necessarily decreased. Had there been a growing industrial centre, people might have moved from the villages to the city for better employment. Because the Dutch exported surplus revenues to Holland, the industrial sector never grew. Now as land pressures increase in the villages and the industrial sector in Jakarta begins to develop, people are migrating to the city to share in a relatively better life. Unfortunately, industrialization must now come from foreign investment which favours extractive and capital intensive industry. There is relatively more money in Jakarta, but jobs are scarce. As the stream from the villages becomes a flood, everyone is finding that there is no place for these people to go. They do not share in the economic improvement reflected in the gross economic indicators.

As Jakarta begins to solve its problems, the problems get worse. There is a vicious circle at play here with Jakarta right in the centre. After all, Jakarta is the centre. It is the centre of political power and government administration. The only difference that is greater than the difference between the rich and poor in Jakarta is the difference between Jakarta and the rest of Indonesia. Jakarta is another world. This is not by accident. Jakarta as a metropolitan city is viewed as a real and important goal by the city administration.[5] Jakarta as a metropolitan city has become an important symbol and a serious goal, in part because a metropolitan city will attract Westerners who will bring their money to invest in the Indonesian economy. This, in turn, is seen as part of the solution to Indonesia's economic malaise. However, this metropolitan city also attracts thousands from the rural areas, which makes it even more difficult to create the metropolitan city. The goal of a metropolitan city also seems to channel resources in such a way so as to increase differences. Jakarta is becoming even more different than the rest of the country. Differences between the rich and the poor in the city are becoming greater.

It could be argued that the increases in differences between the rich and poor in Jakarta are necessary to attain an important social goal. After all, Jakarta is not yet a metropolitan city. Metropolitan cities do not have beggars in the streets, nor do they have vast communities of squatter shacks lining their canals and railroad tracks. Metropolitan cities do not have traffic jams caused by thousands of *becaks* (pedicabs), nor do they have muddy market places and pedlars on the streets. Jakarta does have all of these. They represent a goal not yet fulfilled. They also represent people, citizens and residents of Jakarta who are poor and far removed from that goal. *Becaks* can be prohibited by fiat, but what will happen to the drivers? Squatter shacks can be torn down, but where will the squatters live? Pedlars on the streets can also be prohibited, but where will they sell their wares? How will they live? If the above characteristics are eradicated by administrative fiat, Jakarta will look like a metropolitan city, but is appearance the important goal? This kind of facelifting and the kind of foreign investment which it attracts will not necessarily improve the quality of life for the majority of citizens. These are questions of extreme importance for low income residents because this group is greatly affected by the solutions to the city's problems.

The difficult position of the low income people is most evident when examining their position in the occupational structure. The characteristics of the occupational structure of Jakarta offer little security for the present and even less hope for the future. Because there are too many people in Jakarta for the jobs and resources available, those at the bottom of the occupational structure must scramble for the crumbs that are left. Sociologically speaking, the solution for dividing the economic pie seems to be the urban version of what has been called shared poverty in the rural areas.[6] Most low income people work in so-called tertiary occupations which simply skim money off the top of the industrial sector without being truly productive for the developing economy.[7] While these jobs do render a service, they do not create consumer goods, or capital for the economy. Often the service rendered is redundant, like eight cigarette vendors along one block of a major street. If they were all eliminated, no-one would really miss them. So, wages and/or profits are low, depending on the largesse of richer residents of the city and the buying habits and loyalty of fellow low-income people. The jobs have no future because many will simply be eliminated if development proceeds as planned. In the sample of a small survey which I conducted in Jakarta,[8] the largest work category was *pegawai negeri* (civil servant), which comprised 21 per cent of the total. These were all of very low rank. Given the over-employment situation in government offices we can assume this figure represents some disguised unemployment. Service occupations such as *becak* driver, small trader, and prostitute represent 37 per cent, while more productive occupations such as factory worker, skilled labourer, or unskilled labour represent only 20 per cent. All in all the economic system distributes enough resources to keep people from starving but without increasing productivity in the economy.

The political solution to this problem has been to close Jakarta and thus try to insulate it from the economic problems of the rest of the country. In 1971, Governor Ali Sadikin declared that Jakarta was a closed city. No-one could move to Jakarta any longer unless he could demonstrate that there was a productive job waiting for him. If the flood of people from the villages could be halted perhaps the low income group already in Jakarta would become productive members of the growing industrial sector. Leaving aside obvious abuses of the new regulation, what is the end result? If it succeeds it will slow down the growth of the population to some extent, but the workforce will continue to grow given the age structure of the population.[9] The problem is not so much to limit people as it is to create jobs. This, of course, is the dilemma. Meanwhile, regulations against *becaks* and pedlars lessen job opportunities rather than create more. Their elimination will make Jakarta look more like a metropolitan city, but unless new jobs are created for these people the inequality of income distribution will increase.

Housing is another problem. While not every low-income person is a squatter, the city is constantly plagued with the problem of squatter shacks and houses built on government land without permission. Vacant land, owned by the railroad authority (PNKA) for railroad track right-of-way and for spur tracks and freight yards, does not stay vacant very long. Also land along the canals and creeks is constantly being used by squatters. This is especially choice land because the canal or creek serves as a bathing place or toilet. There are many houses built or bought by people in good faith which are actually *rumah liar* (literally wild house, i.e., illegal). These houses are built on government land without permission. When the government chooses to use that land, the people who own those houses will lose them and receive no compensation from the government.[10] *Kampung* (urban village) improvement projects also displace people from their homes with little or no compensation from the government.[11]

Government action to clean up the city of squatter shacks and to improve the infrastructure often presents quite a burden to low income people. As described above, squatter shacks built along creeks are often raided by the *Team Penertiban*. They are destroyed by the "Team" one day and are rebuilt by squatters soon after the "Team" has left. Other *rumah liar* owned by citizens of Jakarta have been torn down as well. Land is made available at times by the government for purchase by those who have been displaced, but the land must be bought. It is not given to compensate for the loss of the house. Also this land is on the outskirts of the city away from job opportunities and friends or family. This means that low income people must often bear the burden of financing this aspect of development. For people who can hardly afford to eat, this is a heavy burden indeed. While these government actions do improve the infrastructure of the city, perhaps social costs should be weighed against social benefits. Who, in fact, should bear the burden of these improvements: those who use them and benefit most, or those who are displaced by them?

Apart from these wider social considerations, the housing situation and job market form an important part of the day-to-day living of low-income groups in Jakarta. They help to create a social milieu that is wrought with poverty and insecurity. The average income of our sample is between Rp.200 and Rp.300 a day (U.S.$0.50–0.75). While government employees have a fixed income, many low income people work at occupations that are subject to the vagaries of the immediate market. They live from day to day, from hand to mouth. They are pedlars, *becak* drivers, or day labourers. Those less well off beg for money, or collect cigarette butts and papers which they can sell at the port. One informal survey asked members of these occupational groups how much they made on a good day and how much they made on a bad day. The average made on a good day was approximately Rp.150 for cigarette butt collectors, Rp.200 for paper collectors, Rp.200 for shoe shiners, Rp.300 for kerosene pedlars, Rp.350 for construction workers, and Rp.350 for bus conductors. The average income on a bad day was Rp.90 for cigarette butt collectors, Rp.90 for paper collectors, Rp.85 for shoe shiners, Rp.165 for kerosene pedlars, Rp.250 for construction workers, and Rp.200 for bus conductors. The average income for *becak* drivers was Rp.225–250 a day.[12] When you ask low-income people about activities other than work, the usual reply is that there is only time to work, sleep and eat. One must work constantly to simply stay alive.

The housing situation adds to insecurity because many people do not understand why the government is tearing down houses. Actions of the *Team Penertiban* have been highly publicized. Whether they are vulnerable or not, many low-income people are afraid that the *Team Penertiban* will sweep down upon them one day and tear down their house. In one *kampung* that I visited the people were under the impression that I came from the city administration. Their immediate conclusion was that I had come to prepare the way for the destruction of their houses.

Political attitudes and their implications for development

One study of poor people in the United States focused upon grievances as a functional equivalent of ideology for poor uneducated people (Lipsitz 1973, 139–58). This study found that many people had a sense of grievance against the government regarding policies which affected their economic welfare. However, a more specific evaluation of how the situation might be changed, or what had caused it in the first place, was most often lacking. In Jakarta even this sense of grievance does not exist amongst many urban low-income people.[13] Urban poor have no social experience to show them that change to improve their living standards is possible. Even those who might dream are limited by only a vague idea of the relationship between public action and social change. It does not matter whether that action might be government action, anti-government action, or simply community action. In the minds of low-income people there is no cognitive map of the social system which might successfully direct their action toward desired goals. This is not to say that low-income people have no conception at all of how society, government and politics function. I will only try to demonstrate that their life situation coupled with a lack of formal education tends to give them a view of their social world which keeps them from trying to become active political participants, a view which is not necessarily at odds with the social and political realities of Indonesia.

This tendency towards a passive political posture is based on a number of factors which I have alluded to above. I will list them here and discuss them in this last section of the essay. First, the majority of low-income residents of Jakarta have not experienced an improvement in their standard of living. Second, there is very little casual thought about social change which might link government or any kind of public action with social change. Third is a cultural attitude toward acceptance of one's position in society which is reinforced by social and political experience, and last is a political environment which feeds into this whole syndrome. Politics is defined as distant and dangerous by low-income people. Political history has confirmed and reinforced this view.

One is impressed by the fact that the standard of living is rising in Jakarta. There are many cars and motorbikes on the road. The markets are flooded with imported consumer goods. However, it becomes obvious from our survey that a majority of low-income people in Jakarta do not share in this improved standard of living. Respondents were asked to compare the economic situation now with the past. A majority of people answered that it is either harder for them to make a living now than it was before, or that it is the same. Thirty per cent said it was more difficult now to make a living; 39 per cent answered that it was the same as it had been before, while only 24 per cent answered that they had experienced an improvement in their standard of living.

This point can be illustrated by a large number of examples. I will give only one here to add more human dimension to the statistics. Pak Amat (not his real name) works as a low level civil servant for the city. His monthly salary is Rp.3,200 a month (U.S.$8.00). He has a wife and one child. They find it extremely difficult to live on that salary. I asked him to compare the economic situation now with how it had been before. His answer: "In my opinion it was easier to earn a living before. Now it is a bit harder." I probed further in order to find out why he felt this way. I asked him if it was not true that his salary had risen over the years. He answered:

> Yeh, sure it has gone up. But if you compare (it) with the situation before, prices are higher now. While my salary may have just gone up, prices had already gone up three months before. (Jakarta, 27/9/72)

Conversations like this one lead me to believe that the statistics do reflect a real situation. It is not just a reflection of people simply complaining that things are worse or the same, while, in fact, they are really a bit better. However, the important factor is clear. These people feel that they are not better off economically, even if, in fact, they are better off.

The conceptual relationship between government action and social change is very vague. While a majority of the respondents had not experienced an improvement in their living, they did not blame the government. When asked why it was easier or harder to earn money at different times, i.e., why there were economic fluctuations of good times and bad times, almost 30 per cent did not know. Twenty-seven per cent felt that it happened by itself, 24 per cent felt that it was the will of God, 10 per cent said that it was up to fate, while only 6 per cent saw these fluctuations as the responsibility of the government.

In more informal interviews that were not part of the survey, government was mentioned more often as a possible source of help to lessen the burdens of life. The government was seen as a possibility for help in a very immediate way. In direct conversation about *kampung* improvement by the city government, respondents often reacted in a positive manner. They expressed a desire that an improvement project be started in their *kampung*. This may seem to contradict my earlier remarks about the fear of having one's house torn down, but I think it simply further illustrates the unclear picture in the minds of low-income people of projects and actions which come to them from above. Also, government was mentioned as a possibility for help in educating children. People also wanted the government to improve housing and give more jobs. These responses were always to a specific question of how government may help. They are not spontaneous suggestions. Respondents also seem to lack any concept of just how government might go about doing these things. So it seems that the concept of government as a potential for an improved life exists, but it is passive and vague. Finally, when asked if government has helped them, only 35 per cent answered "Yes". Of that 35 per cent, 24 per cent answered "I do not know" when asked to specify the kind of help received.

The concept of public action for low-income groups is more concrete than that which involves city or national government. It is public action which involves the immediate community, often just the surrounding neighbours. This is often a holding action rather than a way of seeking change. This mutual self-help is *gotong-royong*. Anyone familiar with Indonesia knows the word well because it has become a symbol over the years of a bootstraps economy. Now it has become a phrase which in the city refers to almost any situation where neighbours work together. This includes the most traditional sponta-neous activities such as helping a family prepare a funeral or wedding as well as projects instituted by local government officials, the *kepala RW*, and *Kepala RT*,[14] to improve a footpath or clean the gutter. *Gotong-royong* may also refer to credit associations and social clubs in the *kampung* that do charity work. Those activities are political in the sense that they are organized to take care of felt necessities for life in the *kampung*. People participate because it seems a natural activity to them. Ninety per cent of our respondents answered that they participated in *gotong-royong* activities.

However, the important question about these activities concerns whether they have a potential for improving people's living conditions. This, in turn, depends on two factors. The first is whether the people view *gotong-royong* as a way of improving their conditions. The second is whether people in general can actually decide what should be done through those activities. The first factor seems debatable. Respondents to our survey were asked to evaluate the conditions of the roads, gangs, wells, and other facilities in their *kampung*. About 40 per cent answered that they were in disrepair, while about 60 per cent answered that they were in good condition, or good enough condition. Of those who answered that they were in disrepair, 50 per cent gave *gotong-royong* as a way in which they could be fixed. However, of the others, only 28 per cent responded in such a manner. This confirms an impression that I have received during my observations and interviews. *Gotong-royong* is usually seen as an activity to maintain a certain standard of living. It is not as often seen as a way to bring about gross improvements. This may be one reason why the city administration has encountered some resistance to *kampung* improvement projects in which the city supplies materials while the community gives labour through *gotong-royong*.

One also thinks of *musyawarah*, local consultative democracy, in connection with *gotong-royong* especially for official projects. *Musyawarah* brings to mind the idea of spontaneous activity; activity which grows out of the collective will of the majority. It must be remembered, however, that *gotong-royong* includes a large number of activities, not all of which are spontaneous. The most spontaneous seems to be the helping of neighbours in the case of a death in the family. This is also the most traditional in the sense that it exists in most villages as well and is the most accepted. Required work in the neighbourhood can be the spontaneous response of neighbours to a situation which needs repair. It may also simply be a case of people following the instructions of the local official in charge. In poor neighbourhoods people are strongly inclined to simply follow instructions rather than participate in decision-making. Thus one must investigate the power structure and system of administration in each community before he can decide whether these activities are for the general welfare or simply for the advantage of a few people who make the decisions. This is not to imply that there can be no general welfare without local democracy. It is simply to open the possibility that the local system of government can be abused, and used for personal gain. This is especially true in poor neighbourhoods where people tend to play only the role of followers.

Low-income people tend to follow those of higher status and authority uncritically. They tend to accept their lot in life without a sense of tragedy or rebellion. This attitude of acceptance seems to be based upon three factors: feelings of insecurity and powerlessness, a world view which sees life as largely determined by fate which is reinforced by a lack of experiential change, and a feeling that governmental decisions and politics are only for the rich and well educated. It is very tempting to view this acceptance as only a traditional cultural trait unreflected in a changed social system and which is inappropriate to a dynamic developing society.

The word most often used when people discuss the poor is *nrimo*, a Javanese word meaning acceptance with mystical and philosophical overtones. However, when one speaks to a poor person about why he accepts a given social or political situation, it becomes obvious that he accepts it because he can see no way to change it. Acceptance is not only programmed by culture. It is learned from experience. It was demonstrated above that few low-income people have experienced an improvement in their standard of living. They have no experience to show them that an improvement is possible, even though they might indeed hope for such an improvement.[15] The usual response to a question about whether a moral person must accept his station in life is "No". Anyone may try to improve his living conditions. The main problem is that the attempt often does not succeed. One employee of the railroad tried making and selling stoves in his spare time as a way of improving his economic well-being. It did not work and so he gave up.

Two phrases that are repeated over and over again by low-income people demonstrate the above factors. "What can I do? I am only a poor person", and "*Saya tidak mau ambil pusing*" (literally—I do not want to make myself confused). If a person believes that economic life is determined by either the will of God or by fate, what *can* he do? He can only accept. Reinforcing this is the feeling that decision-making in government and all other forms of politics are very complicated and confusing. Because they are only vaguely understood, the results of government decisions seem like arbitrary acts which come down from above without rhyme or reason. From the experience of my observations and interviews this seems to be as true for punishments suffered by followers of the Indonesian Communist Party (PKI) after 1965 as it is for many people who have had their houses torn down. The definition of politics as distant and dangerous pervaded most political discourse. It has been reinforced by past events.

As Clifford Geertz has written, the whole incident surrounding *Gestapu*, the attempted coup put down by the military which led to their formal assumption of power, represents a political catharsis that we know very little about.[16] This event and the actors involved were important for the urban poor in Jakarta because they were one group that the Communist Party tried to organize and represent. Their orientation toward the party before *Gestapu* is an important subject of enquiry, but very difficult to research. Anything that might even slightly resemble a PKI slogan will scare people in most areas, especially those where the PKI had once been strong. When one talks to officials they will readily admit that the PKI was strong or existed in their area before 1965, but they will always add that the people have now changed their thinking. As one official put it: "The trees will always bend in the direction of the wind."

National politics as they come down to the *kampung* have the potential of being personally dangerous. Given the events of 1965–1966, the smartest policy would seem to be avoidance, but even this is not always possible. One woman replied to a question about politics: "Oh, I do not know about politics. I just follow." She went on to explain that she voted for *Golkar*[17] in the general election (1971) because she was a follower, but also because she was scared. Someone had told her that if she did not vote for *Golkar* she would lose her job as a maid in a government-owned university dormitory. In another *kampung* (urban neighbourhood) I found that 80 per cent of the men had belonged to a PKI union before 1965. Now everyone belongs to the union sponsored by the army. The head of the union explained that the people did not really understand the situation after 1965. It was very difficult to get them to attend meetings of the new union. He tried to make the new meetings more interesting by killing a goat each time so there would be food to eat. Still no-one came. Then he asked for help from the government team that watches for communist influences in the population. "They applied a little coercion and sanctions against those who refused to come to the meetings." Now everyone comes.

It is easy to understand why those who had been involved with the PKI are now afraid of politics. It may be harder to explain why those who were not involved with this now stigmatized group are also afraid. One explanation involves the above-mentioned cultural definition of politics. It is for high-status people. Those at the bottom of the social scale only follow. They choose their leaders based upon local political considerations. In the city this is most often determined by one's boss at his place of work, but it may also be based upon local politics in a neighbourhood. There is very little allegiance to an ideology or group cast wider than the local environment, although there is a vague connection to a wider group through a common organizational name.[18] The fall of the PKI was based on national politics to a large extent. Its subsequent destruction was played out on the local stage. In many Javanese villages communal tension exploded into violence and death.[19] In Jakarta violence was at a much lower level. Those who saw what happened to their neighbours who had been unlucky enough to become associated with the PKI realized that it could have happened the other way round. Soldiers could have come to arrest them instead of their neighbours had the drama on the national level ended differently.

To illustrate that the fear of politics is general to all groups, here is part of an interview with a local figure in an urban *kampung*. He is a strong Moslem (compared with most who live in his *kampung*). He has never been connected with the PKI. In fact he now gives required religious teaching to ex-PKI members to reform them.

> *R.* I came here around 1953. So I do not understand political problems. At that time I was busy taking care of my needs, so I just lived here and went along. Just during 1955 after I began to work, did I learn that there were political parties. The only one that I knew was true was the PNI (Indonesian Nationalist Party). I did not understand about PKI.
>
> *I.* Did not understand, or did not want to understand?
>
> *R.* Yes, I did not want to understand. I am afraid to talk about other people's problems. I am a person blind to politics. I am afraid that my

family will be disturbed. I entered the PNI because all the people at work entered.

(Jakarta, 9/9/72)

Conclusion

The main theme of Indonesian politics today is development. President Suharto's Independence Day speech of 17 August 1972, emphasized government action to improve the standard of living of all Indonesians.[20] If this is a real goal of the Indonesian élite then the dilemma is how to include the low-income group in the development process. There is no question that they desire a higher standard of living. They have definite ideas about how their lives could be improved. However, the basic posture is that the decision lies outside the poor community. It is up to the government. Basically, low-income people are accepting and patient, but in most cases they do not really understand that what is going on around them is part of a larger programme of the development effort. What is understood are the physical aspects of development, the new roads and buildings, yet only 35 per cent of the respondents in our survey felt they were helped by those projects. When asked if they, too, were working for development in Indonesia, only 37 per cent answered "Yes". Thus, psychologically, the low-income people of Jakarta are not really involved in development.

Passivity and fear of politics of low-income people are not useful for developing the human potential of the Indonesian population, nor is this situation as safe as it might seem at first glance. Development means a higher standard of living in the end, but the process may require sacrifices and setbacks. Given the nature of uneven development which the Indonesian élite has chosen, it would seem that many low-income people will be forced to sacrifice for the development effort. They will continue to lose houses, jobs, and eventually even their present way of life. If there is no ideology of development which can reach them and which can give meaning to the change in their lives, then the change can only be accomplished by brute force. This will be either through the market mechanism, or a political coercive force. This may result in economic modernization, but it cannot lead to a situation in which a majority of the Indonesian people choose day-to-day activities which can be efficiently coordinated to build a dynamic economy and stable polity.

Notes

1. This essay is based on observations made during a research project to assess the political situation of the urban poor in the developing Indonesian polity during 1972. The data consist of work done in participant observation in a large number of low income neighbourhoods, large numbers of in-depth interviews, and a small random sample survey. The interviews for the survey were carried out by trainees of the Social Science Training Programme at LP3ES, an Indonesian research foundation.

2. This account is based on observation of a *Team Penertiban* action which took place in Jakarta on 1 May 1972.
3. *Penertiban* means to control or curb. It is derived from the word *tertib*, order.
4. From the Western perspective it might seem that the term low-income group would refer to a small minority of the population. In a country like Indonesia they represent the vast majority. In my in-depth interviews I concentrated on people who were obviously not a part of the modern sector, i.e., small traders, *becak* drivers, low-level civil servants, as well as squatters, beggars and prostitutes. In the random sample survey (see note 8 for more details of the survey) 76 per cent of the respondents reported an income below Rp.400 a day, 14 per cent said they did not know, and only 10 per cent reported an income above Rp.400 a day. According to statistics from Jakarta's census bureau 78.4 per cent of the households in Jakarta have incomes of less than Rp.10,000 (U.S.$25.00) a month. See *Hasil Survey Biaja Hidup Di Djakarta*, 1968–1969 (Results of The Survey on Cost of Living in Jakarta), Biro Pusat Statistik, Jakarta. Obviously the group I have labelled as the city's low-income group is very large. In this essay I am emphasizing the similarities based on low income. This may ignore important differences within the group, but I feel at this time, given the present political context, the similarities are more salient than the differences. This is not to say that a change in the context might not change this fact.
5. The term metropolitan city is constantly used in speeches and administrative discourse. For an example of its use by Ali Sadikin, the governor of Jakarta, see *Tempo*, 29 January 1972, 38.
6. See Geertz (1963, 81–103) for a historical account of the development of involution and shared poverty in Javanese villages.
7. For one theory regarding the political implications of this situation, see McGee (1971).
8. The sample consists of 233 heads of households drawn from various local administrative units (*Rukun Tetangga*–RT). The choice of RT was not random. They were chosen to bias the sample to the low end of the economic strata in Jakarta. Within each RT the respondents were chosen randomly. It was very difficult for myself and the researchers to arrive at an operational definition of the low-income group. In our preliminary trial interviews we agreed that this group would be defined by an income below Rp.10,000 per month per household, a house that was a semi-permanent or temporary structure rather than a permanent one, and the lack of certain obvious luxury items such as a television, motor bike, or new furniture. The final sample was taken from neighbourhoods with a reputation for poverty, but because of the homogeneous nature of all Jakarta's neighbourhoods I can only say for sure that the small Jakarta élite was definitely eliminated. At best the sample represents the low end of the income scale of the rest of the population.
9. *Jakarta Dalam Angka 1971* (Jakarta in Numbers), 18, shows that the age group from 0–14 years equates 47 per cent of the population of the city.
10. In fact, during my stay in Jakarta it was revealed by the city administration that "nearly 50 per cent of the land in Jakarta is illegally occupied". See "Billy's Column", *Jakarta Times* (11 October 1972). For another discussion of this problem, see "*Bagaimana Memperoleh Hak Tanah di Jakarta*" (How to Obtain Land Rights in Jakarta), *Merdeka* (25 August 1972), 6.
11. *Kampung* means urban village, but the connotations are rich. *Kampungs* are the neighbourhoods set back from the main roads. Under the colonial system *kampung* referred to the native quarters of the city. Now it simply refers to the non-élite sections of the city. These areas are crowded with narrow paths rather than streets.
12. This survey was conducted by students at the Faculty of Economics, University of Indonesia, in early 1972.
13. This is not to say that there are no grievances. Young adolescent men who live in poor areas and are largely unemployed do have grievances. They will verbalize them if no older adult can hear them. American papers reported that this element joined the student demonstrations against Japanese Prime Minister Tanaka's visit to Indonesia. "Jakarta Youths Riot in Anti-Japanese Protest", *San Francisco Chronicle*, 16 January 1974, 11. However, these youths are not included in the random sample survey because they are not heads of households. This section on political attitudes is representative of people of 20 years old and above. Over 50 per cent of the survey sample were between 30–44 years old.
14. *Kepala RW* (*Rukun Warga*) is the head of a ward which consists of about 20 RTs (*Rukun Tetangga*) which are neighbourhood associations of about 20 households.

232   Dennis J. Cohen

15. This different orientation can remain hidden to a researcher who relies upon a survey for his research only. I saw many questionnaires while I was in Indonesia that used the word *pengharapan* in the sense of expectation. By talking with a number of low-income people I found that this word never carried the connotations of expectation for them. It just meant to hope and dream. If nothing happened, they were not surprised.
16. See his afterword in Holt (1972).
17. *Golkar* is the pseudo-political party organized by elements of the army and government to organize electorial support for Suharto's administration.
18. This pattern is usually referred to as patron-client networks. For example, see Scott (1972, 59–61). I am not using this term here because I am not yet sure if all the implications of the patron–client model apply in this case.
19. For a study of the violence which occurred in the rural areas, see Lyon (1971).
20. Serialized in the *Jakarta Times*, beginning 18 August 1972.

References

GEERTZ, Clifford (1963) *Agricultural Involution*, University of California Press, Berkeley.
HOLT, Claire (1972) *Culture and Politics in Indonesia*, Cornell University Press, Ithaca, N.Y.
LIPSITZ, Lewis (1973) "On political belief: the grievances of the poor", in E. S. Greenberg and R. P. Young, *American Politics Reconsidered*, Duxbury Press, North Scinate, Mass., pp. 139–58.
LYON, Margo (1971) *Causes of Conflict in Rural Java*, Center of South and Southeast Asian Studies Research Monograph, University of California, Berkeley.
McGEE, T. G. (1971) *Urbanization in the Third World*, University of Hong Kong Press, Hong Kong.
SCOTT, James C. (1972) *Comparative Political Corruption*, Prentice-Hall, Englewood Cliffs, N.Y.

CHAPTER 14

A tradition of repression: the street traders of Johannesburg*

C. M. ROGERSON AND K. S. O. BEAVON

The term "informal sector" has entered the lexicon of social science only relatively recently, yet the activities subsumed under the "informal sector" rubric have a long ancestry in many urban areas (see e.g. Jones 1971), not least in South Africa. For nineteenth century Cape Town (Bradlow 1977) and for early Johannesburg during the years 1886–1920 (Van Onselen 1979, 1982), there exist documented studies of the functioning of a thriving "informal" economy. Indeed, from the perspective of an historian, the "informal sector" must be recognized as a regular feature of the South African urban scene (Beavon and Rogerson 1980). That said, it is important to recognize that the "informal sector" has not been involved with the same activities through time (King 1974). The rickshaw puller, the washerman, and the boot-black are some of the several early "informal" operators who have since disappeared from the urban areas of South Africa (Van Onselen 1979, 1982). But counterbalancing these losses are the emergence of relatively recent "informal" income niches such as the driving of pirate taxis, the backyard repair of motor vehicles, and child-minding (Rogerson and Beavon 1980). Amidst what appears as a "moving frontier of informal sector activity" (King 1974), that of street trading remains one of the most persistent "informal" activities in the South African city.

It is the intention in this paper to trace, albeit briefly, the growth and changing nature of street trading in the "City of Gold", Johannesburg. But, more important, attention is focused upon the attitudes and policies of the local municipality and national State towards this group of "informal" operators. Of particular importance in appreciating the tradition of repression towards the street traders of Johannesburg is that since at least 1920 Blacks or Indians, rather than Whites, have been the major race groups engaged in street trading (Beavon and Rogerson 1980). The anti-hawker

*An original essay written especially for this book. The authors thank Mr. P. J. Stickler who prepared the illustrative material, Gordon Pirie for his constructive comments, and the Human Sciences Research Council, Pretoria, for financial assistance.

policies pursued in Johannesburg are thus interwoven into the story of the battle for a pure "White" city in South Africa (Proctor 1979). The policy of racial segregation suggests that an investigation of the experience of the Johannesburg street traders constitutes a study *sui generis*. Nevertheless, the mechanisms of control in Johannesburg find their parallels in many urban areas of the Third World (Bromley 1978a; Forbes 1979, 1981; McGee and Yeung 1977). Moreover, the lesson that may be drawn from studying Johannesburg's experience of attempting to repress street traders, is of the limited success that can be expected of such policies in the face of inadequate alternative employment opportunities.

The tradition of repression

The hawkers or street traders of Johannesburg have traditionally confronted a policy of repression from both municipal authority and national government. The suite of legislative controls introduced by the authorities in South Africa has been aimed at severely curtailing the expansion of street trading in Johannesburg and even, at various times, at eliminating street trading altogether. The negative and restrictive policies historically pursued by city authorities in Johannesburg broadly reflect an official perception that the activities of street traders are antithetical to the creation of a "modern" urban environment. North American or Western European cities have always provided the planning models for Johannesburg rather than those relating to the "Third World" city. Suffused with the powerful ideology of modernization, the planners of Johannesburg have long considered street traders as an "obstacle" in the way of modernization. In viewing street traders largely as a community of law-breakers, a generator of litter, a source of congestion and even, at times, as a health threat, Johannesburg city authorities have been supported variously by complaints both from members of the public and business organizations situated in areas where street traders traditionally operate. A further impetus for the implementation of strict controls stems from the influential voices of established traders protesting at the "unfair trading practises" of street traders. Finally, the city authorities in Johannesburg perforce have responded to national policies intended to preserve urban areas for White South Africans. In terms of so-called Stallardist principles, imprinted upon South African cities from 1923 onwards, Blacks are viewed as "temporary sojourners" in the White urban areas, there only as long as they minister unto the needs of "Whites" (Rich 1978, 1980).

Against this background of national ideology and local pressures, it is not surprising to record the emergence of a battery of controlling legislation, mainly aimed at the activities of Black street traders. It should be noted that this legislation focuses on street traders who do not have a vote in the Whites-only municipal elections. This is in contrast to the situation in some Third World cities where street traders do vote in local elections, occasionally even attracting the support of populist politicians (cf. Bromley 1978a). At the national level the two major instruments of control mirror the official view of Blacks as temporary sojourners. Under the notorious Group Areas Act, one ·of the cornerstone pieces of apartheid legislation, Blacks are not permitted to own land or business in "White" areas, nor may they operate businesses in these areas. In terms of this legislation, it is only as hawkers that Blacks may trade in White areas; however, the Act precludes the possible evolution of successful hawker operations into "formal" retail outlets in fixed premises. Of more direct significance to the aspirant Black hawker is the Black (Urban Areas) Consolidation Act which requires that aspirant hawkers be screened by an Administration Board prior to applying for a hawker licence from the Johannesburg municipality. The function of the Administration Board, in this respect, is to prevent those Blacks "illegally" in the Johannesburg area (in contravention of South Africa's "influx control" legislation) from pursuing legalized hawking. In any event, the possession of a licence for hawking in Johannesburg affords no guarantee of unhindered trading. At the local level, city authorities have introduced a mass of legislation strictly controlling where and at what times hawkers may operate.

The ideal hawker location is one which has a high pedestrian flow, thereby generating a constant stream of potential customers (cf. Bromley 1978b; Forbes 1979). Like their counterparts elsewhere in Third World cities (cf. Bromley 1978b; Forbes 1979; McGee and Yeung 1977) the street traders of Johannesburg, with certain exceptions (see below), traditionally have sought to operate in the core of the city's central business district, more particularly in the retailing heart of that core (Fig. 1). But given the pressures already outlined at both national and municipal levels, city authorities have sought to "defend" the central business area from the perceived threats of street traders. The "defended space" (cf. Bromley 1978a) of Johannesburg is termed the Restricted Area, within which are contained several further restrictions on trading in particular streets. The Restricted Area was established early in the history of Johannesburg. In 1922 the first defended space was demarcated, comprising 23 city blocks. Centred around the City Hall, the area enclosed the retailing core of Johannesburg to the east of Rissik Steet and the office district to its west (Fig. 2). In 1934 the boundaries of the Restricted Area were redrawn to encompass the expansion of the CBD and office district and the loci of the transportation termini situated in the peripheral zones of the CBD, and a similar extension of the Restricted Area took place in 1947 (Fig. 2). It is striking that this spatial extension of the Restricted Area paralleled the growth of the city's retail core, demonstrating that in an expanding Johannesburg there was to be no officially approved role for street traders. Since 1922 no licensed or unlicensed hawker has been permitted to trade in the Restricted Area between the hours of 7 a.m. and 6 p.m., and in the Restricted Streets prohibitions extend to 9 p.m. In seeking to defend the interests of established traders, hawkers have been required by the muncipial "move-on" regulations

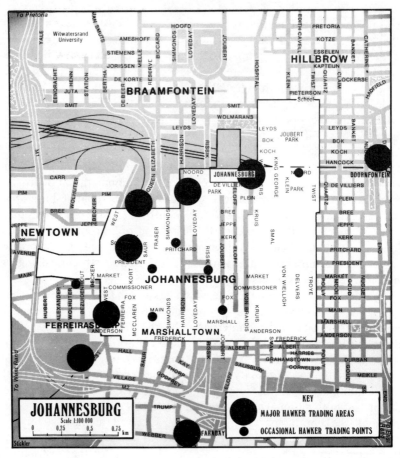

FIG. 1. Geography of hawking in Central Johannesburg.

to transfer their goods and barrow or stall to a new site 25 metres away every 20 minutes. The latter regulation acts as a severe constraint upon hawker operations in the central areas of Johannesburg, the zones of greatest consumer potential for street traders.

Aside from this array of legislative controls on their operations, the hawkers of Johannesburg are confronted by several different agencies of enforcement, each of which tends to view them as committing differing offences or infractions of municipal by-laws. For example, the municipal traffic police see the hawkers as a traffic hazard by virtue of their barrows standing at the kerbside for longer than the designated 20 minute period or because flows of pedestrians may be hindered on the city pavements. Licensing authorities are concerned that the hawkers are selling only those items specified on their licences. Health inspectors constantly perceive the

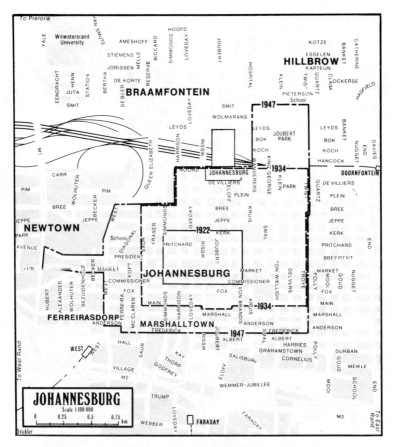

FIG. 2. Changing boundaries of the "Defended Space".

operations of food hawkers as a potential health risk, and the South African police view the hawker community as a possible threat to their crime prevention activities inasmuch as hawking is regarded as encouraging gatherings of crowds and the actions of pickpockets and other petty criminals (Biesheuvel 1979). Each of these law enforcement agencies can be responsible for a surge of arrests and harassment of the hawker community (Fig. 3), and the periodicity of these waves of repression varies according to both local and national circumstances. Most striking was the call made in 1976, after the Soweto uprising, that police should not harass the hawkers in central Johannesburg (*Star* 2/12/1976).

Finally, as if this arsenal of legislation and enforcement were not sufficient to curb the operations of hawkers, the municipal authority has intervened in still other ways to affect their livelihood. In the years 1944–1952 the

FIG. 3. Newspaper clippings *re* the Tradition of Repression.

operations of suburban hawkers in Johannesburg came under threat from municipal mobile food vans. During this period the Johannesburg municipality itself was operating as a hawker and, extraordinarily, did so even in contravention of its own regulations (Pirie and Rogerson 1982). During the early 1960s officials of the City Council further refined their anti-hawker policies through direct pleas to the public for a boycott of the fruits, flowers and vegetables sold by hawkers (*Star* 25/5/1961). This campaign was strengthened in 1967 by publicity orchestrated by the City Council in a further attempt to halt consumer purchases from hawkers (*Star* 25/9/1967; Biesheuvel 1979).   It is against this background of a tradition of repression in Johannesburg that a succession of street traders have sought to obtain a livelihood on the pavements of the city. Attention now turns to a survey of the changing historical character of street trading in Johannesburg.

The evolution of street trading in Johannesburg

The successive rise and fall of a variety of forms of street trading on the streets of the "City of Gold" is a part of the unwritten history of the working class of South Africa. Nevertheless, with the emergence of studies on the "popular history" of the Witwatersrand focused on the lives of the common people (Bozzoli 1979), there are appearing a number of contributions relating to street trading in the city (Tomaselli 1981; Van Onselen 1982). Primary sources of material on hawkers include the records of the Johannesburg City

Council, oral histories and newspaper reports. These various source materials are combined here to sketch the major historical dimensions of street trading in Johannesburg.

From the birth of Johannesburg in 1886 to the present-day it is apparent that street traders, albeit of various forms, have been a continuing feature of the city's life. In the early 1900s it was recorded that there were 2,000 licensed hawkers operating in the city (Johannesburg 1910, 1410). White hawkers were in the majority at this time with Indians constituting the second major group. The operations of Indian hawkers were to form the focus of the first wave of repression undertaken by the municipal authorities. The circumstances surrounding this particular set of repressive actions are especially noteworthy in that these actions were not directed toward hawking as such at this time. Rather they were intended to counter the political challenge mounted by the Indian community against the introduction of legislation designed to control them in the Transvaal. Many prominent members of the Indian community hawked on the streets without a licence in order to provoke arrest and prosecution as part of the passive resistance movement organized at the time by Mahatma Gandhi, later the founder of nationalism in India (Tayal 1981).

It was in the early 1920s that the first in a catalogue of repressive measures were introduced to counter the growth in street trading activity *per se*. The actions taken were directed at what was to become the last group of White hawkers on the streets of Johannesburg. The focus of repression in this instance was the group of hawkers colloquially known as "cheap-jacks". In contrast to the mobile hawker with his barrow, the operating mode of the cheap-jacks was to "stand on stools shouting as loudly as they can, and so attract a crowd (the crowd as a rule being loafers and natives)". *Star* 22/9/1923). Included in the crowd would be assistants to the cheap-jack who would entice others to purchase cheap goods at prices which were very often artificially inflated. The actions of these hawkers-cum-confidence-tricksters were seen by the authorities and shopkeepers as a distinct nuisance in the central area. In order to deal more effectively with the cheap-jacks the hawker by-laws were specifically amended to delimit the first Restricted Area for hawker operations in the city (*Star* 17/5/1922, 18/5/1922; Johannesburg 1922, 308). The demise of the cheap-jacks was swift, accentuated by the withdrawal of all licences to trade under this method. By 1925 the cheap-jacks were no longer (Johannesburg 1925, 96). The legislation that repressed their activities nevertheless continued to affect adversely the operations of succeeding generations of street traders in Johannesburg. Notwithstanding the early restrictions referred to, there occurred an expansion of street trading in Johannesburg. By 1927 the growth of hawking was such as to prompt the report that there was "no problem of municipal government which creates more anxiety and trouble to Transvaal municipalities than the control and regulation of hawkers" (*Star* 21/9/1927).

It appears that the period of the 1920s was a watershed in terms of the history of street trading in the city. During the decade it became absolutely clear that Indians and increasingly Blacks (the so-called Natives) became the major actors in hawking. From this time the repressive measures against street trading increasingly were enmeshed into the web of national controls shaping urban racial segregation in South Africa and particularly in "defending" the White urban areas (Rich 1978, 1980; Proctor 1979). In the early 1930s the community of Indian flower sellers with their flower carts attracted the unwanted attention of city authorities. In 1931 these sellers were classified as hawkers and as such were for the first time subject to the prohibitions on hawking in the Restricted Area and the 20-minute move-on regulations (*Star* 17/8/31). Under the burden of these controls, which resulted in the prosecutions of many Indian hawkers, the sales of cut flowers dropped by an estimated 50 per cent (*Star* 19/8/1931). Without the combined weight of intervention by the flower growers (*Rand Daily Mail* 25/8/1931, *Star* 8/9/1931), organized protests by sellers (*Star* 17/8/1931) and broad-based sympathy from the general public, the flower sellers would have been excised from the city streets. The response by the Council took the form of only a limited set of concessions. Sellers were permitted to operate by vending the flowers from baskets rather than carts (*Rand Daily Mail* 16/11/1931). Notwithstanding the wishes of the sellers that they should be able to trade throughout the central city (*Star* 7/3/1932), the flower sellers were confined to operating in a limited part of Rissik Street near the City Hall (Fig. 2). The area assigned to sellers was unsatisfactory in that it provided no shade, and in the absence of awnings like those on the former carts, the flowers exposed to the sun withered and became unsaleable (*Rand Daily Mail* 19/3/1932). Such was the ferocity of the flower war waged at this time by the municipality that an editorial in the local press opined:

> So many are the regulations they have to obey, and so frequently these regulations changed, that it really seems surprising that the City Council has any time left over to perform its other duties.
>
> (*Rand Daily Mail* 11/3/1932)

The failure of the campaign to eliminate the flower sellers was followed by Council concessions that allowed fixed "stands" (i.e. sites) for flower sellers in the city. Removed from the imperatives of the move-on regulations, flower sellers then continued to operate in central Johannesburg. Again the concession of stands was only a limited one, and the number of stands made available never matched the demand for them from the Indian community. This engendered a continuous conflict against the limitations, and amongst the sellers themselves to preserve a livelihood. The details of these struggles from the 1950s to the present are recounted elsewhere (Tomaselli 1981).

In the history of street trading in Johannesburg discussed so far the focus of attention has been on White and Indian hawkers. There were nonetheless a significant and increasing number of Black hawkers regularly plying their trade in the Black residential areas of Johannesburg in the 1930s (Hellman 1935; Kagan 1978), selling such items as milk, meat, offal, fruit, and vegetables. Occasional harassment of these hawkers took place under public health regulations. In general, however, there was little direct intervention against Black hawkers as long as they operated in the Black rather than the main White areas of the city.

From the mid-1930s there emerged a new and distinct form of street trading that encroached on the White areas of the city. Black hawkers began to sell a mix of foodstuffs and drinks to the growing Black workforce of Johannesburg's inner zone of industries and warehouses. The sale of such foodstuffs as tea, coffee, beans, mielie-meal porridge, meat stew, *maheu*, sour milk, and bread took place from what were styled coffee-carts or cafe-de-move-ons. In their initial evolution the coffee-carts were carts as such; spatially mobile they were trundled daily from residence to trading site in the city. However, with the removal of Blacks from Johannesburg to the segregated "townships" that collectively are known as Soweto, the carts became transformed into permanent pavement kiosks. The coffee-carts entered a niche in the urban economy left open by the absence of feeding facilities for Blacks in "White" Johannesburg. The few existing derogatorily named "Kaffir" or "Native" eating houses were woefully incapable of supplying the expanding demand for refreshments in the early morning when workers entered the city and at the midday-break for lunch. The industrial canteen for Black factory workers was virtually unknown prior to the 1950s in South Africa. The coffee-carts proliferated particularly in the period after the Second World War, reaching a peak of 2,000 carts on the streets of Johannesburg in 1962 (Fig. 4). The spatial distribution of these carts was one that avoided the defended space of the city, being confined to the zones of industrial and mixed land use (Rogerson 1980). The rise of the trade was widely attributed to the fact that coffee-carts were the only source of nourishment and refreshment for Black workers in these zones. The operators of the carts frequently allowed credit to their Black patrons. Relative to their competitors, prices charged were as much as 50 per cent lower for the same foods. Finally, the carts were beneficiaries of the rising tide of African nationalism during the 1950s and associated sentiments to support Black businesses (Rogerson 1980).

Efforts by the City Council to remove the coffee-cart traders date back to the 1930s shortly after their emergence. Later in 1942 the Council took action under a clause of a local government ordinance to refuse licences to businesses conceived as operating in an "unclean and insanitary (*sic*) manner or in a manner inimical to public health" (Freedman 1962). This action led to the rescinding of licences previously granted to the coffee-cart traders in the period 1934 to 1942. The 1950s and 1960s saw increasing attempts by the City Council to remove the coffee-carts. This campaign was launched under the guise of removing a perceived public health nuisance—a reflection of the long-standing imprint upon the South African city of the "sanitation syndrome"

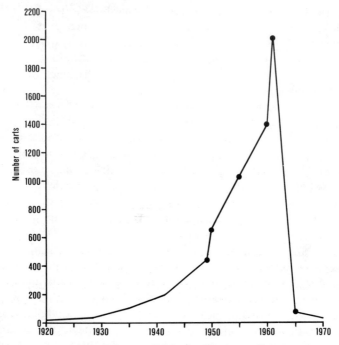

FIG. 4. The rise and fall of coffee-cart trading.

that equates Blacks with a public health hazard for the White population (Swanson 1976, 1977). In addition the City Council authorities objected to the obstruction of pavements caused by the coffee-carts and to the litter associated with them. Attempts to remove the coffee-carts by recourse to existing legislation foundered on the collective resistance of the operators as articulated most importantly through the Association of Coffee-cart Traders (Rogerson 1980). The final demise of coffee-cart trading came swiftly in the period 1962 to 1965 when the authorities resorted to raiding. The traders were then forced to leave their carts unattended, whereupon the authorities would seize what they designated as an "abandoned" cart and subsequently destroy it. Throughout the bitter struggle to remove the carts it was again maintained by officials that the carts were variously an eyesore, a traffic nuisance, and a public health hazard (*Star* 23/9/1963, 25/3/1964; Freedman 1961).

The demise of coffee-cart trading meant that some 2,000 street sellers necessarily had to seek some other avenues of earning a livelihood in the city. Interviews conducted with former coffee-cart traders indicate that perhaps a quarter of them turned to hawking other items. During the middle 1960s the vending of fruit and vegetables experienced a considerable surge. In 1969 surveys by the city council revealed that "illegal street trading is widespread and increasing . . . the coffee-cart has been replaced by the illegal hawker who peddles his wares from trays, moveable stands and the pavement". With the disappearance of the coffee-carts the full weight of the repressive apparatus of controls could turn now to focus upon those alternative forms of street trading mushrooming through the 1960s.

The characteristic form of hawking activities in the 1970s has been the sale of fruit and vegetables, cooked foodstuffs, clothing, flowers, soft goods, and miscellaneous curios and handicrafts (Beavon 1981; Beavon and Rogerson 1982). Less numerous are the hawkers of beverages, furniture, firewood, paper carrier bags, and hub-caps (Biesheuvel 1979). Because of the restrictive actions of the municipal authorities, the number of Black and Indian hawkers selling in central Johannesburg has progressively declined to some 200. Including the suburban areas of White Johannesburg there are estimated to be about 1,000 hawkers now operating. As outlined earlier, the popular sites for Black hawkers are not only in the inner city but also at the peripheral transport termini for Black commuters and at the mini-bus and taxi points that service the central area. It can be postulated that the reduction in the numbers of Black traders operating in White Johannesburg has been accompanied by a corresponding expansion of their activities in the Black townships, particularly Soweto, where it is estimated at least 3,000 hawkers presently operate (Rogerson and Beavon 1982). However, despite raids, arrests, fines and confiscation of goods in the city "the voids so produced are rapidly filled by hawkers from elsewhere, . . . and after paying . . . admissions of guilt the hawkers are back on their old beats within a short time of their removal" (Johannesburg 1969).

In the battle for a "White" city of Johannesburg there is one final chapter in the tradition of repression that deserves attention. There emerged in the Diagonal Street area (the northwestern part of the Restricted Area; Fig. 2) a thriving community of Indian shops and residences. Associated with it were a community of barrow-men who hawked their goods on and near the pavements of this well-known street. This group of traders remained relatively undisturbed during the period of harassment of the coffee-cart traders and the Black fruit and vegetable sellers. However, the decision to relocate the Johannesburg Stock Exchange from the inner core of the city to this peripheral location set in motion a sequence of events leading to the complete removal of these Indian hawkers. In the vision of certain city authorities they were perceived as a potential nuisance or even a threat, easily eradicable, to the more "genteel" clientele of the Stock Exchange (*Rand Daily Mail* 24/4/1979, *Sunday Express* 21/10/1979).

Conclusion

The persistence of street trading as an activity in Johannesburg is inseparable from the material conditions experienced by Blacks, Indians and Coloureds, under the apartheid system. With wage levels for Blacks in regularized wage employment frequently insufficient to meet household needs, the impetus to hawk in the streets has remained strong. Further, in the absence of any satisfactory social welfare and unemployment schemes for Blacks, hawking represents one strategy of survival for the old, infirm and those unable to obtain "formal" employment. The latter factor has strengthened as an impelling force in South Africa since 1945. There exists today a critical problem of the emergence of a group of people surplus to the requirements of capitalist production. In the absence of alternatives, hawking remains in essence a strategy of survival for the Black urban poor.

It is against this background that the tradition of repression directed at street trading in Johannesburg must be evaluated. In the struggle for a "White" city, which was boltered by the election of the National Party with its doctrine of apartheid, the efforts to rid the central area of the perceived menace of street trading has undoubtedly achieved some of its objectives. There has been a continuing decline in the numbers of hawkers, particularly since the heyday of the coffee-cart trade. Against this limited "success" must be set the incalculable human cost borne by the Black populace in the absence of formal earning niches.

References

BEAVON, K. S. O. (1981) "From hypermarkets to hawkers: changing foci of concern for human geographers", *Environmental Studies*, Occasional Paper No. 23, Department of Geography and Environmental Studies, University of the Witwatersrand, Johannesburg.

BEAVON, K. S. O. and ROGERSON, C. M. (1980) "The persistence of the casual poor in Johannesburg", *Contree*, Vol. 7, pp. 15–21.

BEAVON, K. S. O. and ROGERSON, C. M. (1982) "The 'informal sector' of the apartheid city: the pavement people of Johannesburg", in David M. Smith (ed.), *Living under Apartheid*, George Allen and Unwin, London, pp. 106–23.

BIESHEUVEL, S. (1979) Planning for the Informal Sector: Hawking in Johannesburg. Unpublished M.Sc. (T.R.P.) dissertation, University of the Witwatersrand, Johannesburg.

BOZZOLI, B. (1979) "Popular history and the Witwatersrand, in B. Bozzoli (ed.), *Labour, Townships and Protest*, Ravan Press, Johannesburg, pp. 1–15.

BRADLOW, E. (1977) "Cape Town's labouring poor: a century ago", *South African Historical Journal*, Vol. 9, pp. 19–29.

BROMLEY, Ray (1978a) "Organization, regulation and exploitation in the so-called 'urban informal sector': the street traders of Cali, Colombia", *World Development*, Vol. 6, pp. 1161–71. Reprinted in Ray Bromley (ed.) (1979), *The Urban Informal Sector: Critical Perspectives on Employment and Housing Policies*, Pergamon, Oxford.

BROMLEY, Ray (1978b) "The locational behavior of Colombian urban street traders: observations and hypotheses", in William M. Denevan (ed.), *The Role of Geographical Research in Latin America*, Conference of Latin American Geographers Publication, No. 7, Muncie, Indiana, pp. 41–51.

FORBES, D. K. (1979) *The Pedlar of Ujung Pandang*, Monash University, Centre for Southeast Asian Studies, Working Paper No. 17, Melbourne.

FORBES, D. K. (1981) "Production, reproduction and underdevelopment: petty commodity producers in Ujung Pandang, Indonesia", *Environment and Planning A*, Vol. 13, pp. 841–56.

FREEDMAN, M. L. (1961) "The problem of prohibition and control of illegal street trading in urban areas of the Transvaal", *Public Health*, Vol. 61 (12), pp. 7–29.

FREEDMAN, M. L. (1962) "Illegal street trading", *South African Municipal Magazine*, Vol. 44 (533), pp. 14–47.

A tradition of repression   245

HELLMAN, Ellen (1935) "Native life in a Johannesburg slum yard", *Africa*, Vol. 8, pp. 34–62.
JOHANNESBURG (1910) City Council Minutes 24/8/1910.
JOHANNESBURG (1922) City Council Minutes 15/6/1922.
JOHANNESBURG (1925) Mayor's Minute.
JOHANNESBURG (1969) Extract from Health and Amenities Committee 15/1/1969, File No. 8/3/7.
JONES, Gareth Stedman (1971) *Outcast London: A Study in the Relationship between Classes in Victorian Society*, Clarendon Press, Oxford.
KAGAN, N. (1978) African Settlements in the Johannesburg Area 1903–1923. Unpublished M.A. dissertation, University of the Witwatersrand, Johannesburg.
KING, Kenneth (1974) "Kenya's informal machine-makers: a study of small-scale industry in Kenya's emergent artisan society", *World Development*, Vol. 2 (4/5), pp. 9–28.
McGEE, T. G. and YEUNG, Yue-man (1977) *Hawkers in Southeast Asian Cities: Planning for the Bazaar Economy*, International Development Research Centre, Ottawa.
PIRIE, G. H. and ROGERSON, C. M. (1982) "Municipal hawking: Johannesburg's mobile markets, 1944–1952", *Contree*, Vol. 12, pp. 26–31.
PROCTOR, A. (1979) "Class struggle, segregation and the city: a history of Sophiatown 1905–1940", in B. Bozzoli (ed.), *Labour, Townships and Protest*, Ravan Press, Johannesburg, pp. 49–89.
Rand Daily Mail (Johannesburg) Daily.
RICH, P. B. (1978) "Ministering to the White man's needs: the development of urban segregation in South Africa 1913–1923", *African Studies*, Vol. 37, pp. 177–91.
RICH, P. B. (1980) "Administrative ideology, urban social control and the origins of apartheid theory, 1930–1939", *Journal of African Studies*, Vol. 7, pp. 70–82.
ROGERSON, C. M. (1980) "Making out in the 'City of Gold': the coffee-cart traders of Johannesburg". Paper presented at the Annual Meeting, Association of American Geographers, Louisville.
ROGERSON, C. M. and BEAVON, K. S. O. (1980) "The awakening of 'informal sector' studies in Southern Africa", *South African Geographical Journal*, Vol. 62, pp. 175–60.
ROGERSON, C. M. and BEAVON, K. S. O. (1982) "Getting by in the 'informal sector' of Soweto" *Tijdschrift voor Economische en Sociale Geografie*, Vol. 73, pp. 250–65.
Star (Johannesburg) Daily.
Sunday Express (Johannesburg) Weekly.
SWANSON, M. W. (1976) "The Durban system": roots of urban apartheid in colonial Natal", *African Studies*, Vol. 35, pp. 159–76.
SWANSON, M. W. (1977) "The sanitation syndrome: bubonic plague and the urban native policy in the Cape Colony, 1900–1909", *Journal of African History*, Vol. 18, pp. 387–410.
TAYAL, M. (1981) "Indian passive resistance in the Transvaal: 1906–1908". Paper presented at the History Workshop 1981, University of the Witwatersrand, Johannesburg.
TOMASELLI, R. E. (1981) "Johannesburg Indian flower sellers: a history of people on the street". Paper presented at the History Workshop 1981, University of the Witwatersrand, Johannesburg.
VAN ONSELEN, Charles (1979) "The world the mineowners made: social themes in the economic transformation of the Witwatersrand 1886–1914", *Review*, Vol. 3, pp. 289–302.
VAN ONSELEN, Charles (1982) *Studies in the Social and Economic History of the Witwatersrand, 1886–1914*, 2 Vols., Ravan Press, Johannesburg.

Government support and selective uplift

"The injection of planning into a society living in the twilight between feudalism and capitalism cannot but result in additional corruption, larger and more artful evasions of the law, and more brazen abuses of authority."

(P. A. Baran 1959, "On the political economy of backwardness", 89)

"While everybody talks about the necessity of encouraging private enterprise, and while a great number of controls are instituted with this end in view, *most officials have to devote most of their time and energy to limiting or stopping enterprise.* This is like driving a car with the accelerator pushed to the floor but the brakes on. The need for a wide range of negative discretionary controls and for placing so many of the positive controls on a discretionary basis is to a large extent the result of applying excessive positive operational controls. . . . Encouraging private enterprise beyond practical limits makes necessary a gargantuan bureaucratic system of administrative discretionary controls to harness it. . . The widespread existence of conflicting controls has thus the implication that there is a need of more controls . . . than would otherwise be necessary."

(Gunnar Myrdal 1968, *Asian Drama*, 925)

"The social class barrier is particularly crucial because of . . . the particularism of bureaucratic behavior. . . . In such a preindustrial bureaucracy it is crucial to be able to establish a personal relationship with the bureaucrat, and it is precisely this which is made extraordinarily difficult for the person of lower social class by the status order of such societies."

(Lisa R. Peattie 1968, *The View from the Barrio*, 88)

Introduction

The preceding section, on "Physical and Legal Constraints", has a decidedly pessimistic tone, reflecting the realities of small enterprise regulation in the Third World, and emphasizing the special problems of street and market traders and of para-transit operators. Despite the large numbers of unfavourable government-imposed constraints, however, there are also some significant supports, most notably to small handicraft, manufacturing and repair establishments. This section examines the nature, rationale, application and effects of such supports, concentrating on mechanisms of access to, and delivery of, government assistance.

Before evaluating support to small enterprises, it is important to separate out the small minority of enterprises which have been stigmatized by law and by the collective opinion of large sectors of the population as anti-social, inhuman or dangerous. The listing of these "unacceptable enterprises" varies from country to country, but it normally includes such activities as begging, prostitution and theft, and such establishments as brothels, workshops changing the identity of stolen cars, and narcotics processing laboratories supplying traffickers. These enterprises cannot realistically expect to receive government support, though a large proportion of them obtain exemption from government persecution through the judicious bribery of officials, and a minority of the establishments belong to members of the government or the armed forces.

For all small enterprises which are not deemed "unacceptable", there are strong economic arguments to justify the *expectation* of substantial government support. Both those who work in small enterprises and their dependents are normally taxpayers—sometimes through the direct payment of "income" or "head" taxes, but more importantly through "value added", "sales" or "purchase" taxes on consumption goods and public services. Through their labour and their consumption they contribute to the national product, and in many cases they also serve the State as members of the armed forces, the civil defence, or voluntary public service. Even the dependents of those working in small enterprises who are currently unemployed, engaged in occupations with very low remunerations or simply working in unpaid domestic activities, may play an important role as members of the "reserve army of labour", being available for possible future incorporation into the wage–labour force and hence providing a downward pressure on wage levels in the economy as a whole. Additionally, some small enterprises pay taxes as firms, many pay registration and licensing fees to the authorities, and most have a credible argument that they help to hold down the cost of living and increase the quality of life for substantial sectors of the population who consume their goods and services. Furthermore, as subcontractees, pieceworkers, commission sellers and franchisees, and by reducing the costs of living for corporate and State employees, they contribute directly to increasing the profitability and competitiveness of larger-scale enterprises, helping them to make a greater contribution to the national product and exports. Finally, small enterprises contribute significantly to national human resources as training grounds for technical, commercial and managerial skills, as pools for labour recruitment by larger-scale firms, and as components of a competitive environment in which a small minority of small firms can grow into much larger enterprises.

The *expectation* of substantial government support for small enterprises not only derives from the numerous contributions which they make to the economy, but also from basic principles of democracy and social justice. If those who work in small enterprises helped to put a government into power or help to maintain it there through their support, that government has a certain obligation towards them as part of its "power base". More broadly, on the basis of the concept of universal human rights, the State has an obligation to support all citizens who do not actively oppose it, catering especially for the most obvious of their basic needs—an income in money, goods and/or services so as to be able to provide for their own food, drink, clothing and housing. This obligation is particularly pressing when the only alternatives to working in small enterprises are destitution and crime.

Given the strength of these arguments for an *expectation* of substantial government support, it may seem curious that in most countries and contexts support is very limited and selective in character. It is important to remember, however, that small enterprises are very numerous, and that they tend to be geographically dispersed, divided between a wide variety of different economic activities, and highly heterogeneous in terms of the age/sex structure and social composition of their labour force. The prevalent ethic of individualism, competition and petty accumulation also tends to fractionalize any incipient "small enterprise sector" or union of participants, instilling a value structure which is favourable to the continuation of existing socio-economic inequalities. Furthermore, as eloquently explained by Baran, Myrdal and Peattie in the quotes at the beginning of this section, there are numerous problems of corruption, obstruction, overall shortage of government resources, contradictory policy measures, and intense social stratification, all of which make the effective provision of government support extremely difficult.

Whatever *rights* small enterprises may have, there are more pressing *claims* on government from local and foreign élites, and particularly from major financiers, the armed forces, technocrats pushing pet projects, large-scale enterpreneurs, and unionized employees of the State and of large corporations. What is "given" by government to small enterprises, therefore, tends to have the appearance of charitable generosity, though its real character is that of tokenistic paternalism. In many cases it is intended to "selectively uplift" a few small enterprises to a truly petit bourgeois status, demonstrating to the remainder, which are increasingly marginalized as a result, that improvement is achieved through a combination of hard work, initiative, good luck, and compliance with government. "Divide and rule" by providing significant support to a minority and no support to the majority seems to be the underlying rationale of this approach. Its application provides living proof that Samuel Smiles and Horatio Alger success stories come true, encouraging the subservience of petty entrepreneurs to officialdom, the manipulation of social networks to obtain favours, and the corruption of public officials in the allocation of discriminatory supports.

The highly selective nature of most government support is accentuated by widely-applied distinctions between manufacturing (the secondary sector) and services (the tertiary sector). Many intellectuals and officials of both left- and right-wing political persuasions have argued that manufacturing activities are more "productive" and "desirable" than service activities. Manufacturing is considered to be "directly productive" and to "create value", while services are considered to be "unproductive" or only "indirectly productive", merely "recirculating value". Such views are highly questionable, and in many senses the discussion as to whether services are productive is nothing more than a terminological debate about the meaning of the term "productive" (see e.g. the discussion by Hirst 1975, 221–30 of Marx 1969, 155–75, 387–88 and 399–401). Whether or not services can be *produced* like goods, some services must be *provided*, if only to sustain the output of the primary sector (extractive activities) and the secondary sector (manufacturing). No economy could function for long without transport or commercial distribution, and some services are clearly "essential", whether or not they are defined as productive (see Bromley 1982, 66–67). Nevertheless, there is a widespread tendency to view the tertiary sector as overinflated and essentially parasitic, consisting largely of activities "bearing no observable relationship to effective labour demand", where "the supply of labour creates its own employment opportunities (Bhalla 1973, 288). Such negative views are particularly common among governmental élites in relation to the street occupations—numerous forms of petty trading, para-transit, and personal services (e.g. shoe-shining). They are further reinforced by the city planning and urban real estate interests which are concerned to create a spacious, uncongested and modern "city-beautiful", producing a dominant conception of such occupations as "the people who get in the way".

If the "street occupations" are the least favoured small enterprises, apart from those simply classified as "unacceptable", then the opposite group of "most favoured small enterprises" are probably the artisans and small-scale industries. Such enterprises are almost universally viewed as "productive", "labour-intensive", and "skill-generating", and many of them act, or are capable of acting, as subcontractees of larger-scale manufacturing and distribution firms. Those small enterprises which produce handicraft goods reflecting traditional cultures are particularly likely to be the objects of significant governmental support for three major reasons: first, because they preserve age-old skills and designs; second, because they are not easily susceptible to mechanization and the consequent intrusion of factory production; and third, because they provide a boost to the tourist industry.

Whenever small enterprises are selected, or have to apply, for support, the eventual distribution of assistance tends to favour larger-scale and more accessible enterprises, and those enterprises with more articulate and "well-connected" entrepreneurs. However much those who work in small enterprise support programmes may wish to achieve total coverage of enterprises, or to favour the smallest and most remote enterprises, they are hampered by the lack of adequate information, staff, funds and transport, and by a variety of legalistic concerns—for example, not dealing with unlicensed enterprises, entrepreneurs lacking identity papers, or applicants who have not made an income-tax declaration. Comprehensive and up-to-date listings of small enterprises are extremely rare and hard to compile—like finding thousands of needles in a haystack! Even when they do exist it is difficult to ensure that the basic information announcing a support programme reaches them all at the same time. Furthermore, of course, it is precisely the smallest-scale and most remote operators of small enterprises who are most likely to be illiterate, to not have the identity papers, licenses and other documents which are needed to apply for support, to not know the language spoken by government officials, and to not have any income above the margins of subsistence which they can forego by giving up work for a few hours to visit a government office. Very often, when some significant support is available, it has all been exhausted before those who operate the smaller and more remote enterprises have applied for it, or in many cases have even become aware of it.

Government support to small enterprises can be supplemented by the efforts of such non-governmental organizations (NGOs) as charitable foundations, church groups and worker federations. Indeed, in some countries and types of economic activity, NGOs are the only entities providing support to small enterprises, and in many countries it is the NGOs which have the most interesting, innovative and effective small enterprise programmes. Their programmes are often useful experimental or model schemes, but it is unrealistic to expect NGOs to cater for anything more than a small proportion of the needs and expectations of small enterprises. Only national governments, sometimes assisted by bilateral or multilateral aid agencies, have the resources and powers necessary to provide small enterprises with the level of support which their operators can reasonably expect; yet the experience to date in most Third World countries gives little grounds for optimism that such levels of support will be forthcoming. The most important role which NGOs can play may well be in helping to promote the diffusion of ideas and research findings on an international scale, in the hope of changing the prevailing negative views and low priorities assigned to small enterprises, and thus of creating the bases for large-scale governmental support.

Having established both the right to support and the reasons why such support for small enterprises is decidedly limited, it is necessary to define more precisely what forms it can take. Synthesizing the conclusions and recommendations of such authors as Farbman (ed., 1981), Harper and Tan (1979, 89–115), McGee and Yeung (1977, 113–18), Neck (ed. 1977), Sharma (ed. 1979), and the World Bank (1978), sixteen major lines of support to small enterprises can be identified:

1. Designing and building an urban environment which is favourable to small enterprises—without segregation of small-scale manufacturing and commerce from housing, with numerous sites for small enterprises, with high-density and pedestrian areas favourable to markets and street traders, and with a transport mix favourable to para-transit operators;

2. Helping to create new small enterprises by identifying potential business opportunities and entrepreneurs, and by providing seed capital and other forms of "start-up assistance";

3. Promoting the organization of small enterprises into trade unions, cooperatives, associations, federations, or larger self-managed firms;

4. Providing technical and managerial training and advice;

5. Assisting with official procedures for licensing, permits, tax declarations, obtaining credit and public services, and importing and exporting;

6. Giving preference in the allocation of public services (electricity, water supply, sewerage, telephone, refuse disposal, etc.), and/or preferential tariffs for such services;

7. Providing credit at normal or subsidized rates of interest;

8. Providing free or subsidized raw materials, and/or giving preferential access to products handled by government marketing boards and State monopolies;

9. Providing free or subsidized equipment, and/or giving preferential access to scarce imported equipment;

10. Providing suitable premises with subsidized rents or sale prices;

11. Providing free or subsidized advertising, and/or an inter-enterprise and inter-institutional brokering service to link small enterprises to potential purchasers of their goods and services;

12. Directly purchasing goods and services provided by small enterprises for government agencies, marketing boards, export corporations and organized groups of consumers;

13. Imposing constraints on competing larger-scale enterprises within the country, and sometimes also reserving specific economic activities for small enterprises;

14. Prohibiting competing imports, or imposing high tariff barriers on them;

15. Conducting research on appropriate technologies, organizational forms and marketing opportunities for small enterprises, and diffusing the results of such research;

16. Educating the general public on the merits of small enterprises and of the goods and services that they provide, and providing awards and exhibition facilities for outstanding small enterprises.

For supports to small enterprises to be effective, their scale and extent must be very carefully tailored to the total volume of resources available. It is also essential that there be a corresponding reduction in governmental constraints on small enterprises, and particularly in taxation, bureaucratic regulation and policing. More broadly, all support programmes should follow the concluding recommendations of Sharma's (1979, 260) comparative study of Asian small entrepreneurial development:

> Attempts to promote small enterprises should be backed by comprehensive long-term and clear policies, supported by well-organised, effective and purposeful organisations carrying out a balanced programme of stimulatory, support and sustenance activities. Such efforts should also be backed up by systematic research, effective training and educational programmes.

This section consists of two general surveys (Chapters 15 and 16), and two detailed case studies (Chapter 17 and 18). The first general survey, by Bernard Schaffer and Huang Wen-hsien, examines the application of the theory of access to the distribution of government supports. It provides an excellent "recipient's eye view" of small enterprise promotion measures, giving many pointers as to how and why many existing government programmes fail to have their projected impact. In particular, it helps us to understand how the benefits of support programmes are often "hijacked" by the largest of the enterprises falling within the eligibility criteria, or even by larger enterprises, merchants, moneylenders and bureaucrats whose livelihoods are wholly or partly based on appropriating some of the product (in terms of goods and/or money) generated by small enterprises.

Jeffrey Ashe's essay entitled "Extending credit and technical assistance to the smallest enterprises" presents a considerably more optimistic picture, reviewing a wide variety of government and NGO small enterprise support programmes in Africa, Asia and Latin America. He reviews particularly successful pilot programmes, emphasizing the positive lessons to be learnt from such schemes and detailing the mechanisms for providing effective credit, training and technical assistance.

Alan Middleton's case study of the distribution of credit to small enterprises in Ecuador focuses on programmes to assist small-scale industry and artisans (SI & A), taking into account not only one of the more successful pilot schemes discussed by Ashe, but also numerous larger-scale and more bureaucratized efforts. The overall picture for small-scale industry and artisans in Ecuador is relatively depressing, providing an illustration of Schmitz's (1982, 444) generalization that "there is a process of growth and destruction, while the *net* result is one of stagnation".

Richard Batley's case study of "The allocation of public construction contracts in Lima and Caracas" focuses on a little-studied but very important aspect of small enterprise support programmes—the extent to which government contracts can be canalized to small enterprises. He examines a major economic activity which is normally characterized by large amounts of subcontracting and disguised wage-working (see e.g. MacEwen Scott 1979) in two contrasting Latin American countries. In both cases he shows that there are substantial discrepancies between government policy pronouncements and the realities of policy implementation, and that formidable bureaucratic procedural obstacles and social barriers must be overcome if there is to be large-scale effective support to small enterprises.

As a final comment, it is important to emphasize the need for regular evaluations and close supervision of small enterprise support programmes (see Goldmark and Rosengard 1981). If such evaluations and supervision are effectively conducted, and if their recommendations are followed, they can do much to ensure a more equitable distribution of benefits, the avoidance of major corruption in the allocation of discretionary supports, and the application of appropriate levels of subsidies and other forms of support. Too little support may be useless, too much may be patronizing and may create permanent dependence, and poorly designed and badly delivered support may be counterproductive. Without influential critical evaluation, training and technical assistance programmes are particularly vulnerable to qualitative deterioration, in which rote learning replaces thought and discussion, and in which most of what is communicated shows a striking ignorance of the real problems and operating conditions of small enterprises. In many cases the needs and expectations of small enterprises greatly exceed not only the support which governments are willing to give, but also the capacity of government personnel to understand the problems which need to be solved and to design and implement appropriate solutions to those problems.

REFERENCES

BARAN, P. A. (1959) "On the political economy of backwardness", in A. N. Agarwala and S. P. Singh (eds.), *The Economics of Underdeveloped Areas*, Oxford University Press, London.

BHALLA, A. S. (1973) "The role of services in employment expansion", in Richard Jolly, Emanuel de Kadt, Hans Singer and Fiona Wilson (eds.), *Third World Employment*, Penguin, Harmondsworth, pp. 287–301.

BROMLEY, Ray (1982) "Working in the streets: survival strategy, necessity, or unavoidable evil?", in Alan Gilbert (ed.), *Urbanization in Contemporary Latin America*, Wiley, Chichester, pp. 59–77.

FARBMAN, Michael (ed.) (1981) *The PISCES Studies: Assisting the Smallest Economic Activities of the Urban Poor*, Agency for International Development (AID), Office of Urban Development, Washington D.C.

GOLDMARK, Susan G. and ROSENGARD, Jay (1981) *Evaluating Small-Scale Enterprise Promotion*, Agency for International Development (AID), Office of Urban Development, and Development Alternatives Inc., Washington D.C.

HARPER, Malcolm and TAN, Thiam Soon (1979) *Small Enterprises in Developing Countries: Case Studies and Conclusions*, Intermediate Technology Publications Ltd., London.

HIRST, Paul Q. (1975) "Marx and Engels on law, crime and morality", in Ian Taylor, Paul Walton and Jock Young (eds.), *Critical Criminology*, Routledge & Kegan Paul, London, pp. 203–32.

MARX, Karl (1969) *Theories of Surplus Value, Volume 1*, Foreign Languages Publishing House, Moscow.

MACEWEN SCOTT, Alison (1979) "Who are the self-employed?", in Ray Bromley and Chris Gerry (eds.), *Casual Work and Poverty in Third World Cities*, Wiley, Chichester, pp. 105–29.

MCGEE, T. G. and YEUNG, Y. M. (1977) *Hawkers in Southeast Asian Cities: Planning for the Bazaar Economy*, International Development Research Centre (IDRC), Ottawa.

MYRDAL, Gunnar (1968) *Asian Drama: An Inquiry into the Poverty of Nations*, Pantheon/Random House, New York.

NECK, Philip A. (ed.) (1977) *Small Enterprise Development: Policies and Programmes*, Management Development Series No. 14, International Labour Office (ILO), Geneva.

PEATTIE, Lisa R. (1968) *The View from the Barrio*, University of Michigan Press, Ann Arbor.

SCHMITZ, Hubert (1982) "Growth constraints on small-scale manufacturing in developing countries: a critical review", *World Development*, Vol. 10, No. 6, pp. 429–50.

SHARMA, S. V. S. (1979) *Small Entrepreneurial Development in Some Asian Countries*, Light and Life Publishers, New Delhi.

WORLD BANK (1978) *Employment and Development of Small Enterprises: Sector Policy Paper*, World Bank, Washington D.C.

CHAPTER 15

Distribution and the theory of access*

BERNARD SCHAFFER AND HUANG WEN-HSIEN

Most operators of small enterprises are all too familiar with the problems of access to public services—the difficulties of obtaining licences, low-interest credit, adequate premises, electricity and water supplies, technical training and assistance, supplies from government monopolies, and sales outlets through government agencies. Equally, it is common for evaluators of government small enterprise promotion programmes to point out that little or no support reaches the smallest, poorest and most remote enterprises. In the great majority of cases, the distribution mechanisms for government services fail to function in accordance with the oft-repeated but somewhat hollow-sounding objective of "reaching the poorest of the poor".

Both in the provision of support to small enterprises and in the delivery of other services, numerous problems lie between the apparently intended clients or beneficiaries of a programme and their reception of its enjoyment. Many instances could be given indicating other features: the efforts by a client to speed up his case, with all those consequences which often have the opposite effect. "The custom of speed money had become one of the most serious causes of delay and inefficiency" (Myrdal 1968).

Sometimes, again, the need for the programme has become so perpetual and chronic that the beneficiaries have merely become dependents, as reports of relations between U.S. Federal Indian welfare administration and some of the large reservations demonstrate: a ratio of one official to every 18 Indians, while at the same time "with the poverty on most reservations [the Indians] cannot exist without federal financial support. They are terrified of what has come to be known as 'termination'. It is a cannon Indians feel is constantly trained on them."

It is possible to go on giving examples from any country showing the sorts of

*An abridged and slightly amended version of the article with the same title published in *Development and Change*, Vol. 6 (1975), pp. 13–36. Reprinted here with the permission of the editors of *Development and Change*, Sage Publications of London and Beverly Hills, and Bernard Schaffer.

difficulties which come between the members of agencies attempting to tackle problems of poverty and the people themselves. Sometimes government clerks show a marked resistance to playing the role of "servant": that is a member of an agency of public service. As one correspondent writes, "studied elegance, resentment, preoccupation, unconcern, failure to suggest alternative channels when appropriate; all these are much more common than an eagerness to satisfy the applicant, or provide the putative service with speed and objectivity".

This is one aspect of what could be called the problem of access: the difficulties of making organizational connections, the ways in which resources are distributed and the kind of links between clients and institutions (Schaffer 1972). This is an important and neglected area of politics and development studies. This essay indicates one approach by which problems of access can be studied.

Distribution

How do people get the things they value, the prizes they esteem (a piece of land, a house, a career, education, official credits, contracts or licences), from time to time, and place to place, and how does this change?

Insofar as things can be bought in more or less perfect markets, what is needed is disposable income. There is no problem of access as such. There is no question of loyalty, influence, rights or number. Preferences are weakly held (cf. Simon 1957, 170–82). There are no costs of entry, exit or movement. The only question is income. Anyone can enter or leave the market as he will and he knows how to find it. But there are other systems of distribution, and markets are usually imperfect. For some prizes, like land, there may, particularly in underdeveloped countries, be no market at all (see e.g. Griffin 1972). So the resources needed to gain chances are not just disposable income; they include the bases on which rights and claims can be established. The bases of claims may include status, influence, categorization, membership of particular groups and communities, experience or luck.

In non-market systems of distribution, access is problematic. The bases of claims have to be established, demonstrated and checked. Connections have to be secured. In imperfect markets distribution by price is affected by restraints on entry and exit or by product loyalty (cf. Hirschman 1970). In administrative or bureaucratic systems distribution by queue is affected by politics, ascription, lottery or market elements. Furthermore, getting prizes includes avoiding what you do not as well as getting what you do want. It includes the right to minimize the demands, punishments or claims made on you, like the ability to avoid conscription and getting what you want without an admixture of elements of what you do not want: good, not parsons' eggs.

So the actual distribution chances tend to be a result of two things. The first is the resources one possesses: disposable income, status, influence, and knowledge. Resources include the ability to establish organizational connections (Schaffer 1972). The second is the distribution systems which are experienced. These include more or less imperfect markets, and other systems of distribution like administrative allocation, lotteries, commands, elections and inheritance (cf. Dahl and Lindblom 1953). The systems may reinforce or compensate for each other, depending on the nature of the society, whether it is more stratified or more meritocratic, more traditional or more adaptive.

Thus in all distribution systems other than perfect markets there are problems of access, both in imperfect markets and in non-market distribution. In underdeveloped countries there are particularly severe problems of access. Markets are imperfect or are lacking altogether. Bureaucratic-administrative distribution of services is intended to be important; other bases of distribution such as ascription are fundamentally significant. The relations between systems of distribution work out badly; the necessary resources are unequally distributed and the management of organizational connection is accordingly poorly or unfairly handled. This is particularly important for bureaucratic distribution.

Administrative allocation is never completely bureaucratic; and it has imperfections and admixtures of other systems of distribution (Schaffer 1973). What we hope to do is to suggest how to open the institutional envelope which hides what happens within this system of distribution. This means that we must first of all discuss the problems of access which arise from market imperfection, from distribution through non-market systems and, in particular, distribution through bureaucratic administration; and secondly, the peculiar method (of queueing) which bureaucratic distribution is supposed to follow.

Access

The values distributed through a bureaucratic-administrative system can be thought of as packages or items of service. Access to administered services has features which can be distinguished from market alternatives. The potential applicant for a service enters into a different relationship from that of a potential buyer of some goods, available in a price-regulated market.

There is a variety of such situations in which an individual tries to become an applicant who can encounter the boundaries of an administrative system in the hope of acquiring a specific item of service. We can distinguish at least two types of such situations.[1]† In one there is no alternative point of supply at all; hence an applicant cannot choose to leave save by giving up his chances altogether. In a second there may be certain sorts of alternatives. In each case the applicant will have to see what else (than merely leaving) he can do to improve his position or make his application effective.

---

†Superscript numbers refer to Notes at end of chapter.

We begin with the first type of situation. The applicant is interested in a service which is distributed only through a single agency. The applicant cannot turn to any organizational alternative. In such a situation the applicant might attempt some control or influence, aim at redress or correction, or promote improvement of the service. That is to say he can act "politically", speak up for himself, and use his "voice" if he fails to get the service he wants. Alternatively, unhappy applicants may simply not participate in the system. They can decide to avoid it altogether or they might decide to accept it uncritically and invest as much time and resources as seem to be required without question. They establish a sort of "camp", waiting without calculating (Schaffer 1972).

In either case the outcomes and consequences can be unexpected. "Camps" can become riots, quite easily.

What, then, happens to applicants who do attempt to employ activist strategies? Some of these strategies may be prescribed by the organization. There will be procedures for appeal through the hierarchy to supervisors and other levels about the rank and file counter officials whom the applicant first meets (Blau 1955). A dissatisfied applicant can then express himself by following these proper rules, but only if they exist and if he has the resources, like knowing how.

Following these prescribed procedures is distinct from political action. Politically, dissatisfied applicants can team up with similarly frustrated applicants to express an interest in changes in the distribution of this particular service. Alternatively, the applicant can convey his discontent with this service and with many others in alliance with large masses of other people through political parties or rallies, or through military, religious and other aggregating organizations, all of which may be linked to the centre of government decision-making, constitutionally or in other ways.

The strategies vary. Squatters who do not like an existing distribution of local authority housing say they are withdrawing from that system and acquiring an alternative service, namely, empty and unwanted housing.

M. Pompidou said (in the Aranda case),[2] "there are three types of lobbying". There are indeed legitimate processes of administrative feedback which might be assisted by "lobbying" and political linkages; there are uses of political linkages near to the borderline, and then there are political linkages across the border of propriety and civility.

Strategies can become criminal, riotous, rebellious or revolutionary, violent or radical. In many systems of distribution the political linkages are so weak or poorly distinguished from bureaucratic organization that it is the administrative feedbacks which are the more important corrections (Schaffer and Lamb 1974).

An applicant can activate existing social ties to overcome his dissatisfactions with the administered service. The applicant can use ascriptive ties, fellow townspeople, villagers, members of his particular sect. He can attempt to employ authority or influence. He can try his luck, he can exploit knowledge and experience. Or an applicant might attempt to use payments where they are not formally called for. This is stigmatized as corruption.

Where one system of access and distribution is threatened by another the group benefiting by the first will react sharply. "All groups having interests in the status order react with special sharpness precisely against the pretensions of purely economic acquisition . . . Everywhere some status groups . . . consider almost any kind of participation in economic acquisition as absolutely stigmatizing" (Gerth and Mills 1948, 192–93). Status groups can be compared with other categories of rights-holders whose rights are determined differently; e.g. bureaucratically. The problem for the applicant is partly to know at what particular organizational level, place and moment to employ any of these corrective devices. Some may work here, some there. Does the applicant need a representative, a fixer or an agent? Further, it is likely that some corrections are important for some functions within the distribution structure and not for others. Patrons may be useful for providing elements of information; moneylenders for disposable income; tribesmen for contact with fellow tribesmen; priests for fellow members of the church.

Generally the way in which the applicant's relations with the distributive system are arranged tend to determine the way in which his strategy is arranged. Potential applicants who are excluded altogether (i.e. have no access) may use political rather than administrative means. Applicants irritated by rank and file officials (blocked access) might, rather, complain to the superiors. In some situations applicants do that automatically, anticipating irritation or discounting the possibility of satisfactory service in any other way. Secondly, the applicant has to develop a set of these devices depending on the particular mix of resources which he possesses and the effects of the distributive system. So he may feel the need to become a client searching out a patron, a rich man using his disposable income, a tribesman using his fellows and so forth. To some extent it is likely more in some societies than in others, that an applicant will be accustomed to certain beliefs and rituals about bureaucratic administrative distribution. For example, whether it is justified or not, people can learn to believe that ascriptive connections are required.

In some administrative distribution situations there may be a degree of alternative. A different balance of choice and control then is possible.

The services which the applicant is interested in may be offered by more than one agency. There may be parallel civil services. One ministry provides State housing at reduced rents while another dispenses subsidy to tenants of private accommodation. Or, again, an applicant might choose to move between areas where educational housing or other services vary between local governments. There may also be alternatives to the civil service or State agencies which distribute service items in a bureaucratic administrative fashion: political parties, cooperatives, trade unions, the military, religious and ethnic organizations, can offer services that parallel others. So may banks for credit, voluntary bodies and local social work or community development organizations.

Perhaps an applicant can go from an agency organizing self-help housing groups to another, for low-cost rented accommodation. If he can, if he has the resources and the situation permits it, then some of the urgency for political action may well be removed. At the same time, the resources which the applicant may need (such as influence, status, some money, a good record) and the ways in which the situation is arranged, can be as mixed, as complex as they would be where there is no formal alternative for an applicant, as where there is a single distribution agency for housing.

As we have pointed out, such admixtures may be stigmatized as corrupt by those whose rights are threatened. But market elements can be added as a matter of programme design by the administrative authority, as well as being employed as strategies by the applicant himself.

That is to say, an applicant can attempt to introduce the resources available to him within a market as a corrective for his dissatisfaction with his experience of the bureaucratic administrative distribution of the service he is concerned with. This might be legitimate, formal or informal. On the other hand, the policy makers, the authorities designing the whole distribution of a service, can decide that it should be distributed completely in a bureaucratic way; or that some of the service will be distributed in this and some other ways, like a market. Hence, in this situation, some applicants will have a market alternative available to them for a particular service. Others will not, depending on whether they have the resources necessary for entry into the market.

This might be described as either two services, one distributed through a market and one administratively: or as one service distributed in a market way for some applicants and in a bureaucratic-administrative way for others, as where means tests are employed. The outstanding example of services distributed in this way is no doubt housing. Other examples include hospital beds, education, security and personal insurance. But some applicants will have neither the resources for the market nor success in access: what happens to them? (Schaffer and Lamb 1974).

Even where market alternatives are used, other resources than disposable income might be required. For example, those with such resources might also need status to be able to participate in the service, as with some forms of schooling, military recruitment or leisure activities. Other alternatives can also be introduced by design as well as informally; e.g. lotteries.

Where there are alternatives and in particular where there is some market element, two types of outcomes are possible. The first is an important change from the situation of no alternative. In that situation the major corrective to dissatisfaction with the distribution of service was administrative and political strategies. On the whole, it is likely that those applicants who have the resources to employ such action will have other resources (influence, status, disposable income, etc.) as well. If some alternatives and especially some market chances are available, the most resourceful exponents can be removed from this arena of correction. The second point is that applicants who have the resources to use market alternatives tend to adopt least loss strategies. A system where market prevails is likely to be regressive: the distributive effects reinforce existing inequalities.

One distributive system does not always reinforce another. It can compensate for the other. Deliberate bias against inequalities can be built into non-market bureaucratic distribution. This is especially where those with disposable income might not be those with influence or status. This may be intended policy. It can be prejudice—how it will then work out depends on the operation of access methods. Furthermore, market alternatives fit into complicated chains. For example, the consumption of one service can be a condition for applying for another service, as in the movement from primary to secondary to tertiary education. Some of those levels of education will have no or limited alternatives. Others can have market elements, like State schools leading to fee-paying tertiary institutions or fee-paying health maintenance where the State provides only the emergency health services. Here the market is supplementary.

The effects of access will vary. The inequalities and discontinuities of society can be reinforced or qualified, improved and in the end removed by appropriate systems of distribution and access. Such at least is the aim of some services like education, health, insurance, housing, extension and so forth. It is not merely effects, though. Generally the experience and methods of access derive from the cultural setting in which they actually occur. In some situations, for instance, it will be important for an applicant to show (or to hide) his relationships with the rank and file officials: his account will get him to the head of the queue. In others that will not conceivably be relevant. Access is dependent on and revealing about wide and fundamental differences between social situations.

Different access can actually produce different politics. The political point in the end of the distributive systems designed by public authorities, whether they are strictly administrative and bureaucratic or not, is to secure a particular sort of integration and mobilization: loyalty rather than apathy and support rather than revolution. For example the establishment of systems of distribution can be intended or appear to provide access for some who would otherwise be excluded: "To include the excluded", although the service might be inappropriate and the access unreal. The exchanges implied in the actual experience of access and distribution, however oblique or delayed, are profoundly significant. To what sort of politics will this experience give rise; what sort of language and ideology will be available for reinforcing the loyalties which may control or restrain the complaints; what sort of articulation and aggregation can the voice of the disgruntled applicants have to resort to? For example, some will become dependent on the access institutions and feel themselves to be so: special dependency groups, like American Indians on reservations. Some will become incorporated in the institutional processes of access. Indeed, the institutions may initiate and control the political organization of applicants, like trade associations initiated by departments in World War II U.K. industrial policy, and like some types of co-option (Selznick 1949). Others will perceive no relationship at all between the scatter of access offices and functions they, as applicants, know about and quite other political levels or any political channels: little other than occasional violence or sabotage will seem to be available (Peattie 1968).

There is an organizational as well as a political point; thus far, we have been taking the individual applicants, and at the other extreme, the public policy makers. The applicant searches for connections with the points where the services he is interested in are being distributed. But these points occur at one level of whole organizations. The applicant's search, his experience, and his response, express the distinctive nature of the institutional forms which his society employs.

When he becomes "the applicant", his connection with organization is at the point of distribution. But politics operates and is experienced at several levels. At one level of ideology and language, particular patterns or intentions about distribution are enunciated, often in aggregate terms. The legitimacy and efficacy of this language changes from time to time and place to place. Plans, programmes and budgets are worked out. As they are implemented through organization, the processes of institutionalization and the effects of methods and procedures, alter them considerably. Unexpected, unlooked for and indeed painful consequences emerge. What was meant to be benevolent becomes unpleasant, even violent in effect time and again.

The individual outside the organization establishes his connections with it, with varying degrees of disappointment, where the service as item or package is allocated and is made more or less available to him. What in the end is distributed depends partly on what was intended; secondly on what the applicant insists on and complains about, one way or another; and thirdly on the nature of institutional processes. These dimensions are most vivid at the point of connection, where the applicant encounters bureaucratic administrative distribution, where the intentions of the plan in the end meet the test of expectation and outcome. Access to administratively distributed services is not the same as ideology, policy, plan, or programme initiation. But it is where what is crucial in ideology and programme, methods and procedures is revealed.

Queues[3]

When a service is distributed in a bureaucratic administrative situation, access to items is restricted to various applicants who fall into discrete, objective, universalistic categories. Access is possible for those who have the resources to demonstrate that they have those rights. Once individuals have demonstrated their rights to be placed in the category of applicants, there is no further way of distinguishing between one applicant and another: they are in that sense equal. Therefore, systems of distribution of bureaucratic administrative services impose on applicants the acceptance of three conditions. The first is that they have to demonstrate their eligibility for the services being distributed. Categories have been set up and they have to demonstrate their admissibility to the categories.

The second condition is that the applicants have to accept whatever rule is being applied to the serial ordering in which, once they have been admitted, they will be handled and will be brought face to face with the point at which the allocating decisions are made. In all bureaucratic administrative systems of distribution, there will be categorical rules of admissibility and more or less arbitrary, or one-sided, rules of ordering.

These rules for ordering those applicants who have been admitted are frequently the order of arrival: the waiting time. In some situations, though by no means all, people may even stand in line.

The rules of admission and of ordering taken together are meant to simplify the task, to minimize the discretion of the distributive decisions to be taken by the rank-and-file servers. These are the officials behind the counter. An applicant must encounter them once the rules of admission and of ordering have together demarcated that applicant as the next to be dealt with. This is the third condition.

Where these three conditions of admission, ordering and encounter are imposed and accepted, the system can be called a queue. Where the rules about admission, ordering and consideration or encounter work perfectly, all rank-and-file server decision-making is completely simplified. Perfect queues mean perfect routine. What is distinctive here is a number of elements which in their complete form are combined as the ideal type or simple queue.

The simple queue means that the burden of politics and responsibility has been completely removed from the connections between applicant and rank and file servers. The data and predictability which planning requires is met by the routine, reliable and repetitive nature of the distributive decisions taken at the counter. The job of the server has been simplified. So, therefore, has the job of the supervisor between the server and the higher levels of the hierarchy. At the same time, distribution in this way makes the position of the applicant predictable and safer also.

This sort of connection between applicant and public policy means that what is being distributed is something distinctive: items of service. These bits and pieces of service may be tied together in a particular sort of package.

The essential elements of the simple queue are as follows:

(1) A gateway or entry point through which an individual must go before

he can be recognized as an applicant. He can only get through by demonstrating his rights to move in to the defined category of applicant.

(2) The waiting applicants. Where there is more than one they will be arranged according to the ordering rules, such as the line where the ordering rules depend on waiting time.

(3) A counter, grille, *guichet* or table where the applicant conducts exchanges with the rank and file server.

Thus the structure of the simple queue is determined by the following:

(1) The rules of eligibility to pass the entry point: *admission rules.*

(2) The ordering rules which have to be accepted by the individuals who pass the entry point; and other rules on individual behaviour while in the line: *line rules.*

(3) Rules circumscribing exchanges such as rules saying what data will be considered and what disregarded; there can be other rules about passing: *counter rules.*

In a simple queue the admission rules are universally known, unambiguous, not discretionary, finite. They are relatively stable over time. Qualifying under these rules is necessary but not sufficient for the counter. Success at the counter demands success at the entry point, fulfilling the line rules (for example by investing sufficient time) and providing the appropriate data.

It is those characteristics of the simple queue rules which enable the potential applicant to make his calculations about whether he will attempt to apply or not, whether he will delay or refrain altogether from applying, in terms of the time, behavioural, communication, documentation and other costs which might be required of him. In turn it is the possibility that potential applicants can make these sorts of calculations which keep queues relatively limited and reasonable. An endless waiting line is not a queue. Waiting for a local authority house indefinitely (for a hundred years say) is not a queue.

In the simple queue the ordering rule is first in first out: FIFO.[4] Applicants are served in order of their arrival. The applicant will not leave the queue; he will not queue by proxy. Once past the entry point, the applicant in the simple queue does not face supplementary gates. The simple queue does not have priority rules.

Rules regulating permissible exchanges at the counter are clearly defined, limited and relatively stable over time. They are known to applicant and official. There is no third party, broker or advocate in the exchanges between the applicant and the server. The applicant represents nobody other than himself. There is absolute congruence between the applicant's expectations on entering and the actual response of the server.

A complex queue will then differ from the simple queue at the gateway or entry point, in the line and ordering rules, and at the counter where the applicant and the server are brought face to face and have to be reconciled.

Queues are complex where the essentials of the simple queue are all present, but particular elements deviate from the ideal type.

The ways in which the rules work out are unexpected and peculiar. For example, the admission rules can be complicated. Eligibility to enter the queue may be skewed because only particular groups are *au courant* of the rules. Or the rules themselves are vague, or require special expertise to interpret. That may also arise because there is a proliferation of the rules about entry. There could be a gatekeeper who exercises his own discretion or reacts to instructions by turning certain applicants away although they may have qualifications to enter.

In the complex line, FIFO may not prevail or it may operate in conjunction with other rules. Where FIFO is absent, there may be service in random order: SIRO. This means the introduction into bureaucratic-administrative distribution of an element of a lottery. There may also be a last in first out rule: LIFO.

There may be priority rules. Applicants are differentiated, ordered into some hierarchy and move to the counter in categories. Queue jumping may be seen as a claim for such priority categorization which has not been legitimated.

In a complex queue, there can be supplementary gates. There may be political tests, tests of religious affiliation, language competence, ethnicity, social class and so forth. They can result in exclusion or priority. Success in one queue might be the gateway to another, as in schooling. Queue jumping and other correctives may become so organized and subject to strain as to form new queues. Where legitimate correctives are used (as with ombudsmen, inquiry units, Parliamentary Commissioners and M.P. "surgeries"), gateways to them can also be set up: in Britain a constituent can only apply to his Member of Parliament and only someone who has so applied can have his case sent to the Parliamentary Commissioner and only if the Member of Parliament decides to do so.

Frequently, once an applicant has come forward, he can barely afford to leave the queue. Some services are processed into several components. There is a series of channels. Each channel provides one item. The applicant might be able to leave after receiving any one of these, or to continue through the series. In such a serial line the applicant would pass through all the channels in turn beginning with the first.

The line can also assume parallel forms providing a number of identical counters to identical service facilities. Similar counters may be fully available where the applicant has open choice between them. As the number and degree of openness and identity of alternative service counters is increased, so an element of market-like distribution has been introduced into the bureaucratic-administrative situation. An applicant who does not like one can, granted this openness and identity, more or less easily move to another counter, rather like his use of exit in a market. (Compare the introduction of lottery-like elements above.) But there may still be admission rules: all the counters may be fully available to some but not at all to others.

The complex counter may deviate from the simple rules in various other ways. The main modification is the intervention of a third party. He may mediate between applicant and server, or serve the applicant as adviser or as advocate, as representative, fixer or agent. He may intervene as a patron in affecting server performance directly or through administrative superiors, or act as a tout and encourage applicants to come forward. Applicants at the counter may be proxy for other applicants or they may be representatives for families, tribes, communities, villages or other groupings.

In the simple queue, the server is meant to be no more than a routine response to categorically simplified signals. In a complex queue the rank and file server will take a more active role. He might adopt elements of other roles, such as the gatekeeper: e.g. turn an applicant away rather than deal with the case. He might decide to interfere with the line by policing it, or telling an applicant who has fulfilled the ordering rules that he has not yet done so. Or he might widen his area of consideration by breaking the rules which enable the applicant to have much data disregarded.

The rank-and-file server might become a friend or an enemy, in fact an enthusiast. In a complex queue, the rank-and-file server might also tend to be a competitor with the applicant. He might be an *ad hoc* recruit to the counter. He might retain his community membership, sharing relationships with the applicants. In the simple queue, the applicant is content to be reduced to a case to be served, and the rank-and-file server will simply respond by handling the case: that is one of the conditions. In a complex queue, the conflict between the applicants' expectations and the rank-and-file servers' interests are inherent, and there will be a severe problem of reconciliation (Schaffer 1970, 41).

The simple queue does not occur. All actual situations of access contain complications. Some complications might make the access relationship easier to handle. Frequently the relationships are more difficult. Most of the situations we study will no doubt be of this sort, as relationships of access move from patronage to protest, riot or crime enter, queueing breaks down, and alternatives dominate.

The queue becomes more difficult where the item of service is a complex package. With a packaged service, the whole package must be taken and not bits of it. There are at least three ways in which this can make things difficult. Access might include conditions of unpleasant even punitive performance, varying from residence on through tax paying and more positive demands such as conscription. Secondly, the applicant might want a discrete item; but it might be provided by the authority inclusively, things wanted with things unwanted or even opposed (as in some population programmes); and frequently service is combined with supervision. Thirdly, some items might be free but others have relatively heavy costs.

The packaging of unpleasant conditions and items together explain something about the unwilling applicant, taxpayer and citizen. It would be stretching the concept of applicant unnecessarily far to cover all degrees of actual avoidance, like deserters. The avoidant is the opposite of the applicant. Generally, the distinction between items and packages of service helps to explain the different perceptions of applicants and of rank-and-file servers, and the relation between applicants and avoidance. Alternatively, the avoidant can also be seen (as in taxation or conscription or land reform) as someone who is an applicant for exemption.

In practice, there is often a question about the degree to which a service should be broken down into highly discrete items or kept in inclusive packages. The more specialized the less likely it is that unpleasant will be included with pleasant items but the more difficult the whole situation of access is for those individuals and groups relatively lacking in resources for access, like migrants. As the State attempts to solve the problem of inadequate resources for handling access by generalizing the service and creating packages, so the relationship between applicant and administering authority becomes less and less like the momentary, interstitial and passing relationships of the queue and more and more like the inclusive relationship of a total institution (Goffman 1970, 13–117). The more significant and the more habitual these sorts of relationship, the greater the dependency of deprived groups tends to become. The queue may be meant for groups or individuals who are relatively weak in the resources necessary to succeed in access situations, like poverty groups. Generally, it is likely either that the complex queue will actually fail to provide satisfactory access for such groups or that totally dependent relationships between the groups and the authorities will be built up.

The simple queue removes conflict and competition. The conditions are accepted. In complicated queues, conflict and competition re-enter at all points, at the gateway, in the line, at the counter, between one applicant and others, between the rank-and-file server and higher levels of the organization, between applicants and the organization, its political leadership and its political allies: even the stability of the specially dependent group can break out into conflict.

Dimensions of bureaucratization

We have discussed the problem of distribution and access, and the way in which certain systems of access, especially the queue, are used. We now add some hypotheses about ways in which the tendency towards bureaucratization in distribution can be studied, along with three dimensions of access culture: *viz* degrees of diffusion, coherence and intrusion or penetration. As there is less recourse to distribution through price competition and market, as the distribution of publicly administered services becomes more significant, society is bureaucratized, planned, welfare-state-like; as this happens, so there is a tendency for access to be provided through arrangements which approximate more or less to (simple) queues. It might be that queues can be used in less highly bureaucratized societies. It might also be that in highly bureaucratized societies queue-like structures might be used less, or at least more at some than at other levels. In any case, the tendency for access to be provided in this way will be marked by the variations, alternatives and breakdowns indicated above.

This hypothetical tendency of bureaucratization to produce more distribution through queue-like structures has three dimensions.

a. Service spread or *diffusion*. This refers to the number of service outputs present and how frequently they are used. This is a quantity.
b. *Coherence*. This refers to the degree of agreement or similarity between (i) the applicant's perception of what the service item or package is about (how and why to apply and what he is likely to get), and (ii) the administrative authority's reasons for supplying the service in this way and its perceptions, accordingly, of what the service contains and will achieve. This is a matter of agreement or disagreement.
c. *Administrative intrusion* or penetration. Intrusion is a vertical process relating the centre to the periphery, level to level in organization, and the service distributing authorities to more or less encapsulated groups and communities. It refers to the evaluation and awareness of service-distributing authorities in the encapsulated situation. This is a matter of valuation.

For example, we can hypothesize that more diffusion will mean that applicants have more analogous experience. On the whole, the greater the number and use of service outputs (that is to say, the greater the amount of service spread and diffusion) the more effective the applicant strategies should be, and the more the applicant should be able to learn the general rules and formulae for effective applicant behaviour. The fewer the service outputs the applicant is engaged with, the greater the likelihood of his misinterpreting the behaviour which he meets with at the counter.

Then there is a marked difference in degrees of coherence between one situation and another. The less coherence between applicant and authority the more conflict there is likely to be between, for example, the rank-and-file server and the applicant at the counter about "the case"; between one and another applicant in the line about their relative ordering; and between applicant and non-applicant, or applicant and gatekeeper at the gate. There will be conflict between the self-perception of the applicant and the way in which he has to be defined as a case for the service itself. The rank and file server will conflict with the authority supervising him about the way in which he may use the rules about "disregards" which allow "passing" by applicants, and about the amount of attention which he provides for the applicant.

A second aspect of coherence is the conceptualization of the timing of service by the applicant and the authority. The applicant needs some experience and confidence in a service before he can assume that it will have any continuity. This then enables him to make rational calculations about spacing out his applications. His notion of the time at which the service should be applied for should fit the supplying authorities' notions. In the case of education, the service thinks of it as supplied daily and applied for annually. The applicant might think of it as something worthwhile mainly on a seasonal basis.

This coherence of experience and conceptualization is necessary for relatively rational and limited queues. Where queues degenerate either into camps or riots, it might be because these conditions are absent. The greater the coherence about time between applicant and service authorities the less the likelihood of degeneration.

We can distinguish three sorts of situation. At one extreme, the people whom the designers of the services think of as potential applicants are living in encapsulated communities. They do not come forward as applicants, indeed they may seek to avoid situations in which applications and contact are expected of them. At the other extreme, applicants are relatively confident that they can create fresh demands, play a positive role in initiating further services and in shaping the items, that is to say, a pluralist, reformist political culture. Between these two extremes of encapsulated and adaptive societies lie the areas in which we are largely interested. Here the applicants have to develop strategies for procuring the services they want, for avoidance and for redressing their grievances as applicants one way or another. They are variously affected by the intrusion of services into their lives, and by the number of services which become available through processes of diffusion, and there is uncertain coherence between their views of services and the views of the service designers.

Discontinuity and instabilities in the access situation

Discontinuities occur between levels of institutions and public action and between elements of the access structures. The rules will also be subject to constant change. The greater the discontinuities and the more unstable the rules, the greater the modification of the access situation away from the queue. Five categories of modification occur. They may ease or worsen the problems of queue behaviour. Insofar as they worsen them, they can lead to breakdowns or the presence of alternative structures.

    a. *Grouping*. Applicants may act on behalf of groups. They may be treated as members of groups, punitively or otherwise. Grouping might be felt or enforced.

    b. *The use of intermediaries*. These would be employed in interventions at key points of the structure: gateway, line or counter; as alternatives to the structure, or as redress for it. Intervention may occur through the initiative of the applicant or through the initiative of the intermediary, or in other ways.

c. *Role flexibility and instability.* Particular applicants and other actors may from time to time take on different roles, like applicants who become intermediaries on behalf of other applicants; servers who become applicants; applicants who become servers; and so forth.

d. *Ceremonies:* addresses, welcomes, rituals, signs.

e. *Structural breakdowns.* These can be studied quantitatively: for example, numbers of exclusions, length of line or wait. They can also be studied qualitatively: for example, in looking at the difference between expectations and outcomes of service. The breakdowns can also be categorized in opposites, like camps and riots and in patterns, like the entry of alternative systems of distribution; failures, like failures to take up a service, can be studied; training, advertising, and so forth. Most actual breakdowns can then be noted and categorized as either (1) a refusal to queue at all (avoidance etc.), or (2) the entry of non-bureaucratic administrative systems of distribution (corruption, ascription, markets etc.).

Conclusions

The systems which account (partly) for the distribution of life chances have peculiar characteristics in situations of underdevelopment; special problems of entry into markets; and, limitations of resources, knowledge, skill and rationality of applicants, types of group and other loyalties which affect the continuity or ordering of their preferences. They are reflections of gaps and discontinuities, poverty and inequalities. What we are studying is in part such problems of access as indicate and result precisely from these characteristics.

Actual access situations will then reveal a good deal about politics: the strategies and reactions of applicant groups, the sorts of political language, ideologies and other resources which constrain or affect these reactions, the political hopes which lie behind the systems of distribution, like real or mythical efforts to "include the excluded". Again, the gaps between ideology and outcome, between large claims and programmes at one level, and individual experience at another, will be revealed through the levels of institutional arrangements. At one level there is the whole experience of organizational connection. At other political and institutional levels there is the way in which what in the end is provided are discrete, limited and contingent items of bureaucratic output: not so much life chances as bits and pieces of services.

Much of the distributive systems in developing societies are bureaucratic-administrative. These are at once particularly important (the position of the State mechanism, the inadequacy of infrastructure outside the public sector) and difficult to operate (the demands and the withdrawals, the dysfunctions of bureaucratic administration in underdeveloped societies and programmes of development, and complications of combined State/party, central/local, cooperative and other agencies). So we are looking at access in bureaucratic administrative systems where such systems of distribution will have at once extra degrees of significance, an extra difficulty in operation on either side of the counter, and peculiar possibilities and outcomes. As with the imperfections of distributive systems generally, these characteristics will vary situation by situation but the questions will be the same and are of central significance for development: like equality schemes.

The ways in which bureaucratic administrative systems of distribution employ queue structures are likely to be peculiarly complex, and liable to breakdown or alteration in underdeveloped societies. This applies to the very structures or elements of the queue itself, the gatekeepers, the line behaviour, the relations between applicant and official at the counter. On the one hand, methods by which the structures of the queue can be made to operate more easily are likely to be less available in the poorer and discontinuous society. On the other hand, the drive towards complication and difficulty is likely to be greater, and breakdown and alternatives the more frequent. Indeed, in some situations, it is likely that bureaucratic administrative distribution systems will be, despite the decisions of the centre and the content of the plans, totally impossible. Corruption, crime, riot, encapsulation, internal war, lack of civil peace and order; these stand at the opposite remove from the supposed, assumed or intended systems of distribution; but they are frequently how they work. It is of the first importance to understand what these systems actually are, are supposed to be and might become.

Can we look also for changes which are not merely possible but could be recommended? Can we look for some practical applications here including detailed points of design, suggested by the analysis of the access structure? Changes are presumably possible with rules at every stage of gateway, line and counter. At the other extreme, the possibility of changes is wide and very radical indeed. Let us give some instances of what might come out of research into access situations. In the first place, there is the conundrum of the special dependency groups. Those for whom services (like technical training) are ideologically intended, tend to be the least able to gain the benefit and are frequently those more harmed or ignored by the actual operation of the services as they are delivered. On the other hand, those groups which stand in most anguished need of service can become totally dependent on the delivery of services the more significant the services are for them. For some access is liberating, in its rules, methods and distributive effects. For others, the outcome is quite different. The rearrangement of distribution and access might find some answers to problems of special dependency groups like Apache Indians, or Aleuts, or some migrants or Irish itinerants (Schaffer 1974).

Secondly, we see a tendency to unintended exclusion of groups by badly planned definition of the categories. We see too heavy a problem of documentation and demonstration imposed on applicants; we see conflicting roles imposed on rank and file servers. All this can presumably be altered and redesigned. The very definition of a public policy or a planned programme means categorization. The record of implementation is then often disappointing. One reaction is to demand still more data, more documentation, more proceduralization. This is likely to produce still more unexpected and unwanted outcomes. But this can be understood, and it is not inevitable.

Thirdly, applicants do not always come forward to take up the services designed for them. Is this because the service has a stigma? Is it because the service consists not of wanted items but of unwanted and frightening packages? Is it because the general experience of access has been disappointing, painful, even punitive and destructive? Is it because the rank and file officials move out of the simplified role of server into the role of enthusiast or of competitor, rival, opponent, leader or judge?

It is not only in underdeveloped societies that such questions of dependency, planning and stigma are significant. Coincident with the Aranda scandals in France which revealed to the actors themselves the problems of the "blocked society", of the dysfunctions of lobbying and of corruption, the French set up their own (Ripoche) enquiry into the "relations between the administered and the administration". They seemed to seek for solutions in generalized pleas for decentralization, as though access relations are somehow necessarily easier with a local than with a central government bureaucracy. A moment's reflection will show the limitations of this sort of ideological and unanalysed evaluation. But it is possible to design alternative access relationships. Schaffer (1970, 41) has elsewhere discussed the cafeteria as an alternative distribution in certain conditions. Community development and self-help seek to solve these problems of distribution by pretending that the applicant can become the official. The cafeteria suggests ways in which the role of choice by the applicant can be extended. It uses possibilities of participation by the applicant in the serving process which lie well within his limited resources, as long as the service itself is simplified. This is a sort of intermediate technology of public administration.

In the end, there are two points which matter here. The first is that it is a clear implication of this approach that within the structure of implementation and at the level of programme planning, much more attention needs to be given to the design of service as well as to the mere allocation of aggregate resources. In particular the design of service needs to be disaggregated down to the level of task, procedure, method and performance control (Chambers and Belshaw 1973). The way in which this will strike the applicant on the other side of the counter, and indeed outside the queue altogether, has to be found out. The design of services, in fact, has to be built on certain inputs of action and developmental research. Research into access would have to become a central, indeed an initial and an evaluative part of the process of planning, policy-making and design. The implications may reach a long way.

The second point is that bureaucratic and administratively distributed services already have, as a usual matter, opportunities for supervision appeal and administrative referral and feedback. Plural societies assume processes of political articulation and aggregation to provide redress at other levels. The point is partly that the administrative processes do not always work, as they have their own problem of access; and partly that underdeveloped societies tend not to be functional pluralities, systems of constitutional limited and republican politics of this sort. What in the end the argument about access suggests is the significance of political redress to institutional outcomes. Where there are systems of no or limited alternatives, political and social redress will be sought for. What the argument about access amounts to is that where bureaucratic administrative systems of distribution are significant in society, administrative redress will not be sufficient. Existing systems of political and social linkage tend to be inadequate in most societies, and new forms of political redress are therefore required. Research into the point of access provides an indication of why this is so, and what even it might be.

Notes

1. Cf. Schaffer and Lamb (1974). It would not be right to see this as an exclusive sequence (application, rejection, acquiescence or fight). It is a situation in which much is anticipation and coincidence.
2. *The Times*, 29/9/1972, p. 14.
3. The approach outlined here is related to several blocks of work in development studies and the social sciences. The sociology of organizations, for example, has a great deal on relations between clients and closed (or "total") institutions, as industrial sociology does on the possibilities of job enrichment and the criticism of hierarchy. Both are relevant in the understanding of the relationship between applicant and counter official. There is a potential debate between the institution-building school (see e.g. Eaton 1972) and others who hold that institutions are what provide limited access to bad services (e.g. Illich 1972a, 1972b; Reimer 1971). Neither school has taken the studies of collective decision-making or the "strict theory of politics" or of distinct organizational styles fully into account, and for the most part the sociology of queues has looked at them as group situations irrespective of their function of providing access to services.
4. Standard usages in applied mathematical queueing theory, such as FIFO, can be employed usefully in this context (see e.g. Saaty 1961). It should be noted that what we mean here by *the simple queue* is conceptually different from the "simplest" of the theoretical models in mathematical queueing theory, that is $M/M/1$: $(OO/FIFO)$, where the emphasis is on rates of flow and capacity of queueing systems. Our emphasis is on the norms and procedures which determine patterns of output and which influence applicant and administrative behaviour.

References

BLAU, Peter M. (1955) *The Dynamics of Bureaucracy: A Study of Inter-personal Relations in Two Government Agencies*, University of Chicago Press, Chicago.

CHAMBERS, Robert and BELSHAW, Deryke (1973) "Managing rural development", *IDS Discussion Paper* No. 15, Institute of Development Studies, Brighton.

276   Bernard Schaffer and Huang Wen-hsien

DAHL, Robert A. and LINDBLOM, Charles E. (1953) *Politics, Economics and Welfare*, Harper, New York.
EATON, Joseph (ed.) (1972) *Institution-building and Development*, Sage, Beverly Hills.
GERTH, H. H. and MILLS, C. Wright (eds.) (1948) *From Max Weber: Essays in Sociology*, Routledge, London.
GOFFMAN, Erving (1970) *Asylums: Essays on the Social Situation of Mental Patients and Other Inmates*, Penguin, Harmondsworth.
GRIFFIN, Keith (1972) *Economic Aspects of Technical Change in the Rural Areas of Monsoon Asia*, United Nations Research Institute for Social Development, Geneva.
HIRSCHMAN, Albert O. (1970) *Exit, Voice and Loyalty: Responses to Decline in Firms, Organizations and States*, Harvard University Press, Cambridge, Mass.
ILLICH, Ivan D. (1972a) *Deschooling Society*, Calder and Boyars, London.
ILLICH, Ivan D. (1972b) *Celebration of Awareness*, Calder and Boyars, London.
MYRDAL, Gunnar (1968) *Asian Drama: An Enquiry into the Poverty of Nations*, Allen Lane, London.
PEATTIE, Lisa (1968) *The View from the Barrio*, University of Michigan Press, Ann Arbor.
REIMER, Everett (1971) *School is Dead: An Essay on Alternatives in Education*, Penguin, Harmondsworth.
SAATY, T. L. (1961) *The Elements of Queueing Theory with Applications*, McGraw-Hill, New York.
SCHAFFER, Bernard (1970) "Social planning as administrative decision-making", in Raymond Apthorpe (ed.), *People, Planning and Development Studies*, Frank Cass, London, pp. 29-46.
SCHAFFER, Bernard (1972) "Easiness of access: a concept of queues", *IDS Communications*, Institute of Development Studies, Brighton.
SCHAFFER, Bernard (1973) *The Administrative Factor*, Frank Cass, London.
SCHAFFER, Bernard (1974) "Some poverty themes and Irish facts: policy makers have their needs too", *IDS Discussion Paper* No. 50, Institute of Development Studies, Brighton.
SCHAFFER, Bernard and LAMB, Geoff (1974) "Exit, Voice and Access", *Social Science Information*, Vol. 13 (6), pp. 73-90.
SELZNICK, P. (1949) *TVA and the Grassroots*, University of California Press, Berkeley.
SIMON, Herbert A. (1957) *Models of Man, Social and Rational*, Wiley, New York.

CHAPTER 16

Extending credit and technical assistance to the smallest enterprises*

JEFFREY ASHE

One of the most striking features of urban economies in the Third World are the hawkers who shout their wares in the markets and the "micro-entrepreneurs" who repair shoes, make brooms and sew clothing in the back alleys and shanty-towns. Depending on the country, from 20 per cent to 50 per cent of the urban labour force works in these smallest economic enterprises, where start-up capital ranges from a few dollars to a few hundred dollars. In the poorest neighbourhoods, more families own businesses than not and these families make up a substantial part of the city's poor. Net business income often averages that of an unskilled labourer. The man peddling a heavily-laden cargo bike ten hours a day might earn twice that much on a good day, while the woman selling cigarettes, sweets and chewing-gum may earn considerably less. In many countries, the percentage employed in these smallest enterprises is increasing as larger-scale businesses and other sectors

*An original essay summarizing the results of three years of research and programme development on direct assistance to the smallest economic activities of the urban poor carried out in Africa, Asia and Latin America. This effort, known as the PISCES Project (Programme for Investment in the Small Capital Enterprise Sector) was financed by the Agency for International Development, Office of Urban Development, Bureau of Science and Technology, contract number DS-OTR-C-0013, Small Enterprise Approaches to Employment PISCES, Phase I. A second phase of this project (contract number AID-OTR-C-1823) is now underway and demonstration projects that reach the smallest enterprises in six countries will be set up and evaluated. The final report on PISCES, Phase I, is available from the AID Project Manager, Michael Farbman. The Prime Contractor for both phases of the project, ACCION International/AITEC, is responsible for the technical direction of the project, the Latin American fieldwork, and the synthesis of the study results. The African and Asian components have been subcontracted to the Development Group for Alternative Policies and Partnership for Productivity, respectively. All three agencies are Private and Voluntary Organizations (PVOs) with years of experience in small enterprise development. The PISCES team consists of: AID Project Manager, Michael Farbman; Project Director, Jeffrey Ashe, ACCION/AITEC. African team: Fred O'Regan, Douglas Hellinger, The Development Group for Alternative Policies. Asia team: Jason Brown, Partnership for Productivity. Latin American team: Peter Fraser, William Tucker, ACCION/AITEC.

have proved incapable of expanding rapidly enough to meet the employment requirements of growing populations.

Despite their importance, the continued growth and profitability of these smallest enterprises is hindered by several factors. Lack of small amounts of capital is the problem most frequently mentioned by business owners. In the Philippines, for example, 83 per cent of the micro-entrepreneurs interviewed felt credit was their most important need, and the most important service that could be rendered by direct assistance programmes (Farbman (ed.) 1981, 41 and 151). Many mentioned their desire to own their own means of production; a cargo bike peddlar in Santo Domingo complains that he spends one-third of his daily income to rent his bike; a tailor in Indonesia spends U.S. $2 a day on the rental of his sewing machine; a shoemaker in Quito rents a machine at another shop to attach the shoes' uppers to the lowers. With a loan of less than U.S. $300, each of these business owners could purchase the equipment they rent, and for a one-year loan the daily quota would be less than the rental fee.

Other problems include lack of business skills; restrictions, regulation and harassment by local authorities; lack of reliable sources of raw materials and supplies; and lack of adequate markets, especially in areas where population growth and economic development have stagnated or are declining.

Since so many depend on these tiny businesses, some development experts suggest they should be assisted directly. But, direct assistance to the smallest economic enterprises of the urban poor is controversial. Some suggest that scarce development funds would be better spent investing in larger enterprises or in the rural areas with the expectation that benefits would eventually "trickle down" to the urban poor. Others worry that a programme that assists some businesses would necessarily worsen the position of other poor business owners, if the overall demand for the goods and services produced and consumed at this level does not increase.[1]† Most agree that even if it were desirable to assist these businesses, administrative costs would be excessive and the risks of default would be too high.

While the issue of best allocation of scarce development resources and static demand for the products manufactured and sold by micro-businesses are extremely important, they are beyond the scope of this discussion. It will be shown, however, that the smallest economic activities of the urban poor can be assisted effectively and at reasonable cost. Examples of programmes are cited (see also Farbman (ed.) 1981) which reached up to 3,000 businesses in less than two years with initial loans ranging from U.S. $10 to $300. Other types of programmes helped the poor start new businesses by providing loans of less than U.S. $100 to start hawking, or selling prepared food. Our research also shows that it is possible to train poor youths in higher paying skills and help them start new businesses, or help them establish cooperative businesses

---

† Superscript numbers refer to Notes at end of chapter.

where people working together are able to pool resources and equipment, and produce and sell collectively.

The paper is divided into three parts. The first part describes the levels of enterprises that are reached by direct assistance programmes, and the assistance methodologies that attend each level. The second part discusses the programmatic and operational details of specific types of projects. The paper concludes with the implications of these findings for practitioners and donors.

I. Levels of beneficiaries and types of projects

One major finding of PISCES, Phase I, was that within the category of the smaller businesses in Third World cities, there are distinct levels of beneficiaries that correspond closely with the most appropriate type of project assistance. At the lowest level (Level One) people do whatever they must to subsist. They do not perceive themselves as entrepreneurs, nor do they conceive of their money-making activities as "business opportunities". Activities are often extremely ephemeral—selling chewing-gum or cigarettes on a corner, or colas and sweets during parades.

People at the next level (Level Two) have a fundamental understanding of business practices and have a viable going concern. They may make tortillas, or sew clothes on an old treadle sewing machine, or hawk an assortment of clothing or toys, or sell prepared food. Level Two entrepreneurs will invest whatever resources are available—be it capital, raw materials, skills, effort, time or ingenuity—into their businesses.

At Level Three, business owners have better business skills. They understand the basic principles governing their markets better and are flexible enough to expand when the opportunity arises. Examples of businesses at this level might be a shoemaker with a small rented shop who has an assistant, or a family of tailors who divide their living area with a cloth to create a workshop.

People without business, or whose businesses are marginal (Level One), are often assisted by community based development programmes. These efforts are concerned as much with access to such basic services as health, education, nutrition and sanitation, as with enterprise development and income generation. Enterprise development usually involves creating new individual and group businesses to provide enough income to meet basic needs, while helping to increase self-esteem and self worth. In turn, that process, as part of an integrated community development effort, tends to promote the collective solution of problems in the community. Promotion among the very poorest is intensive and long-term. This reflects the time-consuming tasks of directly promoting and organizing projects which include several elements in addition to enterprise development.

Where poor community residents already own very small or Level Two micro-enterprises that have at least a potential to produce enough income to meet basic family needs, programmes often focus on creating small informal groups within the community made up of business owners. Groups are generally set up to collectively guarantee loans.

Level Three micro-entrepreneurs who have an acceptable inventory, a credit history, and/or someone willing to co-sign the loan for them, can be reached by innovative bank programmes. These businesses are far smaller than those traditionally served by banks and government small enterprise assistance programmes but, compared to the typical beneficiaries of community and group programmes, their owners have better developed business skills and more capital.

II. Direct assistance programmes

The programmes studied in PISCES, Phase I, fall into two general categories: (1) *enterprise development programmes* which provide credit and sometimes organizational and rudimentary management assistance to already existing businesses; and (2) *integrated programmes* which, in addition to providing credit and management assistance, often create new individual and collective enterprises and offer vocational training, generally within the context of a community improvement effort.

Enterprise development programmes

Enterprise development programmes which assist existing businesses effectively rely on the ability of the owner of the business to produce more and/or sell more. Existing businesses are assisted because the very process of translating an idea into an enterprise, even if that enterprise consists of little more than a few baskets filled with produce, demonstrates that the owner has the required skills and that the business is viable.

If properly designed and administered, these projects improve on the money-lender, generally the only alternative source of credit for businesses at the smallest levels. They provide money at lower interest rates, in larger amounts, and for longer periods. Often with two or three small loans, the entrepreneur can "think big", and see the potential for progress.

There are two types of programmes reaching existing businesses; group programmes which tend to reach enterprises at Level Two; and individual programmes which tend to reach slightly larger enterprises at Level Three.

Credit or solidarity group programmes[2]

Of the programmes studied, the ones achieving the largest degree of success in reaching Level Two were the Working Women's Forum in Madras[3] and the

PRIDECO/FEDECCREDITO programme in San Salvador.[4] These programmes each provided loans to nearly 3,000 business owners in less than two years. Loans averaged U.S. $10 to $36 in Madras, and U.S. $80 to $200 in San Salvador. Payback in both programmes was close to 99 per cent. Since administrative costs for this type of programme are only 5 per cent to 8 per cent of the total amount lent, this type of programme may be able to cover its costs, and further capitalize its loan fund, assuming a very low default rate and an adequate interest rate.

Directors of a new programme in the Dominican Republic organized by the Dominican Development Foundation,[5] adapted the methodologies used in both these programmes to local conditions. In its first eight months, this programme has enrolled 1,600 hawkers and vendors. Loans have been approved for 450 business owners. Payback is near 100 per cent.

The established programmes in Madras and San Salvador, and the new one in Santo Domingo, use essentially the same mechanisms to extend credit—the solidarity or credit group. These self-formed groups are made up of from five to ten owners of very small businesses who accept collective responsibility to pay the loan made to the group. Each group member uses his or her portion of the loan to invest in his or her individual business. Group members pay their quota to the group leader daily. Depending on the programme a collector/promoter from the programme collects the loans for the group from the group leader, or the group leader pays the bank or loaning institution directly. The solidarity group commitment is the only guarantee required in these programmes.

This simple mechanism avoids the major problems of extending credit to this level, poor payback and high administrative costs. Promotion, group formation and selection are largely in the hands of the beneficiaries. The solidarity group concept can also be easily understood by illiterates or semi-illiterates. It can be boiled down to a few simple concepts—"band together in small groups", "if you do not pay back your loans we all pay"—that can be spread by word of mouth. The experiences in Madras, San Salvador and Santo Domingo demonstrate that after the first few groups are funded, members will take it upon themselves to enroll their friends and neighbours and will do so in a way that conveys an understanding of the requisite sense of responsibility upon which such programmes depend. Furthermore, these experiences show that neighbourhood residents depend on their networks of friendship and kinship in order to decide who is trustworthy and whom to choose to associate with. It has proved extremely difficult for field staff to understand these networks well enough to form viable groups.

The following features of the programmes studied account for their extremely high payback rates:

1. The solidarity group concept and the need for 100 per cent payback is carefully explained at each step in the loan granting process.

2. The first loan is generally very small and is used for working capital that can be paid back in from three months to a year. This first loan is a test for the solidarity group. The risk is minimal for the business owners and for the programme.
3. Groups that do not pay their loans are eliminated from further participation in the programme.
4. Loan payback—often daily to the group leader— is similar to the daily payments made to money-lenders that business owners are familiar with.
5. Loan promoter/collectors consider only the weekly quota for the group, not the amount paid by each individual. If, for example, in a group of seven, only five pay, all the group members are credited with five daily payments. Two more daily payments are added to the next week's quota. Non-payment by individuals in the group quickly becomes a problem to be solved by the group.
6. In the Santo Domingo programme, if a loan payment is late or incomplete, a delegation of group leaders is immediately formed to visit the group. In that programme, all lending activity is halted until the problem is resolved, thus again reinforcing the principle of group solidarity.

This concern with loan payback has several positive aspects. A low default rate avoids the depletion of the loan fund and helps ensure continuing funding from outside sources. Equally important, paying the weekly loan presents a concrete problem for the group to solve which in turn reinforces group cohesion. If an individual has a problem in payment, the group rather than the programme staff must step in to help. This experience has made it easier for the group to take on other roles such as helping members through family emergencies, purchasing, selling or producing collectively, or becoming involved in community activities.

Through the organization of solidarity groups into an association, the other complimentary elements of a programme, such as community development, collective economic activities and the exchange of ideas between groups, progress more rapidly. In the Working Women's Forum, for example, group leaders who make up the Board of Directors have worked to lessen police harassment and improve physical conditions in the markets.

Individual programmes

Slightly larger micro-enterprises are often reached by innovative projects of commercial banks. Experiences in these programmes were also very encouraging. Banks can often cover their costs or even make a profit delivering these loans. Once their first loans are paid, this first success often leads to a subsequent more formal credit arrangement between banks and micro-business owners.

1. *Bank of Baroda, Calcutta*

The Bank's Multi-Service Centre administers its portfolio of 4,000 loans to micro-enterprises with only ten loan officers. Each loan officer is responsible for administering 400 loans and for securing new clients. Interestingly, as in the credit group programmes described earlier, bank officials group their clients by communities, and depend on recommendations from other clients to involve new business owners. Administrative costs average less than 10 per cent of the amount lent because lending requirements specify a minimum of processing and supervision. Loan payback in this programme has been about 90 per cent.

2. *Philippine Commercial and Industrial Bank (PCIB)*

The PCIB, through its seventy "Money Shops" scattered throughout the country, provides credit to established commercial stall holders in public and private markets. To qualify for a minimum loan of U.S. $125, the stall holder must have average daily sales of at least U.S. $7.50 and net profits of at least 25 per cent. Loan instalments are paid daily. Each Money Shop operates from a stall in a public or private market where there is a concentration of 400–800 sellers. A Money Shop has four employees, of which at least one is drawn from the leadership of the local market, thus ensuring that the Bank will know that it is lending to good credit risks. By aggressively expanding into this market, the PCIB gains loyal clients, a significant expansion of its portfolio, and an important source of profits.

The Money Shops were expected to lend U.S. $3 million in 1980 in amounts ranging from U.S. $125 to $1,250. No figures were available from the bank on administrative costs per loan. It is clear, however, that the bank is making a profit on these loans, since seven other financial institutions are now competing for this lucrative and expanding market.

3. *Banco del Pacifico, Ecuador*

This Bank makes small loans to established artisan manufacturers with good credit histories and co-signers. In contrast to the other projects, a credit proposal for each business is completed and a plan for utilizing the loan funds is developed in detail. These steps raise administrative costs to 10 per cent of the value of the loan. All field work is completed by part-time university students with no business training. The Banco del Pacifico has a portfolio of 900 loans to small artisan manufacturers. Nearly 400 new jobs have been created in these businesses, monthly sales have doubled, and income to business owners has increased significantly. Loan payback is well over 90 per cent.

Although the projects directly administered by banks span diverse countries, they share three important characteristics:

1. *A separate unit in the bank with specially oriented, highly dedicated personnel for this type of lending activity.*
2. *Very simple methodologies for processing and administering loans.*
3. *Formal contractual relationships, but with formalities held to a minimum.*

The projects demonstrate that at this level, business owners often have realistic plans for business expansion. They also demonstrate that these businesses can expand sales and cut costs without written records or more formal management skills. Credit is frequently the principal constraint, not entrepreneurial skill. By keeping loans small (generally from U.S. $200 to $1,000), and by having frequent loan repayments and stressing tight supervision, these projects avoid the high default rates which plague so many credit programmes.

Some of those who received credit may eventually want to make more substantial investments in equipment and inventories. The adoption of formal record-keeping and other formal management practices was seen to be a prerequisite for larger loans, in the absence of which borrowers had trouble making repayments, and businesses often failed.

Integrated programmes

Several of the projects studied created new individual and collective businesses, and provided marketing outlets outside the local community and/or job skills training. Most of these efforts are part of comprehensive community development programmes.

Their concern is not only enterprise development *per se* and the increase in income and employment that this might bring; equal emphasis is given to improving the overall socio-economic conditions of those assisted. Consequently, these projects focus on needs ranging from health and housing to active involvement in community improvement activities.

Examples of four of the most innovative of those types of projects are presented below.

1. Bangalur Layout, Bangalore, India[6]

Located in one of the poorest communities in Bangalore, this project moved into enterprise development after five successful years of integrated community development. The project works intensively with 120 families that have a strong interest in "improving themselves". With the assistance of a local bank, the project has facilitated the financing of new businesses, with average loans of U.S. $61.25. These small commercial operations are identical to those commonly found in the community, so no additional skills or management training are necessary. Business ideas are presented to the staff by those who are soliciting the loan, so a commitment to the business to be started has already developed. Administrative costs are nominal for this programme because it is largely run by community volunteers. Loan payback is close to 100 per cent.

2. *National Christian Council of Kenya (NCCK)*[7]

The NCCK works in primary and secondary cities through the country. The vast majority of their beneficiaries are extremely poor women. Most have incomes of approximately U.S. $15 per month and have on the average 6.5 dependents. They have very little "business" experience and very low skill levels.

The NCCK programme both assists existing enterprises and helps in the establishment of new cooperative enterprises in conjunction with other community improvement efforts. These simple cooperative ventures— promoted by NCCK social workers with no special expertise in enterprise development—use the skills people already have, such as sewing and animal husbandry, as their starting point. The groups which are formed market their goods collectively, sometimes through shops run by the NCCK, and have arranged for collective purchase of raw materials. Sometimes group members work in the same shop together. When these groups are successful, administrative costs are only moderate and beneficiaries greatly increase their incomes.

3. *Village Polytechnic Programme, Kenya*[8]

This programme provides training for youth at a low cost compared to traditional vocational education projects. It does so by involving the community in an assessment that determines the skills needed in the local community and utilizes local skilled artisans as trainers. Early in their training, the youth sell part of their products together to defray part of the training costs. Part of the sales income is deposited in a fund that will establish a cooperative enterprise for the group after the training programme has been completed. This fund is also used to purchase tools to help Polytechnic leavers to set up new group and individual businesses.

Village polytechnics are set up at the initiative of the local community with little staff intervention. After two years of successful operation, the polytechnic is eligible for government assistance to expand the programme but the programme is structured so that the initiative remains with the local community.

4. Centre d'Education a la Promotion Collective (CEPAC), and Institut Panafricain pour le Développement (IPD), Cameroon

These two organizations, engaged in community development activities, began in the late 1970s to integrate artisan assistance activities into their respective programmes in two major cities. CEPAC's initial artisan-assistance efforts centred on a poor community of 50,000 people in Yaoundé. Although not primarily a small business assistance organization, CEPAC effectively integrated artisan development activities into its community organizing and training, placing emphasis upon the formation of an artisan organization, the creation of a cooperative for artisan purchasing of raw materials and the guaranteeing of broad-based community control through the coordination of all activities by representative community-action committees. In addition, CEPAC assisted in undertaking local marketing analyses for the identification of viable product lines.

Similarly, in an extremely poor but well organized settlement of 100,000 people in Douala, the IPD has been building up a local artisan association and credit union as a basis for activities designed to enhance community self reliance. It has also assisted in organizing production groups so as to form credit guarantee mechanisms and facilitate the bulk purchase of raw materials; delivered managerial and accounting assistance to local artisans; and helped identify and introduce new product lines.

In contrast to the enterprise assistance programmes described earlier, with the exception of the Bangalur Layout Project, the integrated programmes deliver services through enterprise groups. There are strong arguments in favour of forming enterprise groups in this type of programme.

— They involve the community residents who do not have the entrepreneurial skills or ability necessary to start their own businesses.
— There is a greater possibility of learning new skills and earning more income.
— Cooperatives have better access to national and international markets; problems of competition in the local market are lessened.
— Fixed and variable costs are lessened because equipment can be shared and production can be organized more efficiently.
— Cooperative members will be more inclined to become involved in other community improvement activities because they have learned to work in a group.

Creating any kind of a new enterprise is difficult; a cooperative enterprise often presents particular problems. Group members have to learn to administer a business far more complex than those owned by other poor people with whom they may be acquainted. Formal record-keeping systems must be adopted, and people have to learn to work collectively. In contrast to enterprise development efforts where staff works briefly with each business, each enterprise must be worked with intensively. Benefits to those served, however, may be much greater. A choice seems possible between projects working with individual businesses and group enterprises, depending on local conditions.

Characteristics of effective projects

Despite the diversity of beneficiaries, the different types of implementing organizations and the varied environments in which they operate, in the most effective projects, we found one precept to be universally valid: programme inputs reflect the plans and desires of those they serve, and, to the degree possible, stay close to the level of skills and knowledge that commonly exists in the community. When this precept is violated, project complexity and cost per beneficiary increase, while the number of people who can be served decreases proportionately. Programmes which follow this precept tend to be simple and low cost, and they actively involve the community or groups in the planning process.

The following specific components that reflect this basic precept were present in the effective projects:

1. Design

Every project is a product of an extended process of project design as well as a continuous process of evolution. Most were developed only after an intensive exercise was carried out to identify the problems of poor people. Most important, the major source of programme modifications seems to have been the daily interaction with programme beneficiaries.

2. Staffing

It was frequently observed that the field staff of these programmes are not trained in business. Their most important skills are the ability to relate to people in poor communities and to facilitate grass-roots organizations. Staff must see project beneficiaries as capable and able to advance themselves through their economic activities. Paternalistic staff who see clients as incapable of making major decisions on their own, or who see a need to tightly control the enterprises they assist, were rarely successful.

3. Outreach

No programme we studied simply opened a micro-enterprise office in a central location and started to provide services. It is doubtful that such an effort could be successful, even if tried. To reach the poorest community residents, project staff first have to promote the idea directly in the community. Once the programme and the staff are accepted in the community, and community residents can see positive results, the programme generally spreads rapidly by word of mouth.

4. Selection

Working within the goal of helping the most needy, the most important selection criterion seems to be the individual's reputation among other community residents and local business owners. For example, in group programmes, members determine who is sufficiently credit-worthy to form the group. This is a serious decision, since, depending on the project, either the group leader or other members are responsible in case of default by any individual.

5. Credit

Assuming that the programme has selected a good client, the following generalizations about granting and collecting on very small loans can be drawn from the programmes studied:

a. *Loan amounts:* The first loan should be very small. It tests the individual's ability to repay and avoids over-burdening the business with more money than can be invested wisely.

b. *Terms:* A first loan to existing businesses should be for no more than three to six months. A series of small loans in increasingly larger amounts paid back quickly represents a manageable risk to both the businesses and the programme.

c. *Interest rates:* If interest rates do not cover costs, financial institutions will have little incentive to lend. While those who receive loans at concessionary rates have an important advantage, many others, equally well-qualified, will not receive loans because of lack of funds.

d. *Frequency of loan payback:* The loan payback periods should reflect the cashflow cycle of the economic activity in question, and the time frame in which *the client* is used to thinking. Hawkers and vendors generally pay their group leaders daily, since they purchase and sell their stock daily. In other programmes, loan payback is geared to monthly income.

e. *Loan payback:* Programmes should be very business-like about loan payback if they are to maintain good relations with financial institutions, encourage good habits among beneficiaries and avoid the depletion of the loan fund.

6. Job skills training

Programmes should combine job skills training with business training and intensive follow-up, if the job skills are going to be put into practice.

7. Marketing

Perhaps the most effective approach for dealing with marketing problems is to identify carefully the demand for skills and products within local communities and then match the areas of training and enterprise promotion to these needs. Another effective approach involves the direct intervention of the assistance organization in the identification or establishment of marketing channels for client enterprises, most notably when the best potential markets are located in distant regions of the same country or in foreign countries.

III. Implications for donors

The number of projects studied is small, and their scale is relatively limited in relation to the total needs of the countries concerned. Yet these experimental efforts show that the smallest economic activities of the urban poor *can* be assisted, often very effectively. Assistance is delivered through a variety of programmes, with objectives appropriate to the strikingly different needs of the various levels of beneficiaries.

The diversity of the organizations that implement these programmes is broad: they include small local non-governmental organizations such as the Working Women's Forum and the Bangalur Layout; more sophisticated non-governmental organizations such as the NCCK and the Dominican Development Foundation, government efforts such as the Village Polytechnic Programme, and commercial banks.

Despite their diversity, these organizations share the following characteristics:

1. Strong, highly respected leaders who have a commitment to assisting the poor.
2. An extremely dedicated and hard-working field staff who want to be involved in a programme they believe in.
3. Decentralized organizational structures which extend decision-making responsibility to field staff and a high degree of autonomy which allows field staff the flexibility to adopt strategies they feel are appropriate.
4. Simple, easily understood, cost-effective methodologies that are immediately relevant to people's needs.

If donors want to assist this sector, they will have to find ways to work with these organizations and support their projects. They will have to find ways to accommodate and support very decentralized and flexible small-scale projects.

There are four levels at which donors can facilitate the projects reaching the bottom of the economic scale. They can:

— Strengthen small ongoing local non-governmental business development efforts, or enable small local non-governmental organizations with strong community programmes to begin PISCES level business development efforts. Some of the more successful programmes, for example the Bangalur Layout and the Working Women's Forum, were facilitated by grants provided as they were getting started.

— Enable larger national non-governmental organizations, larger cooperatives, national development foundations, and government agencies with a history of efficient delivery of services and interest in assisting this sector, to set up special units and programmes to reach PISCES level enterprises.

— Strengthen and expand ongoing PISCES level programmes of non-governmental organizations, banks, and government agencies and organizations.

— Establish "umbrella organizations" that can service the needs of a number of small local organizations.

Given the characteristics of these organizations, donors will need to spend a good deal more time just to locate appropriate intermediaries and develop much simpler mechanisms for arranging loans. Also, they will have to restrict the amount of money they try to move and help organizations with complicated paperwork. Many excellent programmes can be facilitated initially with small amounts of additional funds. But, when additional funds are needed, they should be readily available so services can expand with improved organizational capacity. In projects that assist the smallest of existing micro-enterprises, a U.S. $25,000 revolving loan fund can serve approximately 300 clients organized into 40 credit groups. As the organization develops, the loan fund can be increased gradually. With U.S. $800,000, the programme can serve from 2,500 to 5,000 micro-businesses, depending on the average size of the loans.

The PISCES research clearly shows that micro-business owners are reliable and can use small loans and other assistance productively. The research also shows there are effective mechanisms for delivering assistance. The challenge is to identify, train and fund enough programmes to reach a significant number of people living in the poorest communities of the Third World.

Notes

1. Private communication with officials from the World Bank, Agency for International Development, Appropriate Technology Inc., and Private Agencies Collaborating Together.
2. Each of the programmes mentioned briefly in this report is described in detail in the PISCES, Phase I final report (Farbman (ed.) 1981).
3. The Working Woman's Forum is a small non-governmental organization in Madras, organized by Jaya Aranachalam.
4. PRIDECO is a governmental community development agency, FEDECCREDITO is the nation's largest cooperative bank.
5. The Dominican Development Foundation is a non-governmental national development organization with many years of experience in extending credit. The micro-enterprise project of the F.D.D. is one of the six demonstration projects of PISCES, Phase II.

6. A small, local non-governmental organization.
7. A non-governmental organization with projects throughout Kenya.
8. The Village Polytechnic Programme started as a non-governmental organization. It is now administered by the Kenyan government.

Reference

FARBMAN, Michael (ed.) (1981) *The PISCES Case Studies: Assisting the Smallest Economic Activities of the Urban Poor*, Agency for International Development (AID), Office of Urban Development, Washington D.C.

CHAPTER 17

Class, power and the distribution of credit in Ecuador*

ALAN MIDDLETON

A major feature in development economics in the 1970s has been a concern for achieving a more equitable income distribution through the redistribution of assets. Starting from the assumption that half of the poor in the developing world are self-employed and not directly part of the wage economy, it has been argued that assets are an important element for determining family income. It is held that since wage earners are more likely to be in the middle income group, policies which aim to affect the balance between wages and profits have more to do with the better-off sectors of the population than with the working poor.

Such viewpoints are well expressed by Ahluwalia and Chenery (1974, 43–44), who suggest that "a grouping of households according to the type and productivity of their assets provides more insight into the nature of income distribution among the lower income groups than does a narrower focus on the determinants of wages for different types of labour". The same authors go on to contend that the distribution of assets is often more concentrated than the distribution of incomes, that government action tends to assist this concentration, and that greater income equality could be achieved if ownership of private capital and access to public facilities were more equally distributed. Thus, they suggest that policy should operate in favour of those factors of production owned by the lower income groups and attempt to alter the pattern of concentration of physical and human capital. It is argued that investment should be redirected through education, public facilities, access to credit, land reform, etc., towards the poverty groups. Moreover these authors distinguish three sectors at whom development policy should be directed in order to raise the incomes of the poorest groups: large-scale capitalists, small-scale capitalists and the self-employed.[1]† They consider that the incomes of

*An abridged version of the article with the same title published in *SLAS Bulletin* (Bulletin of the Society for Latin American Studies) No. 33, April 1981, pp. 66–100. This essay is published here with the permission of its author and of the editor of *SLAS Bulletin*.
†Superscript numbers refer to Notes at end of chapter.

poverty groups are "determined by (1) wages from the modern (high-income) sector, (2) wages from small-scale producers, (3) self-employment incomes, based on their own stock of physical and human capital, and (4) net transfers from the rich via the fiscal system. It is the combined effect of policy on all these elements that determines the net effect upon the incomes of the poorer groups. However, the general theme which runs through their work is "the need to direct public investment to support incomes of poorer groups by building up their ownership of and access to physical and human resources" (Ahluwalia and Chenery 1974, 47).

In this paper I consider the fate of policy decisions which attempt precisely this through facilitating access to credit for the above subsectors within manufacturing. The category of "self-employed manufacturers" has been redefined and broadened somewhat to "petty manufacturers", a general description which is more in line with the reality I have observed. The paper focuses on the problem of redistribution of credit (as distinct from simply subsectoral increase in value) and the problems confronting each of these sectors as they try to improve their share of available resources.

The distribution of credit in Ecuador between 1972 and 1976

Awareness that the activities of the manufacturing sector were dependent on the expansion of credit facilities was enshrined in the 1973 National Development Plan (hereafter "the *Plan*") which claimed that industry would receive credit "substantially greater than the amounts conceded in the past" (JNP 1972, 277). Indeed the promotion of industrialization was the central platform of the Military government and it was visualized that half of this sector's investment needs would be met by credit from private sector and State banking institutions. However, of the loans authorized by these institutions between 1972 and 1976, 45 per cent were allocated to the commercial sector, leaving only 23.5 per cent for manufacturing (both industry and artisan production), and 17.7 per cent for agriculture.[2] Furthermore, contrary to the emphasis expressed in the *Plan*, credit to the agricultural sector rose fastest between 1972 and 1976, showing an increase of 310 per cent, while manufacturing credit rose by 233 per cent and that destined for commerce by 129 per cent.

Of the total credit authorized by national banking institutions between 1972 and 1976, 60 per cent came from the private sector and 40 per cent from State institutions. Public sector credit increased by 357 per cent over the period. However, the sector which appears to have benefited most from this expansion is not the manufacturing sector. Agriculture received 33 per cent of State credit over the period, while manufacturing got only 27 per cent and commerce 25 per cent. While agricultural credit from the State institutions was less than industrial credit in 1972, by 1976 it had overtaken it. Thus agricultural credit increased by 577 per cent and commercial credit by 380 per cent, while that destined for manufacturing lagged behind at 294 per cent. As the share of agricultural credit in the total distributed by the State rose from 21 per cent to 31 per cent, that allocated to manufacturing actually declined from 31 per cent to 26 per cent, although not so markedly as that of commerce (from 31 per cent to 21 per cent).

It would appear, therefore, that State credit practice was not consistent with original intentions. Although the new oil finances meant a large all-round increase in the volume of credit, the agricultural sector was more successful than the industrial in increasing its share of this credit from the State institutions. There are two main reasons why this should be so. The first is the question of guarantees needed to obtain large loans. Although there are some documented cases where large companies have managed to obtain loans greater than their capital assets, landowners are generally at an advantage in being able to set their lands up against loans, even when the credit solicited is not used for agriculture.[3] The second is the effect of accumulated wealth, not only in making it easier to obtain credit for rational technical banking reasons, but also in permitting individuals and groups to exert influence over State practice. Through patronage, the power of the extended family and the manipulation of friendships and "socio-political leverage" (*palanca*), the landed oligarchies remain capable of influencing government policy, imposing interpretations of policies to further their own interests, and ensuring that their representatives hold key posts within the State apparatus while opponents are removed from office. Using their informal power networks, it was this sector which was best able to take advantage of the increased availability of government loans at negative real rates of interest after 1972, while industry still had to rely on the high interest, private financial sector which provided 54 per cent of industrial loans during the period under study.

If the position of all manufacturing is deteriorating relative to agriculture, then we should expect the same to be true for the category of "small-scale industry and artisans" (SI & A). Unfortunately, there are no figures at the levels of State or private banking institutions which allow us to determine the *overall* fate of the small-scale sector relative to the others, but a look at the data for the National Development Bank (BNF) confirms that within this State institution the same thing is happening as for manufacturing in general. Even though this is the main credit institution for small-scale industry, between 1972 and 1975 BNF agricultural credit grew much more rapidly than SI & A credit, the former rising by 443 per cent and the latter by 311 per cent.[4]

Industrial credit and the expansion of small-scale manufacturing

There has been a general consensus amongst artisans, government technocrats and large-scale private enterprise that the expansion of petty manufacturers into small-scale industries should be the main goal of development planning for this sector. One of the principal stated means of achieving this has been through the attempt to provide generous credit facilities for the small-scale entrepreneur, responding to long-standing demands for credit expressed by the petty producers' representative organizations (see Middleton 1979, Ch. 7).

Just how credit should be distributed, however, is a major problem. The ILO's Regional Employment Programme for Latin America and the Caribbean (PREALC) suggests that it should be given to those who "need it most" and should be combined with a service which offers professional advice. Distribution should depend on "the viability of the project" and the "entrepreneurial capacity" of the solicitant, rather than guarantees (PREALC 1976, 280). Unfortunately, PREALC did not seem to realize that there was not the trained manpower available in Ecuador to carry out professional project evaluation for every small-scale manufacturer applying for credit and they gave no hint as to who was going to judge "entrepreneurial capacity" or on what criteria. But it is the idea that credit should go to those who need it most which suggests a lack of realism only surpassed by local newspaper editorials, which proposed that the "enterprising nature and tenacity" of small-scale producers should be taken into account by the State when it is distributing credit.[5] How are these qualities to be graded and related to numerical scales of finance? Not only do these proposals ignore the fact that other more powerful groups are also competing for these scarce resources, but they also suggest that certain banking procedures central to the capitalist system should be abandoned.

Nevertheless the PREALC team proposed that the extension of the location of credit in this way would be assisted by setting up a register of bad debtors, extending credit allocation to cut operational costs, and through the creation of a national fund. This could be drawn on when creditors defaulted and so serve to encourage the granting of loans to those small-scale producers whose capital goods would not reach the value of the solicited credit if they did have to foreclose. As it happens, the BNF already had an increasing list of bad debtors and the attempt made at setting up such a national fund (before the PREALC team's suggestions) had come to nothing. Once again, a basic failure of the PREALC mission's report was that it was not properly informed about existing and past policy and how it had fared.

Elsewhere, it has been suggested that for Latin America as a whole, new credit procedures need to be evolved and that "one way of improving credit terms for the informal sector might be to set up a properly endowed lending institution exclusively for the purpose" (Souza and Tokman 1976, 355–65). With respect to Ecuador, there are two problems with this. The first is that, while it is easy to propose new procedures and apparently just as easy to incorporate them into policy statements, it is much more difficult to outline *politically realistic* procedures for making funds available. This presupposes a knowledge of existing policy, the extent of its application and the reasons for any breach between the proposals and their applications. The second problem is that there is nothing new about these suggestions, and so new initiatives often merely repeat old mistakes. The provision of new procedures for credit distribution has been long written into the law governing small-scale manufacturing. The 1953 law in support of the artisan stipulated that it was the duty of the Artisan Defence Board "to apply for the establishment, in the *Banco Popular*, of an artisan credit department or, failing this, to endeavour to have an artisan credit bank established". The State was to provide economic assistance through "the granting of long-term loans by the banks of the Development System and the *Banco Popular*".[6] These policies were never carried through.

Nevertheless, through the 1960s, credit was one of the areas where the promotion of small-scale manufacturers was apparently able to make some headway, even if it was not what the State nor the artisans would have wished. The 1963–1973 National Development Plan (JNP 1963) proposed 57.7 million sucres be made available for artisans and a further 90 million to both small-scale industrialists and artisans.[7] According to the ILO assessment of this Plan a total of 90 million sucres had been made available by 1968 (Wall 1975, 29). In the period 1965–1972 credit to SI & A amounted to 29.6 million dollars. Unfortunately, official statistics do not tell us what these loans were used for, nor do they tell us how much actually went to the small non-capitalist producers as distinct from capitalist small-scale industry. According to informal interviews with a number of artisans, the feeling was that these credits did not go to artisans and, as we shall see, there is every reason to believe that the percentage which did was very low. During this period, the majority of the loans were for less than 1,000 dollars and over a period of less than one year.[8] BNF credit to SI & A fell from 7.8 per cent of its total credit to only 1.9 per cent. Again, these loans were mainly short term, 66 per cent being for periods of less than two years. Even less private credit went to SI & A and 95 per cent of the loans were for less than one year (PREALC 1976, 279).

According to the 1973 *Plan*, the State was to provide "integrated credit services" for SI & A, and of the 1,115 million sucres designated by both State and private banks, the State's 75 per cent share amounted to 836 million sucres. The credit was to be distributed by the BNF, the CV-CFN (*Comisión de Valores*) and the Central Bank, but the BNF was to remain the main supplier. The funds were to be directed towards "those activities which would be most convenient for the economy of the country" (JNP 1972, 280 and 285). From 1973 onwards, the credit to the SI & A sector allocated by the BNF alone greatly surpassed the targets set out in the *Plan*. From 149 million sucres allocated in 1972, this increased to 535 millions in 1975 (348 millions at 1972 prices).[9] This was made possible by the fact that the targets set in the *Plan* were drawn up using the 1972 oil prices of 3.60 dollars per barrel and there was a totally unexpected bonus the following year when OPEC raised the price to

13.90 dollars per barrel. Thus, the finance available for all sectors of the economy increased beyond that which was expected. The money was raised, but how was it allocated? The figures by themselves hide a complex mechanism of distribution of credit which acts against the less wealthy and less powerful sectors, irrespective of classical policy decisions which take no account of it.

The problem of SI & A credit allocation 1972–1976

Before June 1972, only the BNF had been involved in the distribution of credit to SI & A, but at this date the CV-CFN became involved. It was initially planned to give credit for up to ten years for fixed capital investment and for up to three years for circulating capital at an interest rate of only 4 per cent.[10] The following month it was reported that 50 million sucres was available through this institution and up to 488,788 sucres each could be borrowed by one-person enterprises and up to 977,556 sucres each by cooperatives.[11] However, it was clarified that interest to the producer would be at a rate of 12 per cent and not at 4 per cent as was at first hoped.

Later in that year, a Guarantee and Development Fund was set up in the Central Bank to distribute a USAID loan for small industry and artisans. One of the channels for the distribution of this loan was the Programme of Fiduciary Funds for Small Industry in the Ministry of Industry, Commerce and Integration (MICEI), but in April of 1973 the members of this programme resigned in protest at "the inefficiency of the Director of the Programme".[12] They claimed that although the USAID loan had been agreed in May of the previous year and the 5.1 million dollars had been available since 31 December of that year, contacts had not been made with small-scale industrialists to promote the loan. There was a list of projects for which loans had been solicited, but the enterprises concerned had not been visited and only three small-scale industrialists had managed to obtain loans in the first three months of that year. Later in this month, the programme's responsibilities were transferred to the CV-CFN. Significantly, the situation of "artisans" did not enter the debate.

At the same time, the small-scale industrialists had been complaining bitterly about the difficulty in obtaining a loan and, despite the reassurances of the Minister, the Association of Small Industrialists of Guayas claimed that the loan was "a complete failure"—a tied credit, limited by bureaucratic organization.[13] From this point on, it was quite clear that, in spite of the intentions of the State and the availability of funds, the distribution of credit towards SI & A was not going to be as simple as was at first thought. The original intentions were reflected in the reformulated Law for the Development of SI & A in August 1973, but it was now stressed that credit should be made available only "assuming a real and potential capacity for repayment".[14] The romanticism of freely available credit was quite clearly rejected in this pragmatic assertion of the importance of guarantees.

Throughout this period, nothing was heard from the Artisans' Chambers and Federations about this loan, but clearly the possibility of these producers obtaining access was even less than that of the small-scale industrialists. In an attempt to promote artisan development the Inter-American Development Bank (BID) made a loan of 70,000 dollars in 1974.[15] A number of experts were brought in, but a major problem which they came up against was that of the problem of bank guarantees. According to these experts, the money which was available for the development of small manufacturing was lying unused in the banks because there were not enough small producers who could offer the necessary guarantees.[16] Indeed, the problem of guarantees had been approached by MICEI in 1973 when they called the major insurance companies to a series of fruitless discussions on ways of forming guarantees and securities for small-scale manufacturers who were seeking loans from the State loan system. Early in 1975 there was already another BID loan arrangement in the pipeline. Two 1.5 million dollar loans for SI & A were being negotiated, one to be made available over 15 years at 8 per cent interest and the other over 40 years at 1 per cent interest. Before these could be made available, however, there remained the problem of 2 million dollars of the USAID loan still waiting to be distributed and, behind that, the need to break the circularity of "lack of capital = lack of guarantees = lack of capital".

From the point of view of the banking institutions, there was only one way out of this situation. Unfortunately, it meant finally renouncing any intention of helping the poorest manufacturing sector. Discussion of the plight of the artisans had notably diminished as the official debate on credit reduced the "small-scale industry and artisan" sector to "small-scale industry" on its own. To bring some financial order to the situation it was necessary to consolidate this tendency formally. The possibility of the vast majority of utilitarian artisans obtaining credit was extremely limited, and at the same time medium-sized industry could use more credit and were better able to offer the guarantees demanded by the financial institutions. In addition, the associations of small-scale industrialists, led by the more successful of their numbers, had been pressing the government to raise the capital ceilings which defined small industries in law. The apparently non-conflictive solution was to redefine small-scale industries for the purposes of obtaining credit.

In June 1975, the Monetary Board decided that small-scale industrialists whose capital was up to 5 million sucres could receive credit up to the same limits from the State institutions. It was claimed that this new resolution "increases the number of enterprises which can receive this type of credit and, in addition, increases the amount that can be obtained.[17] According to the Development Law, however, small-scale industry could not have capital valued at more than 1.5 million sucres.[18] This meant that there was a discrepancy between the way credit was to be distributed and the legal standing of the enterprises which were to receive it, but the fact that a corresponding change in the law was promised meant that an agreement could be reached with the BID for the prospective new loan.

The total programme of the BNF's credit to SI & A was calculated to be in the order of 7.5 million dollars, of which the BID would supply 40 per cent and the BNF the remainder.[19] There was a change in the upper capital limits for "artisans" in 1974 which meant that loans up to 12,000 dollars could be promised for these small producers and in August of 1975 the limits for small-scale industry were brought up to that agreed between the Monetary Board and the BID. The official reason for the change in the law was that it had to be brought into line with agreed financial practice.[20]   Mainly because of the problem of guarantees, the small industry section of the Pichincha branch of the BNF had been closed between March and August of 1975. The redefinition of small industrialists allowed the re-opening of this office for the allocation of funds waiting to be distributed.

Throughout the second half of 1975 registration of small-scale industries with the Development Law surged ahead. These registrations were not merely of new small-scale industrialists keen to take advantage of the new funds for credit. Rather, after the raising of the capital ceiling, there was a rush of medium-sized producers to become classified as "small-scale industries" to obtain the credit and to claim the 100 per cent tax exemption on any new fixed capital investment. One of the original assumptions of the extension of credit to small enterprises was that, since it was more labour intensive than large industry, its promotion would create additional jobs more cheaply. However, the effect of the solution arrived at for guarantees was that the already more capital-intensive industry was stimulated to invest in more labour-saving machinery, to the detriment of the smaller producer and, particularly, of the mass of petty producers whose possibility for obtaining credit had not changed.

By the end of the year the agreed BID/BNF loans were still not in operation, but that did not stop the registration of medium-sized industries as small industries. Early in 1976, the Directive Council of the National Federation of Small Industrialists, in a memorandum sent to the Minister of Industry pointed out that:

> Various enterprises which for their size were initially registered with the Chambers of Industrialists proceeded later to inscribe themselves with the Association of Small Industrialists, in order to obtain additional benefits, especially the credit facilities of the mechanisms of the Financial Funds. This produces a double affiliation which is prejudicial to the real small-scale industrialists, whose credit resources are diminished through them being directed to enterprises whose true category exceeds the level of small-scale industry.[21]

They also complained that the private banks, through which State funds passed, preferred to give large amounts of credit to a few large customers, while the policy best suited to the small industrialists was the distribution of small amounts to many customers. They expressed the fear that loans which were meant for small-scale industry were going to large-scale production by this channel and complained that labour intensive small-scale industry was being discriminated against. Credit was going to more capital-intensive enterprises. The Minister promised to look into this situation, but apparently nothing was done about it.

At the end of 1975, the Credit and Technical Assistance for Small Industry and Artisans Programme of MICEA became The National Centre for the Promotion of Small Industry and Artisans (CENAPIA).[22] The aims of CENAPIA were set out as: (1) The vertical and horizontal integration of SI & A with larger-scale industry; (2) Providing stimulation for the creation of new poles of factory development; (3) Increased use of national raw materials; (4) The promotion of production and the achievement of high quality, to satisfy both local and international demand; and (5) The formulation of norms of control of the use of funds provided by the financial institutions. Despite the inclusion of aims for the artisans, however, CENAPIA had been almost wholly concerned with promoting the development from small capitalist to large capitalist production. Contradictorily, it was set up at a time when government policy was promoting some larger industry to undergo a reclassification downwards.

A few months later the small industrialists began to express the fear that the era of expansion for them was over.[23] While the official pronouncements were considered to be positive, the reality of their situation clearly did not match up to their aspirations. After 1972, small-scale industry had become the most rapidly developing sector of the economy. There was growth of registration with MICEI, a corresponding increase in official employment figures and an extremely rapid increase in investment. Between 1974 and 1975, however, in spite of the availability of funds, there was a decline in the real value of credit from the BNF; and between 1972 and 1975 the real cost of creating one job in small-scale industry rose by 86 per cent.[24]

Despite government intentions, then, the small-scale industrial sector was experiencing a number of difficulties in obtaining loans. The interest rates were higher than was initially expected and the money had not been distributed as was hoped. However, if the lack of guarantees (the underlying reason for this second problem) provided a stumbling block for small industrialists, it was even more important for non-capitalist producers. New credit facilities had been demanded by the latter over many years, yet the main problem of guarantees was solved in such a way that it favoured existing banking procedures and larger capitalist concerns, to the detriment of the small producer. There are no official figures on credit to petty (or artisanal) producers, so in order to understand their situation, let us turn to my own survey material.[25]

The problem of credit for petty manufacturers

We have seen that the petty producers are interested in developing into small-scale industrialists, that their organizations have been promoting this idea and that it has the support of the State.[26] It is an ideal, however, which is nonetheless secondary to the immediate needs of these producers for capital investment on a smaller scale and for the acquisition of raw materials. The expansion into the category of small-scale industrialist is desirable (the problems of employers' obligations notwithstanding), but the pragmatic petty manufacturers are not really concerned with changing categories. They are concerned with improving their means of production, however modestly.

When asked whether they would like a loan and to what use they would put it, 150 small producers (78 per cent) in my sample responded positively,[27] and 55 per cent of these said they would invest in tools and machinery, while 45 per cent mentioned the purchase of raw materials and 19 per cent said they would like to expand into small-scale industries. Seven per cent said they would expand their commercial activities.

Seventy-four per cent of the small producers set up in business using no more than their own savings. A further 12 per cent started off with a loan from another member of their family; in some cases a father and in others a slightly better-off uncle. Nine per cent got money from a variety of sources which included friends, old masters, moneylenders who charged exhorbitant rates of interest, gifts from unspecified sources and the people for whom some produced. Only 5 per cent said that a bank loan had formed a part of the initial capital for their business. In most cases, of course, initial capital amounted to no more than the acquisition of a few hand tools (or a sewing machine where relevant) which were put into production inside the home. Having become set up in business, there was an apparent reluctance even to try to obtain a loan. Of those who did not get a bank loan to set up their enterprise, only one-third had ever attempted to get a loan and of these only one-third had succeeded.

Of those who answered all the questions about financing, (95 per cent of sample), 17 per cent had obtained a loan from a formal banking institution at some time or other. Of the 26 persons who answered questions about the value of their formal loans, 46 per cent had received less than 10,000 sucres (400 dollars). A further 31 per cent had loans between 10,000 and 30,000 sucres and only 23 per cent had loans greater than this. That is, only 3 per cent of the sample said they had obtained loans greater than 1,200 dollars and those using formal sources were not able to get larger loans than those using informal sources.

When we asked about the reasons for the reluctance to seek loans the most frequent response was that the producers were just not interested in applying (39 per cent). A further 20 per cent were afraid of contracting debt or more debt, while 11 per cent were sceptical about the possibility of obtaining a loan if they did apply. Ten per cent thought they would not get one because of lack of guarantees or because they did not have bank accounts (i.e. would not satisfy the bank's requirements) and only 6 per cent said they were thinking about the possibility for the future.

Precisely what lies behind the reply that the artisans are "not interested" could be a matter of some debate. Are they not interested because of a fear of not being able to cope with banking institutions and their bureaucratic requirements such as complicated form-filling? Does the disinterest derive from realistic assessment of their chances of ever getting a loan or from an unwillingness to contract a debt which could easily lead to dispossession of everything the producer owns, as has often happened? PREALC (1976, 280) noted that: "The time, necessary documentation and preparation which is required to obtain a loan, in addition to the guarantees demanded by the banks act against the small manufacturers seeking credit". But the additional fear of debt is also very real. Even among small-scale industrialists, the private banks are notorious for their readiness to institute court proceedings if the debtor falls even slightly behind with repayments, behaviour which contrasts vividly with their readiness to extend large amounts of credit on the basis of a family name.

Where a fear of debt lies behind the reluctance to apply for credit, such a fear is by no means irrational. In a situation of precarious subsistence production, the decision whether to take on debt or not involves risking the means of production which with labour generate that subsistence. An important difference between the capitalist producers and petty producers is that the former are risking the accumulated surplus value produced by other workers and which is employed to generate further surplus, while the petty producers are risking the loss of the means of producing subsistence for themselves and their families. Bankrupt capitalists do not starve, but that is a real possibility for a ruined artisan.

It is likely that a combination of complicated documentation, necessary guarantees, and fear of debt (in addition to old age), lie behind the petty producer's expression of disinterest. The removal of these barriers would probably encourage the petty producers to seek loans. However, it would only make sense to encourage small producers to seek loans when there is a real possibility of obtaining them, for to do otherwise would only encourage the artisan to waste his time in a bureaucratic procedure over a number of months. In the present situation, such encouragement would also only lead to heightened frustration for the petty manufacturers, for clearly those who have applied have not been very successful, most commonly because of their inability to offer the banks the required guarantees.

Conclusions

Policy proposals that credit to small-scale industry should be expanded have come up against the problems of both lack of guarantees and the distribution of power in society. The revenues from oil exports have helped to raise the value of credit to small industry, but relative to other sectors, the significance of this credit has declined. The small industrialists have continued to experience difficulty in obtaining loans, and attempts to improve their situation by raising their capital investment limits, have only succeeded in channelling credit meant for them to medium-sized, less labour-intensive, capitalist enterprises. Changes in the law intended to meet the needs of international finance have operated to the benefit of larger-scale industry, and other institutional changes since 1975 have reinforced this tendency. Meanwhile petty manufacturers in search of loans for raw materials, tools and machinery have found them extremely difficult to obtain.

From experience of the Ecuadorean bureaucracy, it is very likely that the complicated documentation could be reduced substantially. However, the problems of guarantees and fear of debt are inextricably bound together and action on these will meet with stiff resistance from some quarters. Just as the landed oligarchy have stifled attempts at asset redistribution through land reform, the attempts at achieving asset redistribution through reorienting credit provision have come up against the reality of an existing struggle for command of these scarce resources.

In addition, when the BID or the IMF provide loans they require guarantees that international banking standards are being observed. The suggestion by international experts that such standards need not be observed should perhaps be made at the level of international finance with the foreign "donors" offering to bear any losses. But then, we know what the answer to that would be. The question then arises as to why these experts should presume that already poor Third World countries should bear such losses and jeopardize further international loans through charges of unprofessional practice.

On the other hand, provided that guarantees can be given, the distribution of credit is not merely a technical exercise. On the contrary, gaining control of the country's state financial institutions is very much an element of the struggle for power in Ecuador. And it is a struggle which has repercussions throughout all the upper regions of the relevant institutions and Ministries. When a Minister of Finance or Manager of the Central Bank arrives in power, he brings his advisers with him and when he departs, they also depart. It is at this level that the informal mechanisms of patronage, family power and *palanca* are used by powerful groups to ensure that their interests are looked after. Where these fail, bribery can be used as a last resort. To the extent that rational banking practice can be got round, it is the already powerful groups that succeed in bending them in their own interest through these informal mechanisms. To the extent that scarce resources are distributed according to professional practice, the same informal mechanisms ensure priority for the most powerful groups.

This capacity of the most powerful groups in a country like Ecuador to dominate State credit is not just a fact that stands in isolation, but is a reflection of a rather simple general law that the most wealthy and powerful sections of the community will be able to exert most influence on the State in order to increase that wealth and power. As we have seen with the distribution of credit to agriculture and industry, even in the case of a military government committed to national industrialization and the promotion of small-scale manufacturing, it is the fraction of the dominant class at the centre of private accumulation which is best able to increase its share of scarce resources.

To the extent that there is an absolute increase in the resources made available to less powerful sectors or sub-sectors, the same is true within these. Thus, when the government's industrial credit policy functions more effectively the most powerful groups of industrialists will benefit most. When there is a larger-scale credit scheme for small-scale industry in operation the same will be true, and to the extent that credit is made available to "artisans" it will be the few already most developed of these who will benefit most.

On the other hand, within manufacturing, in the struggle for resources the most powerful groups within the less powerful sub-sectors will endeavour to change the law and policy in their interests, but in so doing may leave themselves open to increased domination by already more powerful groups. As we saw in the case where the small industrialists succeeded in obtaining a raise in their capital ceiling, the leading forces of this less developed sub-sector became exposed to pressure from the least developed of the sub-sector classified as large-scale industry. Thus, modifications of the law which may be irrelevant to or perhaps detrimental to the needs of the majority of small producers, may through this process, even be detrimental to the most developed groups of the least developed sub-sectors.

Through this struggle for credit we see a feature of the process which deflects wealth upwards and produces the ruination of small manufacturers. The fundamental element is the collective capacity of certain groups to bend the will of the State in their own interest. In the last analysis, it is the existing distribution of power derived from accumulated wealth which is the basic factor in whether credit policies will be successful or not. This element should be taken much more fully into account in policy proposals.

Notes

1. They omit the non-capitalist wage employer.
2. Based on data from *Superintendencia de Bancos, Boletines* (Quito 1972–1976); *Corporación Financiera del Ecuador, Informes Anuales,* (Quito 1972–1976); and, *Comisión de Valores* (CV-CFN), *Memorias,* (Quito 1973–1976).
3. Not all agricultural loans are in fact used for agriculture. The author knows of a case where a landowner with a *hacienda* just outside Quito obtained a loan from the BNF to start modern chicken production, but used the finance to produce concrete blocks for the booming construction industry in Quito. He received a loan at 3 per cent interest and erected a building where the Indians on his hacienda produced the blocks at agricultural wage rates. When the

BNF inspector came round, he said that the chickens had all died and that since he had to pay back the loan he started up the present business. He was given an extension on his loan.
4. BNF, *Boletín Estadístico* (Quito, BNF, 1971–1976), p. 25.
5. *El Comercio*, 21/10/73.
6. *Ley de Defensa del Artesano, Registro Oficial* 356 (Quito, 5 November 1953), Article 3, (Defence Law), and Article 6d.
7. Between 1970 and 1982 U.S.$1 was equivalent to 25 Ecuadorian sucres at the official rate of exchange.
8. *El Tiempo*, 4/11/73. These loans were distributed to the following types of activity in order of importance: engineering workshops, repair workshops, food products, wood, textiles, clothing manufacturing, chemical products, leather goods and graphical arts (printing).
9. BNF, *Boletín Estadístico* (Quito, BNF, 1972–1975), p. 25. For details of the deflator used see Montaño and Wygard (1976, 246).
10. *El Tiempo*, 17/6/72.
11. *El Comercio*, 4/7/72.
12. *El Comercio*, 11/4/73.
13. *El Universo*, 18/5/74.
14. *El Comercio*, 23/8/73.
15. The loan was to pay for technical experts and consultancy; the creation of artisanal enterprises with adequate technical, managerial and commercial capacity which would incorporate modern work methods, standards of quality and presentation; and the adequate organization of sales. See *El Tiempo*, 7/10/74; *El Universo*, 4/10/74; and *El Tiempo*, 1/12/74.
16. Interviews with UN artisan experts. As a result of this problem, the BID programme turned more towards assisting artistic artisans who were more easily organized into cooperative ventures for the purpose of combining collateral. These were organized mainly outside Quito, and with the expert creation of marketable new designs this programme of relatively modest means was able to make a visible impact on the fortunes of artistic artisans between 1975 and 1978. For the basic programme, see Hamelink (1975).
17. *El Comercio*, 10/6/75.
18. MICEI, *Codificación de la Ley de Fomento de la Pequeña Industria y Artesanía*, Decree No. 921, 2 August 1973 (Quito, MICEI, 1974), Article 5.
19. *El Comercio*, 28/6/75.
20. Supreme Decree No. 734, 22 August 1975.
21. Reprinted in *El Tiempo*, 24/2/76.
22. Decree No. 1020, 8 December 1975.
23. *Pequeña Industria*, July 1976.
24. Based on data from the Directorate of Small Industrial Development of MICEI, the Social Investigation Section of the JNP (National Planning Board), and the Department of Statistics of the BNF.
25. A survey of 273 petty manufacturers and traders was carried out in three areas of Quito in November–December 1975. The areas were chosen after consultation with members of the JNP who knew the city and were interested in the problem of petty enterprise development. The firms were selected by a stratified random sampling technique after all the petty firms in the area had been located on a base map. From 4,181 establishments, 300 were selected for interview and the final sample consisted of 192 petty manufacturers and 81 traders. For a fuller description, see Middleton (1979, Appendix I).
26. Unfortunately, expansion is measured by registration with the Development Law and does not take into account the development, decline or disappearance of companies after registration. Nonetheless, there can be no doubt that the period after 1972 *was* one of rapid expansion.
27. Some did not answer because they had already received a loan, while others were not interested.

References

AHLUWALIA, M. S. and CHENERY, Hollis (1974) "The economic framework", in Hollis Chenery *et al.*, *Redistribution with Growth*, Oxford University Press, New York.

HAMELINK, J. (1975) *Adaptación y Comercialización de Artesanías*, MICEI, Quito.

JUNTA NACIONAL DE PLANIFICACION Y COORDINACION (JNP) (1963) *Plan General de Desarrollo Económico y Social del Ecuador*, JNP, Quito.

JUNTA NACIONAL DE PLANIFICACION Y COORDINACION (JNP) (1972) *Plan Integral de Transformación y Desarrollo, 1973–1977: Resumen General*, JNP, Quito.

MIDDLETON, Alan (1979) "Poverty, Production and Power: The Case of Petty Manufacturing in Ecuador", unpublished D.Phil. thesis, University of Sussex, Brighton.

MONTAÑO, G. and WYGARD, E. (1976) *Visión sobre la Industria Ecuatoriana*, PROCONSULT, Quito.

PROGRAMA REGIONAL DEL EMPLEO PARA AMERICA LATINA Y EL CARIBE (PREALC) (1976) *Situación y Perspectivas del Empleo en el Ecuador*, PREALC/ILO, Santiago de Chile.

SOUZA, Paulo R. and TOKMAN, Victor E. (1976) "The informal sector in Latin America", *International Labour Review*, Vol. 114, pp. 355–65.

WALL, N. C. (1975) *Small-scale Industry Development in Ecuador*, Georgia Institute of Technology, Atlanta.

CHAPTER 18

The allocation of public construction contracts in Lima and Caracas*

RICHARD BATLEY

What better test of the viability of policies to promote employment through small-scale labour intensive operations than to examine practice in an area of government responsibility? Public contracting offers an opportunity for the assertion of government influence directly rather than by attempts to modify the practice of the formal sector. Specifically in the field of urban policy, this sort of approach has underlain the ILO World Employment Programme country and city studies which have all advanced the case for favouring (or withdrawing discrimination against) small traders and producers in public sector contracting and for maximizing labour absorption. The ILO Jakarta and São Paulo studies (Schaefer 1976; Sethuraman 1976) specifically recommended the promotion of informal sector employment in shanty-town improvement programmes.

Similar recommendations have been made by the World Bank with regard to the supply of materials and services by small businessmen in low income housing projects (IBRD 1975).

The question asked here is not whether that sort of policy is right but whether it is feasible—how far does the relationship between public sector agencies and the construction industry permit the implementation of policies to advance small firms and pursue employment policy by the selection of labour-intensive firms? If the informal sector is in a state of "heterogeneous subordination" (Tokman 1978) to the formal sector and survives in activities which allow ease of entry into production and low capitalization, and in the residual areas of oligopolistic markets or in disorganized markets (PREALC

*Pp. 215–27 in Richard Batley (1980) "The allocation of public contracts: studies in Peru and Venezuela" *Development and Change*, Vol. 11, pp. 211–27. Reprinted here with the permission of the author, the editors of *Development and Change*, and Sage Publications of London and Beverly Hills. The research on which this essay is based was financed by the ILO's Regional Employment Programme for Latin America and the Caribbean (PREALC). Fuller versions are available in Batley (1978, 1979, 1981).

1976), can it benefit from a public intervention (such as squatter settlement upgrading or site and service schemes) which has the effect of organizing and enlarging the market, raising technical standards, narrowing the point of entry into the market through contracting, and increasing the earnings of producers? Will the intervention rather have the effect of introducing large producers and material suppliers into areas (for example, the informal housing market) of previously low market organization and of small firm and family production (construction)?[1]†

Indeed, if the informal and formal sector are distinguished partly by the character of their relations with the State and their access to State protection and benefits and exposure to regulation, it cannot be expected either that big firms will give up their privileged relationship easily or that government action to contract work through the informal sector will do more than promote a few small-scale enterprises.

The serious possibility is that an extension of public intervention into previously unorganized sections of the market (e.g. through squatter upgrading) may have the effect of making these markets accessible and interesting to larger companies and of expelling rather than promoting small producers.

The research approach

The questions were examined by looking at the distributional relationship in practice, that is by examining how the terms on which and the processes through which contracts are offered influence the selection of contractors. Whatever the policy plan, the structure of the relationship between the government agency and producers (as contractors) will be an important force in determining outcomes. Agencies offer access to contracts, credit, land and guaranteed markets; the selection of contractors is not an open matter but will be affected by, for example, the agency's preconception about required technologies, scales and timing, by the terms of the contract and by the capacity of firms to respond. The terms on which contracts are offered and the nature of projects may themselves be influenced by the agency's expectations or knowledge about suitable firms' capacity, technology, credit requirements and expected rates of return. Moreover the selection of contractors, once made, will itself contribute to the evolution of a project, to the employment content of production and to decisions about the selection of applicants for housing. Such a two-way relationship can be hypothesized to help confirm the differentiation in the construction and materials industries by contributing to the establishment of rules and procedures which cannot easily be satisfied by small companies and informal organizations.

---

†Superscript number refers to Note at end of chapter.

Policy statements say nothing significant about this relationship; it is policy as implemented which counts. This requires an examination of the procedures which come to compose the relationship between agencies and firms and therefore govern the outcome.

The question is then: if the outcomes are wrong, are the procedures changeable or bound up with mutual interests?

The approach adopted was to consider how agencies distinguish between firms in deciding who has access to contracts. The research was undertaken by the examination of official documents and by the interview of officials to distinguish:

a. the points in the administrative process where selection occurs;
b. the access rules or conditions which applied at the different stages of selection;
c. the implication of these procedures for the inclusion and exclusion of different firms;
d. how the procedures are derived, the interests and assumptions on which they are based and their capacity for change.

Contracting practice in two countries—Peru and Venezuela—was examined inasmuch as it applied to aspects of public utility and housing works in the two capital cities of Lima and Caracas. The particular focus of the study was on works which related to the improvement of squatter settlements in the two cities. With regard to the contracting practice of the public agencies studied, this concern with works related to illegal settlement upgrading implied no sort of special case: (a) because these settlements account for 30 to 40 per cent of the population of Lima and Caracas, and (b) because the contracting practice applied to works in these areas applied equally to other parts of the two cities, and indeed nationally.

Three para-statal agencies were studied in each of the two countries. In both cases they were bodies which had some relation to housing or to the provision of urban services but the precise functions of the agencies chosen differed between the two countries. In Peru, I examined the Lima sanitation and water distribution company (ESAL), the electricity supply company (ELECTROLIMA) and the national agency concerned with "social mobilization" (SINAMOS) which had specific functions in relation to the coordination and implementation of works in recognized squatter settlements (*pueblos jovenes*). In Venezuela, I looked at the Caracas office (*Acueducto Metropolitano*) of the national sanitation and water distribution company (INOS), at the national housing institute (INAVI) and at the semi-private agency (FUNDACOMUN) which coordinated government improvement programmes in squatter settlements (*barrios*). There were variations in the contracting practice of these various agencies but to a considerable degree it is possible to generalize.

Contracting in public construction

Public agencies in both countries were in a strong and even dominant position to influence the employment practice and the development of the construction industry and were certainly of key importance to construction firms' activity. In Venezuela, not only had central government income increased massively as a result of the 1974 increase in petrol prices but also the proportion of public investment devoted to construction grew faster than the increase in income, accounting for 80 per cent of the value of all public investment in 1975 (Palacios *et al.* 1976, 190). Though public investment in residential construction was increasingly channelled via credit and incentives through the private sector, nevertheless throughout the period 1965–1975 almost half of all construction investment was in public works. About the same proportion applied also in Peru.

The potential for influence was apparently great; moreover, in both countries there were formally stated policies which were designed to affect the activities of the construction (and other) industry and its employment impact. Besides general attempts to stimulate the amount of construction, these policies ranged in Venezuela from the use of public investment to promote regional development and the contracting of regionally-based firms, through the requirements that certain agencies working in barrios should employ local workers, to the extension of credit to small firms of any sort.

In Peru, there were formal policies for the promotion of a new sector of collectively-owned "social property" firms, partly through their advance notice of public contracts; there was also a stated intention on the part of the Ministry of Housing and Construction, within the national development plan 1975–1978, to revise the procedures of contracting so as to include a wider range of firms.

What is impressive is that wherever there was any discretion these policies were ignored, that is in all cases except possibly the regional policies (in Venezuela) which did not favour small enterprises or changes in the employment practice of firms. In practice, public agencies did not use their contracting requirements as an opportunity to promote employment or redistribution of wealth through the construction industry, but were concerned rather with the implementation of their own programmes. Even SINAMOS and FUNDACOMUN treated their concern with employment and productive organization in squatter settlements as matters for separate programmes (such as credit allocations) rather than as objectives which could be pursued through their own contracting practice. Their approach and their priorities were not in practice much different from those of any other public agency.

Indeed, the analysis shows how powerful are the processes which tend to decide in favour of the allocation of contracts and incentives to a circle of relatively few, larger firms. The continuity and persistence of these decision-making processes is demonstrated by the absence of important changes in contracting practice in Peru after a "revolution" which brought with it many other structural changes in the productive system.

Among the processes which comprise contracting practice in both countries are the formal rules of selection, but much more powerful are the informal procedures of selection which operate through administrative complexity, the terms of contracts and the more or less private practices of particular agencies.

(a) The formal rules

There was a good deal of similarity between Peruvian and Venezuelan agencies in the formally established procedures for contracting. Peruvian practice was more detailed, in the elaboration in laws and regulations, of general principles for selection between firms; in the Venezuelan case, there were fewer exclusive tests for firms at a general level and more was left to the discretion of the particular contracting agency. But before any firm could be contracted, both systems required that it should be formally registered and, in the Peruvian case, be classified in the register by capital size and permissible maximum contract value; both systems also set out rules for the publication of information on contracts for tender, for tendering procedures and for the means of selecting between candidate firms.

Nowhere do these rules formally exclude any legally-formed company; all are "free" to register, be classified, apply and be selected. But for companies wishing to qualify for public contracts it was a matter of great *administrative complexity* first to demonstrate the firm's eligibility for registration, then to maintain the information annually, and lastly to present updated information at the time of tendering for a particular contract. There were detailed legal, financial, technical and documentary requirements relating to the constitution of the firm, the identity and professional competence of its staff, its balance sheets, list of contracts, bank references, guarantees, equipment chassis numbers, proof of payments in tax and social security etc. Contracting for construction works thus came to be restricted in Peru to 218 registered firms (only 22 of which were eligible for work valued at over U.S. $2m), and in Venezuela to about 1,200 firms.

The point is that these formal rules of registration do act in some degree to exclude from contracting not only enterprises (including the entire informal sector) whose legality and financial and technical capacity were doubtful, but also all those which were uninformed about procedures, unable to deal with administrative complexities and costs, or unable to provide the necessary proofs of experience and professional titles. But while failure to register *excludes* firms from contracting, success has little significance in *qualifying* firms for contracts. Registration is less the basis of their eligibility than is their ability to fulfil much less explicit requirements.

(b) Selection through the terms of contracts

Various elements of the conditions on which contracts are offered tend to operate in favour of larger, better-established firms.

The choice of agencies about the *scale of projects*, about whether they group works into large contracts or divide them into parts, influences the value of the contract and therefore the size of the firm which is permitted to bid for it. In practice agencies find it administratively and technically convenient to put works out to tender in large units or for large geographical areas (for example pipe installations for entire squatter settlements).

In all cases, firms were required by agencies to present their tenders with accompanying *guarantees* against failure to complete, omissions, or bad work. These guarantees comprised deposits by contracted companies of a proportion of the value of works, the withholding of a proportion of the monthly payments by contracting agencies until completion, and the taking-out of insurance or the presentation of guarantees by banks against the possibility of failure by the firm. The guarantees implied at least expense against firms' capital and possibly the need to have a favourable association with a financial institution.

Payment for public works in both countries was customarily delayed by two or three months with the effect that the contracted company has to draw from its own resources or to borrow to cover the cost of current works. Secondly, part of the payment for works may be made in treasury bills or national debt bonds which act as promissory notes for future payment. This implies losses for any contractor whether he holds the bills at below inflation interest rates, sells them at a discounted price or raises bank credit on their strength to cover the period until they mature—for a small company, without a good credit record or strong connection with a bank, the possibility of raising credit against the bills will probably not exist at all.

The scale of works, the guarantees, the payment system and delays tend therefore to select better-resourced and more experienced firms with established connections with financial institutions. What is more, once this selection has occurred, the selected companies benefit from advantages (whether in terms of higher payments or the promise of future contracts) which are intended to compensate for the costs and delays. Ironically, of course, the costs and delays affect unselected firms much more seriously by excluding them altogether.

(c) Direct agency selection

What is really crucial in the business of obtaining contracts to undertake work for all the agencies studied is not the formal rules but the capacity of a firm to engineer a connection with the public agency. Practically all the works of the six agencies examined were below the size where they were required to go through the process of open public tendering to arrive at a choice between companies. Instead they can ask selected companies to submit competitive bids or invite one company to undertake the contract.

In Peru, in 1978, open public tendering was only required for works valued at over U.S. $92,300, in Venezuela at $2.5 million. More closed processes of contracting therefore operate in the contracting of works for which the smaller companies are eligible. They still have to register as public contractors and to conform with the documentary requirements for tendering; the essential point is that to be eligible for a contract issued by restricted competition or invitation, companies have to be known to the contracting agency concerned. In practice, each of the agencies examined held a private list of between 20 and 40 known and approved firms.

These lists are arguably of firms which the contracting agency assesses as technically competent, sufficiently equipped, with qualified personnel, adequately experienced and interested to undertake contracts in that sector. Any firm is said to be free to request inclusion but, unless it is invited, it has of course first to know that the list exists. It has also to have either the opportunity, through a previous contract, to demonstrate its competence and accumulate experience, or the capacity to manipulate and press for inclusion in the list.

Selection depends not only on the expectations of public agencies in establishing requirements but also on the capacity of firms to respond. At one level, this means a sufficient level of information, administrative competence, legal propriety and financial and technical competence, to deal with the formal rules of access to the public register; at another level, it implies a capacity to engineer inclusion in the restricted lists of suitable companies held by all the contracting agencies which were examined; at another, it means the financial capacity to tolerate postponed payment for work.

Interests in restricted access

I would argue that while the exclusive nature of the contracting process might be in part the product of the application of chance selection criteria, it is also lodged in the interests and assumptions of the most significant participants in the process of contracting.

By establishing a special relationship between contracting agencies and a restricted number of firms, the contracting process comes to advance the reputations, competence and experience of those firms. Whether or not they were at first more reputable, competent and experienced than others, the inclusion into the "special relationship" and the opportunity to undertake contracts comes to fulfil the prophecy or to justify the choice.

Once firms have been selected for public contracts they thus come to stand in a relationship of mutual influence and dependence with contracting agencies. The restriction of access to contracts makes the relationship manageable for both the firms and the agencies. The interest of firms in present contracts depends partly on the future promise of work to compensate for the conditions of payment; they are not interested in entering into rigorous competition for small-scale contracts. Once on the short lists, firms are practically assured of a succession of work. From the point of view of agencies, the maintenance of restricted lists of contracting firms offers certain advantages: (a) it gives agencies a certain assurance of the reliability of firms and of their familiarity with the complex contracting requirements and delayed payments; (b) it permits them to cycle a relatively small number of contracts (per agency) in such a way as to retain the interest of known private contractors; (c) it allows them to respond to firms' expectations of continuity in contracting; and (d) it allows agencies to offer some promise of future contracts to firms which, through some means or the other, have been able to demand the attention of the agency, while at the same time restricting to manageable proportions the number of firms which have strong expectations of receiving contracts.

Besides that direct inter-relationship between agencies and firms, there are other interests associated with existing arrangements and which militate against the inclusion of unknown, less experienced, less guaranteed firms.

(i) The pressure which the service agencies experience from their clients is not for the provision of jobs but for the provision of the service as quickly and reliably as possible. Quick, reliable provision is taken by the agency to imply large-scale, well-equipped firms with an established reputation, and, where possible, large-scale projects which attract those firms and allow continuity in their operation.

(ii) This conforms with the view of agency technical staff about the companies in which they are most likely to find their own plans matched by professional standards and "good engineering practice". Moreover, the interconnected nature of urban service networks calls for integration and uniformity which seems simpler to achieve through operations unified in fewer rather than more participant firms.

(iii) It also conforms with agency requirements about the simplicity of administration and supervision of projects. Highly capitalized, experienced firms seem to present less risk of failure; large-scale projects imply less contracting and fewer problems of timetabling and integrating parts of the project.

(iv) Creditors are certainly unlikely to favour the use of their finance for experiments in the promotion of small firms, or new forms of enterprise (direct labour, cooperative or "social property" undertakings). The costs of credit also rise with delays in the implementation of projects. Moreover, creditor agencies (for example, the World Bank or the Peruvian Housing Bank) usually have their own requirements about technical standards, the reliability of firms and even about the process of contracting; the World Bank usually requires international competitive bidding as a condition of its service loans, and itself vets the selection of contractors.

(v) The sections of the construction industry which are already integrated into contracting practice do not expect to have the rules changed so as to promote the entry of previously excluded sections of the same industry.

Indeed, those on the short lists will expect to get their share of going contracts; there will seem to be little point to contracting agencies in promoting more contracting capacity where enough already exists.

Apparently the relationship between these state agencies and their contractors is structured in favour of more established, "better connected" firms. Indeed, change in practice seems to imply costs to those bodies, including para-statal organizations which benefit from present arrangements. The promotion of small firms by these means seems to run counter to the logic of action; the implications are at least that such policies cannot be pursued as a subsidiary to the main aims of public agencies and that they would require constant vigilance in implementation. Yet government policies to promote small and informal enterprises seem unreal if public purchasing itself excludes them.

Conclusion

Whatever the intention, the effect of contracting *practice* appears to have been to protect a reserved number of selected and familiar enterprises which are or become big and sophisticated in their operations. By this process, investment in public works would seem to contribute to the *concentration* of the development of the construction industry. Indeed, some current research indicates that the dominance of a small number of large firms in the Venezuelan construction industry emerged historically precisely as the result of restricted public contracting in important infrastructure works (roads, airports and ports) during 1944–1959 (Acedo 1980). The impact of public investment has increased rapidly since then with the increase in oil revenue in Venezuela and the development of the public sector of the economy in Peru. Of course, the effects of *private* investment may be even more concentrative and less subject to control.

As a by-product of the exclusive nature of public contracting, one effect of intervention in areas (such as squatter settlements) of previously informal productive activity would seem to be the elimination of small enterprises where these were previously undertaking similar works. Sophisticated firms go in on the coat-tails of the administrative intervention which rationalizes, legalizes and increases the scale of local markets. This may affect local informal employment to a small degree where the squatter settlement improvement consists of utility service provision which was previously supplied by standpipes, wells, lorry deliveries or illicit connections; but its effect is likely to be more severe in areas of major informal activity where upgrading involves materials provision and house construction. Improved services for the poor, may therefore *also* mean the decline of locally-controlled enterprises.

Note

1. Winpenny's (1977) review of housing and employment policies suggests that this has happened in site and service schemes. Burgess (1978) suggests similarly that such housing schemes are likely to result in an integration of informal housing into the urban land and industrialized building markets.

References

ACEDO, Clemcy Machado de (1980) "Estructura económica y poder político en Venezuela", *SIC*, Año XLII, No. 421, enero, and Año XLIII, No. 422, febrero.

BATLEY, Richard (1978) "Urban services and public contracts: access and distribution in Lima and Caracas", PREALC/ILO, Santiago de Chile.

BATLEY, Richard (1979) "The allocation of public contracts: studies in Peru and Venezuela", *Development Administration Group Occasional Paper* No. 5, University of Birmingham.

BATLEY, Richard (1981) *Empleo y Necesidades Básicas: Acceso a Servicios Urbanos y Contratos Públicos*, PREALC/ILO, Santiago de Chile.

BURGESS, Rod (1978) "Petty commodity housing or dweller control? A critique of John Turner's views on housing policy", *World Development*, Vol. 6, No. 9/10, pp. 1105–33. Reprinted in Ray Bromley (ed.) (1979) *The Urban Informal Sector: Critical Perspectives on Employment and Housing Policies*, Pergamon, Oxford.

INTERNATIONAL BANK FOR RECONSTRUCTION AND DEVELOPMENT (IBRD) (1975) *Housing Sector Policy Paper*, IBRD, Washington D.C.

PALACIOS, Luis Carlos *et al.* (1976) "Algunos hipótesis sobre las características de desarrollo de Caracas", *Cuadernos de la Sociedad Venezolana de Planificación*, Nos. 138–40, julio-agosto, pp. 173–237.

PROGRAMA REGIONAL DEL EMPLEO PARA AMERICA LATINA Y EL CARIBE (PREALC) (1976) *The Employment Problem in Latin America: Facts, Outlooks and Policies*, PREALC/ILO, Santiago de Chile.

SCHAEFER, Kalmann (1976) *São Paulo: Urban Development and Employment*, ILO, Geneva.

SETHURAMAN, S. V. (1976) *Jakarta: Urban Development and Employment*, ILO, Geneva.

TOKMAN, Victor E. (1978) "An exploration into the nature of informal–formal sector relationships", *World Development*, Vol. 6, No. 9/10, pp. 1065–75. Reprinted in Ray Bromley (ed.) (1979), *The Urban Informal Sector: Critical Perspectives on Employment and Housing Policies*, Pergamon, Oxford.

WINPENNY, James T. (1977) "Housing and jobs for the poor", *Development Planning Unit Working Paper*, No. 2, University College, University of London.

SECTION VI

Conclusion

"The division between 'big' and 'small' business thus represents much more than merely a statistical concept, it actually signifies important differentials between an élite of large, stable concerns operating in lucrative fields and a mass of small enterprises engaged in precarious struggle for survival in the less productive segments of the economy."

(Kurt Mayer 1953, "Business enterprise: traditional symbol of opportunity", 177)

"Survival (of small enterprises) has rested upon continuous adaptation—not always at the level of the individual petit bourgeois, for many have gone to the wall—but at the level of the stratum as a whole. Adaptation has often been born of dire necessity as migrants flock to towns only to find there is no regular work to be had, or as workers are thrown on to the dole queues in times of recession. As with all small fry, the persistence of the collectivity masks the fact of high mortality, and of depredations by governments and larger enterprises which pose continuous threats to the aggregate's survival. But so far it has survived and it is hard to accept that there are any ineluctable forces which will destroy it."

(Frank Bechhofer and Brian Elliott 1981, "Petty property: the survival of a moral economy", 185)

CHAPTER 19

Small may be beautiful, but it takes more than beauty to ensure success

RAY BROMLEY

This concluding chapter attempts to complement, rather than to compete with, the rich and diverse material on small enterprises presented in the preceding chapters. Much of the necessary synthesis and summary has been presented in the Preface and the Introductions to the first five Sections of this book, and the aim of this brief chapter is to provide some additional concluding comments and to open up some new areas of discussion. Our total knowledge of the nature, characteristics and problems of small enterprises and of their relations with larger enterprises and with the State, is remarkably limited. The information available is also very unevenly distributed between countries, and many countries, occupations and social relations of production remain almost unstudied. The most that can be provided here, therefore, are reminders as to the significance of some old ideas and debates, broad orientations for policy, and pointers towards some new lines of investigation and analysis.

The repercussions of early Anarchist–Marxist debates

Discussions of the problems and potentials of small enterprises have been overshadowed for more than a century by the bitter debates between Anarchists and Marxists which led to the division of the First International at the Basel Congress of 1872. These debates have had intellectual and practical implications far beyond the realms of Libertarianism and Socialism, creating a fundamental schism between advocates of small enterprises, "appropriate technology", participatory democracy and decentralization, and advocates of rapid industrialization, "advanced technology", mass production, scale economies, and increasingly centralized government. The bitterness of this debate, as expressed particularly in Marx's (1963) *The Poverty of Philosophy*, in Chapters VI and VII of Lenin's (1936) "The development of capitalism in

Russia", and in Lenin's (1972a) "The handicraft census of 1894–1895 in Perm Gubernia", has led to some very extreme positions being taken up, wholeheartedly condemning either small or large enterprises. In effect, "small" and "large" have been converted through the debate into exclusive opposites, and those who devise policies for the support of small-scale producers have been tarred with Lenin's brush as "petit-bourgeois theorists" wishing to postpone industrialization, proletarianization, workers' revolution and "the dictatorship of the proletariat".

However vivid the polemics between Marx and Engels on the one side and Proudhon and Bakunin on the other (see e.g. Woodcock 1977, 35–42), or between Lenin and the Narodniks and other "Populists" and "Romanticists" (see e.g. Lenin 1972b, 1972c), and however relevant these polemics remain to contemporary development studies (see e.g. Kitching 1982), they cannot possibly be considered to offer the last or the definitive words on small enterprises. The world economy and political system have changed enormously over the last century, and there have been striking technological advances affecting many forms of economic activity. Both the Anarchist dream of the gradual decomposition and eventual overthrow of the State, and the Marxist dream of the global crisis of capitalism and the overthrow of bourgeois rule through proletarian revolution in the most advanced capitalist countries, have been shown to be either false or self-defeating prophesies. There has been a decline of Empire and colonialism, an ascendency of neo-colonialism, and a growing internationalization of capital with increasingly frequent transfers of production between countries. Large numbers of new nation-States have gained Independence and the world has been compartmentalized by the Cold War of the two Superpowers, producing patterns of international interdependence which were, to say the least, difficult to predict in the nineteenth century.

The many and diverse changes which have occurred both at the world level and in individual countries, have been accompanied by a remarkable persistence of small enterprises. Such enterprises have been created, transformed, destroyed and recreated in a great variety of contexts, and they function in substantial numbers in every country of the world. Indeed, given the steady rise in world population, it is reasonable to assert that there are probably more small enterprises in the world today than at any time in history. Small enterprises coexist with large State and private enterprises, sometimes performing subordinate or complementary roles, sometimes competing, and sometimes catering to separate population groups. The numbers, roles and types of small enterprise vary enormously from one country to another, and from one time period to another, but everywhere there are high birth and death rates for small enterprises and notable capacities for adaptation and innovation. The proportional significance of small enterprises in the economy as a whole is higher in capitalist economies (both "core" and "peripheral") than in socialist economies. Even in the COMECON countries, however, there are millions of legal cooperativized, legal unassociated, and illegal small enterprises, and there is little indication that such enterprises are declining in significance (see e.g. Kerblay 1968; Mandel 1970, 555–57 and 592–93; Smith 1976, 53–101).

The slow pace of industrialization in most of the Third World, combined with the global economic crisis of the 1970s and 1980s, the gradual urbanization of the world's population, and the growing proportion of the total labour force working in service occupations (the "tertiarization" of the economy), ensures that the classic Marxist–Leninist scenario of industrialization, proletarianization, workers' revolution and "the dictatorship of the proletariat" is unlikely ever to be fulfilled. Furthermore, of course, "the dictatorship of the proletariat" has been increasingly questioned as both means and end (see e.g. Kautsky 1976), and its use as a guiding principle has lost much of its attraction because of the Soviet experience under Stalin, when there was a "growth of the dictatorship not of but over the proletariat and the peasantry" (Marcuse 1961, 58). There is now overwhelming evidence that Lenin's (1936, 331) generalization that "large-scale machine industry completely squeezes out the small enterprises" is untrue. Instead, small enterprises are continuously in a state of flux, with new foundations, expansions, contractions, take-overs and extinctions continually taking place in adjustment to the expansion and contraction of larger-scale enterprises, so that they play a role in both the causes and the effects of the changing structure of the economy.

The resurgence of right-wing romanticism in Western Europe and North America

In several of the more "advanced" capitalist countries, and most notably in Britain under "Thatcherism" and in the United States under "Reaganomics", there is a resurgence of neo-Liberal, petit-bourgeois Conservative and monetarist thinking. Such thinking romanticizes small enterprises and entrepreneurship and criticizes State controls, the Welfare State, the power of the trade unions, and nationalized industries. It is particularly deeply-rooted in the United States, where there is a vigorous ethic of the "self-made man". According to C. Wright Mills (1951, 44–45), for example:

In any well-conducted Senate hearing on economic issues, someone always says that the small entrepreneur is the backbone of the American economy; that he maintains thousands of small cities, and that, especially in these cities, he is the very flower of the American ways of life. . . . Perhaps giant monopolies do exist, the image runs, but, after all, they are of the big city; it is in the small towns, the locus of real Americans, that the small businessman thrives.

PSE–L

Such views have contributed to enthusiastic attempts by right-wing political parties to recapture the allegiance of small-scale entrepreneurs, their families and their employees, hoping by these means to capture a sufficiently broad electoral coalition so as to both win and retain power. Energy and initiative are praised, and there are numerous promises of reductions in government harassment, less taxation on *earned* income, the vigorous enforcement of law and order, a strong hand with the trade unions, and the termination of State hand-outs to "lame-duck" nationalized industries and bankrupt large companies.

The flowering of right-wing romanticism in major political parties such as the British Conservatives and the U.S. Republicans, has been paralleled by striking changes of attitude amongst big-business corporations, many of which have engaged in lobbying and charitable activities to support the interests of small businesses. Such apparently contradictory behaviour has been explained by Bechhofer and Elliott (1981, 189) as follows:

> They do so out of very mixed motives: from a general wish to see a market economy with lots of small competing units; from a wish to see risk-taking and innovation in the hands of little enterprises rather than their own; from a desire to reduce the power of trade unions and from the knowledge that strike rates and union activity are generally much lower in small concerns. Stability, profitability and social control may all be served by the promotion of the small fry. So, big business gives the appearance of accepting some of the current critiques of the major corporations and joins the boosting of small business. In doing this it distances itself from the strictures about the "unacceptable face of capitalism" and enjoys instead proximity to a defensible, apparently even popular, form of economic organization.

In other words, at least in North America and Western Europe, "the ideology of big business (has) fundamentally changed from the 'rugged individualism', 'public-be-damned' themes of the 1920s to a new, 'stewardship', 'trusteeship' creed" (Rogers and Berg 1961, 108). Such changes of attitude on the part of big-business have accompanied the gradual strengthening of the Welfare State, the real improvements in workers' incomes obtained by the trade union movement, the increase in life expectancy and reduction in morbidity resulting from improved sanitation, health care and pollution control, and the expansion of mass consumption based on the continuous stimulation of consumer demand through "education", "fashion", advertising and the mass media. This transformation of "advanced capitalism" has postponed, and probably avoided, the irremediable crisis of capitalism and the proletarian revolution predicted by Marx and Engels (1965) for the advanced capitalist economies.

The new "niceness" of right-wing governments and big-business towards small enterprises in North America and Western Europe is clearly intended to reawaken petit-bourgeois consciousness, reaffirming the assumed merits of "modern capitalism" and "the market economy" and weakening the trade union movement. Such "niceness" occurs, however, in a context in which the economic and social situation of small businesses is undergoing a long-term decline, summarized in the case of the United States by Mayer (1947, 343–44) as follows:

> Small business continues to provide a living for several million proprietors, but this group of proprietors is undergoing far-reaching changes in its social position. The locus of economic decisions, of initiative and energy is being shifted from numerous small centers to a relatively small number of large units, thereby affecting the entrepreneurial functions traditionally exercised by the small business-man. . . . The freedom of action of small business has diminished. . . . The independence of the small enterprise is declining. The domination by big business takes widely varying forms, ranging all the way from the most unobtrusive forms of leadership to the complete subordination of small enterprises in others.

Mayer goes on to describe "price leadership", moneylending, subcontracting, franchising, and the impact of manufacturers' advertising on the consuming public, all of which contribute to the fact that:

> Small businessmen as a group . . . are being supplanted by, and subordinated to, a small group of big business managers. Small business as a group, while economically stable, is socially mobile—and in a downward direction. . . . With genuine enterprise so blocked, this means that people are struggling for external symbols of 'being enterprising', expressed in such irrelevant ways as running a store and having one's name on a neon sign. . . . Though the small entrepreneur clings desperately to the status symbols of business ownership, it is a status devoid of opportunities for self-fulfilment (Mayer 1947, 347–49).

Right-wing romanticism towards small enterprises is sometimes guided by genuine goodwill, but at least as often it represents a cunning economic and political ploy to reinforce private-sector and State capitalism. Mayer (1953, 180) again provides what may be considered the definitive statement:

> Such tactics might perhaps be discounted as run of the mill political manoeuvres and common incidents of the power struggle. Unfortunately they are also likely to mislead and misdirect the aspirations of millions of people who cherish an outdated concept of business opportunity, resulting inevitably in frustrations and bitter disappointments. More-over, such frustrations may become politically dangerous, as has been amply demonstrated by the example of Germany where the vexations of

the small business enterprisers made them an easy prey of Nazi propaganda.

Romanticism, repression, and different views of "reality" in the Third World

The socio-economic and political processes associated with small enterprises in North America and Western Europe have only limited parallels in the Third World. Large capitalist enterprises are far less "well-behaved" and "benevolent" in the Third World than in the "advanced" Western capitalist countries, where both their workers and the consuming public are more articulate, have easier access to the communications media, represent a considerable electoral force, and have ample information on the perils of labour exploitation, poor-quality and dangerous products, the pillage of natural resources, and environmental pollution. Thus, the unacceptable face of First World capitalist corporations is often turned on the Third World, and the consequences of their exploitative behaviour are reinforced by three additional features of many Third World countries. First, many local capitalist enterprises are as callously exploitative as their First World equivalents were in the nineteenth century. Secondly, First World governments are usually much less subtle in their dealings with Third World governments and populations than they are in dealing with their own electorates. Finally, a high proportion of Third World governments are either dictatorial or elected through some very questionable mechanism involving government-nominated official and opposition candidates and extensive vote-rigging. The potential electoral significance of those associated with small enterprises is therefore reduced, and the subtleties of right-wing romanticism are often replaced with corporate rapacity and government repression.

In the Third World, most operators of, and workers in, small enterprises are much closer to proletarian, sub-proletarian or proto-proletarian status and income levels than to anything resembling a genuine petite bourgeoisie (see e.g. Gerry and Birkbeck 1981; Jelin 1967; McGee 1976). Despite this fact, most left-wing politicians have either ignored them or dismissed them as competitive, individualistic and petit-bourgeois in character, and thus unable to organize and ally with the industrial proletariat and the peasantry against the national comprador bourgeoisie and intruding foreign capitalist interests. In contrast, right-wing politicians and big-business interests have tended to follow a divide-and-rule tactic. They have characteristically persecuted the smallest enterprises and particularly the street occupations, treating them as lumpen-proletarian scum, while they have employed the cunning tactics of right-wing romanticism with the operators of more substantial small enterprises such as well-established shops, workshops and motor transport firms. The latter group has been praised and stimulated to adopt petit-bourgeois roles, most notably in the transport boycotts and waves of speculation which helped to provoke the extreme right-wing military coup in Chile in September 1973.

The operators of small enterprises, whether one-person, family, or employing wage-labour, have a confusing and ambiguous class location. In many senses this location is contradictory, suspended as they are between the bourgeoisie on the one hand and the proletariat, sub-proletariat and peasantry on the other (see Wright 1978, 74–87). Such contradictions are particularly striking in a Third World context, where Western European and North American class structures are difficult to apply and of dubious relevance (see Lloyd 1982, 112–25), and where hard-working poor people operating small enterprises are particularly likely to be the victims of intense persecution (see especially Chapter 13 by Dennis Cohen). In such circumstances, the contradictory class locations of petty entrepreneurs, their families and their employees, are deliberately played upon by diverse interest groups, fractionalizing any incipient union of those involved with small enterprises and facilitating their subordination to the requirements of larger-scale enterprises.

In many Third World countries, ethno-cultural, religious, linguistic or caste factors further complicate the situation of small enterprises, because "outsiders" either have, or had, control over a large part of petty manufacturing, transport and commerce, and particularly over the more substantial small enterprises with a significant capital investment. The best-known examples are probably the Chinese in South-East Asia, the Lebanese in West Africa and parts of Latin America, the South Asians in East Africa, and the Jews in much of Europe, the Middle East and North America (see e.g. Benedict 1968; Glade 1967; Winder 1962). There are, however, numerous other cases, for example the Yoruba in Northern Ghana (see Eades 1979), and, at a much lower status level, the Christian Punjabi sweepers in Pakistan (see Streefland 1973). Such cases create a potential for government-promoted attacks on petty entrepreneurs in general or on enterprises owned by "outsiders", taking advantage of popular resentment of middlemen, money-lenders and the owners of sweat-shops, and of incipient tendencies towards nationalist chauvinism, race hatred and inter-religious conflict. At their worst, such attacks can lead to the sorts of atrocities committed against the Jews in Germany and German-conquered territories before and during the Second World War, or against substantial parts of the Chinese community in Indonesia in 1965–66. In other cases they can lead to the implementation of policies to systematically assist indigenous or majority-group enterprises, as in the promotion of Malay business capacity in Malaysia or in the "Africanization" of small- to medium-scale industry and commerce in various East and West African countries (see Dinwiddy 1974).

Small enterprises in Third World cities are much more diverse, and on average much smaller and operated by much poorer people, than their equivalents in the cities of the First World. It should be obvious by now that their problems are also much more complex, and that "realistic" attitudes must be formulated individually for each type and scale of enterprise. Both right-wing romanticism and the sorts of radical populism inherent in the pro-rural and pro-intermediate-technology views of such great Third World leaders as Mahatma Gandhi and Julius Nyerere, are strikingly inapplicable to the large cities and more urbanized regions of the Third World today. Big-business, enormous socio-economic inequalities, and the growing inter-nationalization of economic activity are ever-present realities. Increasingly large numbers of small enterprises are tied to larger enterprises through such practices as moneylending, rentals, subcontracting, outworking, commission selling and franchising, and the urban economy gradually assumes the form of a complex hierarchical system for the appropriation and accumulation of surplus value, harnessing small enterprises to the objectives of larger ones. Furthermore, the urbanization of the Third World's population is assuming an increasingly "permanent" character—expressed both in terms of the growing significance of indefinite-term migration from rural areas and small towns to cities, relative to seasonal and circular migration, and in terms of the rising number of countries, especially in Latin America and the Middle East, where more than half the total population lives in urban areas.

Whereas the constraints on small enterprises in First World countries usually take the form of bureaucratic red-tape, in many Third World countries there is much more official harassment and persecution. This repressive approach is strikingly paradoxical when related to the functional roles which most small enterprises play in the socio-economic system as a whole: generating employment; contributing to the gross domestic product; increasing the availability of services and the level of competition in the economy; reducing the cost of living; building up entrepreneurial and technical skills; providing a reserve army of labour; and, contributing (through subcontracting, commission selling etc.) to the accumulation processes of larger enterprises. Six factors help to explain the paradoxical relationship between official repression and the evident functionality of most small enterprises:

1. The prevalence on the part of national élites and urban governments of overwhelmingly negative views of the urban poor, considering them variously to be lazy, incapable, dishonest, dangerous, and obstacles to "modernization".
2. The widespread disinterest shown by unionized wage-workers, organized peasant groups and many left-wing political parties for the problems of petty entrepreneurship.
3. Containment intended to give the impression of prohibition while deliberately not taking the steps needed to achieve elimination (see the Introduction to Section IV)—such measures are often applied with

varying force, depending on the level of demand for wage-labour in the economy as a whole (see Chapter 12 by J. S. Eades).

4. The concentration of persecution on enterprises which do not contribute significantly to the accumulation processes of larger enterprises, or which are defined as "unacceptable" (types of economic activity which are prohibited under national law, or widely viewed as immoral).

5. Pressure on government to restrict specific types of small enterprise—for example, bus owners requesting controls on para-transit, supermarket companies requesting controls on competing street traders and shop-keepers, and local industries requesting controls on vendors of imported and contraband goods.

6. Poor communication between leading politicians, bureaucrats, police officers and military commanders, the managers of large-scale enter-prises "using" small enterprises as pieceworkers, commission sellers etc., and scholars studying the socio-economic system.

If we attempt to summarize the situation of small enterprises in Third World cities, no clear pattern emerges. Such enterprises are very diverse, ranging from miniscule one-person "firms" barely able to generate a subsistence income, to moderately substantial firms with up to 19 workers. The economic activities in which they engage are also very varied, covering a wide gamut of manufacturing and service activities, most of them legal but a few of them clearly illegal. Amongst the operators and workers of such enterprises there is no clear concept of a "small enterprise sector" which could serve as a rallying point for discussion, collaborative action and political lobbying. Furthermore, of course, there are many different groups and individuals formulating views about small enterprises, with numerous motivations, political ideologies and intellectual perspectives. The views formulated by the different interest groups are strongly influenced by past debates, and they tend to be complicated by the contradictory class locations of those involved in small enterprises and by the paradoxical relationship between official repression and the evident functionality of many small enterprises. Not surprisingly, the overall result is confusion, with a great diversity of views and policy measures, with constraints and supports to specific types of enterprise having opposite effects, and with no clear definition of issues or opposing camps so as to be able to pursue more informed debates.

There is not one "reality" for small enterprises, but many. Situations are strikingly different in contrasting countries and contexts, and for contrasting types and scales of economic activity. Furthermore, the interpretations of specific situations may vary greatly depending on the ideological perspectives which are employed in their analysis. Small enterprises are diverse, dynamic and controversial, and it would be absurdly idealistic to hope that somehow all the numerous elements can be fitted together like a jig-saw to produce a universally-agreed perspective.

Some pointers for government policies, and for individuals' policies towards governments

The most important realization regarding small enterprises is simply that, as a collectivity, they have existed for a very long time, they exist in substantial numbers now, and, unless there is a nuclear holocaust, they will continue to exist into the far-distant future. The variety of enterprises will change through time as political systems, technologies, market conditions and the roles of larger enterprises all change, with some types of small enterprises declining rapidly (e.g. knife-grinders and hatters), and new types appearing and sometimes expanding rapidly (e.g. micro-electronics assembly workshops and home carpet shampooers). The collectivity of small enterprises should not be evaluated as "good" or "bad", because it is far too varied to permit the application of such blanket terms. What must be recognized, however, is that small enterprises exist, have problems and opportunities, and are affected by every significant change in the economy, social organization, technology, physical environment, and the role of the State. *Even if small enterprises are not supported, they should be planned for.* In other words, they should be taken into account in all official decision-making relating to production, consumption, work, and the economic, social and physical environments. To forget about small enterprises in official decision-making may produce considerable diseconomies, waste, inefficiency and hardship, and may produce no concrete benefits to larger-scale enterprises.

Given the relatively depressed state of the world economy since the mid-1970s, the steady growth of the world's population, and the continuous pressure of technological advances to substitute capital investment for labour, there is a growing unemployment crisis in both the First and Third Worlds (see e.g. Haveman 1978; Sabolo 1975; Weeks 1974). Some of the unemployment problem may be absorbed by growing involvement in household tasks, increased leisure, prolonged education, earlier retirement and the reduction of working hours (see e.g. Burns 1977; Kumar 1979–80; Pahl 1980). All of these solutions, however, seem more suitable to the rich First World countries than to the poorer Third World countries, where the shortage of State financial resources and the desperately low incomes of most households emphasize the urgency of redistributing existing wealth, generating new wealth for capital investment, and increasing the real incomes of the poor majority of the population. The generation of work and income opportunities is necessarily a top priority in the Third World, and reductions in work should be limited to increased controls on child labour and sweat shops, the broader enforcement of minimum wages, and the introduction or universalization of disablement and old-age pensions.

Because of the growing seriousness of the unemployment crisis, it is unrealistic for the governments of Third World countries to depend exclusively on medium- to large-scale private-sector firms, and on State corporations, the bureaucracy and the armed forces, to generate employment opportunities. Indeed, in many cases big-business is unsympathetic to the idea of taking on more workers, and State employment is already over-inflated in relation to the real significance of the tasks being undertaken. Even when there is some genuine employment generation capacity in large enterprises and government, this is usually inadequate in relation to the size of the population willing and able to work for a living, and some of the demand for jobs is best catered for through the creation and expansion of small enterprises. Though they may not be viewed as high priority elements of the economy and employment structure, small enterprises should at least be recognized as significant elements in increasing the national product and in reducing levels of open unemployment, destitution and poverty-induced crime.

In effect, governments have three broad alternatives in dealing with all those small enterprises which are not considered to be unacceptable: "repression", when constraints clearly exceed supports; "tolerance", when constraints and supports are of roughly equal significance; and, "promotion", when supports clearly exceed constraints. At present the great majority of Third World governments have policies and actions which broadly fit the descriptions of "repression" or "tolerance", while only a very small minority can be described as genuinely implementing "promotion".

Given that the repression of small enterprises causes considerable effort, expenditure and hardship, and also reductions in national product, levels of employment and the availability of services, it has no credible justification. When it is applied, it results from a combination of misguided official perceptions of small enterprises with the deliberate persecution of the urban poor and of the members of specific ethnic, cultural, linguistic or religious groups. Any concept of social justice, responsible government for the benefit of those governed, or humanitarianism, leads to the condemnation of repressive policies and of the governments which perpetrate them.

A shift from repression to tolerance or promotion may occur through persuasion of a government in power, or through the replacement of that government with a régime more favourable to small enterprises. Some governments using repression towards small enterprises will obviously never change their fundamental views, and any responsible specialist in employment policy or enterprise promotion would be well advised not to work with such régimes. Repression towards small enterprises is usually accompanied by repression towards various other social groups and types of activity, and the only realistic hope is for the fall or overthrow of the governments involved. The more problematical cases are those governments using repression towards small enterprises which appear to be susceptible to persuasion to shift towards tolerance or even promotion. If they are eventually persuaded, then working with such governments may well be justified, but if not, it has been a wasted effort and it may even prove counterproductive through helping to strengthen that government's hold on power.

Unless a specialist in employment policy or enterprise promotion can persuade a repressive government to change to tolerance or promotion of small enterprises, or it is possible to work with a government which has already adopted tolerance or promotion, there are strong arguments for not working with government. In such circumstances, work with non-paternalistic NGOs in support programmes for small enterprises, or in research oriented at defining and publicizing the mechanisms of repression and exploitation directed towards small enterprises, may be the only means in which positive change can be promoted through the use of professional skills rather than directly political or military action.

Those who advocate tolerance or promotion for small enterprises will always be open to the Leninist accusation that they are "petit-bourgeois theorists" whose policies will "first, mainly benefit the buyer-up (parent firm); second, help to preserve conditions of work and remuneration far worse than those of the workers directly employed by capitalist firms; and, third, retard the development of industry and fully fledged capitalism" (Schmitz, 1982a, 436). Such accusations, however, have a decidedly hollow tone in most Third World countries, where the choice is not so much "small enterprises or accelerated capitalist industrialization", as "small enterprises or increased unemployment and poverty".

A more irresponsible and obnoxious accusation is that advocating tolerance or promotion of small enterprises contributes to ameliorating the suffering of the poor, and hence to postponing or avoiding the "otherwise-inevitable revolution" of the poor against their oppressors. Such re-volutionary idealism and single-mindedness ignore the facts that revolutions of the poor against their oppressors do not necessarily occur, even in the most appalling states of human misery, and that even when they do occur they often result in vicious repression of the poor and in even greater suffering. Extreme poverty is not the best means of combatting modern armaments, and successful popular revolutions or electoral transitions to more egalitarian régimes are most likely to occur where the majority of the population is well nourished, has a moderate basic income, and has some access both to education and to information about government and power structures. Whether through governmental organizations in those countries where official attitudes are not inflexibly oppressive, or through NGOs within specific countries or at the international campaigning level, therefore, advocating tolerance or promotion for small enterprises is a legitimate role, fully compatible with a desire to achieve more egalitarian and democratic forms of socio-economic and political organization.

More specific policy considerations

It should be self-evident by now that small enterprises are not necessarily inefficient, anti-social or lacking in regulatory mechanisms, and that petty entrepreneurs are usually neither incompetent nor inarticulate. Time series statistics on the numbers of small enterprises may indicate growth, stability or decline in the size of the collectivity, but they show nothing of the dynamics of foundation, expansion, collaboration, exploitation, contraction and extinction which affect individual enterprises. Knowledge of these dynamics is generally very limited, and as a result, "micro-intervention" to support or limit individual small enterprises is generally inefficient, highly discriminatory, and susceptible to paternalism, favouritism, corruption and victimization. It is therefore far more important to regulate the broader economic, social and physical environmental conditions which affect the numbers, types and average sizes of small enterprises, than to support or constrain individual enterprises on a highly selective basis. Those constraints which are applied should be few in number, simple in application, and applied to ALL enterprises, or ALL enterprises in a specific economic activity. Similarly, the supports which are applied should be few in number, simple in application, and applied to, or at least potentially available to, ALL enterprises in a specific economic activity, ALL small enterprises, or ALL small enterprises in a specific economic activity or pilot area.

Existing policies towards small enterprises in most countries require substantial revision, and five "policy areas" are particularly worthy of mention here because they are both important and rarely discussed in the available literature on small enterprise policies: "deregulation", "law and order", "urban design", "organizations", and "participatory planning".

Deregulation

There are an excessive number of constraints on most small enterprises, and too many of these are difficult to administer, discretionary in character, or subject to widespread evasion, abuse or corruption. "Get off their backs" is the most obvious piece of advice relating to enterprises which are not simply unacceptable. This implies the abolition or simplification of licensing procedures, by-laws indicating where and how enterprises can operate, and numerous trivial fees and taxes which cost almost as much to collect as they yield in revenues. An effective process of deregulation depends on three major activities: first, the coordination of all government agencies engaged in constraining each type of economic activity, reducing the number of agencies and constraints involved; second, more clearly identifying the powers and responsibilities of the remaining agencies; and, third, trying to ensure that each agency has the resources necessary to apply its constraints to all the enterprises which should be constrained (see Mitnick 1980, 417-47).

Law and order

Of all the constraints which can be applied to the socio-economic system as a whole, there can be little doubt that the most important relate to the enforcement of the basic universal laws prohibiting and punishing: the deliberate killing or injuring of persons; the theft or destruction of personal, corporate and State property; the enslavement or victimization of persons; the manufacture of deliberately defective, dangerous or toxic goods: the sale of unnecessarily dangerous or toxic goods, or of fraudulent, falsified or contraband goods; the extraction of payments through extortion or corruption; and, the creation of a public nuisance which presents a serious threat to the lives, health, work or sleep of others. The efficient enforcement of such laws creates a secure environment within which both small and large enterprises can operate, reducing policing to the "basics" which preserve the rights of both the individual and the State, and avoiding the pettiness and triviality of many existing by-laws designating such things as the height of shop counters, the dimensions of the letters on signs, and the degree to which street traders must "ambulate". Effective enforcement of these basic laws gives those who work in small enterprises considerable protection from criminals, and at the same time removes the basis for accusations that small enterprises are dishonest, dangerous, or gravely exploitative of their workers. Enforcement, however, should be for the whole city, and for all types and sizes of enterprises, so that the control of "petty crime" affecting small enterprises does not draw attention away from the numerous petty and substantial crimes associated with larger enterprises and State bureaucracies.

Urban design

There is a great potential for the design and construction of urban environments which are attractive, human in scale, and strongly favourable to small enterprises. Such environments deliberately integrate small-scale manufacturing and commerce into residential areas through the avoidance of rigid zoning regulations, the construction of houses with rooms appropriate for shops and workshops, and the provision of small neighbourhood service centres. In more central parts of the city, and in major suburban shopping areas, such urban environments include high-density residential areas, pedestrianized streets, pavements and open areas suitable for street traders, sites for daily, nightly and weekly open-air markets, and market buildings incorporating not only stalls and shops, but also a supermarket for mass-consumption durable goods and factory-processed foods. A compatible urban transport system would give priority to buses, various forms of para-transit, and the cheapest forms of personal transport such as bicycles and mopeds, designating segregated direct routes for public transport vehicles, and other such routes for non-motorized vehicles. This orientation of city planning to the requirements of small enterprises has five major elements: (1) making most streets congenial areas for pedestrians, stall and shop traders, and slow-moving traffic, and ensuring that they are areas for social interaction, recreation and commerce as well as axes for the flows of people and goods; (2) creating an urban environment which incorporates considerable diversity of economic and social activities in every neighbourhood; (3) assuring the widespread availability of locations for dispersed small enterprises, and also the availability at focal points of service centres and markets; (4) designing service centres and markets as cheap, simple structures, usually with only one storey, which can be installed in stages, adding an extra section each time the existing area reaches capacity use, and ensuring that the maximum number of shops and stalls face outwards to streets or alleys, rather than inwards to enclosed areas; and, (5) progressively transferring control and ownership of shopping centres and markets to the traders, so that rents are converted into instalment payments on purchase, and so that the traders take an increasing responsibility for refuse disposal, security, maintenance and publicity.

Organizations

The organization of small enterprises, their workers, or petty entrepreneurs, can be promoted by government, larger enterprises or NGO's for a wide variety of reasons related to the interests which organization is intended to serve. At the one extreme, serving private-sector big-business, organization may be promoted to encourage the subordination of small enterprises in the accumulation processes of larger enterprises through patronage, money-lending, renting, subcontracting, franchising, etc. Close to this extreme, and serving right-wing political interests, is the deliberate promotion of organizations of petty entrepreneurs dedicated to promulgating right-wing romanticism and to adopting petit-bourgeois roles in opposition to organized labour and increased State intervention in the economy. At an intermediate level, and more directly serving small enterprises, is the promotion of trade unions of workers in small enterprises or associations of petty entrepreneurs, so as to press for the improvement of working conditions in small enterprises, more reasonable terms for relationships with larger enterprises, the reduction of government constraints, and the increase of government supports. Such measures directly serving small enterprises may be reinforced by more sophisticated forms of economic organization, notably the formation of cooperatives to obtain raw materials, distribute products, handle banking and credit, and/or administer shared physical locations such as small-industry estates, markets and shopping centres. Cooperative manufacturing or commercial activities may even be concentrated in a single location and converted to workers' self-managed medium- to large-scale enterprises (see e.g. Vanek 1975, 1977), or they may be associated with the support of a major State corporation so as to supply that corporation as subcontractors or to distribute for it as commission sellers. Finally, at the opposite extreme to serving private-sector big-business and right-wing political interests, small enterprises may be organized to serve the interests of nationalism and the transition to socialism, with organizations playing a directly political role by strengthening proletarian consciousness and solidarity both with workers in larger enterprises and with the peasantry.[1]†

While there can be little doubt that efforts to create organizations which directly serve small enterprises are highly desirable, opinions will obviously differ greatly as to whether the organization of small enterprises to serve the interests of private-sector big-business, right-wing politics or left-wing politics, is to be recommended. When working in government, urban, regional and national development planners, and specialists in employment policy and enterprise promotion, must work within the broad political and policy objectives of government. They can often raise levels of political conscious- ness, sow the seeds for long-term political change and achieve some significant changes in policy, but outright opposition to government while working within it is a motive for dismissal or worse fates. Even when working in a NGO, such as a charity, a research centre or a trade union federation, planners and other technical specialists are limited in their actions by government political and policy objectives, because actions which effectively oppose those objectives may provoke sanctions against the NGO. The choice of actions in the field of organization, therefore, requires not only a sense of context, but also, if political changes are to be achieved, commitment, courage, and an acute sense of tactics.

Participatory planning

The selection and administration of constraints and supports for small enterprises is an excellent field of governmental activity for the application of "participatory planning" involving representatives of organized groups of small enterprises, their workers, or petty entrepreneurs. Such participation can be especially effective and beneficial if organizations have achieved a coverage of the great majority of enterprises, and the effectiveness of participation can be used as an argument to persuade more of those involved with small enterprises to join key organizations. Through such participation, constraints and supports can be more effectively selected and designed, and complaints about bureaucratic regulation and policing can be voiced and investigated. The very act of calling for participation is a demonstration that government policies towards small enterprises have shifted from harassment to tolerance or even to promotion, and the advice of the participant representatives can do much to ensure that government constraints and supports are applied as widely, as effectively, and as cheaply as possible.

While the development of a "small enterprise sector" with a genuine group consciousness and a common forum for discussion is a worthwhile long-term

†Superscript numbers refer to Notes at end of Chapter.

objective, in the initial stages participation is usually best organized at the level of specific types of economic activity (e.g. metalworking workshops, taxis, or street trading) or at the level of groups of economic activities (e.g. manufacturing and repair; commerce; transport; construction; or, personal and domestic services). For each type or group of economic activity, participation should be conditional on the presence of representatives of the majority of the enterprises in that type or group. In the case of economic activities in which small enterprises employ substantial numbers of wage-workers, it should also be conditional on the representation of broadly-based organizations of these workers. When representation of enterprises or workers is not sufficiently broad-based, then participation should be postponed until organizations can be expanded. This avoids the danger that an organized minority of small enterprises will be assisted in calling for official protection of their interests and the persecution of their "unorganized" competitors, tactics which will further fractionalize the potential "small enterprise sector", and which will reduce overall employment, competition and national product.

Ending at the beginning: priorities for research

It is appropriate to end where perhaps this book should have begun, with some pointers for research which will facilitate the formulation and implementation of more appropriate policies for small enterprises. There is no longer a great need for further general descriptive studies and broad policy formulations at the level of "the small enterprise sector", "the informal sector", "petty commodity production" or other such heterogeneous aggregates. Views on such aggregates and on dualistic divisions of the economy can easily be formulated on the basis of the existing very extensive literature, and in many cases views at this level are already so deeply entrenched that they are unlikely to be changed however much further work is done. The current challenges for research and policy-making lie in exploring newer and more specific subject areas where our existing knowledge is gravely inadequate. In particular, it is worth stressing the need for high-quality studies of the changes affecting small enterprises during a prolonged transition to socialism, of specific groups and types of economic activity in individual cities and in international comparisons, and of specific technological problems, issues in political economy, the evaluation of government intervention, and forms of organization.

Our knowledge of the changes affecting small enterprises during a prolonged transition to socialism is remarkably limited. Numerous travellers' reports and general political and economic studies of the COMECON bloc, China, North Korea, Vietnam, and other countries which have undergone such a transition confirm the presence of substantial numbers of small enterprises and mention that many are now associated into some form of cooperative or collective. In general, however, urban small enterprises have not attracted anything like as much attention as industry, agriculture, the bureaucracy, the class structure, transport systems or urban design, and greater research attention if urgently needed so that we can develop more realistic models of the "evolution" of small enterprises under different types of socio-economic and political system, and of the methods and impact of cooperative organization.

Research on specific groups and types of economic activity is most urgently needed for construction, intra-urban transport, petty trading, and the ubiquitous but almost unknown petty service occupations such as night-watching, shoeshining and queue-standing. In most such cases existing research is limited to a few cities and countries, and there is a particularly grave shortage of analytical studies giving an understanding of the socio-economic organization of the activity as a whole. Also worthy of considerable research priority are the occupations which, in particular countries and contexts, are closely associated with specific ethno-cultural, religious, linguistic or caste groups. These occupations may be both causes and effects of inequality and discrimination, and many of them are potential flashpoints for inter-group violence. Lastly, under types of economic activity, special attention should be given to occupations which are highly age- and sex-specific, both so that we can build up a more detailed knowledge of the generational and sexual division of labour, and also so that employment policies can respond to changes in the structure of the population and of the labour force.

The technological problems affecting small enterprises have already been the subjects of numerous pioneering studies, particularly by the Intermediate Technology Development Group, but there can be little doubt that much more such work is needed, and that research findings require more effective diffusion. In general, the search is for appropriate labour-intensive technologies using equipment which is energy-efficient, cheap and easy to construct, durable, and easy to repair. There is also a great need for the wider international diffusion of the skills available in such countries as India and Turkey to keep old vehicles and machines functioning despite the lack of legitimate spare parts and servicing. Lastly, much could be gained from increased design and experimental construction of cheap, durable and safe modular structures for shop–houses, workshop–houses, markets, service centres, and small-industry estates. Many public sector construction projects are currently economic loss-makers, not because they do not cater to real needs, but simply because they are badly located, poorly designed, and use materials and designs which are much more expensive than is really necessary.

Research on issues in political economy relating to small enterprises should focus on the vertical linkages between small and larger enterprises in hierarchically-organized systems of appropriation and accumulation. The guiding question should be the traditional basis of political economy: "*Who gets what, where, how* and *when* . . . and, *why?*" This research would have an explanatory rather than a simply descriptive character, and there would be more widespread use of in-depth case studies either in addition to, or instead of, the more conventional household and enterprise questionnaire surveys. Particular attention should be paid to the capital accumulation mechanisms of medium- and large-scale enterprises "using" small enterprises, and to the factors influencing decisions as to whether to conduct operations within the firm, to contract them out, or simply to buy on the open market.[2] Following the lead of Epstein and Monat's (1973) survey of labour-only subcontracting, De Grazia's (1980) survey of clandestine employment, and of recent studies of child labour (e.g. Challis and Elliman 1979; Mendelievich 1979), there should be major comparative international surveys of such processes as outworking, commission selling, bonded labour, dependent working and franchising.

Evaluative research on government intervention should examine both the government's role in influencing the broad, general context within which small enterprises function, and also its role in applying specific constraints and supports. In the broad context category fall studies of such topics as: the impact of exchange rates, balance of payments and import–export controls on the conditions for both large- and small-scale enterprises; the effects of urban planning and renewal processes on economic activity in different parts of the city; the impact of, and avoidance mechanisms for, labour legislation, social security provisions, and taxation; and, the allocation of credit and government contracts. In the specific constraints and supports category falls research on such topics as: the delivery of, and access to, official supports; the attitudes, knowledge and performance of personnel working in support programmes; corruption by public officials in dealing with small enterprises; the spatial and socio-economic distribution of policing; and, the impact of specific policy measurements in widening or narrowing socio-economic inequalities.

Finally, research on "forms of organization" requires a wide variety of case studies and pilot "action research" projects to evaluate the potential for associating small enterprises into cooperatives and workers' self-managed enterprises. Such studies and projects are required for each major type of economic activity and for a wide variety of cities and countries, and it is important to take into account not only the obviously successful cases of organization, but also those which show somewhat indifferent results and the outright failures. Through such research and experiments, we can determine whether the association of numerous small enterprises, rather than the mercurial success of a few Samuel Smiles and Horatio Alger "self-made men", may be the key to widespread transition from small to larger-scale enterprises. It would be ironic, but perfectly satisfactory, if such research gave us the solution to the problems of small enterprises by bringing about the disappearance of many such enterprises—not a "downward disappearance" to extinction, but an "upward disappearance" to collective organization, higher status, greater bargaining power, increased security, and the simultaneous enjoyment of scale economies and conviviality.

Notes

1. Such tactics are intended to compensate for the relatively small size of the true proletariat in the Third World, and to "unite the working class, the peasantry, the urban petite bourgeoisie and the national bourgeoisie, form a domestic united front under the leadership of the working class, and advance from this to the establishment of a State which is a people's democratic dictatorship" (Mao Tse-tung 1965, 415).
2. An excellent example of such work on the political economy of small enterprises and the relationships between large and small is Hubert Schmitz's (1982b) recent book, *Manufacturing in the Backyard*. The comparison of his work with the classics on Japanese subcontracting (e.g. Broadbridge 1966; Shinohara 1968) is particularly instructive.

References

BECHHOFER, Frank and ELLIOTT, Brian (1981) "Petty property: the survival of a moral economy", in Frank Bechhofer and Brian Elliott (eds.), *The Petite Bourgeoisie*, Macmillan, London, pp. 182–200.
BENEDICT, B. (1968) "Family firms and economic development", *Southwestern Journal of Anthropology*, Vol. 24, pp. 1–19.
BROADBRIDGE, Seymour (1966) *Industrial Dualism in Japan*, Frank Cass, London.
BURNS, Scott (1977) *The Household Economy*, Beacon Press, Boston.
CHALLIS, James and ELLIMAN, David (1979) *Child Workers Today*, Quartermaine House, Sunbury, Middlesex.
DE GRAZIA, Raffaele (1980) "Clandestine employment: a problem of our times", *International Labour Review*, Vol. 119, pp. 549–63.
DINWIDDY, Bruce (1974) *Promoting African Enterprise*, Croom Helm, London.
EADES, J. S. (1979) "Kinship and entrepreneurship among Yoruba in northern Ghana", in William A. Shack and Elliott P. Skinner (eds.), *Strangers in African Societies*, University of California Press, Berkeley, pp. 169–82.
EPSTEIN, E. and MONAT, J. (1973) "Labour contracting and its regulation", *International Labour Review*, Vol. 107, pp. 451–70.
GERRY, Chris and BIRKBECK, Chris (1981) "The petty commodity producer in Third World cities: petit-bourgeois or 'disguised' proletarian?", in Frank Bechhofer and Brian Elliott (eds.), *op. cit.*, pp. 121–54.
GLADE, William P. (1967) "Approaches to a theory of entrepreneurial formation", *Explorations in Entrepreneurial History*, Vol. 4, pp. 245–59.
HAVEMAN, Robert H. (1978) "Unemployment in Western Europe and the United States", *American Economic Review*, Vol. 68, No. 2, Papers and Proceedings, pp. 44–50.
JELIN, Elizabeth (1967) "Trabajadores por cuenta propia y asalariados: distinción vertical u horizontal?", *Revista Latinoamericana de Sociologia*, Vol. 3, No. 3, pp. 388–410.
KAUTSKY, Karl (1976) *La Dictadura del Proletariado*, Editorial Ayuso, Madrid, Biblioteca de Textos Socialistas, No. 3.
KERBLAY, B. H. (1968) *Les Marchés Paysans en URSS*, Mouton, Paris.
KITCHING, Gavin (1982) *Development and Underdevelopment in Historical Perspective*, Methuen, London.
KUMAR, Krishan (1979–1980) "The social culture of work: work, employment and unemployment as ways of life", *New Universities Quarterly*, Vol. 34, No. 1, pp. 5–28.
LENIN, V. I. (1936) "The development of capitalism in Russia", in V. I. Lenin, *Selected Works, Volume 1*, Lawrence and Wishart, London, pp. 219–385.
LENIN, V. I. (1972a) "The handicraft census of 1894–95 in Perm Gubernia, and general problems of 'handicraft' industry", in V. I. Lenin, *Collected Works, Volume 2*, Lawrence and Wishart, London, pp. 355–458.

LENIN, V. I. (1972b) "The heritage we renounce", in V. I. Lenin, *Collected Works, Volume 2*, Lawrence and Wishart, London, pp. 491–534.

LENIN, V. I. (1972c) A characterization of economic romanticism: Sismondi and our national Sismondists", in V. I. Lenin, *Collected Works, Volume 2*, Lawrence and Wishart, London, pp. 129–265.

LLOYD, Peter (1982) *A Third World Proletariat?* George Allen and Unwin, London.

McGEE, T. G. (1976) "The persistence of the proto-proletariat: occupational structures and planning of the future of Third World cities", in C. Board, R. J. Chorley, P. Haggett and D. R. Stoddart (eds.), *Progress in Geography, Volume 9*, Edward Arnold, London, pp. 1–38.

MANDEL, Ernest (1970) *Marxist Economic Theory, Volume 2*, Monthly Review Press, New York.

MAO TSE-TUNG (1965) "On the people's democratic dictatorship", in *Selected Works of Mao Tse-tung, Volume 4*, Foreign Languages Press, Peking, pp. 411–24.

MARCUSE, Herbert (1961) *Soviet Marxism: A Critical Analysis*, Vintage/Random House, New York.

MARX, Karl (1963) *The Poverty of Philosophy*, New World/International Publishers, New York.

MARX, Karl and ENGELS, Friedrich (1965) *The Communist Manifesto*, Washington Square Press, New York.

MAYER, Kurt (1947) "Small business as a social institution", *Social Research*, Vol. 14, pp. 332–49.

MAYER, Kurt (1953) "Business enterprise: traditional symbol of opportunity", *British Journal of Sociology*, Vol. 4, pp. 160–80.

MENDELIEVICH, Elias (ed.) (1979) *Children at Work*, International Labour Office (ILO), Geneva.

MILLS, C. Wright (1951) *White Collar: The American Middle Classes*, Oxford University Press, New York.

MITNICK, Barry M. (1980) *The Political Economy of Regulation*, Columbia University Press, New York.

PAHL, R. E. (1980) "Employment, work and the domestic division of labour", *International Journal of Urban and Regional Research*, Vol. 4, pp. 1–20.

ROGERS, David and BERG, Ivar E. (1961) "Occupation and ideology: the case of the small businessman", *Human Organization*, Vol. 20, pp. 103–11.

SABOLO, Yves (1975) "Employment and unemployment, 1960–90", *International Labour Review*, Vol. 112, pp. 401–17.

SCHMITZ, Hubert (1982a) "Growth constraints on small-scale manufacturing in developing countries: a critical review", *World Development*, Vol. 10, No. 6, pp. 429–50.

SCHMITZ, Hubert (1982b) *Manufacturing in the Backyard: Case Studies on Accumulation and Employment in Small-scale Brazilian Industry*, Frances Pinter, London.

SHINOHARA, Miyohei (1968) "A survey of the Japanese literature on small industry", in Bert F. Hoselitz (ed.), *The Role of Small Industry in the Process of Economic Growth*, UNESCO/Mouton, Paris, pp. 1–113.

SMITH, Hedrick (1976) *The Russians*, Times Books, London.

STREEFLAND, Pieter H. (1973) *The Christian Punjabi Sweepers*, University of Amsterdam, Antropologisch-Sociologisch Centrum, Amsterdam, Voorpublikatie Nr. 6, Afdeling Zuid-en Zuidoost Azië.

VANEK, Jaroslav (ed.) (1975) *Self-management: Economic Liberation of Man*, Penguin, Harmondsworth.

VANEK, Jaroslav (1977) *The Labour-managed Economy*, Cornell University Press, Ithaca, N.Y.

WEEKS, John (1974) "A brief note on the unemployment crisis in poor countries", *Manpower and Unemployment Research in Africa*, Vol. 7, No. 1, pp. 32–38.

WINDER, R. Bayley (1962) "The Lebanese in West Africa", *Comparative Studies in Society and History*, Vol. 4, pp. 296–333.

WOODCOCK, George (1977) "Anarchism: a historical introduction", in George Woodcock (ed.), *The Anarchist Reader*, Fontana/Collins, London, pp. 11–56.

WRIGHT, Erik Olin (1978) *Class, Crisis and the State*, New Left Books, London.

Author index

Acedo, C. M. de (1980) 317, 318
Achebe, C. (1971) 133
Adams, W. (1959) 188, 190
Agarwala, A. N. (1959) 256
Ahluwalia, M. S. (1974) 293, 294, 306
Alavi, H. (1975) 63
Amin, S. (1974) 114, 121, 133
Anti-Slavery Society (1978) 171
Apthorpe, R. (1970) 276
Armstrong, W. (1968) 132, 133
Arn, J. (1977) 127, 135
Asiwaju, A. I. (1976) 207, 216

Bademli, R. R. (1977) 153
Banerjee, S. (1979) 97, 105
Baran, P. A. (1959) 247, 250, 256
Batley, R. (1978), 309, 318; (1979) 309, 318; (1980) 309; (1981) 309, 318
Bauer, P. T. (1954) 207, 216
Beavon, K. S. O. (1980) 233, 244; (1981) 243, 244; (1982) 243, 244
Bechhofer, F. (1981) 105, 169, 217, 319, 324, 340
Beer, C. F. (1976) 207, 216
Belshaw, D. (1973) 274, 275
Benedict, B. (1968) 327, 340
Berg, E. J. (1968) 209, 216
Berg, I. E. (1961) 324, 341
Berger, E. L. (1974) 133, 134
Berger, S. (1981) 41
Berkman, A. (1929) 1
Berry, S. S. (1975) 207, 216
Berthomieu, C. (1980) 100, 105
Bhalla, A. S. (1973) 251
Bhattacharya, S. S. (1969) 59, 63
Bienefeld, M. (1974) 47, 50, 60, 63; (1975) 53, 63, 115, 129, 134, 189, 190; (1976) 133, 134, 138, 152, 153
Biesheuvel, S. (1979) 237, 238, 243, 244
Birkbeck, C. (1978) 125, 133, 134; (1979) 127, 133, 134, 167; (1981) 99, 105, 156, 159, 169, 204, 217, 326, 340

Blau, P. M. (1955) 260, 275
Blaxter, L. (1979) 205, 216
Board, C. (1976) 341
Boeke, J. H. et al. (1961) 44, 62, 63
Bosanquet, N. (1972) 217
Bose, A. N. (1974) 52, 53, 63; (1978) 117, 133, 134
Bozzoli, B. (1979) 238, 244, 245
Bradlow, E. (1977) 233, 244
Breman, J. (1974) 39, 41, 47, 60, 61; (1976) 39, 43; (1977) 39, 41, 55, 133
Brett, S. (1974) 47, 63
Broadbridge, S. (1966) 340
Bromley, R. (1978) 39, 41, 115, 133, 134, 156, 168, 185, 187, 190, 234, 235, 244; (1979) 39, 41, 42, 99, 101, 105, 108, 113, 132, 133, 134, 135, 139, 153, 156, 168, 190, 217, 244, 318; (1980) 184, 190, 203, 216; (1981) 184, 190, 203, 216; (1982) 251, 256
Buchanan, I. (1972) 211, 216
Buckley, K. (1978) 216
Bujra, J. M. (1978-1979) 123, 124, 126, 134
Burgess, R. (1978) 318
Burman, S. B. (1979) 216
Burns, S. (1977) 330, 340

Campbell, B. (1978) 207, 216
Cardoso, F. H. (1970) 93, 95; (1980) 40, 42
Challis, J. (1979) 339, 340
Chambers, R. (1973) 274, 275
Chan, H. C. (1976) 211, 216
Chenery, H. (1974) 293, 294, 306
Cherry, G. E. (1980) 190
Chorley, R. J. (1976) 341
Clark, C. (1957) 81, 95
Clinard, M. B. (1966) 115, 134
Cohen, A. (1966) 206, 216
Cohen, D. J. (1974) 219
Collins, P. (1975) 210, 216
Coquery-Vidrovitch, C. (1971) 207, 216
Coutsinas, G. (1975) 63
Crowder, M. (1970) 207, 216

343

Subject index

349

Other titles in the series

The terms of our inspection copy service apply to all the above books. A complete catalogue of all books in the Pergamon International Library is available on request. The Publisher will be pleased to consider suggestions for revised editions and new titles.

N